HUMAN DIGNITY

Human dignity is now a central feature of many modern constitutions and international documents. As a constitutional value, human dignity involves a person's free will autonomy, and ability to write his life story within the framework of society. As a constitutional right, it gives full expression to the value of human dignity, subject to the specific demands of constitutional architecture.

This analytical study of human dignity as both a constitutional value and a constitutional right adopts a legal-interpretive perspective. It explores the sources of human dignity as a legal concept, its role in constitutional documents, its content and its scope. The analysis is augmented by examples from comparative legal experience, including chapters devoted to the role of human dignity in American, Canadian, German, South African and Israeli constitutional law.

AHARON BARAK is a faculty member at the Interdisciplinary Center (IDC) Herzliya, Israel, and a visiting professor at Yale Law School. In 1975 he was appointed Attorney General of the State of Israel, becoming Justice of the Supreme Court of Israel in 1978 and serving as President from 1995 until his retirement in 2006. He has also served as a lecturer, professor and Dean at the Law School of the Hebrew University of Jerusalem.

HUMAN DIGNITY

The Constitutional Value and the Constitutional Right

AHARON BARAK

Translated from the Hebrew by

DANIEL KAYROS

CAMBRIDGE
UNIVERSITY PRESS

University Printing House, Cambridge CB2 8BS, United Kingdom

Cambridge University Press is part of the University of Cambridge.

It furthers the University's mission by disseminating knowledge in the pursuit of education, learning and research at the highest international levels of excellence.

www.cambridge.org
Information on this title: www.cambridge.org/9781107090231

First published 2015

Based on *Human Dignity: The Constitutional Right and its Daughter-Rights*, published in 2014 by Nevo Publishing, Israel.

Printed in the United Kingdom by Clays, St Ives plc

A catalogue record for this publication is available from the British Library

Library of Congress Cataloguing in Publication data
Barak, Aharon author.
[Kevod ha-adam. English]
Human dignity : the constitutional value and the constitutional right / Aharon Barak ; [translated by Daniel Kayros].
pages cm
Includes bibliographical references and index.
ISBN 978-1-107-09023-1 (hardback) – ISBN 978-1-107-46206-9 (paperback)
1. Respect for persons–Law and legislation–Israel. 2. Human rights–Israel.
3. Respect for persons–Law and legislation. 4. Human rights. I. Title.
KMK2097.B3713 2015
342.569408′5–dc23
2014036812

ISBN 978-1-107-09023-1 Hardback
ISBN 978-1-107-46206-9 Paperback

CONTENTS

PREFACE

The concept of human dignity has a 2,500 year history.[1] As it has moved through history, the concept has been influenced by different religions which held it as an important component of their theological approach. It was also influenced by the views of philosophers who developed human dignity in their contemplations. In the twentieth century, the concept encountered a new phenomenon. The atrocities of the Second World War, and particularly the Holocaust of the Jewish people, brought human dignity into the forefront of legal discourse. As a result, constitutional and international legal texts began to adopt the concept, and jurists appeared alongside the theologians and the philosophers. Legal scholars were called upon to determine the theoretical basis of human dignity as a constitutional value and as a constitutional right. Judges were required to solve practical problems created by the constitutionalization of human dignity, as a value or as a right.

This book discusses the legal-constitutional aspect of human dignity. It makes no theological or philosophical contribution. I do not argue with Jewish or Christian religious sages; I have no dispute with Kant. I attempt, through legal analysis, to explain human dignity as a constitutional value and as a constitutional right. Of course, law is not detached from life. Legal understanding is influenced by theological and philosophical views. It is not, however, identical to them. Aquinas and Kant were not dealing with the interpretation of a constitutional bill of rights in which the value of human dignity, or the right to human dignity, is entrenched. Of course, the legal solutions for practical problems at times overlap the solutions that theologians or philosophers promote. This is the Rawlsian phenomenon of "overlapping consensus."[2] However, the theoretical points of departure are different: the point of departure for understanding human

[1] See Bodo Pieroth and Bernhard Schlink, *Grundrechte Staatsrecht II* (Heidelberg: C. F. Müller Verlag, 2006).

[2] See John Rawls, *Political Liberalism* (New York: Columbia University Press, 2005), 144.

dignity in a constitutional bill of rights is the constitution, not theological or philosophical considerations.

A constitution is a legal text. The language of the constitution is not a metaphor. Legal interpretation is the tool utilized by jurists to give meaning to human dignity in a constitution. In the absence of a "true" meaning,[3] each legal system must independently determine the interpretation it finds appropriate. In modern interpretational theory we find three main systems for understanding constitutional texts:[4] Intentionalism, Originalism and Purposivism. The first understands the constitutional text according to the intent of the framers. The second understands the text based on its public understanding at the time of framing. The third understands the text based on the purpose that it is intended to fulfill. Purposive constitutional interpretation lies at the foundation of this book.[5] This interpretation considers the language of the constitutional text, its architecture and the purpose underlying its provisions. On the basis of all these factors, constitutional language is imbued with meaning that fulfills its purpose and allows it to meet the needs of the present. Constitutions are interpreted with a spacious view.

In many constitutions human dignity is not a constitutional right. Nonetheless, it is recognized as a constitutional value either expressly (such as in Spain[6]) or implicitly (such as in the USA[7] and Canada[8]). The value of human dignity has several roles within a constitution. It serves as a foundation for the constitutional rights. It serves as a value by which the constitutional rights are interpreted; for example, the right to equality may be interpreted based on the value of human dignity.[9] It influences

[3] Aharon Barak, *Purposive Interpretation in Law* (Princeton University Press, 2005), 30.

[4] See Chapter 5.

[5] See *ibid.*

[6] See Constitución Española, B.O.E. n. 311, December 29, 1978, §10.

[7] See Walter F. Murphy, 'An Ordering of Constitutional Values' (1979–80) 53 *Southern California Law Review* 703; Louis Henkin, 'Human Dignity and Constitutional Rights', in Michael J. Meyer and William A. Parent (eds.), *The Constitution of Rights: Human Dignity and American Values* (Ithaca, NY: Cornell University Press, 1992), 228; Maxine Goodman, 'Human Dignity in Supreme Court Constitutional Jurisprudence' (2006) 84 *Nebraska Law Review* 740; Leslie Meltzer Henry, 'The Jurisprudence of Dignity' (2011) 160 *University of Pennsylvania Law Review* 169; Erin Daly, *Dignity Rights: Courts, Constitutions, and the Worth of the Human Person* (Philadelphia: University of Pennsylvania Press, 2012). See also Chapter 11, section 3.

[8] See Dierk Ullrich, 'Concurring Visions: Human Dignity in the Canadian Charter of Rights and Freedoms and the Basic Law of the Federal Republic of Germany' (2003) 3 *Global Jurist Frontiers* 1. See also Chapter 12, section 2.

[9] See Laurie Ackermann, *Human Dignity: Lodestar for Equality in South Africa* (Cape Town: Juta, 2012).

the various factors that determine whether a limitation of a constitutional right is constitutional. What is human dignity in constitutions that recognize it solely as a constitutional value? This book's answer is that human dignity is the humanity of a person as such. Underlying that humanity is a person's free will and autonomy. It is a person's freedom to write her life story. This humanity always sees a person as an end unto herself and not merely as a means. It is the humanity of a person in the framework of the society in which she lives.

In a number of constitutions human dignity is not solely a constitutional value. It is recognized as a constitutional right. Examples are the Constitutions of Germany,[10] Colombia,[11] Russia,[12] Switzerland,[13] South Africa[14] and Israel.[15] According to purposive interpretation, the content of the right to human dignity is the fulfillment of the constitutional value of human dignity. Therefore, the purpose of the right to human dignity is fulfillment of the humanity of a person as such. Human dignity as a constitutional right is a person's freedom to write her life story. It is her free will. It is her autonomy and her freedom to shape her life and fulfill herself according to her own will rather than the will of others. This humanity is expressed in the framework of the society in which she lives.

The conception of the constitutional right to human dignity as the humanity of a person leads to a spacious view of the right. There is considerable overlap – complementary or conflicting – between the right to human dignity and the other constitutional rights. Complementary overlap is a welcome phenomenon. It reinforces each one of the overlapping rights. However, this spacious view of human dignity often leads to conflicting overlap between the right to human dignity and other constitutional rights (such as the rights to privacy and personal liberty) or the public interest (such as security and public welfare). Should that not narrow the scope of the right to human dignity? According to my approach, that conflict is natural to human existence. It does not reflect a constitutional mistake. It does not narrow the scope of the right to human dignity or the scopes of the other rights. At the constitutional level, the conflict

[10] Grundgesetz für die Bundesrepublik Deutschland [Grundgesetz] [GG] [Basic Law], May 23, 1949, BGBl. I, § 1(1). See also Chapter 13, section 1A.

[11] Constitution of Colombia, 1991, § 21.

[12] Constitution of Russia, 1993, § 21.

[13] Constitution of Switzerland, 1999, § 7.

[14] Constitution of South Africa, 1996, § 10. See also Chapter 14, section 1A.

[15] Basic Law: Human Dignity and Liberty, 5752–1992, SH No. 1391, 150 1992, § 2, 4. See also Chapter 15, section 1A.

will continue without a constitutional solution: let a thousand flowers bloom. The solution to the conflict will not be found at the constitutional level. It will be found at the sub-constitutional level. A sub-constitutional norm (statute or common law) that limits human dignity in order to protect another conflicting constitutional right or to fulfill a conflicting public interest will be constitutional only if it is proportional.

This spacious view of the right to human dignity is of course subject to another interpretational conclusion, resulting from the constitutional structure and architecture. This is the case in the German Basic Law. The right to human dignity in the German Basic Law is an absolute right.[16] It is not subject to the rules of proportionality. Any limitation of the right is unconstitutional. The right to human dignity in such a constitutional structure requires that a narrower construal of the value of human dignity be applied in understanding the constitutional right of human dignity. The right must be interpreted narrowly, because otherwise social life would be impossible. Thus the Constitutional Court of Germany uses the object formula (*Objektformel*) in order to understand human dignity as a constitutional right. According to this formula, human dignity is limited when a person is seen as a mere means for fulfilling someone else's ends. This formula reflects the absolute character of the right to human dignity in the German Constitution. This formula will not apply where human dignity, as a constitutional value, fulfills its task regarding the other constitutional rights recognized in the German Basic Law.

Interpretation of the right to human dignity with a spacious view, and understanding that right as the humanity of a person, grant the right to human dignity a broad application covering many issues. In most constitutions it constitutes both a negative right and a positive right. It covers aspects that are at the core of the right and aspects that are at its periphery. It covers both civil and social aspects. It applies to all conduct of the state vis-à-vis every person. The right to human dignity is seen as a framework right and a mother-right. Daughter-rights gather together under its wings. These daughter-rights express the various aspects of human dignity on different levels of generality. In a constitution with a comprehensive bill of rights, there will be complementary overlap between these daughter-rights and the independent freestanding rights recognized in the constitution. This does not make the right to human dignity superfluous, and should not turn it into a residual right. A statute that limits the constitutional right to human dignity and another independent constitutional

[16] See Grundgesetz, § 1(1). See Chapter 13, section 1B.

right will be constitutional only if it fulfills the requirements of proportionality that apply to human dignity as well as those that apply to the other right. However, the main role of the right to human dignity in a constitution with a full bill of rights is reinforcing the other, independent constitutional rights and serving as a source of daughter-rights where they are not recognized as independent rights. Thus, for example, in South Africa the constitution does not recognize a freestanding right to reputation. That right is recognized as a daughter-right of human dignity.[17] Of course, in a constitution with a comprehensive bill of rights, the right to human dignity will at times conflict with other constitutional rights. A conflict among daughter-rights of human dignity might also occur. Such conflict will not be solved at the constitutional level. The solution is found at the sub-constitutional level. A statute or common law that limits a constitutional right in order to protect human dignity will be constitutional only if it is proportional.

The spacious view of the constitutional right to human dignity is of course subject to criticism. Many critics point out that human dignity is a vague and flexible concept; they claim it grants the interpreter – the judge – undesirably broad discretion. My response to that criticism is that most constitutional rights "suffer" from similar traits. The right to equality and the right to liberty – like the right to human dignity – are vague and flexible rights that grant a judge broad discretion. Professional judges are accustomed to this phenomenon, and have the interpretational tools to handle it. What appears to the theologian and the philosopher as a limitless right appears to the judge as a right that is hemmed in by the rules of interpretation. These rules of interpretation do not prevent judicial discretion. Such discretion is innate to the judicial process, and constitutes an inseparable part of it.[18] Indeed, the problem of the scope of judicial discretion is not unique to human dignity, and it exists wherever there is a constitutional bill of rights based upon "majestic generalities."[19]

Another, intra-constitutional, criticism is that the spacious view of human dignity will ultimately lead to limitation of human rights. Protection of human dignity, which constitutes a positive right, will justify limitation of the negative constitutional rights. This criticism is not unique to human dignity. The conflict between constitutional rights is

[17] See *Khumalo* v. *Holomisa* 2002 (5) SA 401 (CC), para. 27. See Chapter 14, section 1E(1).

[18] See Aharon Barak, *Judicial Discretion* (Yale University Press, 1989); Marisa Iglesias Vila, *Facing Judicial Discretion: Legal Knowledge and Right Answers Revisited* (Dordrecht: Kluwer, 2001).

[19] See *Fay* v. *New York*, 332 US 261, 282 (1947) (Jackson J).

a healthy physiological phenomenon, not a negative pathological condition. Solution to the conflict will be found at the sub-constitutional level. This is made possible, of course, only if all of the constitutional rights are relative, and only if human dignity is not an absolute right. A great majority of constitutions are constructed in this way. German constitutional law is the exception, and there indeed human dignity as a constitutional right has a narrow scope.[20]

This book, like my book *Proportionality: Constitutional Rights and their Limitations*, is the product of both legal scholarship and legal practice. It reflects my thoughts on human dignity as I expressed them in articles and judgments I wrote. I served for twenty-eight years as a justice in the Supreme Court of Israel. The enactment of Basic Law: Human Dignity and Liberty, which granted constitutional status to the value and the right to human dignity, marked the beginning of the second half of my term. Along with my colleagues in the Supreme Court, I wrote scores of judgments dealing with human dignity. The theoretical analysis of the constitutional value and the constitutional right to human dignity is the result of their practical implementation.

This book focuses on human dignity as a constitutional value and a constitutional right. It is the first part of a larger volume on human dignity originally written in Hebrew. The second part of the Hebrew volume is dedicated to the eleven daughter-rights of human dignity that have been recognized in Israel so far: the rights to personality, dignified human subsistence, reputation, family life, equality, freedom of expression, freedom of conscience and religion, freedom of movement, education, employment and due process. This reflects vast judicial activity, which is based entirely on human dignity. This book is of course not limited to Israeli law; it is based upon comparative law. It can provide assistance to every legal system that has a constitution recognizing human dignity – whether as a value or as a right – in understanding its own approach to human dignity.

Like proportionality, human dignity as a constitutional right underwent particularly extensive development in German constitutional law. It seems that we all owe thanks to the German Constitutional Court and the German legal literature, which enriched our collective knowledge regarding human dignity. Nonetheless, we must be cognizant of the great difference between human dignity as a constitutional right in most modern constitutions and human dignity in German constitutional law. While

[20] See Chapter 13, section 1F.

in most constitutions human dignity is a relative right and is thus subject to proportional limitation, in the German Basic Law the right to human dignity is absolute and is thus not subject to proportional limitation. Every limitation is a violation. Despite this difference, understanding the German judgments and literature regarding the constitutional value of human dignity is very worthwhile. This value continues to have a broad meaning in German constitutional law. The German legal literature will likely be of great benefit to every legal system that has a similar approach.

The literature on human dignity is most extensive. Is another book on the subject really necessary? Many of the books and articles on the subject deal with human dignity from a perspective of theology or general philosophy. As noted, these are not the perspectives I examine in this book. The focus of this book is human dignity as a constitutional value and a constitutional right. The legal literature on this aspect of human dignity is sparse. Again, the German legal constitutional literature is exceptional, particularly the volumes by Enders[21] and Mahlmann.[22] The books by Ackermann,[23] Waldron,[24] Eberle[25] and Daly[26] stand out in the English landscape. Most of the literature is edited books.[27] They do not present

[21] Christoph Enders, *Die Menschenwürde in der Verfassungsordnung: zur Dogmatik des Art. 1 GG* (Tübingen: Mohr Siebeck, 1997), 501.

[22] Matthias Mahlmann, *Elemente einer ethischen Grundrechtstheorie* (Berlin: Nomos, 2008).

[23] Ackermann, *Human Dignity*.

[24] Jeremy Waldron, *Dignity, Rank, and Rights*, ed. by Meir Dan-Cohen (Oxford University Press, 2012).

[25] Edward J. Eberle, *Dignity and Liberty: Constitutional Visions in Germany and the United States* (Santa Barbara: Praeger, 2002).

[26] Daly, *Dignity Rights*.

[27] The most important among these are Michael Meyer and William Parent (eds.), *The Constitution of Rights: Human Dignity and American Values* (Ithaca, NY: Cornell University Press, 1992); David Kretzmer and Eckart Klein (eds.), *The Concept of Human Dignity in Human Rights Discourse* (The Hague: Kluwer Law International, 2002); Berma Klein Goldewijk, Adalid Contreras Baspineiro and Paulo Cesar Carbonari (eds.), *Dignity and Human Rights: The Implementation of Economic, Social and Cultural Rights* (Antwerp: Intersentia, 2002); Robert P. Kraynak and Glenn E. Tinder (eds.), *In Defense of Human Dignity: Essays for our Times* (University of Notre Dame Press, 2003); Silja Vöneky and Rüdiger Wolfrum (eds.), *Human Dignity and Human Cloning* (Leiden: Brill, 2004); Jeff E. Malpas and Norelle Lickiss (eds.), *Perspectives on Human Dignity: A Conversation* (Dordrecht: Springer, 2007); Paulus Kaufmann, Hannes Kuch, Christian Neuhäuser and Elaine Webster (eds.), *Humiliation, Degradation, Dehumanization: Human Dignity Violated* (Dordrecht: Springer, 2011); Christopher McCrudden (ed.), *Understanding Human Dignity* (Oxford University Press, 2013); Marcus Düwell, Jens Braarvig, Roger Brownsword and Dietmar Mieth (eds.), *The Cambridge Handbook of Human Dignity: Interdisciplinary Perspectives* (Cambridge University Press, 2014).

a coherent constitutional thesis focusing upon the constitutional value and right to human dignity. It is in this area that I see the contribution of this book.

The book is divided into four parts: Part I is dedicated to fundamental concepts (Chapter 1) and the intellectual history of human dignity (Chapter 2). This part also includes a review of human dignity in international documents and the constitutions of various states (Chapters 3 and 4). Part II is dedicated to human dignity as a constitutional value. The scope of this value and its role are determined through interpretation of the constitution. Thus, Part II opens with an analysis of the method of purposive interpretation, which serves as the legal mechanism for understanding human dignity (Chapter 5). On the basis of purposive interpretation I analyze the various roles of the constitutional value of human dignity (Chapter 6). The central role of the value is the interpretational task of revealing the meaning of the various rights, primarily the meaning of the right to human dignity. The seventh chapter, which is the central chapter in this part, deals with the content of human dignity as a constitutional value. This is not theological or philosophical content. It is the content of human dignity as a constitutional value with a constitutional role. According to this view, human dignity is the humanity of a person. It is her humanity as a free being, with unbridled autonomy. It is her freedom to write her life story. This humanity expresses the conception of a person as an end, and rejects viewing her as mere means. This humanity is humanity in the framework of society.

Part III deals with the constitutional right to human dignity. It examines the various ways of recognizing human dignity as a constitutional right (Chapter 8). The central chapter in this part is Chapter 9, which examines the content of the constitutional right to human dignity. The point of departure is that it is intended to fulfill the constitutional value of human dignity. This broad interpretation raises problems regarding the relationships between the right to human dignity and other constitutional rights. Various aspects of these relationships are examined in this chapter. The broad interpretation of human dignity as a framework right or mother-right sees human dignity as a bundle of rights that includes daughter-rights of human dignity. The chapter examines both the relationships between these daughter-rights and the relationships between them and the other constitutional rights. Chapter 10 focuses on the question of whether the right to human dignity covers an exclusive area of application.

Part IV examines human dignity's place in five constitutions. It opens with an examination of two constitutions – the US Constitution (Chapter 11) and the Canadian Charter of Rights and Freedoms (Chapter 12) – in which human dignity is solely a constitutional value. It then examines three additional constitutions – the German Basic Law (Chapter 13), the South African Constitution (Chapter 14) and the Israeli Basic Law: Human Dignity and Freedom (Chapter 15) – in which human dignity serves both as a constitutional value and as a constitutional right. In these three legal systems, it examines the traits of human dignity as a constitutional value, as well as its traits as a constitutional right, both as an absolute right (in German law) and as a relative right (in South African and Israeli law). In this light it examines the scope of the constitutional right to human dignity in these constitutions.

I am neither a theologian, nor a philosopher. I am a legal scholar and judge interested in comparative constitutional law. This is not a book on jurisprudence or political theory. It is an analytical book on constitutional law regarding the constitutional value and the constitutional right to human dignity. The book is intended for legal scholars, judges and practitioners. I hope that the comparative analysis enriches the readers and brings them closer to the fundamental value and right of human dignity.

ACKNOWLEDGEMENTS

I am grateful, first and foremost, to the Interdisciplinary Center Herzliya and its President, Uriel Reichman, and the Yale Law School and its Dean, Robert Post, who opened their doors to me and provided me with the research environment that enabled the writing of this book. I thank my research assistants Lior Hadas, Ori Kivity, Adi Koppel-Aviv, Stav Cohen, Tom Kohavi, Joey Lightstone and Liron Koren, as well as Esther Tammuz who coordinated the editing efforts and Dina Zahury who worked hard deciphering my handwriting. I also thank Daniel Kayros, who translated the Hebrew manuscript into English and the Oscar M. Ruebhausen Fund at Yale Law School that sponsored the translation. And, as always, I thank Elika, who is the embodiment of human dignity as the humanity of a person.

TABLE OF CASES

Israel

CA 7155/96 *A.* v. *the Attorney-General*, 13 IsrLR 115 (1997) 127, 288

HCJ 5373/08 *Abu Levada* v. *The Minister of Education* (6.2.2011) 299

CA 9535/06 *Abu Musa'ed* v. *The Water Commissioner* (5.6.2011) 289, 290, 291

HCJ 8276/05 *Adalah* v. *Minister of Defense* 2006-2 IsrLR 352 (2006) 127

HCJ 7052/03 *Adalah* v. *Minister of Interior* 2006-1 IsrLR 443, 486–7 (2006) 151, 160, 179, 293, 295

HCJ 5631/01 *AKIM* v. *the Minister of Labor and Social Welfare* IsrSC 58(1) 936 (2003) 291

LCA 4740/00 *Amar* v. *Yoseph*, LCA 4740/00, IsrLR 401 (2001) 165

FH 13/60 *Attorney-General* v. *Aharon Matana*, 4 IsrLR 112, 123 (1962) 100

PPA 4463/94 *Avi Hanania Golan* v. *Prisons Service*, 1995–1996 12 IsrLR 489 (1996) 41

HCJ 4593/05 *Bank HaMizrahi* v. *The Prime Minister* (20.9.2006) 282

CA 6821/93 *Bank Mizrahi* v. *Migdal Cooperative Village*, IsrLR 1, 43 (1995) 148, 284

RT 3032/99 *Baranes* v. *State of Israel*, IsrSC 56(3) 354 (2002) 300

HVJ 1181/03 *Bar-Ilan University* v. *the National Labor Court* (28.4.2011) 290, 299

HCJ 531/77 *Baruch* v. *The Supervisor of Transportation*, IsrSC 32(2) 160 (1978) 298

HCJ 428/86 *Barzilay* v. *Government of Israel*, IsrSC 40(3) 505 (1986) 86

LCA 10520/03 *Ben Gvir* v. *Dankner* (12.11.2006) 157, 179

HCJ 1890/03 *Bethlehem Municipality* v. *Ministry of Defense*, 2005-1 IsrLR 98 (2005) 296

LCrimA 8295/02 *Biton* v. *Sultan*, IsrSC 59(6) 554 (2005) 296

HCJ 366/03 *Commitment to Peace and Social Justice Society* v. *Minister of Finance* 2005-2 IsrLR 335 (2005) 140, 148, 280

HCJ 164/97 *Conterm Ltd.* v. *Finance Ministry*, 14 IsrLR 1 (1998) 290

HCJ 7444/03 *Daka* v. *The Minister of Interior* (22.2.2010) 294

LabCH 4-10/98 *Delek* v. *Histadrut*, IsrLabC 33, 338 (1998) 300

CrimA 3632/92 *Gabay* v. *State of Israel*, IsrSC 46(4) 487, 490 (1992) 20, 21

LCA 4905/98 *Gamzu* v. *Yeshayahu*, IsrSC 55(3) 360 (2001) 290

CrimFH 2316/95 *Ganimat* v. *State of Israel*, IsrSC 49(4) 589 (1995) 307

LCA 2687/92 *Geva* v. *Walt Disney*, IsrSC 48(1) 251, 265 (1993) 296

Australia

Canada

England

European Court of Human Rights

Germany

India

South Africa

The United States

Glass v. *Louisiana*, 471 US 1080 (1985) 201
Glasser v. *United States*, 315 US 60 (1942) 194
Goldberg v. *Kelly*, 397 US 254 (1970) 200
Gompers v. *United States*, 233 US 604 (1914) 100
Gonzales v. *Carhart*, 550 US 124 (2007) 199, 203
Gregg v. *Georgia*, 428 US 153 (1976) 110, 201
Griswold v. *Connecticut*, 381 US 479 (1965) 77, 141, 186, 189, 205
Hampton v. *Mow Sun Wong*, 426 US 88 (1976) 200
Harris v. *United States*, 331 US 145 (1947) 197
Heart of Atlanta Motel Inc. v. *United States*, 379 US 241 (1964) 199
Hewitt v. *Helms*, 459 US 460 (1983) 199
Homma v. *Patterson, Secretary of War*, 327 US 759 (1946) 196
Hope v. *Pelzer*, 536 US 730 (2002) 199
Hudson v. *Michigan*, 547 US 586 (2006) 198
Hudson v. *Palmer*, 468 US 517 (1984) 199
In re Yamashita, 327 US 1 (1946) 196
Indiana v. *Edwards*, 554 US 164 (2008) 199
Irvin v. *Dowd*, 366 US 717 (1961) 199
Irvine v. *California*, 347 US 128 (1954) 197
J.E.B. v. *Alabama ex. rel. T.B.*, 511 US 127 (1994) 199, 202
Johnson v. *Eisentrager*, 339 US 763 (1950) 197
Jones v. *Barnes*, 463 US 745 (1983) 201
Kennedy v. *Louisiana*, 554 US 407 (2008) 199
Korematsu v. *United States*, 323 US 214 (1944) 195
Lawrence v. *Texas*, 539 US 558 (2003) 199, 202
Lochner v. *New York*, 198 US 45 (1905) 86
Louisiana ex. rel. Francis v. *Resweber*, 329 US 459 (1947) 197
McCulloch v. *Maryland*, 17 US 316, 407 (1819) 71
McDonald v. *City of Chicago*, 561 US 3025 (2010) 199
McKaskle v. *Wiggins*, 465 US 168 (1984) 199
McNabb v. *United States*, 318 US 332 (1943) 194
Miller v. *Johnson*, 515 US 900 (1995) 199
Miranda v. *Arizona*, 384 US 436 (1966) 199
Missouri v. *Holland*, 252 US 416, 433 (1920) 87
NAACP v. *Claiborne Hardware Co.*, 458 US 886 (1982) 199
National Treasury Employees Union v. *Von Raab*, 489 US 656 (1989) 198
New York Times v. *Sullivan*, 376 US 254 (1964) 107
O'Lone v. *Estate of Shabazz*, 482 US 342 (1987) 200
Ohio v. *Akron Center for Reproductive Health*, 497 US 502 (1990) 199
Osborn v. *United States*, 385 US 323 (1966) 198
Oyama v. *California*, 332 US 633 (1948) 197

Winston v. *Lee*, 470 US 753 (1985) 200
Woodford v. *Ngo*, 548 US 81 (2006) 199

Others

94–343/344 DC of 27 July 1994 (France) 58
CE, October 27, 1995, Rec. Lebon 372, Conseil d'État statuant au contentieux, n. 143578, n. 136727 (France) 123
Conseil Constitutionnel, no. 71-44 DC du 16 juillet 1971 (France) 58
Kingdom of the Netherlands v. *European Parliament & Council of the European Union*, Case C–377/98, 2001 ECR I–7079 (ECJ) 54
SC 58/2005 *Hansen* v. *The Queen*, [2007] NZSC 7 (New Zealand) 153

PART I

Fundamental concepts and sources

1

The various aspects of human dignity

1. Theology, philosophy and constitutional law

A. The difference between the intellectual history and the constitutional interpretation

The roots of the English term "dignity" are found in the Latin word *dignus, dignitas.* In romance languages the words *dignité* (French), *dignità* (Italian), *dignidade* (Portuguese) and *dignidad* (Spanish) are used.[1] In English dictionaries the definitions of dignity appear as honor, glory and respect.[2]

This abundance of meanings stems from the complexity of the concept of "human dignity."[3] Over the course of its long history, it has been used primarily as a social value.[4] The appearance of human dignity as a constitutional value and as a constitutional right is new: it is only as old as modern constitutions. Human dignity benefitted from special

1 See Margareta Broberg, 'A Brief Introduction', in Margareta Broberg and J. B. Ladegaard Knox (eds.), *Dignity, Ethics and Law* (Copenhagen: Centre for Ethics and Law, 1999) 7, 8.

2 In the Oxford English Dictionary there are five definitions of dignity: *The New Shorter Oxford English Dictionary*, ed. by Lesley Brown (Oxford: Clarendon Press, 1993). See also Aurel Kolnai, 'Dignity' (1976) 51 *Philosophy* 251; Gloria L. Zúñiga, 'An Ontology of Dignity' (2004) 5 *Metaphysica* 115.

3 See *Egan* v. *Canada*, [1995] 2 SCR 513, 545 ("Dignity being a notoriously elusive concept"); David Feldman, 'The Developing Scope of Article 8 of the European Convention on Human Rights' (1997) 3 *European Human Rights Law Review* 265; *National Coalition for Gay and Lesbian Equality* v. *Minister of Justice*, 1999 (1) SA 6 (CC), para. 28: "Dignity is a difficult concept to capture in precise terms" (Ackermann J); Michael Meyer, 'Dignity as a (Modern) Virtue', in David Kretzmer and Eckart Klein (eds.), *The Concept of Human Dignity in Human Rights Discourse* (The Hague: Kluwer Law International, 2002) 195.

4 For the differentiation between a social value and a social ideal, see Drucilla Cornell, 'Bridging the Span toward Justice: Laurie Ackermann and the Ongoing Architectonic of Dignity Jurisprudence' (2008) *Acta Juridica* 18.

development in light of the severe violations that took place during the Second World War.[5]

Those dealing with human dignity – whether theologians (like Thomas Aquinas) or philosophers (such as Immanuel Kant) – did not deal with the constitutional value of and right to human dignity as part of a constitutional bill of rights. This is because there was no constitutional bill of rights whatsoever at the time, and there certainly was no discussion of the constitutional meaning – whether as a value or as a right – of human dignity. That discussion has been underway for only a short time, and is still at its very early stages. Of course, the modern discussion of the constitutional value and constitutional right rests upon the long theological and philosophical history of human dignity. However, the constitutional discussion is unique, and is decisively influenced by its constitutional character. This is the source of both the importance of the intellectual history to the constitutional discourse, and its limited applicability. Justice M. Cheshin, of the Israeli Supreme Court, discussed this difference between the legal-constitutional and other points of view in one case[6] in which he examined the question of whether freedom of expression is part of the constitutional right to human dignity:

> The subject incorporates not only the meaning of the concept of "human dignity" in its linguistic, moral, political, historical and philosophical senses, but also – or should we say, mainly – the meaning of the concept in the special context of the Basic Law: Human Dignity and Liberty. This special context – which is bound up with the relationship between the organs of the State – can also directly affect the sphere of influence of "human dignity."[7]

Indeed, the intellectual process of understanding the meaning of the constitutional value and the constitutional right to human dignity is a process of constitutional interpretation.

B. *The similarity between the intellectual history and the constitutional interpretation*

Despite the essential difference between the long theological and philosophical history of the concept of human dignity and its short

[5] See James Q. Whitman, 'On Nazi "Honour" and the New European "Dignity"', in Christian Joerges and Navraj S. Ghaleigh (eds.), *Darker Legacies of Law in Europe: The Shadow of National Socialism* (Oxford: Hart Publishing, 2003) 243.

[6] See PPA 4463/94 *Avi Hanania Golan* v. *Prisons Service*, 1995–1996 12 IsrLR 489 (1996).

[7] *Ibid.* at 550.

constitutional history, there are a number of similarities between these two "histories." First, they both involve an intellectual process with a moral[8] and ethical[9] basis that is entrenched in the culture of a society. Human dignity in a western culture is not the same as human dignity in a non-western culture;[10] human dignity in one western culture is not the same as human dignity in another western culture.[11] It is a concept that is in a constant state of development.[12] Justice Brennan correctly noted that "the demands of human dignity will never cease to evolve."[13] In a similar spirit the German Constitutional Court noted in *Life Imprisonment*:

> Recognizing what the command to respect human dignity requires cannot be separated from history. A judgment regarding what corresponds to human dignity can only be based on the current state of knowledge and cannot lay claim to interminable validity.[14]

8 See Bertram Morris, 'The Dignity of Man' (1946) 57 *Ethics* 57. For a different approach, see Meyer, 'Dignity as a (Modern) Virtue'. See also, Rachel Bayefsky, 'Dignity, Honour, and Human Rights: Kant's Perspective' (2013) 41 *Political Theory* 809.

9 See Abraham Edel, 'Humanist Ethics and the Meaning of Human Dignity', in Paul Kurtz (ed.), *Moral Problems in Contemporary Society: Essays in Humanistic Ethics* (Englewood Cliffs: Prentice-Hall, 1969) 232; Thomas W. Platt, 'Human Dignity and the Conflict of Rights' (1972) 2 *Idealistic Studies* 174; Paulo C. Carbonari, 'Human Dignity as a Basic Concept of Ethics and Human Rights', in Berma K. Goldewijk, Adalid C. Baspineiro and Paulo C. Carbonari (eds.), *Dignity and Human Rights: The Implementation of Economic, Social and Cultural Rights* (Antwerp: Intersentia, 2002) 35; Jeff Malpas and Norelle Lickiss, 'Human Dignity and Human Being', in Jeff Malpas and Norelle Lickiss (eds.), *Perspectives on Human Dignity: A Conversation* (Dordrecht: Springer Publication, 2007) 19.

10 See Jack Donnelly, 'Human Rights and Human Dignity: An Analytic Critique of Non-Western Conceptions of Human Rights' (1982) 76 *American Political Science Review* 303; Stephen Angle, *Human Rights and Chinese Thought: A Cross Cultural Inquiry* (Cambridge University Press, 2002); Man Yee Karen Lee, 'Universal Human Dignity: Some Reflections in the Asian Context' (2008) 3 *Asian Journal of Comparative Law* 1932. See also Raul S. Manglapus, 'Human Rights Are Not a Western Discovery' (1978) 21(10) *Worldview* 4.

11 See Giovanni Bognetti, 'The Concept of Human Dignity in European and US Constitutionalism', in George Nolte (ed.), *European and US Constitutionalism* (Cambridge University Press, 2005) 85; Stéphanie Hennette-Vauchez, 'When Ambivalent Principles Prevail: Leads for Explaining Western Legal Orders' Infatuation with the Human Dignity Principle' (2007) 10 *Legal Ethics* 193.

12 See Alan Gewirth, 'Human Dignity as the Basis of Rights', in Michael J. Meyer and William A. Parent (eds.), *The Constitution of Rights: Human Dignity and American Values* (Ithaca, NY: Cornell University Press 1992) 10.

13 See Stephen J. Wermiel, 'Law and Human Dignity: The Judicial Soul of Justice Brennan' (1998) 7 *William & Mary Bill of Rights Journal* 223, 239.

14 BVerfGe 45, 187, 229 (1997). See also the First Abortions case (BVerfGE 39, 1 (1975)).

Indeed, human dignity is a contextually dependent value. It is a changing value in a changing world.[15] It may be that the concept of human dignity in a given society was initially based upon the religious view that sees God's image in man. Eventually a change may have taken place in that society's view, and it now bases human dignity upon Kantian rationality. This view as well might change. Indeed, any understanding of human dignity is based upon a given society's understanding at a given time, which might change as times change.[16] Therefore, I do not accept the opinion that human dignity is an axiomatic, universal concept.[17] In my opinion, human dignity is a relative concept,[18] dependent upon historical,[19] cultural,[20] religious, social[21] and political[22] contexts.[23] This relativity of

[15] See Matthias Mahlmann, *Elemente einer ethischen Grundrechtstheorie* (Berlin: Nomos, 2008) 5.

[16] See David P. Currie, *The Constitution of the Federal Republic of Germany* (University of Chicago Press, 1994) 315.

[17] See Abraham I. Melden, 'Dignity, Worth, and Rights', in Michael J. Meyer and William A. Parent (eds.), *The Constitution of Rights: Human Dignity and American Values* (Ithaca, NY: Cornell University Press 1992) 29; Nazeem M. Goolam, 'Human Dignity – Our Supreme Constitutional Value' (2001) 4 *Potchefstroom Electronic Law Journal* 1, 5; Anton De Baets, 'A Successful Utopia: The Doctrine of Human Dignity' (2007) 7 *Historein* 71.

[18] See Jackie Jones, '"Common Constitutional Traditions": Can the Meaning of Human Dignity under German Law Guide the European Court of Justice?' (Spring 2004) *Public Law* 167.

[19] See Henk Botha, 'Human Dignity in Comparative Perspective' (2009) 2 *Stellenbosch Law Review* 171, 178; Juliane Kokott, 'From Reception and Transplantation to Convergence of Constitutional Models in the Age of Globalization – With Particular Reference to the German Basic Law', in Christian Starck (ed.), *Constitutionalism, Universalism and Democracy: a Comparative Analysis* (Baden-Baden: Nomos Publication, 1999) 71.

[20] See Rhoda E. Howard, 'Dignity, Community, and Human Rights', in Abdullahi Ahmed An-Na'im (ed.), *Human Rights in Cross-Cultural Perspectives – A Quest for Consensus* (Philadelphia: University of Pennsylvania Press, 1992) 81; David Weisstub, 'Honor, Dignity and the Framing of Multiculturalists Values', in David Kretzmer and Eckart Klein (eds.), *The Concept of Human Dignity in Human Rights Discourse* (The Hague: Kluwer Law International, 2002) 263; Kokott, 'From Reception and Transplantation'.

[21] See Kokott, 'From Reception and Transplantation'; Doron Shultziner, 'Human Dignity – Justification, not a Human Right' (2007) 11 *Hamishpat* 527 (Heb.); Antonio S. Cua, 'Dignity of Persons and Styles of Life' (1971) 45 *Proceedings of the American Catholic Philosophical Association* 120; Paolo G. Carozza, 'Human Dignity in Constitutional Adjudication', in Tom Ginsburg and Rosalind Dixon (eds.), *Comparative Constitutional Law* (Cheltenham: Edward Elgar, 2011) 459.

[22] See Rhoda E. Howard and Jack Donnelly, 'Human Dignity, Human Rights, and Political Regimes' (1986) 80(3) *American Political Science Review* 801; Mette Lebech, 'What is Human Dignity?', in Mette Lebech (ed.), *Maynooth Philosophical Papers* (National University of Ireland Maynooth, 2004) 59.

[23] See Cua, 'Dignity of Persons and Styles of Life'; Kokott, 'From Reception and Transplantation', at 81; Carozza, 'Human Dignity in Constitutional Adjudication'. See also Shultziner, 'Human Dignity'.

human dignity does not diminish its importance. On the contrary: this relativity intensifies the position of human dignity in each society, while expressing the special experiences of the society and influencing its conclusions. Thus, for example, human dignity in post-Second World War Germany expresses disgust toward Nazism and constitutes the basis for the development of German post-war society. Similarly, human dignity in post-apartheid South Africa reflects the detachment from that regime and the lodestar by which the new South Africa wishes to progress. Furthermore, despite the relativity of human dignity and its dependence upon social context, human dignity in various societies – certainly in societies based upon liberal democracy[24] – has common foundations. It can therefore be said that despite the fact that there are different conceptions of human dignity, they all express a similar concept.[25]

Second, the intellectual history of human dignity as a social value is based upon different theological and philosophical approaches. As human dignity as a constitutional value and a constitutional right developed, the constitutional aspect joined this history. Despite the difference in approaches, the social and constitutional values often lead to overlapping results and share a common core.[26] Thus, for example, different, and even conflicting, traditions lead to the conclusion that human dignity preserves the physical and psychological integrity of a person,[27] their personal identity[28] and their basic subsistence, and ensures equality between people.[29]

[24] See Jeremy Waldron, 'The Dignity of Groups' (2008) *Acta Juridica* 66; Christopher McCrudden, 'Human Dignity and Judicial Interpretation of Human Rights' (2008) 19 *European Journal of International Law* 655.

[25] See McCrudden, 'Human Dignity and Judicial Interpretation'; Howard and Donnelly, 'Human Dignity, Human Rights, and Political Regimes', at 801; Ernst L. Winnacker, 'Human Cloning from a Scientific Perspective', in Silja Vöneky and Rüdiger Wolfrum (eds.), *Human Dignity and Human Cloning* (Leiden: Martinus Nijhoff, 2004) 55; Meir Dan-Cohen, 'A Concept of Dignity' (2011) 44 *Israel Law Review* 9.

[26] See Carozza, 'Human Dignity in Constitutional Adjudication'; Horst Dreier, *GG Grundgesetz Kommentar* (Tübingen: Mohr Siebeck, 2006) 20.

[27] See Daniel Statman, 'Humiliation, Dignity, and Self Respect', in David Kretzmer and Eckart Klein (eds.), *The Concept of Human Dignity in Human Rights Discourse* (The Hague: Kluwer Law International, 2002) 209; Aart Hendriks, 'Personal Autonomy, Good Care, Informed Consent and Human Dignity – Some Reflections from a European Perspective' (2009) 28 *Medicine and Law* 469, 472.

[28] See Steven Wheatley, 'Human Rights and Human Dignity in the Resolution of Certain Ethical Questions in Biomedicine' (2001) 3 *European Human Rights Law Review* 312.

[29] See Statman, 'Humiliation, Dignity, and Self-Respect'.

Third, all of the meanings of human dignity – the theological, philosophical and constitutional meanings – deal with human dignity within society. Indeed, it does not exist in a void. Human dignity is the dignity of a person in a given society.[30] It is not the human dignity of the solitary Robinson Crusoe. It is the human dignity of a person in his or her relations with others. It is a "relational" concept.[31]

2. Criticism of the use of the concept of human dignity and response to it

A. *The criticism*

The concept of human dignity is the subject of sharp disagreement.[32] On the one hand, there are those who see it as one of the most important social concepts[33] and as a concept that serves as a basis and justification for all human rights.[34] On the other hand, there are those who hold that it is an elusive concept,[35] devoid of all content.[36] Criticism of human dignity comes from various directions. Philosophers criticize it. Schopenhauer's statement is well known:

[30] Edward J. Eberle, *Dignity and Liberty: Constitutional Visions in Germany and the United States* (Santa Barbara: Praeger Publishers, 2002) 42.

[31] See Laurie Ackermann, *Human Dignity: Lodestar for Equality in South Africa* (Cape Town: Juta, 2012) 75.

[32] See Botha, 'Human Dignity in Comparative Perspective'.

[33] See Ronald Dworkin, *Justice for Hedgehogs* (Cambridge, MA: Harvard University Press, 2011); Walter F. Murphy, *Constitutional Democracy: Creating and Maintaining a Just Political Order* (Baltimore: The Johns Hopkins University Press, 2007).

[34] See Gewirth, 'Human Dignity as the Basis of Rights'; Christoph Enders, *Die Menschenwürde in der Verfassungsordnung: zur Dogmatik des Art. 1 GG* (Tübingen: Mohr Siebeck, 1997) 501; Christoph Enders, 'A Right to Have Rights – The German Constitutional Concept of Human Dignity' (2010) 3 *NUJS Law Review* 253.

[35] See Edward J. Eberle, 'Human Dignity, Privacy and Personality in German and American Constitutional Law' (1997) 4 *Utah Law Review* 963, 965; Michael Rosen, *Dignity: Its History and Meaning* (Cambridge, MA: Harvard University Press, 2012).

[36] See Joern Eckert, 'Legal Roots of Human Dignity in German Law', in David Kretzmer and Eckart Klein (eds.), *The Concept of Human Dignity in Human Rights Discourse* (The Hague: Kluwer Law International, 2002) 41; Ruth Macklin, 'Dignity Is a Useless Concept' (2003) 327 *British Medical Journal* 1419; Mirko Bagaric and James Allan, 'The Vacuous Concept of Dignity' (2006) 5 *Journal of Human Rights* 257; Reiner Anselm, 'Human Dignity as a Regulatory Principle of Bioethics: A Theological Perspective', in Nikolaus Knoepffler, Dagmar Schipanski and Stefan L. Sorgner (eds.), *Human-Biotechnology as Social Challenge: An Interdisciplinary Introduction to Bioethics* (Aldershot: Ashgate Publishing, 2007) 109.

> The expression, dignity of man, once uttered by Kant, afterward became the shibboleth of all the perplexed and empty headed moralists who concealed behind that imposing expression their lack of any real basis of morals, or, at any rate, of one that had any meaning. They cunningly counted on the fact that their readers would be glad to see themselves invested with such a dignity and would accordingly be quite satisfied with it.[37]

Jurists claim that the concept of human dignity is dangerous for human rights.[38] In the opinion of the jurist-critics, human dignity can be seen as a Trojan horse that will lead to severe limitation of human rights.[39] According to that approach, it is inappropriate to use human dignity in the rights discourse.[40] The use of the concept grants judges the power to do with it as they please.[41] All the critics – and even some of the supporters – point out that human dignity is an equivocal,[42] vague[43] and flexible[44] concept that grants the interpreter wide discretion.[45]

[37] Arthur Schopenhauer, *On the Basis of Morality* (Indianapolis: Bobbs-Merrill, 1965) 100.

[38] See Carozza, 'Human Dignity in Constitutional Adjudication', at 459; Neomi Rao, 'On the Use and Abuse of Dignity in Constitutional Law' (2008) 14 *Columbia. Journal of European Law* 201; Matthias Mahlmann, 'The Basic Law at 60 – Human Dignity and the Culture of Republicanism' (2010) 11 *German Law Journal* 9; Neomi Rao, 'Three Concepts of Dignity in Constitutional Law' (2011) 86 *Notre Dame Law Review* 183.

[39] See Mahlmann, *Elemente einer ethischen Grundrechtstheorie*, at 11; Anselm, 'Human Dignity as a Regulatory Principle of Bioethics', at 110.

[40] Shultziner, 'Human Dignity'; Eberle, 'Human Dignity, Privacy and Personality', at 963; Macklin, 'Dignity Is a Useless Concept', at 1420; Lorraine E. Weinrib, 'Human Dignity as a Rights-Protecting Principle' (2004) 17 *National Journal of Constitutional Law* 325, 339; Dreier, *GG Grundgesetz Kommentar*, at 17; Hennette-Vauchez, 'When Ambivalent Principles Prevail'; Rory O'Connell, 'The Role of Dignity in Equality Law: Lessons from Canada and South Africa' (2008) 6 *International Journal of Constitutional Law* 267; Susanne Baer, 'Dignity, Liberty, Equality: A Fundamental Rights Triangle of Constitutionalism' (2009), 59 *University of Toronto Law Journal* 417, 465.

[41] D. M. Davis, 'Equality: The Majesty of Legoland Jurisprudence' (1999) 116 *South African Law Journal* 398, 413 ("The Constitutional Court ... has given dignity both a content and a scope that make for a piece of a jurisprudential Legoland – to be used in whatever form and shape is required by the demands of the judicial designer").

[42] O'Connell, 'The Role of Dignity in Equality Law'; Rao, 'Three Concepts of Dignity in Constitutional Law'.

[43] Mahlmann, *Elemente einer ethischen Grundrechtstheorie*, at 11.

[44] Botha, 'Human dignity in Comparative Perspective', at 187.

[45] Botha, 'Human dignity in Comparative Perspective'; Feldman, 'The Developing Scope of Article 8'.

B. *The response*

There is no doubt that human dignity is a complex concept.[46] This complexity stems, inter alia, from the lack of consensus regarding its essence. The lack of consensus is found primarily on three levels: there is no consensus regarding human dignity's content;[47] there is no consensus regarding human dignity's underlying rationale beyond a common core;[48] and there is no consensus regarding the results to which human dignity leads.

This complexity is not a sufficient reason to justify a negative approach toward human dignity. Equality, liberty and life are also complex concepts, and their content, underlying rationales and results are also controversial. That cannot justify ignoring them.[49] Similarly, proportionality is a complex concept, but that does not prevent its use. Quite the opposite: it is an expression par excellence of laws' migration from one system to another.[50] This is the case regarding human dignity. Its complexity does not make it useless. Indeed, equality, liberty and life are concepts that have been with us for centuries, whereas human dignity is a new concept in constitutional law.[51] This novelty passes quickly; society gets accustomed to the new concept, with all its problems. What in the past appeared vague and unclear becomes natural and accepted in the present.

In any case, what philosophers consider to be unclear and vague is not necessarily unclear and vague to jurists. Judges do not enjoy the extent of discretion granted to theologians and philosophers. They live in a legal framework, which determines rules on whose opinion is decisive and whose is not. The judge who must give meaning to human dignity in a constitution does not have the freedom of the philosopher to agree with Kant or to reject his approach. The original complexity of the concept disappears, replaced by concepts that must be implemented. This complexity,

[46] Meyer, 'Dignity as a (Modern) Virtue', at 196; O'Connell, 'The Role of Dignity in Equality Law'; Rao, 'Three Concepts of Dignity in Constitutional Law', at 192.

[47] McCrudden, 'Human Dignity and Judicial Interpretation', at 712.

[48] See section 1B of this chapter.

[49] Arthur Chaskalson, 'Human Dignity as a Constitutional Value', in David Kretzmer and Eckart Klein (eds.), *The Concept of Human Dignity in Human Rights Discourse* (The Hague: Kluwer Law International, 2002) 133, 135; Paolo G. Carozza, 'Human Dignity and Judicial Interpretation of Human Rights: A Reply' (2008) 19 *European Journal of International Law* 931.

[50] Aharon Barak, *Proportionality: Constitutional Rights and their Limitation*, Doron Kalir trans. (Cambridge University Press, 2012) 181.

[51] Rao, 'Three Concepts of Dignity in Constitutional Law', at 190.

which is seen by non-jurists as a negative factor, is seen by the constitutional jurist as a necessity, and as an advantage that allows human dignity to fulfill its function in a changing society.

More difficult is the "internal" criticism, by jurists themselves, who see human dignity not only as a source for protecting rights, but also as a source for limiting them. This criticism is based in law. At times an argument regarding the right to human dignity constitutes a basis for limiting a constitutional right.[52] At times human dignity appears on both sides of the constitutional balance.[53] This criticism is not unique to human dignity. Protection of any constitutional right can be a constitutional cause for limiting other constitutional rights, provided that the limitation is proportional. Human dignity is by no means unique in this regard. Indeed, every constitutional value and every constitutional right are both a source for protection of other constitutional rights and a source for their limitation. The constitutionality of such a limitation is decided according to the rules of proportionality.

The internal criticism is unique to human dignity only in those legal systems in which human dignity is an absolute constitutional right,[54] that is, a right whose entire scope is protected and any limitation is unconstitutional. That is the case in the German Constitution.[55] In its framework, protection of the right to human dignity justifies any limitation of any other constitutional right, without consideration of the proportionality of the limitation. Indeed, in the framework of the German Constitution, protection of human dignity is so strong that it can lead to disproportionate limitations of other rights. In such a state of affairs, the internal criticism is justified. However, this criticism is not of the concept of human dignity, rather of the absolute character of the right to human dignity in German constitutional law.[56] This criticism does not apply to the constitutions of most of the states that recognize a constitutional right to human dignity, because within their frameworks human dignity is a relative right.[57] A relative right is a right that is not protected in its full scope.

[52] For example: as justification for limiting the freedom of expression due to the limitation of human dignity, from which the right to reputation is derived. See Chapter 9, section 2E(4)(a).

[53] See Chapter 9, section 2E(4)(a).

[54] Regarding the essence of the absolute right, see Barak, *Proportionality*, at 27.

[55] See Chapter 13, section 1B.

[56] On the question whether human dignity should be recognized as an absolute right, see Mahlmann, *Elemente einer ethischen Grundrechtstheorie*, at 232.

[57] On the essence of the relative right, see Barak, *Proportionality*, at 32.

It can be limited. Not every limitation constitutes a violation. Limitations are constitutional if they are proportional.

Finally, in recent years great developments in medical research have taken place that raise bioethical problems in areas such as cloning, stem cell research and other techniques of genetic engineering.[58] Many oppose this development, as they are concerned for the future of the human race. One of the constitutional mechanisms used by this opposition is the right to human dignity. If the protection of the human race falls within the scope of the right to human dignity, then legislation that allows various developments in the bioethical field may limit that right. Such activity may then become unconstitutional at a certain phase. The response to this argument is twofold. First, the question whether human dignity applies to the protection of the human race has not yet been decided. Second, even if the legislation allowing the bioethical research might limit human dignity, that does not necessarily prevent such research. The decision – in this area as in every other area – will ultimately be made according to the rules of proportionality. Of course, this answer does not hold regarding German law, but it is an appropriate answer in all other legal systems.

3. Human dignity – a social value, a constitutional value and a constitutional right

Human dignity, according to its modern meaning, has three aspects: it is a social value, it is a constitutional value and it is a constitutional right. Human dignity as a social value reflects human dignity's place among the values of a given society at a given time. The intellectual history of human dignity, which will be discussed later,[59] is its history as a social value. It is expressed in religious and philosophical texts, in literature and in the poetry of nations and societies.

As constitutions were being developed – primarily during the second half of the twentieth century – it became possible to speak not only of the social value of human dignity, but also of the constitutional value of human dignity. This value focuses upon the aspect of human dignity as a social value that has been expressed – explicitly or implicitly – in the constitution of the state. By its very nature, the scope of the constitutional

[58] See Horst Dreier, 'Does Cloning Violate the Basic Law's Guarantee of Human Dignity?', in Silja Vöneky and Rüdiger Wolfrum (eds.), *Human Dignity and Human Cloning* (Leiden: Martinus Nijhoff, 2004) 77.

[59] See Chapter 2, section 1.

value is narrower than the scope of the social value. The reason for this is that only those aspects of the social value of human dignity that are (explicitly or implicitly) expressed in the constitution, and comport with its language and structure, are included within the constitutional value of human dignity.

The right to human dignity stands beside the (social and constitutional) value of human dignity.[60] Of course, the constitutional right to human dignity is based upon the constitutional value of human dignity. However, the two are not necessarily identical. In a number of constitutions, the constitutional value of human dignity is recognized, without the constitutional right to human dignity also being recognized.[61] That is the case regarding the constitutions of Spain[62] (in which the constitutional value of human dignity is recognized expressly) and of Canada[63] and the United States[64] (in which the constitutional value of human dignity is implied). In these three legal systems the constitutional right to human dignity is not recognized. Furthermore, even when a constitution recognizes the constitutional value of human dignity, the scope of this value will at times be broader than the scope of the constitutional right. The reason for this is found in the structure of the constitution

[60] On the distinction between human dignity as a constitutional value and human dignity as a constitutional right, see Chaskalson, 'Human Dignity as a Constitutional Value'; Nicholas Haysom, 'Dignity', in Halton Cheadle, Dennis Davis and Nicholas Haysom (eds.), *South African Constitutional Law: The Bill of Rights* (Durban: Butterworths, 2002) 131; Donnelly, 'Human Rights and Human Dignity', at 306. The difference between the constitutional value and the constitutional right is not similar to the difference between a principle and a rule. For a different approach, see Rao, 'On the Use and Abuse of Dignity in Constitutional Law', at 223; Francois Venter, 'Human Dignity as a Constitutional Value: A South African Perspective', in Jörn Ipsen, Dietrich Rauschning and Edzard Schmidt-Jortzig (eds.), *Recht, Staat, Gemeinwohl: Festschrift für Dietrich Rauschning* (Munich: Heymann 2001) 341 ("[A] proper understanding of the effect on constitutional interpretation and application of the founding value of the constitution, especially of human dignity as value, requires the recognition of both the distinction between and the inter-dependence of rights and values"); Stuart Woolman, 'Dignity', in Stuart Woolman, Michael Bishop and Jason Brickhill (eds.), *Constitutional Law of South Africa*, 2nd edn, Revision Series 4 (Cape Town: Juta, 2012) chapter 36, p. 19.

[61] See David Feldman, 'Human Dignity as a Legal Value: Part 1' (Winter 1999) *Public Law* 682; David Feldman, 'Human Dignity as a Legal Value: Part 2' (Spring 2000) *Public Law* 61.

[62] See Jesus Gonzalez Perez, *La Dignidad de la Persona* (Madrid: Civitas Ediciones S.L., 1986); Alberto Oehling de los Reyes, 'Algunas Reflexiones Sobre la Significación Constitucional de la Noción de Dignidad Humana' (2006) 12 *Pensamiento Constitucional* 327.

[63] See Chapter 12, section 2. [64] See Chapter 11, section 3.

and its architecture, which might be interpreted as adopting only certain aspects of the constitutional value of human dignity. That is the situation in the German Constitution, in which the constitutional value of human dignity has a broader meaning than the constitutional right to human dignity.[65]

[65] See Chapter 13, section 1F.

2

The intellectual history of the social value of human dignity

1. The ancient world

A. *History of ideas*

Understanding the concept of human dignity requires an understanding of its long history.[1] Knowledge of this concept's origins can assist us

[1] The literature on this subject is extensive. See Richard C. Dales, 'A Medieval View of Human Dignity' (1977) 38 *Journal of the History of Ideas* 557; Andrew Cuschieri, 'Endorsement of Human Dignity in the Jurisprudence of the Sacred Roman Rota in the XVI–XVII Centuries' (1982) 42 *Jurist* 466; Louis Henkin, *Human Dignity and Human Rights* (Jerusalem: The Israel Academy of Sciences and Humanities, 1995); Izhak Englard, 'Human Dignity: From Antiquity to Modern Israel's Constitutional Framework' (1999) 21 *Cardozo Law Review* 1903; Teresa Iglesias, 'Bedrock Truths and the Dignity of the Individual' (2001) 4 *Logos* 114; Yehoshua Arieli, 'On the Necessary and Sufficient Conditions for the Emergence of the Dignity of Man and His Rights', in David Kretzmer and Eckart Klein (eds.), *The Concept of Human Dignity in Human Rights Discourse* (The Hague: Kluwer Law International, 2002) 1; Hubert Cancik, '"Dignity of Man" and "Persona" in Stoic Anthropology: Some Remarks on Cicero, *De Officiis* I, 105–107', in David Kretzmer and Eckart Klein (eds.), *The Concept of Human Dignity in Human Rights Discourse* (The Hague: Kluwer Law International, 2002) 19; Joern Eckert, 'Legal Roots of Human Dignity in German Law', in David Kretzmer and Eckart Klein (eds.), *The Concept of Human Dignity in Human Rights Discourse* (The Hague: Kluwer Law International, 2002) 41; Christian Starck, 'The Religious and Philosophical Background of Human Dignity and its Place in Modern Constitutions', in David Kretzmer and Eckart Klein (eds.), *The Concept of Human Dignity in Human Rights Discourse* (The Hague: Kluwer Law International, 2002) 179; Milton Lewis, 'A Brief History of Human Dignity: Idea and Application', in Jeff E. Malpas and Norelle Lickiss (eds.), *Perspectives on Human Dignity: A Conversation* (Dordrecht: Springer, 2007) 93. See also Carlos R. Miguel, 'Human Dignity: History of an Idea' (2002) 50 *Jahrbuch des öffentlichen Rechts der Gegenwart* 281; Göran Collste, *Is Human Life Special? Religious and Philosophical Perspectives on the Principle of Human Dignity* (Berlin: Peter Lang, 2002); Don Chalmers and Ryuichi Ida, 'On the International Legal Aspects of Human Dignity', in Jeff E. Malpas and Norelle Lickiss (eds.), *Perspectives on Human Dignity: A Conversation* (Dordrecht: Springer, 2007) 157; Matthias Mahlmann, *Elemente einer ethischen Grundrechtstheorie* (Berlin: Nomos, 2008); Michael Rosen, *Dignity: Its History and Meaning* (Cambridge, MA: Harvard University Press, 2012).

in understanding where it is leading us.[2] Pieroth and Schlink[3] correctly noted that the concept of human dignity is loaded with 2,500 years of history. I would like to follow the development of this concept. I would also like to understand it in places where human dignity was referred to not by that express term, but by ideas that express our understanding of it today. The historical examination of human dignity, however, should be approached very cautiously.[4] This is due not only to my lack of expertise on the history of ideas, but also to the objective difficulty in knowing, with the proper level of caution, if this same idea is being developed consecutively throughout the history. Tracking the term "human dignity" (*Menschenwürde*) is neither a necessary nor a sufficient condition for examining this history. It is also difficult to determine the historical point of departure, which at times is arbitrary. Furthermore, we naturally proceed from the modern concept of human dignity backward, to those conceptions that might help us to understand the modern concept. We thus skip over those historical aspects that have no modern expression, but might be expressed in the future. Our examination is, therefore, to a great extent arbitrary.

Ultimately, as jurists interpreting a constitutional text, we are interested in the meaning of the constitutional value or the constitutional right in our modern constitutions. That is not what the theologians and the philosophers who dealt with human dignity were dealing with. While acknowledging the importance of their examination, its bearing on understanding the modern constitutional meaning is not decisive. Ultimately, as interpreters of a constitutional text, we are interested in knowing the content of the modern constitutional value or the constitutional right. The importance of the information regarding the intellectual history of human dignity is limited.

After these words of "warning," I will focus on the framework of western culture. Even here, due to a lack of personal knowledge, I cannot perform an in-depth examination of the approaches to the character of human beings from which the conceptions of human dignity are derived.[5]

[2] See Laurie Ackermann, *Human Dignity: Lodestar for Equality in South Africa* (Cape Town: Juta, 2012) 18, 27, 49.

[3] See Bodo Pieroth and Bernhard Schlink, *Grundrechte Staatsrecht II* (Heidelberg: C. F. Müller Verlag, 2006) 81.

[4] See Horst Dreier, *GG Grundgesetz Kommentar* (Tübingen: Mohr Siebeck, 2006) 144.

[5] See James Burgh, *The Dignity of Human Nature: Or, a Brief Account of the Certain and Established Means for Attaining the True End of Our Existence* (London: J. Johnson and J. Payne, 1767; New York: J. O. Ram 1812); Herschel C. Baker, *The Image of Man: A Study of the Idea of Human Dignity in Classical Antiquity, the Middle Ages, and the Renaissance*

My analysis shall naturally only skim the surface. I was greatly assisted on this issue by the books by Mahlmann,[6] Dreier[7] and Ackermann.[8] I shall begin with the Greek and Roman periods, including Stoic philosophy.

B. *The Stoics and Cicero*

According to the Stoics, what sets humans apart are their rationality.[9] Only humans have the ability to think and create concepts; be subject to moral dictates and ethical responsibility; have language and the ability for aesthetic creation. They live not only in the present, but also in the past and in the future. Human beings constitute an ethical community of rational beings. All people are part of this community – including slaves. Within the framework of the community of human beings, only the wise have the capability of philosophical understanding. They – as opposed to the ignorant – are truly free. The other creatures are intended to provide for the needs of man.

Cicero followed the Stoics. He shared the opinion that the ability to think is what sets man apart. Humans are rational creatures who see the results of their actions, understand the connections between cause and effect, and thus control their lives. Only human beings aspire to the truth, and have access to the moral good. While animals were intended for human beings, human beings were intended for one another. To live well is not to live as an animal seeking out pleasures; human life is directed by logic. This is the root of the connection between people acting as part of a human community with the goal of improving it.

The term "*dignitas*" appears in Cicero's writings – and the literature of that period in general.[10] That term deals with the status of a person within the community.[11] However, discussion of the universal meaning of

(New York: Harper, 1961); William Davis, *The True Dignity of Human Nature: Or, Man Viewed in Relation to Immortality* (London: General Books, 2009).

6 Mahlmann, *Elemente einer ethischen Grundrechtstheorie.*

7 Dreier, *GG Grundgesetz Kommentar.*

8 Ackermann, *Human Dignity.*

9 On the Stoics, see Steven K. Strange and Jack Zupko (eds.), *Stoicism: Traditions and Transformation* (Cambridge University Press, 2004).

10 Oliver Sensen, 'Human Dignity in Historical Perspective: The Contemporary and Traditional Paradigms' (2011) 10 *European Journal of Political Theory* 71, 76.

11 See Marcus T. Cicero, *De Inventione: De Optimo Genere Oratorum: Topica* (London: W. Heinemann, 1949) 323. See also Miguel, 'Human Dignity'; Iglesias, 'Bedrock Truths'. On the relationship between the Roman *dignitas* and the *dignitas* of other classes, and the modern meaning of human dignity, see Stéphanie Hennette-Vauchez,

"*dignitas*" can also be found in his writings.[12] According to his approach, due to their rationality, humans bear a similarity to God ("*cum deo similitudo*"). Nature granted us reason. This reason is universal. Cicero discussed the source of universality, stating that:

> [A]rising from the fact of our being all alike endowed with reason and with that superiority which lifts us above the brute [bastiis]. From this all morality and propriety are derived, and upon it depends the rational method of ascertaining our duty.[13]

According to Cicero's view, duties regarding the ways humans conduct themselves stem from the human dignity of the individual.

C. *The world religions*

(1) Judaism

Judaism is not the first religion that recognized the concept of human dignity. In Hinduism, Buddhism[14] and Confucianism[15] one can find ideas that can be expressed in terms of human dignity.[16] Similarity can also be found between human dignity and concepts such as *ubuntu*,[17]

'A Human Dignitas? Remnants of the Ancient legal Concept in Contemporary Dignity Jurisprudence' (2011) 9 *International Journal of Constitutional Law* 32.

[12] See Sensen, 'Human Dignity in Historical Perspective', at 76; Cancik, 'Dignity of Man'; Englard, 'Human Dignity', at 1905. On the transition from one meaning to the other, see Nathan Rotenstreich, *Man and His Dignity* (Jerusalem: Magnes Press, Hebrew University, 1983).

[13] Marcus T. Cicero, *De Officiis* (Cambridge, MA: Harvard University Press, 1975) 107; Cancik, 'Dignity of Man'.

[14] See Andrew Huxley, 'The Pali Buddhist Approach to Human Cloning', in Silja Vöneky and Rüdiger Wolfrum (eds.), *Human Dignity and Human Cloning* (Leiden: Martinus Nijhoff, 2004) 13; Jens Schlieter, 'Some Aspects of the Buddhist Assessment of Human Cloning', in Silja Vöneky and Rüdiger Wolfrum (eds.), *Human Dignity and Human Cloning* (Leiden: Martinus Nijhoff, 2004) 23.

[15] See, Man Yee Karen Lee, 'Universal Human Dignity: Some Reflections in the Asian Context' (2008) 3 *Asian Journal of Comparative Law* 1932.

[16] See Raul S. Manglapus, 'Human Rights Are Not a Western Discovery' (1978) 21(10) *Worldview* 4; Jack Donnelly, 'Human Rights and Human Dignity: An Analytic Critique of Non-Western Conceptions of Human Rights' (1982) 76 *American Political Science Review* 303.

[17] See Rosalind English, 'Ubuntu: The Quest for an Indigenous Jurisprudence' (1996) 12 *South African Journal on Human Rights* 641; Yvonne Mokgoro, 'Ubuntu and the Law in South Africa' (1998) 4 *Buffalo Human Rights Law Review* 15; Irma J. Kroeze, 'Doing Thing with Values (Part 2): The Case of Ubuntu' (2002) 13 *Stellenbosch Law Review* 252; Paolo G. Carozza, 'Human Dignity in Constitutional Adjudication', in Tom Ginsburg

dharmal,[18] *tomgata* and *mani* in the Maori culture.[19] However, these ideas did not influence the understanding of the constitutional value of human dignity and the constitutional right to human dignity in western culture. There is no doubt that Judaism and Christianity made an important contribution to the development of the concept of human dignity as we understand it today.

Judaism uses the term "*kavod*" (honor/dignity) extensively.[20] This term relates to God's honor.[21] It entails a description of God as the king of "*kavod*."[22] At times the Jewish sources use the term "*kavod*" for a description of man's stature.[23] But what is the meaning of "*k'vod ha'adam*" (human dignity) in Judaism? Man has dignity because human dignity is derived from his creation in the image of God.[24] "So God created humankind in his image, in the image of God he created them" (Genesis 1:27).

> He [Rabbi Akiva] used to say, beloved is man in that he was created in the image of God, but it is a mark of a greater love that it was made known to him that he had been created in the image of God, as it is said (Genesis 9:6), "For in the image of God He made man."[25]

and Rosalind Dixon (eds.), *Comparative Constitutional Law* (Cheltenham: Edward Elgar, 2011) 459, 462; Ackermann, *Human Dignity*.

18 See Carozza, 'Human Dignity in Constitutional Adjudication'.

19 See Jonathan Barrett, 'Dignatio and the Human Body' (2005) 21 *South African Journal on Human Rights* 525.

20 See Nahum Rakover, *Human Dignity in Jewish Law* (Jerusalem: Library of Jewish Law, 1998); England, 'Human Dignity'; 'God's Honour', in *The Biblical Encyclopedia: A Treasury od Knowledge on the Bible and that Era* (Jerusalem: Bialik Institute, 1963) vol. IV, 3 (Heb.); Yehiel Kaplan 'Basic Law: Human Dignity and Liberty – Balance between Conflicting Jewish Values and Conflicting Human Rights' (2009) 8 *Kiryat HaMishpat* 145, 156 (Heb.).

21 See England, 'Human Dignity'; Gerald Blidstein 'The Honour of the Creations and the Dignity of Man', in Yosef David (ed.) *A Question of Dignity – Human Dignity as a Supreme Ethical Value in Modern Society* (Jerusalem: The Israel Democracy Institute, 2006) 97 (Heb.).

22 Psalms, 27:7–10.

23 See Menachem Elon, Yaira Amit, Eliezer Shvid and Israel Knohel, 'Human Dignity and Liberty in Hebraic Tradition', in *Human Dignity and Liberty in Hebraic Tradition* (Jerusalem: The President's House Press for Bible and Hebraic Liturgy, 1995) 15, 16 (Heb.); Rakover, *Human Dignity in Jewish Law*, at 3.

24 See England, 'Human Dignity', at 1906; David Rosenberg and Ken Levy, 'Capital Punishment: Coming to Grips with the Dignity of Man' (1978) 14 *California Western Law Review* 275; Doron Shultziner, 'A Jewish Conception of Human Dignity: Philosophy and its Ethical Implications for Israeli Supreme Court Decisions' (2006) 34 *Journal of Religious Ethics* 663.

25 Ethics of the Fathers (Pirkei Avot), 3, 14.

What is "in His image?" What is "in God's image?" Jewish religious legal sources deal with this question extensively.[26] Maimonides stated that "the soul of every person is his form, which was given to him by God; and the additional wisdom found in man's soul is the form of a man who is complete in his wisdom. The Torah says about that form: 'man was made in My image and in My likeness'."[27] In Rakover's opinion, "God's image" was thus exchanged for "God's dignity" (*kavod*) and in the corresponding rabbinical language – according to the *halakha* – "the dignity of God's creations (*k'vod ha'briot*)."[28]

What is "dignity of God's creations?"[29] Who are these "creations?" The accepted approach is that the "creations" are human beings.[30] All the creations – not as an incorporated body, but rather each and every person separately, whether or not they are Jewish.[31] Thus, "*k'vod ha'briot*" is – in Elon's words – "the dignity of the created, of every one created in G–d's image."[32]

Humankind is not like all the other creations created by God. Humankind was created in the image of God in order to rule over the other creations. "Yet you have made them a little lower than God, and crowned them with glory and honor" (Psalms 8:5). Humankind is of special value as "great love is reserved for he who was created in God's image" (Mishna Avot 3:14). Thus Judaism deduced, inter alia, the value of the sanctity of life,[33] and the value of equality.[34] These values apply to every person;[35] including the dead.[36] So important is human dignity, that the individual cannot renounce it. "So great is the dignity of the creations,"[37] – that

26 See Rakover, *Human Dignity in Jewish Law*, at 19; Yair Lorerboim, *Image of God: Halakhah and Aggadah* (Tel Aviv: Shoken, 2004) (Heb.).

27 Maimonides, The Code of Maimonies, Book of Knowledge, The Laws of the Funamental Principles of the Torah, Chapter Four, Law 8.

28 See Rakover, *Human Dignity in Jewish Law*, at 22.

29 See *ibid.*

30 See David Kretzmer, 'Human Dignity in Israeli Jurisprudence', in David Kretzmer and Eckart Klein (eds.), *The Concept of Human Dignity in Human Rights Discourse* (The Hague: Kluwer Law International, 2002) 161.

31 See Rakover, *Human Dignity in Jewish Law*, at 29.

32 See Elon *et al.*, 'Human Dignity and Liberty in Hebraic Tradition', at 21; Rakover, *Human Dignity in Jewish Law*, at 4.

33 See Genesis 9:6: "Whoever sheds the blood of man, by man shall his blood be shed, for God made man in his own image"; Rakover, *Human Dignity in Jewish Law*, at 18.

34 See CrimA 3632/92 *Gabay* v. *State of Israel*, IsrSC 46(4) 487, 490 (1992) ("a foundation of the world of Judaism is the idea of creation of humankind in the image of God … So opens the Torah of Israel, and from it the *halakha* deduces foundational principles regarding the value of man – every human being, as a human being – his equality and love" (Elon D. P.).

35 See Rakover, *Human Dignity in Jewish Law*, at 5.

36 See *ibid.*, at 22.

37 See *ibid.*, at 18.

is, the dignity of man who was created in God's image – "that it overrides prohibitions from the Torah."[38] Anyone who violates human dignity degrades the image of God in humankind. The approach of Judaism on the issue of human dignity can be summed up in the following passage by Justice M. Elon written in an Israeli case:

> A basic element in Judaism is the idea that man was created in the image of god (Genesis 1:27). The *Torah* so opens, and from this concept the *halakha* derives certain fundamental principles regarding the value of man – every human being as such – his equality and the love of him: He [R. Akiva] used to say, beloved is man in that he was created in the image of God, but it is a mark of a greater love that it was made known to him that he had been created in the image of God, as it is said (Genesis 9:6), "For in the image of God He made man" (Mishna, *Avot* 3:18). And it was by reason of this verse that the sons of Noah were prohibited from spilling blood, even before the *Torah* was given. Very instructive is the difference of opinion between two leading [mishnaic scholars] as to the crowning value in human relations: "And you shall love your neighbor as yourself" [Leviticus 19:18]. R. Akiva said, this is a major rule of the *Torah*. Ben Azai said, "This is the book of the generations of Adam" [on the day God created man He did so in the image of God – Genesis 5:1] – this is the greater rule (Sifra, *Kedoshim*, 4:10). According to R. Akiva the supreme value in human relations is love of one's fellow man; and according to Ben Azai, the supreme and preferred value is the equality of man, since every man was created in the image of God. And these two values – equality and love of one's fellow – came together as one at the hands of the Jewish nation, together forming a cornerstone of Judaism throughout its generations and history.[39]

(2) Christianity

Christianity took the concept of the creation of humankind in the image of God (*imago dei*) from Judaism.[40] The image of God is revealed in Jesus

[38] See *ibid.*, at 5; Elon *et al.*, 'Human Dignity and Liberty in Hebraic Tradition', at 22; Gerald I. Blidstein '"Great is Human Dignity" – the Peregrination of a Law' (1982) 15 *Annual of the Institute for Research in Jewish Law Publication* 127 (Heb.).

[39] EA 2/84 *Moshe Neiman et al.* v. *Chairman of the Central Elections Committee for the Eleventh Knesset*, 8 IsrLR 83, 148 (1985). See also CrimA 3632/92 *Gabay* v. *State of Israel*; VCrimH 2145/92 *State of Israel* v. *Gueta*, IsrSC 46(5) 704, 716 (1992) (Heb.); CA 506/88 *Yael Shefer (a Minor) by Her Mother and Natural Guardian, Talila Shefer* v. *State of Israel*, 11 IsrLR 170, 204 (1993).

[40] See Collste, *Is Human Life Special?*, at 31; Sensen, 'Human Dignity in Historical Perspective', at 78 (on the approach of Pope Leo I); Robert P. Kraynak, 'Made in the Image of God: The Christian View of Human Dignity and Political Order', in Robert P. Kraynak and Glenn E. Tinder (eds.), *In Defense of Human Dignity: Essays for our Times* (University of Notre Dame

of Nazareth, and through him to humankind.[41] Thomas Aquinas was central to the development of the idea of human dignity.[42] According to the approach of Thomas Aquinas (1225–1274), in his work *Summa Theologia*, God is rational and determines his goals for himself. Man was created in the image of God, and he too is rational and determines his own goals, subject to the goals of God as a rational creation. Man has freedom of will. This is his *dignitas*. He is free to choose his goals, and he himself is a goal. His supreme goal is to know God. Thus he is set apart from a slave and from all the creations under him. When a man sins, he loses his human dignity. He becomes an object.

In the eyes of the Catholic theologians, man is a goal in and of himself, and the wellspring of this goal is God. He has the dignity of man: an eternal soul, free will, rational action and the ability to act morally. Despite original sin, human nature has not been completely corrupted.[43]

Press, 2003) 81. On the development in the Catholic Church, see Sharon Holland, 'Equality, Dignity and Rights of the Laity' (1987) 47 *Jurist* 103; Martin Rhonheimer, 'Fundamental Rights, Moral Law, and the Legal Defense of Life in a Constitutional Democracy' (1998) 43 *American Journal of Jurisprudence* 135; George P. Fletcher, 'In God's Image: The Religious Imperative of Equality under Law' (1999) 99 *Columbia Law Review* 1608; Miguel, 'Human Dignity'; Dierk Ullrich, 'Concurring Visions: Human Dignity in the Canadian Charter of Rights and Freedoms and the Basic Law of the Federal Republic of Germany' (2003) 3 *Global Jurist Frontiers* 1; Kenneth L. Grasso, 'Saving Modernity from Itself: John Paul II on Human Dignity, the Whole Truth About Man, and the Modern Quest for Freedom', in Robert P. Kraynak and Glenn E. Tinder (eds.), *In Defense of Human Dignity: Essays for Our Times* (University of Notre Dame Press, 2003) 207. On the relationship between the Jewish approach to "God's image" and the Christian approach to this concept, see Alexander Altmann, 'Homo Imago Dei in Jewish and Christian Theology' (1968) 48 *Journal of Religion* 235. On Christianity's contribution to the discourse on human rights, see Cuschieri, 'Endorsement of Human Dignity'; Jurgen Moltmann, *On Human Dignity: Political Theology and Ethics* (Minneapolis: Alban Books Limited, 2007); John Witte, Jr. and Frank Alexander (eds.), *Christianity and Human Rights: An Introduction* (Cambridge University Press, 2010).

41 On the image of man in Judaism and Christianity, see Kraynak, 'Made in the Image of God'; Collste, *Is Human Life Special?* This image was predominant in the Middle Ages; see Dales, 'A Medieval View of Human Dignity'. It of course also has implications for us today; see Jeremy Waldron, 'The Image of God: Rights, Reason, and Order', New York University Public Law and Legal Theory Working Papers, Paper 246 (2010).

42 See Collste, *Is Human Life Special?*, at 47; Miguel, 'Human Dignity', at 285. See also John Finnis, *Aquinas: Moral, Political and Legal Theory* (Oxford University Press, 1998).

43 See Englard, 'Human Dignity', at 1908; Cuschieri, 'Endorsement of Human Dignity'.

Protestant theology also sees humankind as having been created in the image of God.[44] Unlike Catholic theology, it puts forth the proposition that as a result of original sin, man's nature has been completely corrupted, has lost the link to the image of God, and has become similar to the image of Satan (*imago diaboli*). According to Luther, man's characteristics, such as his rationality, are not the basis of his similarity to God, as Satan too is rational, and about him as well it must be said that he was created in God's image. Only faith can save man. God's image is Jesus – and it is he that humankind must hold before its eyes. Human dignity is given by God via God's act of grace. It is not man's internal characteristics that provide a basis for his dignity as a human being, but rather his connection with God, and God's act of grace.[45]

(3) Islam

God created man. He gave him life at his birth. Man was not created in God's image, but he is proof of the existence of God.[46] At the time of his creation man was given special ability – the ability to think. Thus man has a special status before God. Because man is a creation of God, he should not be harmed. Harm to a human being is harm to God. God promised the Prophet that he created the heavens and the earth in order to serve man. Harm to man means that the world that God created is useless. God, as an act of love, created man. He wishes to grant him recognition, dignity and authority. Human dignity stems from the belief that man is a creation of God – the creation that God loves more than any other.

[44] See Collste, *Is Human Life Special?*, at 47; John Witte, 'Between Sanctity and Depravity: Human Dignity in Protestant Perspective', in Robert P. Kraynak and Glenn E. Tinder (eds.), *In Defense of Human Dignity: Essays for our Times* (University of Notre Dame Press, 2003) 119; Nicholas P. Wolterstorff, 'Modern Protestant Developments in Human Rights', in John Witte, Jr. and Frank Alexander (eds.), *Christianity and Human Rights: An Introduction* (Cambridge University Press, 2010) 155.

[45] See Englard, 'Human Dignity', at 1908.

[46] See Collste, *Is Human Life Special?*, at 18; Mohammad Hashim Kamali, *The Dignity of Man: An Islamic Perspective* (Kuala Lumpur: Ilmiah Publishers, 1999); Reza Sheikholeslami, 'The Creation and the Dignity of Man in Islam', in Silja Vöneky and Rüdiger Wolfrum (eds.), *Human Dignity and Human Cloning* (Leiden: Martinus Nijhoff, 2004) 3; Muddathir Abd Al-Rahim, *Human Rights and the World's Major Religions: The Islamic Tradition* (Westport: Praeger, 2005), vol. III; Abdullah al-Ahsan, 'Law, Religion and Human Dignity in the Muslim World Today: An Examination of OIC's Cairo Declaration of Human Rights' (2009) 24 *Journal of Law and Religion* 569; Hamidreza Salehi and Mahmoud Abbasi, 'Human Dignity: The Final Word on the Religious Ideas and Moral Thinking' (2012) 1 *Iranian Journal of Medical Ethics* 14.

2. Philosophical approaches

A. *Philosophical approaches until Kant*

(1) The Renaissance

Some argue that modern man was born in the Renaissance (between the fourteenth and seventeenth centuries).[47] Human dignity was instilled with new and rich content.[48] The sinning man who requires God's salvation of medieval theology was replaced by a dynamic man, who shapes his world, and whose human dignity is based upon his rationality.[49] One can see the connection between the religious and the humanistic view of man in the writings of Petrarch (1304–1374).[50] In the following years, the gap between the two widened. Emphasis was relocated to the centrality of man and his power to develop his abilities. This is the basis of humanism, at the center of which stands man and his dignity. According to Petrarch, the soul of man is similar to God. This is humanism's religious aspect. Alongside it there is an additional aspect. The dignity of man stems from his rationality, and from man's power to build his own world.

Manetti (1396–1459) dedicated four volumes to the dignity and excellence of man (*De Dignitate et Excellentia Hominis*).[51] He emphasized the rationality in the soul of man, and its inherent intellect and willpower, resulting in man's creativity in science and art. According to his approach, humankind's main goal is thought and action. The sensual instinct of man is limited by his rationality and morality.

The concept of human dignity was expressed fully in the writings of Ficino and Pico della Mirandola. Ficino (1433–1499) discussed man's power over nature. He noted the glory in humankind's achievements in various areas, such as language, mathematics and art. He emphasized freedom, through which man uses his talents.

[47] For another approach, see Hershel Baker, *The Dignity of Man: Studies in the Persistence of an Idea* (Cambridge, MA: Harvard University Press, 1947). For the image of man in the Middle Ages, see Paul Oskar Kristeller, *Renaissance Concepts of Man and Other Essays* (New York: Harper & Row, 1972). For human dignity in medieval Russia, see Serge Levitsky, 'Protection of Individual Honour and Dignity in Pre-Petrine Russian Law' (1972) 40 *Legal History Review* 341.

[48] See Ullrich, 'Concurring Visions'; Miguel, 'Human Dignity', at 288; Mordechai Kremnitzer and Michal Kramer, *Human Dignity as a Supreme and Absolute Constitutional Value in German Law – In Israel Too?* (Jerusalem: The Israel Democracy Institute, 2011) 28.

[49] See Dreier, *GG Grundgesetz Kommentar*, at 148.

[50] See Englard, 'Human Dignity', at 1910.

[51] See Cancik, 'Dignity of Man', at 28.

Pico (1463–1494) published the oratory on human dignity in his 1486 book *Oratio De Hominis Dignitate*.[52] According to Pico, having created man, God granted him the freedom to act according to his own will. Man's dignity stems from his ability to choose his path. This is God's message to man, according to Pico:

> The nature of all other creatures is defined and restricted within laws which We have laid down; you, by contrast, impeded by no such restrictions, may, by your own free will, to whose custody We have assigned you, trace for yourself the lineaments of your own nature. I have placed you at the very center of the world, so that from that vantage point you may with greater ease glance round about you on all that the world contains. We have made you a creature neither of heaven nor of earth, neither mortal nor immortal, in order that you may, as the free and proud shaper of your own being, fashion yourself in the form you may prefer. It will be in your power to descend to the lower, brutish forms of life; you will be able, through your own decision, to rise again to the superior orders whose life is divine.[53]

(2) The Enlightenment

The philosophers of the Renaissance were mainly religious. They believed in the creation of humankind in the image of God. This was the source of their view on the rationality of man and his freedom of choice. In their writing, there is tension between the religious aspect of man and his humanistic aspect. This tension disappeared during the Enlightenment (the mid seventeenth to eighteenth centuries), which was characterized by the unification of man and the humanity within him.[54] The emphasis was no longer the creation of man in God's image. The emphasis became his part in society. The transition was from man as a creation, to man as human being.[55] The main voices of the Enlightenment – from Spinoza to the founding fathers of the American Constitution (Franklin, Hamilton, Jefferson and Madison) – believed in human reason, and in man's power to overcome ignorance, superstition and tyranny. The Enlightenment wished to free itself from the binds that restricted human knowledge while

[52] Giovanni Pico della Mirandola, *Oration on the Dignity of Man* (The University of Adelaide, 2005). See also Francesco Borghesi, Michael Papio and Massimo Riva (eds.), *Giovanni Pico della Mirandola, Oration on the Dignity of Man: A New Translation and Commentary* (Cambridge University Press, 2012).

[53] Giovanni Pico della Mirandola, *Oration on the Dignity of Man* (Washington DC: Regnery Publishing, 1996) 7.

[54] See Arieli, 'On the Necessary and Sufficient Conditions', at 7.

[55] See Englard, 'Human Dignity', at 1917.

granting man freedom to develop himself, and recognizing tolerance between people and reason's control over human behavior. Recognition of human rights developed during the period of the Enlightenment, and reached full bloom in the Declaration of the Rights of Man and of the Citizen (1789) and the Bill of Rights in the American Constitution (1791).

Within this framework, Locke (1632–1704) noted that the rationality of man is the basis of his individuality.[56] This individuality is common to all human beings. Thus there is a need for equality in preserving life and in political life.[57] A similar approach can be found in the work of Pufendorf (1632–1694),[58] who derived from human dignity the equality and liberty of human beings,[59] all of whom are instilled with rationality.[60] Thus the transition was made from a person's duties toward his creator, to a person's rights in society.[61] However, it was Kant who provided a firm basis for the ideas regarding the rationality of man and his free will.

B. Kant

The modern conception of human dignity was affected by the philosophy of Kant.[62] Kant's moral theory had particular influence on the understanding of the provision regarding human dignity in the German Constitution. Kant's moral theory is divided into two parts: ethics and right (jurisprudence). The discussion of human dignity took place within his doctrine of ethics and does not appear in his jurisprudence.[63] Kant's

[56] John Locke, *An Essay Concerning Human Understanding* (London: The Baffet, 1690) Book II, ch. 27.

[57] John Locke, *Two Treatises of Government* (London: Awnsham Churchill, 1690) Book II, ch. 2.

[58] See Englard, 'Human Dignity', at 1917.

[59] See Starck, 'The Religious and Philosophical Background of Human Dignity', at 181.

[60] Samuel Pufendorf, *De Jure Naturae et Gentium Libri Octo* (Amsterdam: David Mortier, 1684) Book II, chapter 1, 35.

[61] See Englard, 'Human Dignity', at 1918.

[62] See Tomas E. Hill, 'Humanity as an End in Itself' (1980) 91 *Ethics* 84; Allen Wood, 'Humanity as an End in Itself', in Paul Guyer (ed.), *Kant's Groundwork of the Metaphysics of Morals: Critical Essays* (Lanham: Rowman and Littlefield, 1998), 165; Andrew Clapham, 'Human Rights Obligations of Non-State Actors', in Andrew Clapham, *Human Rights Obligations of Non-State Actors* (Oxford University Press, 2006), 535; Arthur Ripstein, *Force and Freedom: Kant's Legal and Political Philosophy* (Cambridge, MA: Harvard University Press, 2009); Dietmar von der Pfordten, 'On the Dignity of Man in Kant' (2009) 84 *Philosophy* 371; B. Sharon Byrd and Joachim Hruschka, *Kant's Doctrine of Rights: A Commentary* (Cambridge University Press, 2010). See also Kremnitzer and Kramer, *Human Dignity as a Supreme and Absolute Constitutional Value*, at 29.

[63] See Pfordten, 'On the Dignity of Man in Kant'.

jurisprudence features the concept of a person's right to freedom as a human being.

According to Kant, a person acts ethically when she acts by force of a duty that a rational agent self-legislates onto his own will. This self-legislated duty is not accompanied by any right or coercion, and is not correlative to the rights of others. For Kant, ethics includes duties to oneself (e.g. to develop one's talents) and to others (e.g. to contribute to their happiness). This ability is the human dignity of man. This is what makes a person different than an object. This ability makes a person into an end, and prevents her from being a mere means in the hands of another.

Alongside the doctrine of ethics, Kant dealt, within the doctrine of morality, with right or jurisprudence.[64] As opposed to ethics, in jurisprudence there are rights and there is coercive force. The universal principle of a right is a person's freedom to choose her ends and to realize them, on the condition that they comport with the identical freedom of other people to choose and realize their own ends.[65] This free will is the right of every person as a person (*angeborn*). This is the humanity in a person.[66] This is the independence of a person in relation to others. In order to enjoy this freedom of choice, law grants people the ability to attain acquired rights, such as property or contracts. In order to enjoy these rights, a state and governmental institutions are needed to establish, interpret and enforce the rights and duties of its members. The right to independence is an innate right, not an acquired one. It is inherent in a person, and no act is needed on his part to obtain it. All other rights are acquired.[67]

The freedom of the individual – as long as comports with the identical freedom of every other individual – is the independence of a person. This freedom is innate in every person, who may use the power of choice as she desires,[68] so long as it comports with other people's freedom to do so. This free choice is a person's independence – her right to be her own master. The freedom of the individual protects her from the will of other individuals. When a person is viewed as subject to another person, she serves as a means for fulfilling the desires of that other person. That subjugation is at odds with a person's free will. From this stems the view that the meaning of human dignity is the rejection of the possibility that a person will be but a means for fulfilling the will of another person. People are equal,

[64] See Joachim Hruschka, 'Kant and Human Dignity', in B. Sharon Byrd and Joachim Hruschka (eds.), *Kant and Law* (Aldershot: Ashgate, 2006) 69; Thomas Christiano, 'Two Conceptions of the Dignity of Persons' (2008) 16 *Jahrbuch Fuer Recht Und Ethik* 101.

[65] See Ripstein, *Force and Freedom*, at 13.

[66] *Ibid.* [67] See *Ibid.*, at 9. [68] See *Ibid.*, at 17.

in the sense that no person is master over his fellow man.[69] From this also stems the conclusion that a person has a duty not to turn himself into a mere means for the fulfillment of another's free will.[70]

A person's right to her own humanity means that she, and no other person, makes decisions regarding her goals. A person's innate right to her humanity means her freedom to do with her body as she pleases, as long as that will comports with the freedom of others. A person's right to be her own master is violated if she is subject to another's will.

C. *Dworkin*

Human dignity is expressed in Dworkin's writing.[71] This is important for the history of the idea, as Dworkin is a philosopher-jurist who is aware of the idea of a constitution and of a constitutional right to human dignity. As far back as his book *Taking Rights Seriously* (1978), he noted that everyone who takes rights seriously must give an answer to the question why human rights vis-à-vis the state exist. In order to give such an answer one must accept, as a minimum, the idea of human dignity. Dworkin writes:

> [H]uman dignity ... associated with Kant, but defended by philosophers of different schools, supposes that there are ways of treating a man that are inconsistent with recognizing him as a full member of the human community, and holds that such treatment is profoundly unjust.[72]

In his book *Life's Dominion: An Argument about Abortion, Euthanasia and Individual Freedom* (1994), he examines, inter alia, the questions of abortion and euthanasia. He notes that both supporters and critics accept the idea of the sanctity of life. The concept of human dignity stands on both sides of the argument:

> Dignity – which means respecting the inherent value of our own lives – is the heart of both arguments.[73]

Decisions regarding death – whether by abortion or by euthanasia – affect our human dignity. In Dworkin's opinion, proper recognition of human

[69] See *Ibid.*, at 36. [70] See *Ibid.*, at 37.

[71] See Collste, *Is Human Life Special?*, at 154.

[72] Ronald Dworkin, *Taking Rights Seriously* (Cambridge, MA: Harvard University Press, 1978) 198.

[73] Ronald Dworkin, *Life's Dominion: An Argument About Abortion, Euthanasia, and Individual Freedom* (New York: Vintage Books, 1994) 238.

dignity leads to the recognition of the freedom of the individual. Freedom is a necessary condition for self worth. Dworkin adds:

> Because we cherish dignity, we insist on freedom ... Because we honor dignity, we demand democracy.[74]

Dworkin returns to the concept of human dignity in his book *Is Democracy Possible Here?* (2006).[75] In this book, Dworkin presents two principles, which in his opinion are commonly held by every American. One principle regards the intrinsic value of every person. According to it, every person has special objective value. A person's value is important not only to himself. The success or failure of the lives of every person is important to all of us. The second principle is that of personal responsibility. According to it, every person has the responsibility for success in his own life. Thus, he must use his discretion regarding the way of life that will be successful from his point of view. In Dworkin's opinion, these two principles together define the basis of, and the conditions for, human dignity.

These two principles are further developed and expanded in Dworkin's book *Justice for Hedgehogs* (2011).[76] In this book Dworkin provides a basis for a philosophical approach with a general standard that will integrate morality (which deals with the standard by which man should treat his fellow man)[77] and ethics (which deals with the standard by which man should live his own life).[78] These two standards are connected and interdependent.[79] This connection is not based upon a balance between opposing principles. It is based upon a general view that is common to these principles. This view is interpretative in character. It attempts to create a good life while ensuring one lives well. According to Dworkin's approach, the two principles that provide the basis for living well are as follows: the first principle is the principle of self-respect:[80] every person must take his life seriously; he must recognize the objective importance of his life with self-respect.[81] The second principle is the principle of authenticity: in his relations with others every person must express himself in his life, while identifying and pursuing his own conception of what it is to live well.[82]

[74] *Ibid.*, at 239.

[75] Ronald Dworkin, *Is Democracy Possible Here? Principles for a New Political Debate* (Princeton University Press, 2006).

[76] Ronald Dworkin, *Justice for Hedgehogs* (Cambridge, MA: Harvard University Press, 2011).

[77] *Ibid.*, at 191. [78] *Ibid.*, at 255. [79] *Ibid.*, at 1.

[80] *Ibid.*, at 203. [81] *Ibid.*, at 205. [82] *Ibid.*, at 209.

The principle of self-respect requires similar respect for other people. If you have respect toward yourself, then you must also respect the lives of others. In Dworkin's words:

> [S]elf-respect … entails a parallel respect for the lives of all human beings.[83]

Dworkin learns this from Kant, according to whom:

> [W]e cannot adequately respect our own humanity unless we respect humanity in others.[84]

The principle of authenticity is an objective, relational principle[85] – it is the flip side of self-respect.[86] It imposes upon man responsibility for his actions toward others.

The interpretational principle[87] that unites self-respect and authenticity is that of human dignity. Dworkin sees human dignity as an organizing idea, as it enables us, through interpretation, to assemble ethical principles and gather them under the one roof of human dignity.[88]

D. Waldron

Waldron dedicated a number of books and articles to the examination of the concept of human dignity.[89] According to his approach, human dignity reflects rank. In his first article on this issue – *Dignity and Rank* – Waldron wrote:

> [T]he distinctive contribution that "dignity" makes to human rights discourse is associated, paradoxically, with the idea of *rank*; once associated with hierarchical differentiations of rank and status, "dignity" now conveys the idea that all human persons belong to the same rank and that rank is a very high one indeed, in many ways as high as what were formerly regarded as ranks of nobility.[90]

[83] *Ibid.*, at 255. [84] *Ibid.*, at 14. [85] *Ibid.*, at 213.

[86] *Ibid.*, at 209. [87] *Ibid.*, at 204. [88] *Ibid.*, at 205.

[89] See Jeremy Waldron, 'Dignity and Rank' (2007) 48 *European Journal of Sociology* 201; Jeremy Waldron, 'The Dignity of Groups' (2008) *Acta Juridica* 66; Jeremy Waldron, 'Dignity and Defamation: The Visibility of Hate' (2010) 123 *Harvard Law Review* 1596; Jeremy Waldron, 'Dignity, Rights, and Responsibilities' (2011) 43 *Arizona State Law Journal* 1107; Jeremy Waldron, *Dignity, Rank, and Rights*, ed. by Meir Dan-Cohen (Oxford University Press, 2012); Jeremy Waldron, 'How Law Protects Dignity' (2012) 71 *Cambridge Law Journal* 200; Jeremy Waldron, *The Harm in Hate Speech* (Cambridge, MA: Harvard University Press, 2012).

[90] Waldron, 'Dignity and Rank', at 1.

Waldron argues in this first article that his understanding of human dignity constitutes the "best account of what is now going on" regarding the use of the term human dignity – the usage which presents it in the best light. Waldron does not claim that this is the best or most correct interpretation of human dignity. He presents his position as a possible hypothesis.

In a different article[91] Waldron recognized the importance of views different than his own on human dignity as rank – he referred to the approaches of Kant and Dworkin – and proposed an approach that unites the three, according to which:

> As a foundational idea, human dignity might ascribe to each person a very high rank. Associated with the sanctity of her body, her control of herself and her determination of her own destiny, values and capacities that are so important that they must not be traded off for anything.[92]

In his book on *Dignity, Rank and Rights*, Waldron returns to the approach that human dignity expresses the idea of the high and equal rank[93] of every person. According to this approach, human dignity is a high normative status that belongs to every person in society. Waldron writes:

> [T]he modern notion of *human* dignity involves an upwards equalization of rank, so that we now try to accord to every human being something of the dignity, rank, and expectation of respect that was formerly accorded to nobility ... Every man a duke, every woman a queen, everyone entitled to the sort of deference and consideration, everyone's person and body sacrosanct, in the way that nobles were entitled to deference or in a way that an assault upon the body or the person of a king was regarded as a sacrilege.[94]

In his book, he presents various aspects of the field of law that express this view. Thus, for example:

> High-ranking persons might be regarded as capable of participating fully in something like a legal system; they would be trusted with the voluntary self-application of norms; their word and testimony would be taken

[91] Waldron, 'The Dignity of Groups'. [92] *Ibid.*, at 9.

[93] See Waldron, 'Dignity, Rank, and Rights', at 18, 30. See also Bertram Morris, 'The Dignity of Man' (1946) 57 *Ethics* 57.

[94] Waldron, 'Dignity, Rank, and Rights', at 33–4. Compare with James Whitman, according to whom the phenomenon that characterizes American law is actually "leveling down." James Whitman, '"Human Dignity" in Europe and the United States: the Social Foundations', in George Nolte (ed.), *European and US Constitutionalism* (Cambridge University Press, 2005) 108.

> seriously; they would be entitled to the benefit of elaborate processes, and so on.[95]

In an article on *Dignity, Rights and Responsibilities*, Waldron reiterated his approach on human dignity as reflecting a conception of rank. However, as a result of proposals made in England, he discussed the relationship between rights and responsibility. In this context Waldron noted – while referring to the writings of H. L. A. Hart – that it should not be assumed that a single view can explain the entire analysis of rights. He notes that "rights" constitute a heterogenic category, and sometimes one form of analysis will be appropriate and sometimes another one will be.

In the article on *How Law Protects Dignity*, Waldron explains his understanding of the concept dignity – without defining it – in the following manner:

> Dignity is the status of a person predicated on the fact that she is recognized as having the ability to control and regulate her actions in accordance with her own apprehension of norms and reasons that apply to her; it assumes she is capable of giving and entitled to give an account of herself (and of the way in which she is regulating her actions and organizing her life), an account that others are to pay attention to; and it means finally that she has the wherewithal to demand that her agency and her presence among us as human beings be taken seriously and accommodated in the lives of others, in others' attitudes and actions towards her, and in social life generally.[96]

In this article, he discusses the relationship between human dignity and the right to be heard and the status to sue.

Finally, in his book *The Harm in Hate Speech* Waldron notes that the right to freedom of expression is derived from human dignity.[97] Regarding the understanding of the term "human dignity," Waldron restates his position that human dignity is a status. However, he clarifies that according to his approach to freedom of expression and its limitations, the term human dignity "is not being used legislatively."[98] Waldron emphasizes that he makes use of the human dignity concept "as a value or principle embedded in political argument" regarding the relationship between human dignity and freedom of expression.[99]

[95] Waldron, 'Dignity, Rank, and Rights', at 55.

[96] Waldron, 'How Law Protects Dignity', at 202–3.

[97] Waldron, *The Harm in Hate Speech*, at 139.

[98] *Ibid.*, at 138. [99] *Ibid.*

Waldron's approach is important for our study as, like Dworkin, Waldron is also a philosopher-jurist who looks upon human dignity not only as a social value, but also as a constitutional value and right.

3. The lessons learned from the intellectual history

The intellectual history of human dignity demonstrates the complexity of human dignity. From this history we learn of the extreme caution that we must exercise when using this term. It is apparent from this history that the theologian's understanding is different than the philosopher's. Each one makes fundamental assumptions – religious or ethical – and builds his arguments upon them. We jurists are neither theologians nor philosophers. Our fundamental assumptions are the constitution and its interpretation. It is appropriate for us to learn the approaches of theologians and philosophers from the intellectual history. There are many upstanding members of modern society who possess religious or philosophical perspectives. We would do well to internalize the various perspectives when we attempt to discern what our constitution is telling us. Nonetheless, we must see ourselves as constitutional interpreters who are tasked with giving meaning to the constitutional value or constitutional right to human dignity – each with his own constitution.

3

Human dignity as a value and as a right in international documents

1. Human dignity in legal discourse

Until the middle of the twentieth century, the history of human dignity was part of the history of ideas. From the middle of the twentieth century it also became an inseparable part of legal history. It became a central factor in the discourse on rights – both on the international and the national plane. Indeed, scores of multilateral international conventions expressly include human dignity – whether in the preamble or in the body of the convention. In many of the constitutions that were enacted or amended after the Second World War, human dignity was established as a key concept.[1]

What caused this change? The atrocities of the Second World War, particularly the Holocaust of the Jewish people, are the primary factors that led human dignity to become a central factor in legal discourse. The recognition that those interested in protecting democracy must protect human rights, and that those who wish to protect human rights must recognize human dignity, became more prevalent. In its wake the Second World War brought the human rights revolution, and it was in this framework that the human dignity revolution took place.

The primary push for this change can be identified in three legal texts – two international documents and one constitutional provision. The beginning of the change can be found in the preamble to the Charter of the United Nations.[2] This charter was enacted in 1945, right after the end of the Second World War. The preamble of the Charter expressed the determination of the peoples of the United Nations to:

> [R]eaffirm faith in fundamental human rights, in the dignity and worth of the human person, in the equal rights of men and women.

[1] See Oscar Schachter, 'Human Dignity as a Normative Concept' (1983) 77 *American Journal of International Law* 848; Lorraine E. Weinrib, 'Human Dignity as a Rights-Protecting Principle' (2004) 17 *National Journal of Constitutional Law* 325.

[2] 1 UNTS XVI (October 24, 1945).

The second international document that recognized human dignity was the Universal Declaration of Human Rights. This declaration – of December 1948 – determined that:

> All human beings are born free and equal in dignity and in rights. They are endowed with reason and conscience and should act towards one another in a spirit of brotherhood.[3]

The third legal document is the German Basic Law (the *Grundgesetz*), which entered into effect in 1949. Article 1(1) of the Basic Law determines:

> The dignity of man (*die Würde des Menschen*) shall be inviolable (*unantastbar*). To respect and protect it shall be the duty of all state authority.

It was additionally determined that the basic principles entrenched in this provision may not be amended.[4]

These three documents outlined the development of human rights after the Second World War in general, and the development of the right to human dignity in particular. Indeed, the development of human dignity as part of legal discourse took place on two paths. The first was the international path. Human dignity was expressed in international declarations and conventions that recognized it – whether as a value or as a right – as part of the bill of human rights. The second was the national path. Human dignity was expressed in the constitutions of various states. These constitutions recognized human dignity – whether as a value or as a right – as part of the constitutional bill of rights. These two paths crossed more than once, when international declarations or conventions had influence upon the drafting and interpretation of the constitutions of the various states. For this reason, each path is important in terms of interpretation for the understanding of the other.

These three documents – the preamble to the Charter of the United Nations, the Universal Declaration of Human Rights and the German Basic Law – ushered in the age of human dignity in legal discourse in the middle of the twentieth century. Scores of multinational conventions have since been adopted that include provisions regarding human dignity. Many constitutions include a provision regarding human dignity. Every legal document has its own special history, and each one's recognition of human dignity has its own characteristics. Within the

[3] The Universal Declaration of Human Rights, GA RES. 21A (III), UN DOC A/810 (1948), at 71.

[4] See Art. 79(3) GG.

framework of this book I cannot carry out a historical analysis of this phenomenon, its special reasons and its results. I shall present only the main developments.

In this context, I should like to make four comments. First, even prior to the Second World War there were a small number of constitutions that mentioned human dignity. Second, some of the express provisions in international documents or constitutions regarding human dignity refer to the value of human dignity without recognizing it as a right, and some of them relate to human dignity as a right as well. Each legal document requires an individual and precise analysis, while examining the special factors that led to its creation. Third, even without an express provision regarding human dignity, the interpretation of the text might justify the conclusion that human dignity – as a value or as a right – is implied. Here too an individual examination of every convention and every constitution is needed. Fourth, the distinction between the express provisions regarding human dignity in international documents and various constitutions, and the reality "on the ground" should be well noted. At times there is a large gap between rhetoric and practice. In totalitarian states, the constitution might determine provisions regarding human rights in general, and human dignity particularly. De facto, the provisions of the law are not applied, and there is no possibility of enforcing them. Indeed, human dignity's place in the life of a given society is determined more by the way human dignity is fulfilled in daily life and in the relations between the individual and the government than by the (explicit or implicit) meaning of the legal text. The existence of a provision in the constitution on this matter is neither a necessary nor a sufficient condition for the existence of human dignity, de facto, in the life of a society. It is not a necessary condition, as even lacking a written constitution – and certainly if there is no constitutional provision regarding human dignity – it is possible to protect human dignity. England and New Zealand are good examples of this. It is not a sufficient condition, as in many of the states in which the constitution mentions human dignity, this dignity is, de facto, crushed with an iron fist. Historically, Latin America has been a good example of that.[5]

[5] See Allan R. Brewer-Carías, *Constitutional Protection of Human Rights in Latin America: A Comparative Study of Amparo Proceedings* (Cambridge University Press, 2009) 2.

2. Human dignity in international conventions

A. *Human dignity discourse in international conventions*

Human dignity has developed in international law[6] since the end of the Second World War.[7] Human dignity is seen today as one of the general principles of international law.[8] Its first appearance in international law was, as we have seen, in the preamble to the Charter of the United Nations (1945) and the Universal Declaration of Human Rights (1948).[9] It was

[6] See Herbert C. Kelman, 'The Conditions, Criteria, and Dialectics of Human Dignity: A Transnational Perspective' (1977) 21 *International Studies Quarterly* 529; Frowein Abr. Jochen, 'Human Dignity in International Law', in David Kretzmer and Eckart Klein (eds.), *The Concept of Human Dignity in Human Rights Discourse* (The Hague: Kluwer Law International, 2002) 121; John O. McGinnis, 'The Limits of International Law in Protecting Dignity' (2003) 27 *Harvard Journal of Law and Public Policy* 137; Jeremy Rabkin, 'What We Can Learn about Human Dignity from International Law' (2003) 27 *Harvard Journal of Law and Public Policy* 145; Don Chalmers and Ryuichi Ida, 'On the International Legal Aspects of Human Dignity', in Jeff E. Malpas and Norelle Lickiss (eds.), *Perspectives on Human Dignity: A Conversation* (Dordrecht: Springer, 2007) 157; Niels Petersen, 'Human Dignity, International Protection', in *Max Planck Encyclopedia of Public International Law* (Oxford, 2007); Viviana Bohrquez Monsalve and Javier Aguirre Romcan, 'Tensions of Human Dignity: Conceptualization and Application to International Human Rights Law' (2009) *International Journal on Human Rights* 39.

[7] Human dignity was mentioned as far back as the Dijon Declaration (1936). In 1944 the American Jewish Committee adopted a Declaration of Human Rights that mentioned human dignity. For additional examples of declarations that refer to human dignity prior to the Universal Declaration of Human Rights, see Christopher McCrudden, 'Human Dignity and Judicial Interpretation of Human Rights' (2008) 19 *European Journal of International Law* 655, 665.

[8] See Petersen, 'Human Dignity, International Protection', at para. 28.

[9] The Universal Declaration of Human Rights, note 3 above. The Universal Declaration of Human Rights was preceded by the American Declaration of the Rights and Duties of Man, discussed below in section 2.D.(2). On the Universal Declaration of Human Rights, see Johannes Morsink, 'The Philosophy of the Universal Declaration' (1984) 6 *Human Rights Quarterly* 309; Marry Ann Glendon, '*Propter Honoris Respectum*: Knowing the Universal Declaration of Human Rights' (1998) 73 *Notre Dame Law Review* 1153; Johannes Morsink, *The Universal Declaration of Human Rights: Origins, Drafting and Intent* (Philadelphia: University of Pennsylvania Press, 1999); Klaus Dicke, 'The Founding Function of Human Dignity in the Universal Declaration of Human Rights', in David Kretzmer and Eckart Klein (eds.), *The Concept of Human Dignity in Human Rights Discourse* (The Hague: Kluwer Law International, 2002) 111; Kevin J. Hasson, 'Religious Liberty and Human Dignity: A Tale of Two Declarations' (2003) 27 *Harvard Journal of Law and Public Policy* 81; William J. Wagner, 'Universal Human Rights, the United Nations and the Telos of Human Dignity' (2005) 3 *Ave Maria Law Review* 197; Johannes Morsink, *Inherent Human Rights: Philosophical Roots of the Universal Declaration* (Philadelphia: University of Pennsylvania Press, 2009); Adrienne Anderson, 'On Dignity and whether the Universal Declaration of Human Rights Remains a Place of Refuge after

from these documents that human dignity spread to additional documents, including conventions prepared by the United Nations and its specialized agencies (e.g. the International Labour Organization (ILO), the UN Educational, Scientific, and Cultural Organization (UNESCO) and the World Health Organization (WHO)). Human dignity was also incorporated into regional documents (like those of the Council of Europe), and into international documents dealing with particular issues such as international humanitarian law and medical and bioethical law.

This chapter discusses the main international documents that mention human dignity, whether in the preamble or in the body of the text. Only multilateral international conventions will be discussed; bilateral declarations and conventions are excluded from the examination. In this survey of international law I will not distinguish between human dignity as a right and human dignity as a value. Indeed, in some international documents human dignity is a right. In others it is a value.[10]

B. United Nations conventions

(1) The UN conventions on human rights of 1966

The two most important United Nations conventions on human rights were adopted in the General Assembly in 1966: the International Covenant on Civil and Political Rights[11] (ICCPR) and the International Covenant on Economic, Social and Cultural Rights[12] (ICESCR). In their preambles,

60 Years' (2009) 25 *American University International Law Review* 115; Glenn Hughes, 'The Concept of Dignity in the Universal Declaration of Human Rights' (2011) 39 *Journal of Religious Ethics* 1; Jenna Reinbold, 'Political Myth and the Sacred Center of Human Rights: The Universal Declaration and the Narrative of "Inherent Human Dignity"' (2011) 12 *Human Rights Review* 247.

[10] See Schachter, 'Human Dignity as a Normative Concept'. An extensive discussion of human dignity can be found in Harold D. Lasswell and Myres S. McDougal, *Jurisprudence for a Free Society: Studies in Law, Science and Policy* (Dordrecht: Martinus Nijhoff, 1992) vol. II, 737, 1017.

[11] 999 UNTS 171 (December 16, 1966). See also, Egon Schwelb, 'Civil and Political Rights: The International Measures of Implementation' (1968) 62 *American Journal of International Law* 827; Manfred Nowak, *U.N. Covenant on Civil and Political Rights: CCPR Commentary* (N. P. Engel Verlag, 1993); Sarah Joseph, Jenny Schultz and Melissa Castan, *International Covenant on Civil and Political Rights*, 2nd edn (Oxford University Press, 2005).

[12] 993 UNTS 3 (December 16, 1966). See also, Matthew Craven, *The International Covenant on Economic, Social and Cultural Rights: A Perspective on its Development* (Oxford: Clarendon Press, 1998); Audrey Chapman, 'A "Violations Approach" for Monitoring the International Covenant on Economic, Social and Cultural Rights' (1996) 18 *Human Rights Quarterly* 23.

both covenants refer to the content of the Charter of the United Nations, according to which:

> recognition of the inherent dignity and the equal and inalienable rights of all members of the human family is the foundation of freedom, justice and peace in the world.

Article 10(1) of the ICCPR states:

> All persons deprived of their liberty shall be treated with humanity and with respect for the inherent dignity of the human person.

Article 13(1) of the ICESCR, dealing with the right to education, states:

> [E]ducation shall be directed to the full development of the human personality and the sense of its dignity.

These two conventions influenced the content of the constitutions of many states.

(2) United Nations conventions on particular issues

In 1965 the International Convention on the Elimination of all Forms of Racial Discrimination[13] was adopted by the General Assembly. The preamble to the convention notes consideration of the fact that the Charter of the United Nations is based upon the values of human dignity and equality, which are inherent in all human beings. The Universal Declaration of Human Rights, which declares that all human beings are born free and equal in dignity and rights, is also taken into consideration.

In 1979 the General Assembly adopted the Convention on the Elimination of all Forms of Discrimination against Women.[14] Human dignity is mentioned in the preamble to that convention. In 1984 the Convention against Torture and Other Cruel, Inhuman or Degrading Treatment or Punishment was adopted.[15] The preamble to this convention determines, inter alia, that human rights:

> derive from the inherent dignity of the human person.

In 1986 the General Assembly passed a resolution setting guidelines for new conventions regarding human rights. Inter alia, the guidelines determined that the new conventions would be:

[13] 660 UNTS 195 (December 21, 1965).
[14] 1249 UNTS 13 (December 18, 1979).
[15] 1465 UNTS 85 (December 10, 1984).

> [O]f fundamental character and derive from the inherent dignity and worth of the human person.[16]

In 1989 the Convention on the Rights of the Child[17] was adopted. Human dignity appears in the preamble to the convention, which notes that inherent dignity is the basis for freedom, justice and world peace. An additional paragraph in the preamble states that "[t]he peoples of the United Nations have, in the charter, reaffirmed their faith in fundamental human rights and in the dignity and worth of the human person."[18]

In 1990 the International Convention on the Protection of the Rights of All Migrant Workers and Members of their Families[19] was adopted. Article 17(1) of this convention determines that:

> Migrant workers and members of their families who are deprived of their liberty shall be treated with humanity and with respect for the inherent dignity of the human person and for their cultural identity.

Article 70 of the convention states that the working and living conditions of migrant workers and their families shall be in keeping with the standards of fitness, safety, health and principles of human dignity.

In 1993 the United Nations held the Vienna World Conference on Human Rights. The conference adopted the Vienna Declaration and Programme of Action.[20] The preamble to the declaration states:

> [A]ll human rights derive from the dignity and worth inherent in the human person.

The body of the declaration determines a number of issues that require international action in the future. In some of those issues human dignity plays a considerable role.[21]

In 2005 the International Convention for the Protection of All Persons from Enforced Disappearance[22] was adopted. Article 19 of the convention

[16] Setting International Standards in the Field of Human Rights, GA Res. 41/120 (December 4, 1986), s. 4(b).

[17] 1577 UNTS 3 (November 20, 1989). See Judith Karp, 'Matching Human Dignity with the UN Convention on the Rights of the Child', in Ya'ir Ronen and Charles W. Greenbaum (eds.), *The Case of the Child: Towards a New Agenda* (Antwerp: Intersentia, 2008).

[18] On this paragraph and proposals to amend it, see Jordan J. Paust, 'Human Dignity, Remedies, and Limitations in the Convention' (1989) 7 *New York Law School Journal of Human Rights* 116.

[19] 2200 UNTS 3 (December 18, 1990).

[20] A/CONF.157/23 (July 12, 1993).

[21] See Arts. 11, 18, 20, 25 and 55 of the Declaration.

[22] UN Doc. A/61/488 (December 20, 2006).

deals with personal information discovered during searches for people who have been forcibly disappeared. Sub-Article (2) determines that the collection, processing, use and storage of this information shall not infringe upon:

> the human rights, fundamental freedoms or human dignity of an individual.

In 2007 the General Assembly adopted the Convention on the Rights of Persons with Disabilities.[23] In its preamble, this convention quotes the content of the Charter of the United Nations regarding human dignity. The preamble also notes that discrimination against any person on the basis of disability is a violation of the "inherent dignity and worth of the human being." Article 3 of the convention determines its general principles. Sub-Article (a) establishes "respect for inherent dignity" as one of the principles of the convention.

(3) Conventions of the United Nations' specialized agencies

Alongside the conventions adopted by the General Assembly of the United Nations, there are conventions that were adopted by the United Nations Specialized Agencies. Thus, for example, the Declaration of Philadelphia[24] of 1944, which served as a basis for the establishment of the ILO, determined, inter alia, in Article II(a):

> All human beings, irrespective of race, creed or sex, have the right to pursue both their material well-being and their spiritual development in conditions of freedom and dignity, of economic security and equal opportunity.

This declaration is part of the constitution of the ILO.[25] It appears in a number of conventions adopted by the ILO.[26]

The United Nations Educational, Scientific and Cultural Organization (UNESCO), established in 1945, often refers to human dignity. The organization's constitution determines, inter alia, that the Second World War was made possible by:

[23] 2515 UNTS 3 (December 13, 2006).

[24] Declaration Concerning the Aims and Purposes of the International Labour Organization, adopted at the 26th session of the ILO (May 10, 1944).

[25] See *ibid.*, Art. 1(1).

[26] See ILO Discrimination (Employment and Occupation) Convention, C111 (1958); ILO Employment Policy Convention, C122 (1964); Convention concerning Equal Opportunities and Equal Treatment for Men and Women Workers: Workers with Family Responsibilities, C156 (1981).

> the denial of the democratic principles of the dignity, equality and mutual respect of men.

The preamble also states that:

> the wide diffusion of culture, and the education of humanity for justice and liberty and peace are indispensable to the dignity of man.

UNESCO adopted a number of conventions in which human dignity is mentioned. For example, in 1960 the Convention Against Discrimination in Education was adopted.[27] In describing the term "discrimination," the convention notes that discrimination is any distinction with the purpose of impairing equality of treatment in education by:

> inflicting on any person or group of persons conditions which are incompatible with the dignity of man.

Within the framework of its activity, UNESCO has published many declarations, including declarations regarding bioethics, in which human dignity plays an important role. Thus, for example, the Universal Declaration on the Human Genome and Human Rights[28] determines (in Article 1) that:

> The human genome underlies the fundamental unity of all members of the human family, as well as the recognition of their inherent dignity and diversity. In a symbolic sense, it is the heritage of humanity.

Article 2 states:

> (a) Everyone has a right to respect for their dignity and for their rights regardless of their genetic characteristics.
> (b) That dignity makes it imperative not to reduce individuals to their genetic characteristics and to respect their uniqueness and diversity.

Additional declarations deal with human genetic data, bioethics and human rights. In each of these declarations, human dignity has an important role.

C. *Conventions on particular issues*

There are many multilateral international conventions dealing with particular issues. Human dignity appears in most of them. I shall focus upon one, which deals with international humanitarian law.

27 UNESCO Convention against Discrimination in Education, December 14, 1960, 429 UNTS 93.

28 UNESCO Gen. Conf. Res. 29 C/Res.17, 29th Sess. (November 11, 1997).

The Fourth Hague Convention (1907)[29] deals with the laws of war. In this convention there was no mention of human dignity. This changed soon after the Second World War. Four conventions covering broad areas of international humanitarian law were adopted in 1949.[30] These conventions include provisions regarding care for the wounded, protection of prisoners of war and protection of civilians during times of combat. All these conventions have a common provision. The content of "Common Article 3" in each of the conventions is identical. This article prohibits, inter alia:

> 1(c). Outrages upon personal dignity, in particular humiliating and degrading treatment.

In 1977 two protocols were adopted that added provisions regarding international humanitarian law.[31] In the two protocols the wording appearing in Common Article 3 regarding human dignity is repeated. This wording, to the extent that it relates to human dignity, was also adopted in the establishment of special criminal courts,[32] and in legislation regarding the International Criminal Court.[33]

Human dignity is also a part of customary international law. It is part of the principles of humanity.[34] Indeed, a state has a duty to act humanely, and this humanity means, inter alia, safeguarding human dignity.

[29] See Hague Regulations on the Laws and Customs of War on Land, October 18, 1907, 205 Consol. T.S. 277.

[30] See Geneva Convention (I) for the Amelioration of the Condition of the Wounded and Sick in Armed Forces in the Field (August 12, 1949); Geneva Convention (II) on the Wounded, Sick and Shipwrecked of Armed Forces at Sea (August 12, 1949); Geneva Convention (III) on Prisoners of War (August 12, 1949); Geneva Convention (IV) on Protection of Civilian Persons in Time of War (August 12, 1949).

[31] See Arts. 75 and 85 to the Protocol Additional to the Geneva Conventions of 12 August 1949, and Relating to the Protection of Victims of International Armed Conflicts (Protocol I), June 8, 1977, 1125 UNTS 3; Art. 4(2)(1) to the Protocol Additional to the Geneva Conventions of 12 August 1949, and Relating to the Protection of Victims of Non-International Armed Conflicts (Protocol II), June 8, 1977, 1125 UNTS 609.

[32] See The Agreement for and Statute of the Special Court for Sierra Leone, January 16, 2002, Art. 3; Statute of the International Criminal Tribunal for the Prosecution of Persons Responsible for Genocide and Other Serious Violations of International Humanitarian Law Committed in the Territory of Rwanda and Rwandan Citizens Responsible for Genocide and Other Such Violations Committed in the Territory of Neighboring States, Between 1 January 1994 and 31 December 1994, Art. 4; Rome Statute of the International Criminal Court, July 17, 1998, Art. 8.

[33] See Art. 8(2)(b)(xxi) to the Rome Statute of the International Criminal Court, which defines "war crimes."

[34] On the principle of humanity see Theodor Meron, 'The Martens Clause: Principles of Humanity and Dictates of Public Conscience' (2000) 94 *American Journal of International*

D. *Regional conventions*

(1) Europe

Human dignity plays an important role not only in the constitutions of many European states, but also in supranational activity on the Continent. The European Convention for the Protection of Human Rights and Fundamental Freedoms (1950)[35] does not include any express mention of human dignity. Only in 2002, in the framework of amendments to the convention made in the 13th Protocol[36] dealing with annulment of the death penalty, was it noted in the preamble that annulment of the death penalty is essential:

> for the full recognition of the inherent dignity of all human beings.

It is generally accepted that human dignity is an implied value in this European convention.[37]

The Council of Europe adopted a considerable number of conventions and resolutions in which human dignity plays a central part. I shall mention in this context its basic convention: the Convention for the Protection of Human Rights and Dignity of the Human Being with Regard to the Application of Biology and Medicine (the Oviedo Convention).[38] The preamble mentions, inter alia, the need to respect the human being both as an individual and as a member of the human species, and recognizes:

> the importance of ensuring the dignity of the human being.

The first article of the convention states:

> Parties to this Convention shall protect the dignity and identity of all human beings.

Law 78; Jean-Marie Henckaerts and Louise Daswald-Beck, *Customary International Humanitarian Law* (ICRC, 2005), 315.

[35] Convention for the Protection of Human Rights and Fundamental Freedoms, CETS No. 005 (November 4, 1950).

[36] Protocol No. 13 to the Convention for the Protection of Human Rights and Fundamental Freedoms, Concerning the Abolition of the Death Penalty in All Circumstances, CETS No. 187 (May 3, 2002).

[37] See David J. Harris, Michael O'Boyle, Edward P. Bates and Carla M. Buckley, *Harris, O'Boyle & Warbrick: Law of the European Convention on Human Rights*, 2nd edn (Oxford University Press, 2009) 335; Catherine Dupré, 'Human Dignity in Europe: A Foundational Constitutional Principle' (2013) 19 *European Public Law* 319, 320.

[38] Convention for the Protection of Human Rights and Dignity of the Human Being with Regard to the Application of Biology and Medicine: Convention on Human Rights and Biomedicine (Oviedo Convention), CETS No. 164 (April 4, 1997).

The protocols annexed to the convention also mention human dignity.[39]

Human dignity has a considerable status in the European Union. The proposal for the European Constitution (2004) – a proposal that was not ratified – stated:[40]

> The Union is founded on the values of respect for human dignity, freedom, democracy, equality, the rule of law and respect for human rights.

The proposed constitution included a bill of rights. The opening article of that bill of rights dealt with human dignity:[41]

> Human dignity is inviolable. It must be respected and protected.

The proposed constitution was not ratified. In its stead, the Treaty of Lisbon[42] was signed (in 2007). The text regarding human dignity that appeared in the proposed constitution was preserved in the treaty's preamble. The Treaty of Lisbon applied the Charter of Fundamental Rights of the European Union,[43] which had already been ratified in 2000. The preamble to the charter determines, inter alia:

> [T]he Union is founded on the indivisible, universal values of human dignity, freedom, equality and solidarity; it is based on the principles of democracy and the rule of law.

The first article of the charter determines:

> Human dignity is inviolable. It must be respected and protected.

(2) America

The American Declaration on the Rights and Duties of Man[44] was adopted in 1948, a number of months before the Universal Declaration of Human Rights. The preamble to the declaration determines, inter alia, that:

> All men are born free and equal, in dignity and in rights.

[39] See the Additional Protocol to the Convention on Human Rights and Biomedicine, Concerning Biomedical Research, CETS No. 195 (January 25, 2005).

[40] Art. 2-I. [41] Art. 6-II.

[42] Treaty of Lisbon Amending the Treaty on European Union and the Treaty Establishing the European Community, December 13, 2007, 2007/C306/01.

[43] Charter of Fundamental Rights of the European Union, 7 December 2000, Official Journal of the European Communities, December 18, 2000 (2000/C 364/01).

[44] American Declaration of the Rights and Duties of Man, OAS Res. XXX, adopted by the Ninth International Conference of American States (1948).

The American states are organized in the Organization of American States (OAS). In this framework, the American Convention on Human Rights was adopted in 1969.[45] It entered into effect in 1978. Human dignity is mentioned in the convention. Article 2 states:

> All persons deprived of their liberty shall be treated with respect for the inherent dignity of the human person.

The article on privacy (Article 11) states:

> Everyone has the right to have his honor and his dignity recognized.

A protocol on economic, social and cultural rights was annexed to this convention.[46] The preamble to this protocol notes that there is a close relationship between civil and political rights and social and economic rights. This relationship is manifest in the fact that the various categories of rights:

> constitute an indivisible whole based on the recognition of the dignity of the human person.

In the framework of the activity of the OAS, the Inter-American Convention to Prevent and Punish Torture (1985)[47] was adopted. Human dignity is mentioned in the first lines of the preamble. In 1994 the Inter-American Convention on the Prevention, Punishment and Eradication of Violence against Women[48] was adopted. The preamble to the convention states that violence against women is an offense against their human dignity. Article 4(e) of the convention determines, inter alia, that every woman has:

[45] Organization of American States, American Convention on Human Rights, "Pact of San Jose," Costa Rica (November 22, 1969).

[46] See Additional Protocol to the American Convention on Human Rights in the Area of Economic, Social and Cultural Rights "Protocol of San Salvador," OAS Treaty Series No. 69 (November 17, 1988); Additional Protocol to the Convention for the Protection of Human Rights and Dignity of the Human Being with regard to the Application of Biology and Medicine, on the Prohibition of Cloning Human Beings, CETS No. 168 (January 12, 1998); Additional Protocol to the Convention on Human Rights and Biomedicine Concerning Transplantation of Organs and Tissues of Human Origin, CETS No. 186 (January 24, 2002); Additional Protocol to the Convention on Human Rights and Biomedicine Concerning Genetic Testing for Health Purposes, CETS No. 203 (November 27, 2008).

[47] Organization of American States, Inter-American Convention to Prevent and Punish Torture, December 9, 1985, OAS Treaty Series, No. 67.

[48] Organization of American States, Inter-American Convention on the Prevention, Punishment and Eradication of Violence against Women ("Convention of Belem do Para"), June 9, 1994.

> the rights to have the inherent dignity of her person respected and her family protected.

The Inter-American Convention on the Elimination of All Forms of Discrimination against Persons with Disabilities[49] was adopted in 1999 by the OAS. The convention determines, in its preamble, that a person with disabilities has all the rights that any other person has, and that those rights, including the right not to be discriminated against based on disability:

> flow from the inherent dignity and equality of each person.

(3) Africa

The Organization of African Unity (OAU) prepared the African Charter on Human and Peoples Rights.[50] The proposal was accepted and confirmed by the states of Africa. It entered into effect in 1986. The preamble to the charter states, while quoting the document that established the OAU, that:

> [F]reedom, equality, justice and dignity are essential objectives for the achievement of the legitimate aspirations of the African peoples.

Article 5 of the charter states:

> Every individual shall have the right to the respect of the dignity inherent in a human being and to the recognition of his legal status.

The OAU prepared a number of protocols that added rights to the charter. One of the protocols deals with the rights of women in Africa.[51] Article 3 states:

> Every woman shall have the right to dignity inherent in a human being and to the recognition and protection of her human and legal rights.

[49] Organization of American States, Inter-American Convention on the Elimination of All Forms of Discrimination against Persons with Disabilities, June 7, 1999, AG/RES. 1608 (XXIX-O/99).

[50] African [Banjul] Charter on Human and Peoples' Rights, adopted June 27, 1981, OAU Doc. CAB/LEG/67/3 rev. 5, 21 ILM 58 (1982).

[51] Protocol to the African Charter on Human and Peoples' Rights on the Rights of Women in Africa (2000) (Maputo Protocol).

(4) The Arab League

The Arab League was established in 1945. It includes the Arab states in Africa and in Asia. In 1994 the Arab League adopted the Arab Charter of Human Rights.[52] It came into effect in 2008. Its preamble states:

> [S]temming from the Arab Nation's faith in the dignity of man; from what God favored it by making the Arab nation the cradle of monotheistic religions and the birthplace of civilization; which has reaffirmed [man's] right to a life of dignity based on freedom, justice and peace.

(5) The Organization of Islamic Cooperation

The Organization of Islamic Cooperation is an international organization with fifty-seven member states. It is intended to reflect the voice of the Islamic world. In the framework of this organization, the Cairo Declaration of Human Rights in Islam was adopted.[53] Article 1(a) of the declaration states:

> All human beings form one family whose members are united by submission in God and descent from Adam. All men are equal in terms of basic human dignity and basic obligation and responsibilities, without any discrimination on the grounds of race, colour, language, sex, religious belief, political affiliation, social status or other considerations. True faith is the guarantee for enhancing such dignity along the path to human perfection.

Article 6 of the declaration states:

> Woman is equal to man in human dignity.

[52] League of Arab States, Arab Charter on Human Rights, September 15, 1994.

[53] Cairo Declaration on Human Rights in Islam, August 5, 1990, UN GAOR, World Conference on Human Rights, 4th Session, Agenda Item 5, UN Doc. A/CONF.157/PC/62/Add.18 (1993).

4

Human dignity as a value and as a right in constitutions

1. Pre-Second World War developments

A. *Pre-First World War developments*

The intellectual history of human dignity is found predominantly in religious, philosophical and social discourse.[1] Human dignity was not part of the legal discourse. Almost none of the national constitutions included any mention of human dignity before the First World War. In those rare cases in which human dignity was mentioned in a constitution or in a document of constitutional importance, it related to human dignity as honor. Thus, for example, in the English Bill of Rights of 1689, a succession arrangement was determined "to hold the crown and royal dignity." The term "dignity" here is not the human dignity that is the subject of this book. The same is true regarding the Declaration of the Rights of Man and of the Citizen adopted during the French revolution in 1789. It determines, inter alia:

> Tous les Citoyens étant égaux à ses yeux sont également admissibles à toutes dignités, places et emplois publics, selon leur capacité, et sans autre distinction que celle de leurs vertus et de leurs talents.[2]

The "*dignités*" in this article pertains to honor, and not the dignity that we are discussing.

B. *Development from the First World War until the Second World War*

A change in the constitutional status of human dignity occurred after the First World War. The first constitution[3] that related to dignity seems to

[1] See Chapter 2, section 1A. [2] Art. 6.

[3] Many see the Constitution of Mexico (1917) as the first source of recognition of human dignity in a constitution after the First World War. Art. 3(c) of that constitution indeed refers to human dignity, but that provision was added to the Mexican constitution in 1948.

be the Constitution of Finland (July 1919). One of its provisions[4] determined that every Finnish citizen shall have the law's protection of his life, dignity, personal liberty and property. In the same year, the Weimar Constitution (August 1919)[5] determined that the organization of economic life must fit the principles of justice in order to ensure that everyone may lead a life suitable for a human being. The term used in this respect was *menschenwürdigen*, regarding human dignity. A similar provision was added in 1920 to the permanent constitution of Estonia.[6] In the Constitution of Lebanon (1926), the dignity of religion was safeguarded.[7] The Constitution of Ecuador (1929)[8] included a provision similar to that in the Weimar Constitution, according to which the organization of economic life must be based upon the principles of justice in order to ensure general growth, and through it to ensure a quality of life that is in line with human dignity (*dignidad humana*).

A provision regarding human dignity was included in the preamble of the Constitution of Ireland (1937), worded as follows:

> In the Name of the most Holy Trinity, from Whom all authority and to Whom, as our final end, all actions both of men and States must be referred, We the people of Éire, humbly acknowledging all our obligations to our Divine Lord, Jesus Christ, Who sustained our fathers through centuries of trial, Gratefully remembering their heroic and unremitting struggle to regain the rightful independence of our Nation, and seeking to promote the common good, with due observance of Prudence, Justice and Charity, so that the dignity and freedom of the individual may be assured, true social order attained, the unity of our country restored, and concord established with other nations, Do hereby adopt, enact, and give to ourselves this Constitution.

This preamble is seen as part of the constitution itself.[9] Various proposals to amend the preamble did not materialize.

The Constitution of Nicaragua (1939) determined a provision regarding the human dignity of the worker.[10] The Constitution of Cuba (1940) determined equality of all under the law.[11] It determined that any discrimination on the basis of sex, race, color, class or any other basis that diminishes human dignity (*dignidad humana*) is illegal and punishable.

[4] Art. 6. [5] Art. 151. [6] Art. 25.

[7] Art. 10. [8] Art. 151(18).

[9] Teresa Iglesias, 'The Dignity of the Individual in the Irish Constitution: The Importance of the Preamble' (2000) 89 *Studies: An Irish Quarterly Review* 19, 20.

[10] Art. 100(4). [11] Art. 20.

2. Development from the Second World War until the present

A. *The scope of the development*

Human dignity became a central feature of human rights discourse after the Second World War. Many newly independent states inserted chapters on human rights that included reference to human dignity into their constitutions.[12] States that moved from totalitarian regimes to democracy included a bill of human rights in their constitutions, in the framework of which appeared provisions regarding human dignity. Alongside the influence of the preamble of the Charter of the United Nations, the Universal Declaration of Human Rights and the German Basic Law,[13] additional international documents became more influential, predominantly the International Covenant on Civil and Political Rights (1966) and the International Covenant on Economic, Social and Cultural Rights (1966).[14] Regional developments which included human dignity began in different parts of the world. I shall discuss these developments, while distinguishing between the various regions.

In some of the new constitutions, human dignity is a constitutional right. This is the case, for example, in the constitutions of Namibia,[15] Russia,[16] Switzerland,[17] South Africa,[18] Ethiopia,[19] Colombia,[20] Poland,[21] Hungary,[22] Israel,[23] and Germany.[24] In other new constitutions, human dignity serves as a constitutional value without it being recognized as a constitutional right.[25]

12 I face a severe problem of translation. Due to language restrictions, I always refer to the English text of the constitutions. However, I cannot be certain if these are precise translations of the original wording and whether the English term "dignity" indeed reflects the original term in the language of the constitution.

13 See Art. 1(1) of the German Basic Law (1949). See also Arts. 2 and 4 of the Israeli Basic Law: Human Dignity and Liberty.

14 993 UNTS 3 (December 16, 1966).

15 Art. 8 of the Constitution of Namibia (1990).

16 Art. 21 of the Constitution of Russia (1993).

17 Art. 7 of the Constitution of Switzerland (1999).

18 Art. 10 of the Constitution of South Africa (1996).

19 Art. 24 of the Constitution of Ethiopia (1995).

20 Art. 21 of the Constitution of Colombia (1991).

21 Art. 30 of the Constitution of Poland (1997).

22 Art. 1 in Ch. 1 of the Constitution of Hungary (2011).

23 Arts. 2 and 4 of Basic Law: Human Dignity and Liberty (1992).

24 Art. 1 of the German Basic Law (1949).

25 Art. 10 of the Constitution of Spain (1978).

It is unclear to what extent there was mutual influence between the various constitutions regarding the use of human dignity. For example, was there European (primarily Spanish and Portuguese) influence on the use of human dignity in the constitutions of Latin America; was there (English and French) influence on the use of human dignity in Africa and Asia? It appears that the answer to these questions is no. To the extent that there was external influence on the constitutions of the states of Latin America, it did not come from Spain or Portugal – as those states only enacted democratic constitutions in the 1980s – but rather from the spirit of the French and American revolutions of the end of the eighteenth century[26] and the influence of the development of the understanding of human dignity in German constitutional law.[27] Similarly, it is very doubtful whether the colonial states had influence on the constitutions of their former colonies in Africa and Asia that had just attained independence. To the extent that it is possible to indicate external influence, it came, primarily in the case of Africa and Asia, from international documents.

B. Development of human dignity in the constitutions of the European states

(1) The 1940s

Soon after the end of the Second World War (July 1945), Spain adopted its charter of basic rights (Fuero de los Españoles). The charter contains a number of references to human dignity. Thus, for example, Article 1 of the charter determines that:

> The Spanish state proclaims as a guiding principle of its acts, respect for the dignity, integrity, and liberty of the human person.

Franco initiated this charter so that Spain would gain international credibility. The attempt was unsuccessful.

The next change came about in France. In 1946 the French Constitution was enacted (The Constitution of the Fourth Republic). The preamble of the constitution determined:

> On the morrow of the victory of the free peoples over the regimes that attempted to enslave and degrade the human person, the French people

[26] See Allan R. Brewer-Carías, *Constitutional Protection of Human Rights in Latin America: A Comparative Study of Amparo Proceedings* (Cambridge University Press, 2009), 13.

[27] See Erin Daly, 'Dignity in the Service of Democracy', Widener Law School Legal Studies Research, Paper no. 11-07 (2010), 5.

> proclaims once more that every human being, without distinction of race, religion or belief, possesses inalienable and sacred rights. It solemnly reaffirms the rights and freedoms of man and of the citizen consecrated by the Declaration of Rights of 1789 and the fundamental principles recognized by the laws of the Republic.

This provision – which bases itself upon the Declaration of the Rights of Man and of the Citizen (1789) – was interpreted years later by the French Constitutional Court as granting constitutional status to the value of human dignity.[28]

In 1948 the Italian Constitution was enacted. Human dignity is mentioned in three of its articles.[29] Article 3 of this constitution determines:

> All citizens have equal social dignity [*dignità sociale*] and are equal before the law, without distinction of sex, race, language, religion, political opinions, personal and social conditions.

Article 27 of the constitution deals with penal rights. It determines, inter alia, that:

> Punishment cannot consist in treatment contrary to human dignity [*senso di umanità*] and must aim at rehabilitating the condemned.

Finally, Article 41 of the constitution, which deals with free economy, determines:

> Private economic initiative is free. It cannot be conducted in conflict with public will or in such manner that could damage safety, liberty or human dignity [*dignità umana*].

The main development during this period took place in Germany, first in the constitutions of a number of German states (*Länder*) that included human dignity, and then in the provision of Article 1(1) of the German Basic Law (*Grundgesetz*), which determines:

> The dignity of man [*die Würde des Menschen*] shall be inviolable [*unantastbar*].[30] To respect and protect it shall be the duty of all state authority.

It was also determined that the fundamental principles determined in this provision of the Basic Law cannot be changed through constitutional

[28] See section 2B(4) below.

[29] See Paolo Becchi, *Il Principio Dignità Umana* (Brescia: Morcelliana, 2009).

[30] This expression has been translated into English in the official publication as "inviolable." See Chapter 13, section 1B.

amendment.[31] I shall discuss the interpretation of this provision and its centrality in the German Basic Law further on in this book.[32]

(2) The 1950s – the European Convention for the Protection of Human Rights and Fundamental Freedoms

The next development in Europe arrived when the European Convention for the Protection of Human Rights and Fundamental Freedoms (1950)[33] entered into effect. This convention is influenced by the Universal Declaration of Human Rights. Nevertheless, it contains no express reference to human dignity.[34] The accepted view is that human dignity is an underlying value of the convention.[35] It serves as a basis for all of the rights determined within it. It is also used in the interpretation of the provisions of the convention.[36] Over the years, human dignity's effect has intensified in Europe. It is expressly determined as a right or as a value in the constitutions of many states.

(3) The 1960s, 1970s and 1980s

During these years, two major developments took place. The first relates to the European Convention for the Protection of Human Rights and Fundamental Freedoms (1950) and the law of the European Community. The European Court of Human Rights determined that human dignity constitutes a legal value underlying the European Convention.[37] The European Court of Justice ruled in a similar spirit.[38]

The second development is found in the constitutions of a number of states that adopted the concept of human dignity. The Constitution of Turkey (1961) determines that punishment incompatible with human

[31] See Art. 79(3) of the Basic Law of Germany.

[32] See Chapter 13, section 1C.

[33] See Francis Jacobs and Robin White, *Jacobs & White: The European Convention on Human Rights*, 3rd edition (Oxford University Press, 2002), 3.

[34] Only in the preamble to the 13th protocol of the convention regarding annulment of the death penalty is it stated that annulment of the death penalty is essential "for the full recognition of the inherent dignity of all human beings."

[35] See Conor A. Gearty, *Principles of Human Rights Adjudication* (Oxford University Press, 2006), 91; *S.W.* v. *United Kingdom* (1995) 21 EHRR 363, paras. 42, 44; *Prety* v. *United Kingdom* (2002) ECHR 427 (April 29, 2002).

[36] See Frowein Abr. Jochen, 'Human Dignity in International Law', in David Kretzmer and Eckart Klein (eds.), *The Concept of Human Dignity in Human Rights Discourse* (The Hague: Kluwer Law International, 2002) 121, 124.

[37] See section 2B(4) above.

[38] See *Kingdom of the Netherlands* v. *European Parliament & Council of the European Union*, Case C-377/98, 2001 ECR I-7079, paras. 70–77.

dignity cannot be imposed.[39] The transition from dictatorship to democracy in Greece led to the enactment of the Greek Constitution in 1975. Human dignity has an important role in this constitution. Article 2 of the constitution determines, in Sub-Article (1):

> Respect and protection of the value of the human being constitute the primary obligations of the state.

Article 7 of the Constitution of Greece deals with penal rights. Sub-Article (2) determines that:

> Torture, any bodily maltreatment, impairment of health, or the use of psychological violence as well as any other offence against human dignity are prohibited and punished as provided by law.

Finally, Article 106 of the Constitution of Greece deals with the relations between the state and the economy. Sub-Article (2) determines, inter alia, that:

> Private enterprise may not be exercised in any way detrimental to liberty, human dignity and the national economy.

The transition from dictatorship to democracy in Portugal led to the enactment of a new constitution in 1976. The first article of the Portuguese constitution states:

> Portugal is a sovereign Republic, based on the dignity of the human person and the will of the people and committed to building a free, just and solidary society.

In the other articles of this constitution, human dignity is not mentioned. It is therefore interpreted as a constitutional value that did not reach the status of constitutional right.[40]

In 1978 a new constitution was enacted in post-Franco Spain. Human dignity is expressly entrenched in this constitution. Article 10(1) of this constitution states:

> The dignity [*dignidad*] of the person, the inviolable rights which are inherent, the free development of the personality, respect for the law and the rights of others, are the foundation of political order and social peace.

[39] See Art. 14(4) of the Constitution of Turkey (1961).

[40] See Jose Manuel Cardoso Da Costa, 'The Principle of Human Dignity in European Case-Law', in European Commission for Democracy through Law, *The Principle of Respect for Human Dignity* (Strasbourg: Council of Europe, 1999) 50.

This article recognizes human dignity as a constitutional value, but not as a constitutional right.[41]

In 1982 a new constitution was enacted in Turkey. The constitution states, inter alia, that:

> No one shall be subjected to torture or ill treatment; no one shall be subjected to penalties or treatment incompatible with human dignity.[42]

At the end of the 1980s the Constitution of Sweden was amended, determining, inter alia, that:

> Public power shall be exercised with respect for the equal worth of all and for the liberty and dignity of the individual.[43]

(4) The 1990s

The central event of the 1990s, from the viewpoint of human rights in general and human dignity specifically, was the break-up of the Soviet bloc in central and eastern Europe, the fall of communism in those states and the transition to democracy. In each of those states a new constitution was enacted, or important amendments were made to existing constitutions. In all these constitutions there is a chapter on human rights. In the framework of that chapter, human dignity is protected.

The first post-communist constitution was enacted – by way of amendment to the constitution of 1949 – in Hungary.[44] Article 54 of the Hungarian Constitution (1989),[45] which opens the chapter on human rights, states that:

> In the Republic of Hungary everyone has the inherent right to life and to human dignity.

[41] See Alberto Oehling de los Reyes, 'Algunas Reflexiones Sobre la Significación Constitucional de la Noción de Dignidad Humana' (2006) 12 *Pensamiento Constitucional* 327.

[42] Art. 17. [43] Art. 2(1).

[44] Regarding human dignity in the Hungarian constitution, see Catherine Dupré, *Importing Law in Post-Communist Transitions: The Hungarian Constitutional Court and the Right to Human Dignity* (Oxford and Portland, OR: Hart Publishing, 2003); Catherine Dupré, 'The Right to Human Dignity in Hungarian Constitutional Case-law', in European Commission for Democracy through Law, *The Principle of Respect for Human Dignity* (Strasbourg: Council of Europe Publishing, 1999) 68.

[45] On January 1, 2012 a new constitution entered into effect in Hungary. Art. II of the chapter on freedom and responsibility states: "Human dignity is inviolable. Everyone has the right to life and human dignity; the life of a fetus will be protected from conception."

In a similar spirit, provisions on human dignity were determined in the constitutions of Croatia (1990),[46] Albania (1991),[47] Bulgaria (1991),[48] Slovenia (1991),[49] Macedonia (1991),[50] Estonia (1992),[51] Lithuania (1992),[52] Slovakia (1992),[53] the Czech Republic (1992),[54] Russia (1993),[55] Belarus (1994),[56] Moldova (1994),[57] Armenia (1995),[58] Azerbaijan (1995),[59] Georgia (1995),[60] Bosnia-Herzegovina (1995),[61] Ukraine (1996)[62] and Poland (1997).[63]

In the mid 1990s human dignity was added to the Belgian constitution (1994), stating:

> Everyone has the right to lead a life in conformity with human dignity.[64]

At the end of the 1990s (1999), a radical change took place in the Federal Constitution of Switzerland. A comprehensive chapter on human rights was added. The chapter states, inter alia:

> Human dignity is to be respected and protected.[65]

The new Constitution of Finland (1999) states:

> The constitution shall guarantee the inviolability of human dignity.[66]

An important development took place in France. In 1958 a new constitution was enacted (Constitution of the Fifth Republic). The preamble to this constitution states:

> The French people solemnly proclaim their attachment to the Rights of Man and to the principles of national sovereignty as defined by the

[46] Arts. 25 and 35. [47] Ch. 1, Art. 2, and Ch. 4, Art. 15.
[48] In the Preamble and Arts. 4(2), 6(1) and 32(1).
[49] Arts. 21 and 34. [50] Arts. 11 and 25.
[51] Art. 10. [52] Arts. 21, 22 and 25.
[53] Arts. 12(1), 19(1) and 36(a). [54] In the Preamble.
[55] Art. 21(1). [56] Arts. 25, 28, 50 and 53.
[57] In the Preamble and Arts. 1(3), 9(2) and 32(2).
[58] Arts. 3, 14, 17 and 47. [59] Arts. 13(3), 18(2) and 46.
[60] Arts. 17(1) and 24(4). [61] In the Preamble.
[62] Arts. 3, 21, 28, 41 and 68.
[63] In the Preamble and Art. 30. See also Biruta Lewaszkiewicz-Petrykowska, 'The Principle of Respect to Human Dignity', in European Commission for Democracy through Law, *The Principle of Respect for Human Dignity* (Strasbourg: Council of Europe, 1999) 15.
[64] Art 23. See Francis Delpérée, 'The Right to Human Dignity in Belgian Constitutional Law', in European Commission for Democracy through Law, *The Principle of Respect for Human Dignity* (Strasbourg: Council of Europe, 1999) 57.
[65] Art. 7. [66] Art. 1(2).

> Declaration of 1789, confirmed and completed by the Preamble to the Constitution of 1946 …
>
> By virtue of these principles and that of the self-determination of peoples, the Republic offers to the overseas territories that express the will to adhere to them new institutions based on the common ideal of liberty, equality, and fraternity and conceived with a view to their democratic development.

Further on in that constitution there are provisions regarding governmental agencies. It does not have a constitutional bill of rights. It established the Constitutional Council (the Conseil Constitutionnel), which was authorized, inter alia, to examine the constitutionality of statutes (*lois*) legislated by the National Assembly that have not yet been published.

Against the backdrop of this constitutional structure, which rests on the preamble to the Constitution of the Fourth Republic, the preamble to the Constitution of the Fifth Republic, as well as making reference to the Declaration of the Rights of Man and of the Citizen of 1789, the Constitutional Council decided that the rights in the Declaration are of constitutional status.[67] The constitutional bill of rights was constructed upon these foundations. This bill of rights does not include an express right[68] to human dignity. A 1994 decision of the Conseil Constitutionnel[69] held that the value of human dignity is part of the "*bloc de constitutionnalité*."[70] A committee of experts established by the President of the Republic proposed, inter alia, to amend the preamble to the Constitution of the Fifth Republic to include an express provision regarding the value of human dignity.[71] That proposal has yet to materialize.

(5) The start of the twenty-first century

In the twenty-first century the trend of recognition of human dignity as a constitutional value or right continues. Some of the new constitutions reflected the developments in central and eastern Europe, primarily the events in Serbia. Against that backdrop, the Constitution of Serbia was

[67] Decision no. 71-44 DC of July 16, 1971.

[68] See section 2B(2) above.

[69] Decision no. 94-343/344 DC of July 27, 1994.

[70] Giovanni Bognetti, 'The Concept of Human Dignity in European and US Constitutionalism', in George Nolte (ed.), *European and US Constitutionalism* (Cambridge University Press, 2005) 85, 97. See also Jacques Robert, 'The Principle of Human Dignity', in European Commission for Democracy through Law, *The Principle of Respect for Human Dignity* (Strasbourg: Council of Europe, 1999) 43.

[71] Comité de réflexion sur le Préambule de la Constitution, Rapport au Président de la République (2008).

enacted in 2006. It includes a chapter on human rights and minority rights. Regarding human dignity, it states:

> Human dignity is inviolable and everyone shall be obliged to respect and protect it.[72]

The Constitution of Kosovo was enacted in 2008. Regarding human dignity it determines that:

> Human dignity is inviolable and is the basis of all human rights and fundamental freedoms.[73]

(6) In retrospect

Out of forty-five European states, thirty-two mention human dignity expressly in their constitutions, whether only as a constitutional value or as a constitutional right. In twelve states the constitution does not expressly refer to human dignity. These states are Iceland, Denmark, Holland, the Vatican, Luxemburg, Lichtenstein, Monaco, Malta, Norway, San Marino, France and Cyprus. All these states, as well as the United Kingdom, are signatories of the European Convention for the Protection of Human Rights and Fundamental Freedoms. As we have seen, human dignity is a constitutional value pursuant to that convention. Seven of these states are members of the European Union, the international documents of which – including the Treaty of Lisbon and the Charter of Fundamental Rights of the European Union – recognize human dignity.

C. *Development of human dignity in the constitutions of Latin American states*

(1) Until the end of the 1940s

The first constitution in South America that mentioned human dignity (*dignidad humana*) was the constitution of Ecuador in 1929. Similar to the Weimar Constitution, the Constitution of Ecuador also stated that the organization of economic life must provide for growth that will ensure a standard of living consistent with human dignity. In 1940 human dignity appeared in the constitutions of Cuba and Paraguay. The Constitution of Cuba establishes the principle of equality of all people under the law, and prohibits discrimination that detracts from human dignity.[74] The

[72] Art. 23. [73] Art. 23. [74] Art. 20.

Constitution of Paraguay prohibits the exploitation of people, and determines that the state must ensure a standard of living that is compatible with human dignity for every worker.[75]

The widespread use of human dignity in the constitutions of South America took place after the Second World War. The Constitution of Ecuador (of 1945) in Article 141(2) prohibits discrimination that impinges upon human dignity. It further states, in Article 148, that the state must ensure dignified (*digna*) working conditions.[76] The Constitution of Guatemala (1945) determines that the list of rights in the constitution does not exclude other rights of analogous character, or those derived from the principle of popular sovereignty, the republican and democratic form of government or human dignity.[77] The Constitution of Panama (1946) includes a provision on education as a means to instill consciousness of the dignity of Panamanian citizenship. Within the framework of the constitutional amendment in late 1946, Article 3(IIc) relating to human dignity was added to the Mexican Constitution.[78] The Preamble of the Constitution of Venezuela of 1947 states that the fundamental reason for the existence of the Venezuelan nation is:

> the spiritual, political, and economic liberty of man, based on human dignity, social justice, and the fair participation of all the people in the enjoyment of the national wealth.

Human dignity is mentioned in the Constitution of Nicaragua of 1948, in the context of a provision regarding minimum wage for workers that will ensure them minimal subsistence that is in line with human dignity.[79] The Constitution of Argentina of 1949 also refers to human dignity in the context of labor relations. This constitution determines a right to work, noting that said right is protected by society:

> and it should be considered with the dignity that it deserves.[80]

The Constitution of Costa Rica of 1949 also mentions human dignity in the context of the right to work.[81]

Along with the recognition of human dignity in the 1940s as part of the constitutional discourse in Latin America, human dignity's status in the constitutions of Latin American states increased. The development was

[75] Art. 14.

[76] Human dignity is also mentioned in Art. 148 of the Constitution of Ecuador (1945).

[77] Art. 50.

[78] Diario Oficial, October 8, 1946.

[79] Art. 83(3).

[80] Art. 37(1).

[81] Art. 56.

fast, and passed from the constitution of one state to another, and within states from one constitution to the next. Indeed, there are many Latin American constitutions. Of all the states of Latin America, only in the Constitution of Uruguay is there no mention of human dignity, although there is a mention of honor.[82] I shall analyze human dignity as it appears in the constitutions of Latin America in the form in which they existed at the end of the first decade of the twenty-first century.

(2) Human dignity in modern constitutions

All the constitutions of Latin America – with the exception of the constitution of Uruguay – mention human dignity. The intensity of the use of human dignity of course varies from one constitution to another. At one end of the spectrum is Panama, which mentions human dignity only in the preamble to the constitution.[83] At the other end of the spectrum are the constitutions of Ecuador[84] and Bolivia,[85] which mention human dignity in the preamble and in a large number of articles throughout the entire constitution. Characteristic of the constitutions of a number of Latin American states[86] – primarily Colombia, Peru, Mexico, Argentina and Brazil – is the central role of human dignity in their bills of rights and their view of democracy.

Most of the constitutions declare that the state is based upon respect of human dignity (*respeto de la dignidad humana*).[87] There are constitutions that state that democracy is based upon the recognition of human dignity.[88] A number of constitutions declare that human dignity is inalienable.[89] At times the general right to human dignity is

[82] See Art. 66 of the Constitution of Uruguay (1966).

[83] See the Constitution of Panama (1972), as amended in 1994. The Preamble states that the goal of the constitution is, inter alia, to promote human dignity (*dignidad humana*).

[84] The Constitution of Ecuador (2008). Human dignity is mention in the Preamble and in Arts. 7, 30, 33, 37(7), 39, 42, 45, 56, 57(14), 57(21), 60, 66(2), 84, 158, 171, 189, 229, 329, 375 and 408.

[85] The Constitution of Bolivia (2009). Human dignity is mentioned in the Preamble and in Arts. 8(2), 9(2), 21(2), 22, 23(2), 46(1), 54(1), 67(1), 70(4), 73(1), 98(3).

[86] See Daly, 'Dignity in the Service of Democracy'.

[87] See Art. 1 of the Constitution of Brazil (1988); Art. 1 of the Constitution of Colombia (1991); Art. 1 of the Constitution of Peru (1993); the Preamble of the Constitution of Paraguay (1994); the Preamble of the Constitution of Panama (amended in 1994); Art. 3 of the Constitution of Venezuela (1999); the Preamble of the Constitution of Ecuador (2008); the Preamble and Art. 8(2) of the Constitution of Bolivia (2009).

[88] See Art. 1 of the Constitution of Paraguay (1992).

[89] See Art. 42 of the Constitution of Colombia (1991); Art. 59 of the Constitution of Honduras (1982, amended in 1991); Art. 22 of the Constitution of Bolivia (2009).

recognized.[90] At times this right is recognized regarding prisoners,[91] workers,[92] people with disabilities[93] and children.[94] At times human dignity is granted to the family.[95]

In a number of constitutions, human dignity is associated with equality. At times it is stated that the recognition of human dignity is intended to ensure equality,[96] or to ensure equal human dignity to all.[97] At times it is stated that discrimination contradicts human dignity.[98] At times it is stated that people are born with equal human dignity.[99] Finally, at times human dignity serves as a standard for defining discrimination. Thus, for example, the Constitution of Mexico prohibits discrimination on the basis of sex, age, social status, health, religion, opinion, preference, or any other discrimination that infringes upon human dignity.[100]

A number of constitutions state that the human rights determined in them do not preclude the existence of other rights found outside the constitution that are based on human dignity.[101]

D. *Development of human dignity in the constitutions of African states*

The first African constitution was the Constitution of Liberia (1847). This constitution does not mention human dignity. It appears that the first constitution in Africa that includes reference to human dignity is the

90 See for example Art. 21(2) of the Constitution of Bolivia (2009).

91 See for example Art. 19 of the Constitution of Guatemala (1985); Art. 44(1) of the Constitution of Haiti (1987); Art. 46 of the Constitution of Venezuela (1999); Art. 73 of the Constitution of Bolivia (2009).

92 See for example Art. 83(3) of the Constitution of Nicaragua (1948); Art. 53 of the Constitution of Costa Rica (amended in 1999); Art. 37 of the Constitution of El Salvador (1983); Art. 23 of the Constitution of Peru (1993); Arts. 33 and 329 of the Constitution of Ecuador (2008); Art. 53 of the Constitution of Colombia (1991); Art. 37(1) of the Constitution of Argentina (1949).

93 See Art. 81 of the Constitution of Venezuela (1999); Art. 7 of the Constitution of Peru (1993).

94 See Art. 45 of the Constitution of Ecuador (2008).

95 See Art. 42 of the Constitution of Colombia (1991).

96 See Art. 1 of the Constitution of Paraguay (1992).

97 See Art. 9 of the Constitution of Bolivia (2009).

98 See Art. 33 of the Constitution of Costa Rica (amended in 1999).

99 See Art. 1 of the Constitution of Chile (1980); Art. 4 of the Constitution of Guatemala (1985); Art. 9(2) of the Constitution of Bolivia (2009).

100 See Art. 1 of the Constitution of Mexico (amended in 2011).

101 See for example Art. 3 of the Constitution of Peru (1993); Art. 11(7) of the Constitution of Ecuador (2008).

Constitution of Egypt (1956). The preamble of that constitution refers to the members of the Egyptian population:

> with our sacred belief in equality, justice and dignity as fundamental roots of liberty and peace.

Since then, human dignity has appeared in most of the constitutions of African states. Only seven of the constitutions of African states do not refer to human dignity.[102] Most of the constitutions state that human dignity constitutes a human right.[103] In some of them human dignity appears as a constitutional value that must be maintained, and is mentioned only in the preamble.[104]

Human dignity is at times associated with equality, when it is stated that human beings are of equal human dignity.[105] Equality of human dignity is determined particularly between men and women.[106] Human dignity also appears in provisions regarding people with disabilities,[107] the elderly,[108] family members,[109] and imprisoned or detained people.[110]

102 These are Botswana, Djibouti, Zimbabwe, Mauritius, Senegal, Cameroon and Rwanda.

103 See Art. 12(2) of the Constitution of Tanzania (1977); Art. 5 of the Constitution of Guinea (1990); Art. 8 of the Constitution of Namibia (1990); Art. 13(e) of the Constitution of Sierra Leone (1991); Art. 11 of the Constitution of Togo (1992); Art. 9(1) of the Constitution of Malawi (1994); Art. 10 of the Constitution of South Africa (1996); Art. 16 of the Constitution of Eritrea (1997); Art. 34(1) of the Constitution of Nigeria (1999); Art. 2 of the Constitution of Ivory Coast (2000); Art. 21 of the Constitution of Burundi (2005); Art. 17 of the Constitution of Madagascar (2010); Art. 28 of the Constitution of Kenya (2010); Art. 31(2) of the Constitution of Angola (2010); Art. 11 of the Constitution of South Sudan (2011); Art. 22 of the Constitution of Morocco (2011).

104 See the Constitution of Liberia (1955); the Constitution of Mauritania (1991); the Constitution of Congo (1992); the Constitution of Nigeria (1996); the Constitution of Chad (1996).

105 See Art. 22 of the Constitution of Cape Verde (1992); Art. 13 of the Constitution of Burundi (2005); Art. 11 of the Constitution of Democratic Republic of Congo (2006).

106 See Art. 33(1) of the Constitution of Uganda (1995); Art. 28(1) of the Constitution of Gambia (1997); Art. 16(1) of the Constitution of South Sudan (2011).

107 See Art. 35(1) of the Constitution of Uganda (1995); Art. 30(1) of the Constitution of Swaziland (2005); Art. 31(1) of the Constitution of Gambia (1997); Art. 54(1) of the Constitution of Kenya (2010); Art. 30(2) of the Constitution of South Sudan (2011).

108 See Art. 57(c) of the Constitution of Kenya (2010); Art. 30(2) of the Constitution of South Sudan (2011).

109 See Arts. 119(3) and 120(1) of the Constitution of Mozambique (amended in 2007).

110 See Art. 42 of the Constitution of Egypt (1971); Art. 13(6) of the Constitution of Tanzania (1984); Art. 42(b) of the Constitution of Malawi (1994); Art. 30 of the Constitution of Sudan (1998); Art. 18 of the Constitution of Zaire (2006).

In a number of constitutions there are provisions regarding the right to work and labor relations. Human dignity appears among these provisions.[111] Human dignity also appears in a provision stating that the rights in the constitution do not preclude rights that are not mentioned and are intended to secure human dignity.[112]

Human dignity appears in a considerable number of constitutions in the context of honor, such as dignity of the state, nation, parliament or office.[113] Human dignity is also mentioned in the context of dignifying language.[114]

E. *Development of human dignity in the constitutions of Asian states*

Human dignity is mentioned in most of the constitutions of Asian states.[115] It was first mentioned in the Constitution of Lebanon (1926), according to which the dignity of religion must be preserved.[116] Next came Japan. Article 24 of its constitution (1946) states that in family life, the dignity of each individual must be preserved. The use of human dignity in the constitutions of Asian states has been expanding since the 1950s. A number of constitutions recognize the (negative) right to human dignity, or the (positive) right requiring the state to protect human dignity.[117] A number of constitutions have also established an inalienable right to human

[111] See Art. 30(2)(d) of the Constitution of Tanzania (1984); Art. 4 of the Constitution of Cape Verde (1992); Art. 36 of the Constitution of Zaire (2006).

[112] See Art. 23(5) of the Constitution of Ghana (1992); Art. 37(8) of the Constitution of Gambia (1997).

[113] See Art. 8(2) of the Constitution of Tanzania (1984); Arts. 31(d)(b) and 60(1) of the Constitution of Namibia (1990); Art. 97 of the Constitution of Sierra Leone (1991); Art. 177(c) of the Constitution of Mozambique (amended in 1997); Art. 73(1) of the Constitution of Kenya (2010); Art. 152(2)(d) of the Constitution of Angola (2010).

[114] See Art. 21(n) of the Constitution of Angola (2010).

[115] Human dignity is missing from the Constitutions of Australia, Taiwan, Jordan, Singapore, Qatar, The United Arab Emirates, Brunei, Micronesia, Tonga, Nauru, Vanuatu, Samoa, Palau, Kiribati and the Marshall Islands. As New Zealand does not have a written constitution, there is also no Bill of Rights.

[116] See Art. 10 of the Constitution of Lebanon (1926).

[117] See Art. 28(g) of the Constitution of Indonesia (1945); Art. 33 of the Constitution of Syria (1973); Art. 9 of the Constitution of South Korea (1980); Art. 48(a) of the Constitution of Yemen (1991); Arts. 2 and 4 of Basic Law: Human Dignity and Liberty (1992); Art. 71 of the Constitution of Vietnam (1992); Arts. 3 and 46 of the Constitution of Turkmenistan (1992); Art. 17 of the Constitution of Mongolia (1992); Art. 27 of the Constitution of Uzbekistan (1992); Art. 18 of the Constitution of Kazakhstan (1995); Art. 1(1) of the Constitution of East Timor (2002); Art. 6 of the Constitution of Afghanistan (2004); Art. 37 of the Constitution of Iraq (2005); Art. 12 of the Constitution of Nepal (2007); Arts. 4 and 26 of the Constitution of Thailand (2007).

dignity.[118] Specific provisions regarding human dignity can be found in the context of prohibiting criminal punishments that violate human dignity[119] or preservation of the human dignity of persons who have been deprived of their liberty.[120] Torture and other methods of investigation that infringe upon human dignity are similarly prohibited.[121] The human dignity of women,[122] children,[123] mothers of children,[124] workers,[125] minorities[126] and senior citizens[127] is protected in a number of constitutions. At times it is stated that protection of the right of human dignity justifies limiting other constitutional rights.[128] At times the term dignity is associated with the dignity of the state, one of its agencies or officials,[129] or with the dignity of religion.[130]

[118] See Art. 14 of the Constitution of Pakistan (1973); Art. 38 of the Constitution of China (1982); Art. 5 of the Constitution of Tajikistan (1994); Art. 17 of the Constitution of Kazakhstan (1995); Art. 24 of the Constitution of Afghanistan (2004); Art. 29(1) of the Constitution of Kirgizstan (2010).

[119] See Art. 46(3) of the Constitution of Azerbaijan (1995); Art. 24 of the Constitution of Afghanistan (2003); Art. 44 of the Constitution of Myanmar (2008).

[120] See Art. 37(17) of the Constitution of Papua New Guinea (1975); Art. 48(b) of the Constitution of Yemen (1991); Art. 57 of the Constitution of the Maldivian Islands (2008); Art. 22(2) of the Constitution of Kirgizstan (2010); Art. 13(1)(j) of the Constitution of Fiji (2013).

[121] See Art. 28(3) of the Constitution of Syria (1973); Art. 17(2) of the Constitution of Kazakhstan (1995); Art. 17 of the Constitution of Turkey (amended in 2004).

[122] See Art. 63 of the Constitution of Vietnam (1992); Art. 46 of the Constitution of Cambodia (1993).

[123] See Art. 39(f) of the Constitution of India (1950).

[124] See Art. 39(4) of the Constitution of East Timor (2002).

[125] See Art. 30(d) of the Constitution of South Korea (1980).

[126] See Art. 34 of the Constitution of Uzbekistan (1992).

[127] See Art. 20(2) of the Constitution of East Timor (2002).

[128] See Arts. 38 and 39 of the Constitution of Papua New Guinea (1975); Art. 23 of the Constitution of Laos (1991); Art. 39 of the Constitution of Saudi Arabia (1992); Art. 41 of the Constitution of Cambodia (1993); Art. 34(1) of the Constitution of Kazakhstan (1995); Art. 45 of the Constitution of Thailand (2007); Art. 17(3)(b) and (d) of the Constitution of Fiji (2013).

[129] See Art. 24(b) of the Constitution of Indonesia (1945); the Preamble of the Constitution of China (1982); Art. 36 of the Constitution of Mongolia (1992); Art. 106 of the Constitution of Azerbaijan (1995); Art. 46 of the Constitution of Kazakhstan (1995); Art. 59 of the Constitution of Oman (1996); Art. 38(4) of the Constitution of Malaysia (amended in 2006); Art. 34(6) of the Constitution of Nepal (2007); Art. 248 of the Constitution of Thailand (2007); Art. 10(20) of the Constitution of Bhutan (2008).

[130] See Art. 10 of the Constitution of Lebanon (1926).

PART II

Human dignity as a constitutional value

5

Purposive constitutional interpretation

1. Constitutional uniqueness and its influence on constitutional interpretation

A. *Human dignity as a constitutional value and constitutional interpretation*

Is human dignity a constitutional value? This is the question that I shall examine in this chapter. The answer to this question is interpretative. It is subject to interpretational tools. We must answer the question through a holistic interpretation of the constitution – each constitution according to its own interpretation. There is no single interpretive method for understanding the constitution. However, comparative constitutional experience indicates that there are three primary approaches to constitutional interpretation.[1] The first method is interpretation according to the intent of the constitution's framers: *Intentionalism*. Intentionalism's answer to the question of whether or not human dignity is a constitutional value will be decided according to the intention of the constitution's framers. The second interpretive method, which is prominent in American constitutional law, is interpretation according to the original public understanding: *Originalism*.[2] Human dignity is a constitutional

[1] See Aharon Barak, *Purposive Interpretation in Law* (Princeton University Press, 2005) 30.

[2] See Daniel A. Farber, 'The Originalism Debate: A Guide for the Perplexed' (1989) 49 *Ohio State Law Journal* 1085; Jack N. Rakove, *Original Meanings: Politics and Ideas in the Making of the Constitution* (New York and Toronto: Random House, 1996); Jeffrey Goldsworthy, 'Originalism in Constitutional Interpretations' (1997) 25 *Federal Law Review* 1; Dennis Goldford, *The American Constitution and the Debate over Originalism* (Cambridge University Press, 2005); Steven G. Calabresi (ed.), *Originalism: A Quarter Century of Debate* (Washington DC: Regnery Publishing, 2007); Jack Balkin, *Living Originalism* (Cambridge, MA: Harvard University Press, 2011); Grant Huscroft and Bradley Miller, *The Challenge of Originalism: Theories of Constitutional Interpretation* (Cambridge University Press, 2011); Antonin Scalia and Bryan A. Garner, *Reading Law: The Interpretation of Legal Texts* (St. Paul: West Publishing, 2012).

value, according this approach, if that was society's understanding at the time of the constitution's adoption. The third interpretative method is the functional approach: *Purposive Interpretation*. Human dignity is a constitutional value if that is what is indicated after assessing the role, the function and the purpose that the constitution fills at the time of interpretation. Dworkin provided another important theory of constitutional interpretation. Due to its intricate nature, I will not delve into it in this book. In principle I would argue – and it certainly is open to argument – that Dworkin's approach presents a specific aspect of purposive interpretation. The same holds true for Posner's pragmatism. For the purposes of this book, I see it as an aspect of purposivism. The same is true for the American approach called The Living Constitution.

I shall focus on purposive constitutional interpretation. This is the accepted interpretative approach in many modern democracies. I shall address the details of this method so far as they pertain to constitutional interpretation generally, and to the interpretation of "human dignity" within a constitution specifically. As we shall see, purposive interpretation considers both the intent of the constitution's framers and the original public understanding. However, it does not attribute significant weight to either of them. Decisive weight is given to the fundamental purpose underlying the constitution at the time of interpretation. I shall discuss this later in the book.

B. *A constitution as a supreme norm*

I assume that the constitution is a written legal text.[3] From it, the constitutional norm is extracted.[4] It should be interpreted like any other legal text. However, a constitution is a unique legal text: it determines a unique norm. It stands at the top of the normative pyramid. It shapes the image of society and its aspirations throughout history.[5] It determines the basic political views of the state. It lays the foundations for its values. It determines its aspirations, its commitments and its trends.[6] It is intended to direct human conduct over the course of a long time. It determines the

[3] See Thomas C. Grey, 'The Constitution as Scripture' (1984) 37 *Stanford Law Review* 1, 14; Jed Rubenfeld, 'Reading the Constitution as Spoken' (1995) 104 *Yale Law Journal* 1119.

[4] See Barak, *Purposive Interpretation in Law*, at 12.

[5] See William J. Brennan, Jr., 'Construing the Constitution' (1985) 19 *University of California Davis Law Review* 2.

[6] See Rubenfeld, 'Reading the Constitution as Spoken'.

framework within which statutes are legislated[7] and national government is run.[8] It reflects the events of the past. It lays the foundations for the present. It forms the face of the future. It is philosophy, politics, society and law combined. This requires a unique interpretational approach to constitutional text,[9] as "it is a constitution we are expounding."[10] Professor Freund correctly noted that the court must be careful:

> [N]ot to read the provisions of the Constitution like a last will and testament, lest indeed they become one.[11]

Chief Justice Dickson of the Supreme Court of Canada reiterated the same idea in one of the first decisions interpreting the Canadian Charter of Rights and Freedoms:

> The task of expounding a constitution is crucially different from that of construing a statute. A statute defines present rights and obligations. It is easily enacted and as easily repealed. A constitution, by contrast, is drafted with an eye to the future. Its function is to provide a continuing framework for the legitimate exercise of governmental power and, when joined by a Bill or a Charter of rights, for the unremitting protection of individual rights and liberties. Once enacted, its provisions cannot easily be repealed or amended. It must, therefore, be capable of growth and development over time to meet new social, political and historical realities often unimagined by its framers. The judiciary is the guardian of the Constitution and must, in interpreting its provisions, bear these considerations in mind.[12]

Indeed, the constitution has a unique status in the legal system. It has a role that no other legal text can play.[13]

[7] See *Attorney General (NSW)* v. *Brewery Employees Union of NSW (Union Label)*, (1908) 6 CLR 469, 612 ("it is a constitution, a mechanism under which laws are to be made, not a mere act which declares what the law is to be") (Higgins J).

[8] See Anthony Mason, 'Trends in Constitutional Interpretation' (1995) 18 *University of New South Wales Law Journal* 237, 283.

[9] See Laurence H. Tribe and Michael C. Dorf, *On Reading the Constitution* (Boston, MA: Harvard University Press, 1991); Bruce Ackerman, *We The People: Foundations* (Boston, MA: Harvard University Press, 1991) 90.

[10] In the words of Chief Justice Marshal in *McCulloch* v. *Maryland*, 17 US 316, 407 (1819).

[11] Paul A. Freund, 'The Supreme Court of the United States' (1951) 29 *Canadian Bar Review* 1080, 1086. See also Justice Harlan's opinion in *Poe* v. *Ullman*, 367 US 497 (1961).

[12] *Hunter* v. *Southam Inc* [1984] 2 SCR 145, 156.

[13] See Farber, 'The Originalism Debate', at 1101.

C. *The uniqueness of a constitution and its purposive interpretation*

This unique status of a constitution should influence the way it is interpreted.[14] What is the character of this influence? How can we reconcile the approach that a constitution is a legal text that should be interpreted like any other legal text with the view that a constitution is a unique legal text that requires a unique interpretational approach? The answer to these questions is found in purposive interpretation. This interpretation reflects, on the one hand, the uniformity of the interpretational approach toward all legal texts. On the other hand, this interpretation allows expression of the uniqueness of the constitutional text.

This uniqueness is manifest in the relationship between the subjective purpose and the objective purpose. Indeed, purposive interpretation of the constitution – like purposive interpretation of any legal text – takes into account both the intention of the creator of the text (the subjective purpose) and the "intention" of the system (the objective purpose). It does not hold that the intention of the framers of the constitution alone determines the interpretation. To the same extent, its attitude is not that only the understanding of the modern reader determines the interpretation. In its holistic approach, purposive interpretation takes into account both the subjective purpose and the objective purpose. The purpose of the constitutional text, which determines its interpretation, is a normative concept. It is determined by the subjective purpose, as learned from the language of the text and its external sources. The purpose is also determined according to the objective purpose, as learned from the language of the text and its external sources. The uniqueness of a constitution is manifest in the internal relationship between the subjective purpose and the objective purpose; between the intention of the framers of the constitution and the intention of the legal system.

D. *Purposive interpretation of a constitution – comparative law*

A constitution should be given a purposive interpretation.[15] Thus the Supreme Court of Canada has repeatedly ruled that the Canadian Charter of Rights and Freedoms is a purposive document and should be given

[14] See Lord Wilberforce's opinion in *Minister of Home Affairs* v. *Fisher* [1980] AC 319, 329.

[15] On purposive interpretation see Barak, *Purposive Interpretation in Law*, at 370. See also Jeffrey Goldsworthy, *Interpreting Constitutions: A Comparative Study* (Oxford University Press, 2006) 88 (Canada), 190 (Germany), 226 (India), 293 (South Africa). On the development of purposive interpretation in Australia, see Mason, 'Trends in Constitutional Interpretation'; Anthony Mason, 'The Interpretation of the Constitution in a Modern

purposive interpretation.[16] According to this approach, the court must examine the interest that the constitution is intended to fulfill.[17] It is by this standard that the language of the constitution is to be interpreted.[18] The German Constitutional Court takes a similar approach. It grants decisive weight to the purpose (*Telos*) of the constitutional provision, and the function it is intended to fulfill at the time of the interpretation.[19] This is also the approach of the Constitutional Court of South Africa[20] and the Supreme Court of Israel.[21]

2. Constitutional meaning

A. *Express and implied meaning*

Every (written) text has two meanings: an express meaning and an implied meaning.[22] This we learn both from linguistics and from doctrines of legal

Liberal Democracy', in Charles Sampford and Kim Preston (eds.), *Interpreting Constitutions: Theories, Principles and Institutions* (Sydney, Australia: The Federation Press, 1996) 13; Goldsworthy, 'Originalism in Constitutional Interpretations', at 1; David Lloyns, 'Original Intent and Legal Interpretation' (1999) 24 *Australian Journal of Legal Philosophy* 1; Jeremy Kirk, 'Constitutional Interpretation and a Theory of Evolutionary Originalism' (1999) 27 *Federal Law Review* 323; David Tucker, 'Textualism: An Australian Evolution of the Debate Between Professor Ronald Dworkin and Justice Antonin Scalia' (1999) 21 *Sydney Law Review* 567; Michael Kirby, 'Constitutional Interpretation and Original Intent: A Form of Ancestor Worship?' (2000) 24 *Melbourne University Law Review* 1.

16 *Hunter* v. *Southam Inc.*, at 156–7.

17 *R* v. *Big M Drug Mart*, [1985] 1 SCR 295, para. 116 ("The proper approach to the definition of the rights and freedoms guaranteed by the Charter was a purposive one. The meaning of a right or freedom guaranteed by the Charter was to be ascertained by an analysis of the purpose of such guarantee") (Dickson CJ). See also Justice Lamer's opinion in *Reference re Motor Vehicle Act (British Columbia)*s. 94(2), [1985] 2 SCR 486, 499.

18 See Peter W. Hogg, *Constitutional Law of Canada*, 5th edn (Toronto: Thomson Carswell, 2007) vol. II, 56.

19 See Karl Heinrich Friauf, 'Techniques for the Interpretation of Constitutions in German Law', in *Proceedings of the Fifth International Symposium on Comparative Law* (University of Ottawa Press, 1968) 12 ("The *teleological* method is today probably the most important technique of interpretation in German constitutional law … The teleological method might also be characterized as 'functional', because it asks for the function which a certain rule has to accomplish within the context of the Constitution … Today the teleological method asks for the *present* purpose and the present meaning of a rule") (emphasis in original).

20 See Lourens Du Plessis, 'Interpretation', in Stuart Woolman, Michael Bishop and Jason Brickhill (eds.), *Constitutional Law of South Africa* 2nd edition, Revision Series 4 (Cape Town: Juta, 2012) chapter 32, p. 52; *S* v. *Zuma* 1995 (2) SA 642.

21 See Barak, *Purposive Interpretation in Law*, at 378.

22 See Reed Dickerson, *The Interpretation and Application of Statutes* (Boston: Little Brown, 1975) 40; Jeffrey Goldsworthy, 'Implications in Language, Law and the Constitution', in

interpretation. According to both theories, the legal norm is extracted both from the text's express meaning and from its implied meaning. The distinction between these two meanings is not easy to make,[23] but its existence in every text, including any written constitutional text, is undisputed. For example the Australian Supreme Court inferred the recognition of an implied constitutional right to freedom of political expression from the structure of the constitution, even in the absence of a bill of constitutional rights.[24] Examples of constitutional implication are the implication of constitutional values such as separation of powers and judicial independence, the implication of constitutional rights such as the right of access to the courts, and the implication of judicial review of the constitutionality of statutes. Let us now explore the difference between express and the implied meanings, and purposive interpretation's approach to understanding them.

B. *Express meaning*

The express meaning of the constitutional text is the meaning obtained directly through reading the constitutional language. This is the literal meaning indicated by semantics and syntax. This is the dictionary meaning of the text.[25] The express meaning has a limit that cannot be exceeded. The text must not be given an express legal meaning that does not align with its linguistic meaning.[26]

Constitutional language is no different than any other language. It is the natural and accepted language in a given society at a given time. However, an inspection of constitutions reveals that they contain more "vague" terms than other legal texts.[27] A constitution has many "valve concepts" (*ventilbegriffe*; *concetti valvola*) and many of its provisions are

Geoffrey Lindell (ed.), *Future Directions in Australian Constitutional Law* (Sydney: The Federation Press, 1994) 150, 170–1; Jeffrey Goldsworthy, 'Constitutional Implications Revisited' (2011) 30 *University of Queensland Law Journal* 9, 12.

[23] See Jeremy Kirk, 'Constitutional Implications (I): Nature, Legitimacy, Classification, Examples' (2000) 24 *Melbourne University Law Review* 645, 647.

[24] *Lange* v. *Australian Broadcasting Corporation* (1997) 189 CLR 520.

[25] See Dickerson, *The Interpretation and Application of Statutes*, at 40 ("[A] communication is 'express' so far as it is directly conveyed by language taken in its relevant dictionary sense").

[26] See Barak, *Purposive Interpretation in Law*, at 18.

[27] See Siegfried Magiera, 'The Interpretation of the Basic Law', in Christian Starck (ed.), *Main Principles of the German Basic Law* (Baden-Baden: Nomos, 1983) 89.

"open textured"[28] and "vague." In constitutional texts, human rights are usually expressed as "majestic generalities."[29]

These generalities are characterized by the inability to know how they will apply to individuals solely from the express language of the constitutional text. Take the constitutional right that protects property. What is property? The constitutional norm itself does not elucidate the legal and factual situations to which it will apply. A simple interpretative act will certainly establish that it applies to real estate, but does it apply to obligations? Is a person's right to a pension from the national social security plan his property right? Answering these questions requires complicated interpretative action that will grant meaning to the express meaning of the constitutional text based on its underlying modern purpose.

Indeed, applying a generality to a specific set of facts raises complicated questions.[30] The framers of a constitutional text established a generality. The interpreter must determine the generality's application to a specific case. The generality always includes situations that differ from those envisioned by the text's framers, because otherwise it would have been sufficient to list the specific circumstances. This is the main difficulty that the interpreter faces regarding the express meaning of constitutional texts – establishing the meaning of the generality regarding a specific set of facts.[31] Aristotle discussed this, saying:

> [A]ll law is universal but about some things it is not possible to make a universal statement which shall be correct. In those cases, then, in which it is necessary to speak universally, but not possible to do so correctly, the law takes the usual case, though it is not ignorant of the possibility of error. And it is none the less correct; for the error is not in the law nor in the legislator but in the nature of the thing, since the matter of practical affairs is of this kind from the start ... For when the thing is indefinite the rule also is indefinite.[32]

[28] See William J. Brennan Jr., 'The Constitution of the United States: Contemporary Ratification' (1986) 27 *South Texas Law Review* 433; Beverley M. McLachlin, 'The Charter: A New Role for the Judiciary' (1990) 29 *Alberta Law Review* 540, 545.

[29] As expresssd by Justice Jackson in *Fay* v. *New York*, 332 US 261, 282 (1947).

[30] See Barak, *Purposive Interpretation in Law*, at 25.

[31] See Harry W. Jones, 'Statutory Doubts and Legislative Intention' (1940) 40 *Columbia Law Review* 957, 961.

[32] Aristotle, 'Ethica Nicomechea', in *The Works of Aristotle Translated Into English*, ed. by William D. Ross and John A. Smith (Oxford: Clarendon, 1912).

C. *Constitutional silence*

If the interpretation of the constitutional text leads to the conclusion that the text's explicit meaning does not provide an answer – affirmative, negative or otherwise – to a legal problem that the interpreter seeks to solve, what is to be concluded from this silence? The answer is that constitutional silence "speaks" in different voices[33] and offers several interpretive solutions that are selected according to the various methods of interpretation. The first solution is that in the absence of a solution to a legal problem within the limits of the explicit meaning, the solution must be external to the constitution. Thus, for example, many constitutions contain no explicit arrangement concerning remedies for unconstitutional infringement of constitutional rights. In cases like these, the interpreter is referred to laws that are external to the constitution, such as common law, under which the relief will be determined. The second solution is that the absence of a solution indicates the existence of a gap (lacuna, *Lücke*) in the constitution, which must be filled in, in accordance with the applicable "gap-filling rules."[34] Continental law has thoroughly developed the concept of lacuna.[35] A lacuna exists where a legal arrangement that aspires for completeness is incomplete, and this incompleteness negates its purpose. The gap-filling rules refer the judge – who is authorized to fill in the gap – to analogy, and in its absence, to general legal principles.[36] The gap-filling doctrine – as developed in continental law – is not accepted in common law countries, and this solution cannot be taken into account. When a common law jurist notes that there is a gap in a written text,[37] he or she is not referring to this gap-filling doctrine. A lacuna exists where there is no

[33] See Barak, *Purposive Interpretation in Law*, at 67; Dennis Rose, 'Judicial Reasonings and Responsibilities in Constitutional Cases' (1994) 20 *Monash University Law Review* 195.

[34] See Barak, *Purposive Interpretation in Law*, at 66.

[35] See Chaim Perelman, *Le Problème des Lacunes en Droit* (Brussels: Établissements Émile Bruylant, 1968); Alfred E. Von Overbeck, 'Some Observations on the Role of the Judge Under the Swiss Civil Code' (1977) 37 *Louisiana Law Review* 681; W. Canaris, *Die Feststellung von Lucken im Gesetz: Eine Methodologische Studieuber Voraussetzungen und Grenzen der Rechtsfortbildung Praeter Legem*, 2nd edition (Berlin: Duncker & Humblot, 1983).

[36] See the Italian Civil Code Art. 2 (M. Beltremo *et al.*, trans. 1969) "If a controversy cannot be decided by a precise provision, consideration is given to provisions that regulate similar cases or analogous matters; if the case still remains in doubt, it is decided according to the general principles of the legal order of the state." See also the Swiss Civil Code Art. 1; the Austrian Civil Code Art. 7.

[37] See *Reference re Remuneration of Judges of the Provincial Court of Prince Edward Island*, [1997] 3 SCR 3, para. 95. Chief Justice Lamer maintained that the role of the unwritten

text, and the text must be completed on the basis of extra-interpretational doctrines. This is an important distinction. It determines the boundaries of interpretational activity, which the interpreter may not cross. Indeed, whatever the interpretational system, it must respect the boundaries of the constitution's language. The third solution is that an implicit meaning can be inferred from the explicit meaning; what seems like the silence of the explicit meaning is not silence at all, rather an implied meaning that provides a positive solution ("positive implication") or a negative solution ("negative implication") to the legal problem that the interpreter seeks to solve can be inferred from it.[38]

D. *Implied meaning*

Legal interpretation extracts the legal meaning – the legal norm – not only from the express meaning of the written constitutional text, but also from its implied meaning. What is implied meaning? The implied meaning of the text is obtained – like the express meaning – from the language of the constitutional text. However, it is not directly obtained from the language. It is not revealed by applying the rules of semantics and syntax. The dictionary does not help us in understanding the text. The implied meaning is obtained by understanding the constitutional text against the background of the relevant context.[39] In the Australian example of freedom of expression, the implied meaning concerns the question of whether the right to freedom of political expression is recognized. The dictionary is useless in providing an answer to this question, because constitutional rights cannot be extracted from the express meaning of the constitutional text. The answer is found in the relevant context according to which the interpreter understands the implied meaning of the text, and from which she extracts the constitutional norm.

principles is "to fill out gaps in the express terms of the constitutional scheme." Justice Douglas's theory in *Griswold* is not based on gap-filling. See *Griswold* v. *Connecticut*, 381 US 479 (1965).

[38] Implication is different than gap-filling. Implication gives a meaning to what the constitutional text contains. Gap-filling completes what is missing in the text. See John H. Merryman, 'The Italian Legal Style III: Interpretation' (1966) 18 *Stanford Law Review* 583, 593 ("The problem of interpretation is to supply meaning to the norm; that of lacunae is to supply the norm").

[39] See Dickerson, *The Interpretation and Application of Statutes*, at 40 ("Implied meaning ... is meaning carried other than by express language taken in its dictionary sense ... Implied meaning ... is meaning that exists only by virtue of specific context. Implications may attach to sentences, paragraphs, or whole documents").

The implied meaning, like the express meaning, has a limit that cannot be exceeded. What is this limit? In the absence of meaning arising directly from the language of the constitution, what is to stop the interpreter from extracting any meaning she wishes from the constitutional language? My answer is that the implied meaning must arise from the constitutional structure. This is the meaning of the language – the words, clauses, articles, parts, the whole – against the background of the constitutional architecture. This constitutional structure creates the necessary nexus between the constitutional language and its implication. To quote Tribe: "The constitutional structure is ... that which the text shows but does not directly say."[40] This structural implication does not have to be essential or necessary.[41] The implied meaning must reasonably emerge from the structure of the constitution.

The existence of a nexus between the constitutional language and its implication is what gives constitutional implication constitutional legitimacy. Indeed, just as the constitutional text imparts legitimacy to the interpretation given to the express meaning of the constitutional language, the constitutional structure imparts legitimacy to the interpretation given to the implied meaning of the constitutional text. What can be read directly from the constitutional language can be read from the constitutional structure as it emerges from the language. Where the meaning is explicit, the nexus between the constitutional text and the constitutional norm extracted from it is created by the direct connection between the explicit meaning and the constitutional norm. Where the meaning is implied, the nexus between the constitutional text and the constitutional norm extracted from it is created by the direct connection between the implied meaning, as informed by the constitutional structure, and the constitutional norm. The content of the structure and its implications are decided by the theory of interpretation.

According to purposive constitutional interpretation, the question is not whether the implied meaning is necessary, or whether it is obvious; it is whether the implied meaning fulfills purpose of the interpreted text. Thus, for example, it has been held that the constitution as a whole

[40] Laurence Tribe, *American Constitutional Law*, 3rd edn (New York: Foundation Press, 2000) 40.

[41] See Kirk, 'Constitutional Implications (I)', at 65. See also Jeffrey Goldsworthy, 'Constitutional Cultures, Democracy and Unwritten Principles' (2012) *University of Illinois Law Review* 683, 702.

implies the principles of separation of powers,[42] independence of the judiciary[43] and rule of law.[44] It was held that the American Bill of Rights implicitly includes the value of human dignity;[45] it was similarly held that the

[42] See *South African Association of Personal Injury Lawyers* v. *Heath*, 2001 (1) SA 883 (CC), paras. 20–22 ("I cannot accept that an implicit provision of the Constitution has any less force than an express provision … The Constitutions of the United States and Australia, like ours, make provision for the separation of powers by vesting the legislative authority in the Legislature, the executive authority in the Executive, and the judicial authority in the Courts. The doctrine of separation of powers as applied in the United States is based on inferences drawn from the structure and provisions of the Constitution, rather than an express entrenchment of the principle. In this respect, our Constitution is no different … There can be no doubt that our Constitution provides for such a separation, and the laws inconsistent with what the Constitution requires in that regard, are invalid") (Chaskalson P). See also Aharon Barak, *The Judge in a Democracy* (Princeton University Press, 2006) 45 ("The democratic value of separation of powers, and not just the de facto division of authority among the different branches, is itself a constitutional concept, superior to legislation. True, the constitution may not contain an explicit provision recognizing the principle of separation of powers. Nevertheless, the principle of separation of powers is a constitutional principle. Such recognition is required by the purposive interpretation of the constitution. This principle may not be written in the lines of the constitution, but it is written between the lines. It derives implicitly from the language of the constitution. It is a natural outgrowth of the structure of the constitution – which distinguishes between three branches of government and discusses each of them in a separate chapter – and from the entirety of the provisions").

[43] See *HDS-TAL Party* v. *Chairman of the Central Elections Committee to the 17th Knesset*, HCJ 2257/04, IsrSC 56(6) 685 (2004), 704 ("Our basic laws imply separation of powers, the rule of law and judicial independence. Indeed, the language of a legal text is not merely the words that are defined in the dictionary. The language of the text is also what is implied by it, by its structure, its organization and the relationship between its various provisions … It can be said that the implicit language of the text is written between the lines in invisible ink") (Barak P). See also *Reference re Remuneration of Judges of the Provincial Court (PEI)*, [1997] 3 SCR 3; *Reference re Secession of Quebec*, [1998] 2 SCR 217.

[44] See *Reference Re Manitoba Language Rights*, [1985] 1 SCR 721, 752; *Reference Re Remuneration of Judges of the Provincial Court (P.E.I.)*, [1997] 3 SCR 3; Mark Walters, 'Written Constitutions and Unwritten Constitutionalism', in Grant Huscroft (ed.), *Expounding the Constitution: Essays in Constitutional Theory* (Cambridge University Press, 2008) 245; Horst Dreier, *GG Grundgesetz Kommentar* (Tübingen: Mohr Siebeck, 2006) 256; BVerfGE 2, 380 (1953); Tribe, *American Constitutional Law*, at 84 ("The proposition that ours is a government of laws, not men – that we live under the 'rule of law' … is a principle that, by just about any imaginable account, would have to be reckoned part of our Constitution").

[45] See Walter F. Murphy, 'An Ordering of Constitutional Values' (1979–80) 53 *Southern California Law Review* 703; Louis Henkin, 'Human Dignity and Constitutional Rights', in Michael J. Meyer and William A. Parent (eds.), *The Constitution of Rights: Human Dignity and American Values* (Ithaca, NY: Cornell University Press, 1992) 228; Maxine Goodman, 'Human Dignity in Supreme Court Constitutional Jurisprudence' (2006) 84 *Nebraska Law Review* 740; Leslie Meltzer Henry, 'The Jurisprudence of Dignity'(2011) 160 *University of Pennsylvania Law Review* 169; Erin Daly, *Dignity Rights:*

Canadian Charter of Rights and Freedoms implicitly includes the value of human dignity.[46]

Implication is not limited solely to implied values. Purposive interpretation – which is based on the constitutional structure as a whole – may recognize implied rights as well.[47] It may also recognize the principle of judicial review of the constitutionality of laws as implied from the constitution's structure.[48] The source of governmental authority may be implied.

E. Constitutional structure

Constitutional structure plays a role in interpreting both the express and the implied meaning of the constitutional text. However, the interpretive role of the constitutional structure is different in each of the meanings. Regarding the express meaning, the constitutional structure plays a role in extraction, that is the transition from the express meaning of the constitutional text to the constitutional norm. The structure is not alone at this stage, and purposive interpretation recognizes other considerations alongside it. Regarding the implied meaning, the constitutional structure plays a role in crystallizing the linguistic meaning, that is the transition from the express meaning to the implied meaning. It is the only consideration at this stage. Once the implied meaning has been established, the constitutional structure may be a consideration, alongside other considerations, in extraction, that is the transition between the implied meaning of the constitutional text to the constitutional norm. The content of the structure and its implications are decided by purposive interpretation.

Courts, Constitutions and the Worth of the Human Person (Philadelphia: University of Pennsylvania Press, 2012).

[46] See Dierk Ullrich, 'Concurring Visions: Human Dignity in the Canadian Charter of Rights and Freedoms and the Basic Law of the Federal Republic of Germany' (2003) 3 *Global Jurist Frontiers* 1. See also *R* v. *Oakes*, [1986] 1 SCR 103; *R* v. *Morgentaler*, [1988] 1 SCR 30; *Rodriguez* v. *British Columbia (Attorney General)*, [1993] 3 SCR 519; *Egan* v. *Canada*, [1995] 2 SCR 513; *Law* v. *Canada (Minister of Employment and Immigration)*, [1999] 1 SCR 497; *Blencoe* v. *British Columbia (Human Rights Commission)*, [2000] 2 SCR 307.

[47] See section 2E below.

[48] See Laurence H. Tribe, *The Invisible Constitution* (New York: Oxford University Press, 2008).

What is this structure?[49] At the outset, of course, this is the words, paragraphs, articles, and chapters that make up the constitutional whole.[50] This structure produces the implied meaning as well as the express meaning. Implied meanings are the "bridges overs waters that separate islands of constitutional text, creating a unified and useable surface."[51] The implied meaning of the constitutional text is based on the fundamental assumptions upon which the constitutional text rests.[52] These are the "postulates which form the very foundation of the constitution."[53] Frankfurter explained that the most fundamental question in statutory interpretation – and in my opinion *a fortiori* regarding constitutional interpretation – is "what is below the surface of the words and yet fairly a part of them?"[54] The express constitutional meaning teaches us about the architecture underlying the constitutional scheme,[55] the constitutional principles that support this scheme and their underlying assumptions.[56] Thus for example, from the branches of government established by the express meaning of the constitutional text we can deduce the principle of separation of powers that lies at their foundation; from the express

[49] On structural interpretation, see: Charles Black, *Structure and Relationship in Constitutional Law* (Baton Rouge: Louisiana State University Press, 1969); Philip Bobbit, *Constitutional Fate: Theory of the Constitution* (Oxford University Press, 1982); Tribe, *The Invisible Constitution*; Maxwell O. Chibundu, 'Structure and Structuralism in the Interpretation of Statutes' (1993–1994) 62 *University of Chicago Law Review* 1439; George H. Taylor, 'Structural Textualism' (1995) 75 *Boston University Law Review* 321; Laurence H. Tribe, 'Taking Text and Structure Seriously: Reflections on Free-Form Method in Constitutional Interpretation' (1995) 108(6) *Harvard Law Review* 1221; Ernest A. Young, 'Alden v. Maine and the Jurisprudence of Structure' (1999–2000) 41 *William and Mary Law Review* 1601; Akhil Reed Amar, 'Foreword: The Document and the Doctrine' (2000) 114 *Harvard Law Review* 26; Robin Elliot, 'References, Structural Argumentation and the Organizing Principles of Canada's Constitution' (2001) 80 *Canadian Bar Review* 67; Michael C. Dorf, 'Interpretive Holism and the Structural Method, or How Charles Black Might Have Thought about Campaign Finance Reform and Congressional Timidity' (2003) 92 *Georgetown Law Journal* 833; Casey L. Westover, 'Structural Interpretation and the New Federalism: Finding the Proper Balance between State Sovereignty and Federal Supremacy' (2005) 88 *Marquette Law Review* 693.

[50] See Tribe, *American Constitutional Law*, at 40.

[51] Walters, 'Written Constitutions and Unwritten Constitutionalism', at 267.

[52] See *Reference re Secession of Quebec*, [1998] 2 SCR 217, paras. 49, 52.

[53] See *Reference re Manitoba Language Rights*, [1985] 1 SCR 721, 749 (Lamer JC). See also Tribe, *The Invisible Constitution*, at 210 ("Invoking the tacit postulates of the constitutional plan … is an enterprise that should unite all who see the Constitution as their lodestar").

[54] Felix Frankfurter, 'Some Reflections on the Reading of Statutes' (1947) 47 *Columbia Law Review* 527, 533.

[55] See Akhil Reed Amar, 'Architexture' (2002) 77 *Indiana Law Journal* 671.

[56] See Tribe, *American Constitutional Law*, at 55.

meaning that distinguishes between the constitutional level (of the constitution that establishes the legislature and judiciary) and the sub-constitutional level (of the regular legislature's statutes), we can infer the implied recognition of judicial review over the constitutionality of legislation that contradicts the constitution; from the express meaning that establishes the legislature, its election and its powers, we can infer the implied meaning that the constitution is based on representative democracy for which the implied constitutional right to freedom of political expression is a prerequisite. From the structure of the branches of government and human rights it can be determined that substantive rule of law lies at the foundations of the constitution, and that implies constitutional rights such as equality and due process.[57]

3. The constitution's subjective purpose

A. Its essence

Purposive interpretation considers the intent of the constitution's framers. It refers to this as the subjective purpose. This subjective purpose is certainly considered one of the components of the constitution's ultimate purpose, but it bears only minor weight. The subjective purpose of the constitution comprises the goals, interests, values, objectives, policies and functions that the framers of the constitutional text wished to achieve. It is the intent of the framers of the constitution. It is an empirical fact, based upon historical-biological reality. It is not approximated intent; it is not hypothetical intent; it is not the intent that they would have had if they had considered it or if they had acted reasonably. It is the intent that they actually had.

There are those who think that such intent does not exist or cannot be identified.[58] I do not accept that approach. Such intent does exist, and it is the basis for enacting the constitution. Without it, the constitution would not have been adopted. If we have reliable historical data, it can be identified.[59] This intent must be at a high level of generality. It is the abstract intent of the framers of the constitution. It is not their concrete

[57] See T. R. S. Allan, *Constitutional Justice* (Oxford University Press, 2001).

[58] See Kent Greenawalt, 'Are Mental States Relevant for Statutory and Constitutional Interpretation?' (2000) 85 *Cornell Law Review* 1609.

[59] On problems caused by the passage of time, see H. Jefferson Powell, 'Rules for Originalists' (1987) 73 *Virginia Law Review* 659.

or interpretational intent.[60] When a constitutional provision deals with human rights, the question is: what was the intent of the framers regarding the (abstract) goal that the right was intended to achieve? The question is not whether the framers of the constitution visualized the application of the right in a given factual situation (i.e. – it is not concrete intent).[61] The abstract intent might be at various levels of generality.[62] The purposive interpreter considers this entire spectrum.

B. *Its sources: structure*

Where does the interpreter learn of the constitution's subjective purpose? Purposive interpretation's answer is: from any reliable internal or external source. The most reliable source is the language of the constitution and its structure. The constitutional structure is not only the source for understanding the implied meaning of the constitutional language;[63] it is also a source for understanding the underlying purpose of the constitution altogether. This underlying purpose informs the interpretation of both the express and implied constitutional meaning. It is presumed that the framers of the constitution expressed their (abstract) intent in the language of the constitution. It is from the express and implied meaning of the constitution that the interpreter learns the framers' intent. Through this intent, she gives meaning to the language of the constitution. Indeed, we approach our understanding of the constitution equipped with values – including our interpretational approach – that are the result of prior understanding. These values allow us to understand the essence of the abstract intent from within the language that is being interpreted according to that intent. The text should be considered as a whole. The structure of the text – its division into various provisions that have various roles – assists in understanding the intent of the framers of the text.

[60] See Tribe, *American Constitutional Law*, at 54.

[61] See Michael J. Perry, 'The Legitimacy of Particular Conceptions of Constitutional Interpretation' (1991) 77 *Virginia Law Review* 669, 681; Ronald Dworkin, *Freedom's Law: The Moral Reading of the American Constitution* (Oxford University Press, 1996) 131; Paul Brest, 'The Misconceived Quest for the Original Understanding' (1980) 60 *Boston University Law Review* 204. See Brennan's criticism of consideration of the concrete (interpretational) intent of the constitutional framers: Brennan, 'The Constitution of the United States'.

[62] Terrance Sandalow, 'Constitutional Interpretation' (1981) 79 *Michigan Law Review* 1033. On levels of generality, see Laurence Tribe, and Michael Dorf, 'Levels of Generality in the Definition of Rights' (1990) 57 *University of Chicago Law Review* 1057.

[63] See section 2E above.

The use of identical or dissimilar terms might reveal the framers' intent.[64] The natural and regular language of the constitution – and at times its technical or exceptional language – is an important source from which the interpreter learns the subjective purpose of the constitution.

C. *Its sources: constitutional history*

The subjective purpose of the constitution can be learned from its history. Indeed, a constitution is not an ahistoric document. A constitution is the product of the history of the people and the nation. The subjective purpose at the foundations of the constitution can be learned from its history. This includes the pre-constitutional history, namely – the social and legal background from which the constitution stemmed. The history of the constitution includes the history of the proceedings that led to its establishment. These are the proceedings of the constituent assembly that created the constitution. These can be learned from the protocols of the assembly's meetings. From all these sources one can derive the revealed intent of the framers of the text. Finally, the intent of the framers can be learned from post-constitutional developments. Thus, for example, an amendment of the constitution might reveal the original intent.[65]

4. The constitution's objective purpose

A. *Its essence*

Purposive interpretation grants decisive weight to the constitution's objective purpose. The objective purpose of the constitution is the interests, goals, values, objectives, policy and functions that the constitutional text achieves in a democracy. This purpose is not determined only by the intent of the framers of the constitution. It is not simply a manifestation of the original public understanding. The objective purpose is mainly determined according to the fundamental views of a democratic regime as embodied in the constitution. It thus reflects the "intent of the system" at the time of interpretation.

[64] This is the "intratextualism" discussed by Professor Amar: Akhil Reed Amar, 'Intratextualism' (1999) 112 *Harvard Law Review* 747; Amar, 'Foreword: The Document and the Doctrine'. For criticism of this view see Adrian Vermeule and Ernest A. Young, 'Hercules, Herbert, and Amar: The Trouble with Intratextualism' (2000) 113 *Harvard Law Review* 730.

[65] See Tribe, *The Invisible Constitution*, at 67.

B. The sources of the objective purpose

(1) Internal sources: the constitution as a whole and the search for constitutional unity

The objective purpose has internal and external sources. The internal source is the text of the constitution. By looking at the constitution as a whole one can learn what its objective purpose is. By examining the structure of the constitution, one can learn what values and principles it is (objectively) intended to fulfill.[66] By examining the interaction between the parts of the constitution, one can learn what functions it is meant to perform. Justice Lamer expressed this well in a Canadian case:

> Our constitutional Charter must be construed as a system where "Every component contributes to the meaning as a whole, and the whole gives meaning to its parts" ... The court must interpret each section of the Charter in relation to the others.[67]

Indeed, the interpretational point of departure is one of constitutional unity.[68] A constitutional norm does not stand alone. It is part of the constitutional system and is embedded in a constitutional structure. A specific constitutional provision influences the understanding of the whole constitutional structure, which in turn influences the interpretation of the specific provision integrated within. Indeed, in formulating the purpose of the constitutional text, the aspiration should be to formulate the purpose that will best promote constitutional unity and optimally preserve constitutional harmony. This, however, should not be taken to extremes. Social life is not perfect, and the constitutional text is certainly not perfect. The constitutional text is at times based upon disharmony and a lack of integration. In formulating the purpose of a constitutional text it is inappropriate to bring about unity that does not belong. Both constitutional disintegration and constitutional hyper-integration are undesirable, extreme situations.[69] A constitution is based upon political, philosophical, social and legal views. These views do not always reflect

66 *Ibid.*, at 40; Black, *Structure and Relationship in Constitutional Law*; Bobbitt, *Constitutional Fate*; Dorf, 'Interpretive Holism and the Structural Method'.

67 *Dubois* v. *R* [1985] 2 SCR 350, 356.

68 See Friauf, 'Techniques for the Interpretation of Constitutions in German Law', at 18. See also Konrad Hesse, *Grundzüge des Verfassungsrechts der Bundesrepublik Deutschland* (Heidelberg: C. F. Muller, 1999) 28; Murphy, 'An Ordering of Constitutional Values', at 746.

69 See Tribe and Dorf, 'Levels of Generality in the Definition of Rights', at 19.

a coherent approach; quite the opposite. A constitution is the product of compromise between philosophical, political, social and legal views. Most of the time it does not reflect one philosophical view or a uniform social view. As Justice Holmes famously said:

> The Fourteenth Amendment does not enact Mr. Herbert Spencer's Social Statics ... [A] constitution is not intended to embody a particular economic theory, whether of paternalism and the organic relation of the citizen to the State or of laissez faire.[70]

Indeed, a constitution reflects a comprehensive national attempt to unite around a common core. Any attempt to achieve constitutional perfection will end in failure, but constitutional unity must be the aspiration, to the extent possible under the existing circumstances and within the framework of the national compromise that has been attained.

(2) External sources: other constitutional provisions

At times a constitution is "scattered" in various documents that were enacted in different periods. This is also the case where amendments were made to the constitution throughout the years. Purposive interpretation attempts to look at all of the parts of the constitution as a unified whole.[71] It discovers the purpose of one provision of the constitution from the purposes of the other provisions in separate constitutional texts or in later amendments to the unified text. The Israeli Supreme Court discussed this in one case:

> Constitutional legislation must be interpreted against the backdrop of the structure of the [legal] system as a whole. A law is a "creature that lives in its environment" ... the "environment" of a piece of constitutional legislation is, inter alia, the other constitutional legislation that determines the essence of the regime. Each piece of constitutional legislation is but one brick of an entire structure, constructed on given foundations of regime and law. Thus, the role of the judge-interpreter when interpreting a piece of constitutional legislation is to make it "harmonious with the foundations of the constitutional regime that exists in the state."[72]

The constitutional norm does not stand alone. It is part of a constitutional structure that might cover a number of constitutional texts. Together, all

[70] *Lochner* v. *New York*, 198 US 45, 75 (1905).

[71] Regarding interpretation of amendments to the US Constitution that comprise the Bill of Rights, see: Akhil Reed Amar, *The Bill of Rights: Creation and Reconstruction* (New Haven: Yale University Press, 1998).

[72] HCJ 428/86 *Barzilay* v. *Government of Israel*, IsrSC 40(3) 505, 595 (1986) (Heb.) (Barak P).

of the constitutional texts constitute one unified whole, from which the judge-interpreter learns the purpose of each part. Indeed, a later constitutional text might influence our understanding of an earlier constitutional text.[73] An implied constitutional provision may influence our understanding of an express constitutional provision. This influence expresses the desire to prevent internal contradictions in the text. The (objective) presumption, while refutable, is that the various provisions of the state's constitution do not contradict each other. The influence of this presumption is expressed in the need to evaluate the old constitutional text anew, from the point of view of the new constitutional text.

(3) External sources: post-constitutional history

The post-constitutional history of a constitutional text is important in formulating the objective purpose of the constitution. In order to understand the objective purpose of the constitution today, one must study its development throughout history. One cannot understand the present without understanding the past. A constitution is an organism that develops in a constantly changing constitutional environment. Understanding the constitution requires understanding the historical continuum, or breaking this continuum and starting a new continuum. Indeed, a constitution does not act in a void; a constitution is not ahistoric. A constitution is the product of the history of a people and society. Justice Holmes discussed this, saying:

> The case before us must be considered in the light of our whole experience and not merely that of what was said a hundred years ago.[74]

Indeed, the entire historical continuum is a source from which the judge-interpreter learns the objective purpose of the constitution.[75] We understand ourselves by understanding our roots. The past is the key to understanding the present. We do not search history for answers to modern questions. We search history for guidance regarding the formulation of the objective and modern purpose of the constitution.

(4) External sources: precedent

An important external source from which the interpreter learns the objective purpose of the constitutional text is precedents which construe

[73] See Tribe, *American Constitutional Law*, at 67.

[74] *Missouri* v. *Holland*, 252 US 416, 433 (1920). See also Frankfurter J's opinion in *Rochin* v. *California*, 342 US 165, 171 (1952).

[75] See Sandalow, 'Constitutional Interpretation', at 1050.

the constitution. A judgment that interprets the constitution contains not only an operative instruction regarding the meaning of the specific constitutional text. The judgment also contains a general part, which leads the rationale toward the operative result. This rationale, in turn, contains value-laden generalities that serve as sources for determining the objective purpose of the constitutional text.[76] Indeed, the modern interpreter does not act in a void. The judicial history does not begin with the modern judge. Her judgment is but a link in the chain.[77] This chain has both a direct and an indirect effect on the modern interpreter.[78] The direct influence is via *stare decisis*. Once the purpose of a constitutional provision has been decided, the modern judge is not at liberty to ignore it, even if she does not agree with it. It must influence her, at various levels of intensity. Prior judgments are indeed a source that the judge must consider. The indirect influence is caused by the need to maintain constitutional unity. Thus, for example, if the purpose of a constitutional text has been determined in the past, that determination has implications for similar constitutional texts.[79] Indeed, the various holdings that interpret constitutional provisions constitute a continuum, which (directly or indirectly) influences the constitutional purpose to be determined in the present.

This influence is especially important when the question for judicial decision is what is the right level of generality for the objective constitutional purpose.[80] A level of generality determined in the past regarding other constitutional provisions might influence the level of generality in the present.[81] A past judicial decision regarding the level of generality of one constitutional provision might influence the determination of the level of generality of another constitutional provision to which it is indirectly connected.

[76] See Richard Fallon, 'A Constructive Coherence Theory of Constitutional Interpretation' (1987) 100 *Harvard Law Review* 1189, 1202; David A. Strauss, 'Common Law Constitutional Interpretation' (1996) 63 *University of Chicago Law Review* 877; David A. Strauss, *The Living Constitution* (Oxford University Press, 2010).

[77] See Ronald Dworkin, 'Law as Interpretation' (1982) 9 *Critical Inquiry* 179, 195; Ronald Dworkin, *Law's Empire* (Cambridge, MA: Harvard University Press, 1986) 229.

[78] See Strauss, 'Common Law Constitutional Interpretation'; Rubenfeld, 'Reading the Constitution as Spoken'.

[79] Compare with J. M. Balkin, 'The Rule of Law as a Source of Constitutional Change' (1989) 6 *Constitutional Commentary* 21; Balkin, *Living Originalism*.

[80] See Tribe and Dorf, 'Levels of Generality in the Definition of Rights', at 78.

[81] Thus, for example, the level of generality established for the interpretation of provisions regarding freedom of expression might influence the level of generality regarding freedom of movement. American law applies different levels of scrutiny for constitutional examination. Decisions interpreting one constitutional provision might be relevant to

Furthermore, at times various constitutional provisions are based on a common constitutional principle. In determining that principle, assistance should be sought in the constitutional purposes that have been determined for the individual express and implied constitutional provisions. Once the principle has been determined, it in turn influences the purposes of these provisions. Indeed, law is a system, and the various provisions must fit together within it. A past precedent that interpreted various constitutional provisions is a major waypoint[82] in formulating the modern determination of the constitutional purpose.[83]

(5) External sources: fundamental values

A constitution breathes fundamental values. They comprise, explicitly or implicitly, part of the constitution. These values are an important mechanism for interpreting the constitution.[84] They also hold a central position in the constitutional structure. Their main position is in the objective purpose of the constitution. The fundamental values reflect the bedrock views of society.[85] They are a manifestation of the national ethos, cultural heritage, social tradition and the entirety of historical experience. The judge-interpreter learns of these fundamental values from the constitutional text itself. They can be identified through understanding the text's direct express meaning, or through understanding the text's indirect implied meaning. Various constitutions are saturated with fundamental values determined in their language, such as liberty, human dignity, privacy and equality. In these cases, the fundamental values constitute both

the examination of another constitutional provision at the same level of constitutional scrutiny.

[82] Subject, of course, to considerations regarding deviation from *stare decisis*: see Stephan Reinhardt, 'The Conflict Between Text and Precedent in Constitutional Adjudication' (1988) 73 *Cornell Law Review* 434; Henry Paul Mongham, 'Stare Decisis and Constitutional Adjudication' (1996) 88 *Columbia Law Review* 877.

[83] See Louis H. Pollak, '"Original Intention" and the Crucible of Litigation' (1989) 57 *University of Cincinnati Law Review* 867, 870; Harry H. Wellington, *Interpreting the Constitution: The Supreme Court and the Process of Adjudication* (New Haven: Yale University Press, 1992).

[84] See Tribe, *American Constitutional Law*, at 70; Luanne A. Walton, 'Making Sense of Canadian Constitutional Interpretation' (2001) 12 *National Journal of Constitutional Law* 315. See also Robert C. Post, *Constitutional Domains: Democracy, Community, Management* (Boston, MA: Harvard University Press, 1995) 23.

[85] Australian law refers to "community values" in constitutional and statutory interpretation: see Anthony Mason, 'The Role of a Constitutional Court in a Federation: A Comparison of the Australian and the United States Experience' (1986) 16 *Federal Law Review* 1; Haig Patapan, 'Politics of Interpretation' (2000) 22 *Sydney Law Review* 247.

the constitutional language that the interpreter is interpreting and the (objective) purpose according to which the interpretation is made.

In this context, I should like to make three comments. First, the fundamental values are interpreted according to their meaning at the time of interpretation. The content assigned to them is modern content that reflects the needs of the present.[86] The question is not: what is the concept of liberty as the constitutional framers envisioned it or as it was originally understood. The question is: what is the meaning of liberty according to our modern understanding. Second, the modern understanding focuses on the fundamentals of the values. It does not consider the fleeting currents of opinion. The interpreter is referred to the long-term beliefs of society, and to the basic and essential rather than the temporary and passing.[87] Finally, only fundamental values that can be fulfilled through the constitutional text's express or implied meaning are taken into consideration. A constitutional text is not an empty frame to be filled with any new value, important as it may be.

(6) External sources: comparative law

The objective purpose is influenced by comparative law.[88] Democratic states have common fundamental values. Legal institutions fill similar roles within them. One can learn about the purpose of a constitutional institution in one democratic system from the purpose of that same constitutional institution in another democratic system.[89] Indeed, comparative constitutional law is fertile ground for cross-pollination of ideas and expanding horizons.[90] This is the case where

[86] See Brennan, 'Construing the Constitution'.

[87] See Sandalow, 'Constitutional Interpretation', at 1061.

[88] See *ibid.*, at 218. See also Tania Groppi and Marie-Claire Ponthoreau (eds.), *The Use of Foreign Precedents by Constitutional Judges* (Oxford: Hart Publishing, 2013).

[89] In *Stanford* v. *Kentucky*, 492 US 361 (1989) the Eighth Amendment to the US Constitution, which prohibits "cruel and unusual punishment," was interpreted. The accepted test for this is, inter alia, the "evolving standards of decency that mark the progress of a maturing society" (*Trop* v. *Dulles*, 356 US 86, 101 (1958)). Justice Scalia noted (in *Stanford* v. *Kentucky* at 369) that: "[I]t is *American* conceptions of decency that are dispositive, rejecting the contention … that the sentencing practice of other countries are relevant." Indeed, the decision is "American," but, as determined in the dissenting opinion in that case (*Stanford* v. *Kentucky* at 389), in making it, it is appropriate to find interpretational inspiration in the law of the states with views on the sanctity of human life particularly and human rights generally that are similar to those of the United States. See also *Thompson* v. *Oklahoma*, 487 US 815 (1988); *Printz* v. *United States*, 521 US 898 (1997).

[90] See Anne-Marie Slaughter, 'A Typology of Transjudicial Communication' (1994) 29 *University of Richmond Law Review* 99; George P. Fletcher, 'Comparative Law as a Subversive Discipline' (1998) 46(4) *American Journal of Comparative Law* 683; Vicki C.

a constitutional text of one state was influenced by the constitutional text of another state[91] or an international document.[92] But even without one constitutional text's direct or indirect influence on another, there is still room for interpretational inspiration. This is certainly the case when a constitution expressly refers to democratic ideals[93] or

Jackson and Mark V. Tushnet, *Comparative Constitutional Law* (New York: Foundation Press, 1999); Sujit Choudhry, 'Globalization in Search of Justification: Toward a Theory of Comparative Constitutional Interpretation' (1999) 74 *Indiana Law Journal* 819; Kathryn A. Perales, 'It Works Fine in Europe, So Why Not Here? Comparative Law and Constitutional Federalism' (1999) 23 *Vermont Law Review* 885; Mark V. Tushnet, 'The Possibilities of Comparative Constitutional Law' (1999) 108 *Yale Law Journal* 1225; Christopher McCrudden, 'A Common Law of Human Rights? Transnational Judicial Conversations on Constitutional Rights' (2000) 20 *Oxford Journal of Legal Studies* 499; Christopher McCrudden, 'A Part of the Main? The Physician-Assisted Suicide Cases and Comparative Law Methodology in the United States Supreme Court', in Carl E. Schneider (ed.), *Law at the End of Life* (Ann Arbor: University of Michigan Press, 2000) 125; Lorraine E. Weinrib, 'Constitutional Conceptions and Constitutional Comparativism', in Vicki C. Jackson and Mark V. Tushnet (eds.), *Defining the Field of Comparative Constitutional Law* (Westport: Praeger, 2002) 23; Vicki C. Jackson, 'Constitutional Comparisons: Convergence Resistance, Engagement' (2005) 119 *Harvard Law Review* 109; Jeremy Waldron, 'Foreign Law and the Modern Ius Gentium' (2005) 119 *Harvard Law Review* 129; Vicki C. Jackson, *Constitutional Engagement in a Transnational Era* (Oxford University Press, 2010) 114; Günter Frankenberg, 'Comparative Constitutional Law', in Mauro Bussani and Ugo Mattei (eds.), *The Cambridge Companion to Comparative Law* (Cambridge University Press, 2012) 171; Jeremy Waldron, *'Partly Laws Common to All Mankind': Foreign Law in American Courts* (New Haven: Yale University Press, 2012).

[91] For example, the influence of the US Constitution on the constitutions of a number of states, such as Japan and Argentina. These are situations of "migration of law." Judge Calabresi noted that "wise parents do not hesitate to learn from their children" (see *United States* v. *Then*, 56 F. 3d 464, 469 (1995)). But great caution should be employed (see Jackson and Tushnet, *Comparative Constitutional Law*, at 169). See also the effect of Canadian constitutional law on South African constitutional law: Johan De Waal, 'A Comparative Analysis of the Provisions of German Origin in the Interim Bill of Rights' (1995) 11 *South African Journal of Human Rights* 1; Peter W. Hogg, 'Canadian Law in the Constitutional Court of South Africa' (1998) 13 *South African Public Law* 1; Halton Cheadle, 'Limitation of Rights', in Halton Cheadle, Dennis Davis and Nicholas Haysom (eds.), *South African Constitutional Law: The Bill of Rights* (Durban: Butterworths, 2002) 693. See also the effect of German constitutional law on the constitutional law of Spain and Portugal: Juliane Kokott, 'From Reception and Transplantation to Convergence of Constitutional Models in the Age of Globalization – With Particular Reference to the German Basic Law', in Christian Starck (ed.), *Constitutionalism, Universalism and Democracy: A Comparative Analysis* (Baden-Baden: Nomos, 1999) 71.

[92] See s. 2(1)(a) of the Human Rights Act (1998), which requires the British courts to refer to the judgments of the European Court of Human Rights.

[93] See the Preamble of the South African Constitution, which states that the constitution's purpose is to "[h]eal the divisions of the past and establish a society based on democratic values, social justice and fundamental human rights."

democratic societies.[94] Even without such a reference, the interpretational influence of comparative law is appropriate.[95] However, interpretational inspiration is appropriate only if the legal systems being compared have a common ideological basis and common loyalty to fundamental values.[96]

Note that a common basis of democracy is a necessary but insufficient condition. One must assess whether there is a difference in the historical development or social circumstances of the local or foreign system that distinguishes it enough to challenge interpretational inspiration.[97] Furthermore, it is necessary to examine whether the constitutional architecture of the legal system affects the relevance of the comparative law.[98] Such interpretational inspiration should come both from the law of other democratic states and from international law. As is well known, various international conventions enshrine constitutional values and thus affect the understanding of the constitutional text. Past judgments of international and national courts that interpret these conventions should serve as inspiration for the interpretation of the national constitution. At times a constitution contains a special provision allowing or requiring

[94] See Art. 1 of the Canadian Charter, which states: "The Canadian Charter of Rights and Freedoms guarantees the rights and freedoms set out in it subject only to such reasonable limits prescribed by law as can be demonstrably justified in a free and democratic society." See also David M. Beatty, 'The Forms and Limits of Constitutional Interpretation' (2001) 49 *American Journal of Comparative Law* 79.

[95] See Donald P. Kommers 'The Value of Comparative Constitutional Law' (1976) 9 *John Marshall Journal of Practice and Procedure* 685.

[96] See Frank Iacobucci, 'The Charter: Twenty Years Later' (2002) 21 *Windsor Yearbook of Access to Justice* 3.

[97] See La Forest J's opinion in *R* v. *Rahey*, [1987] 1 SCR 588, 639 and Dickson CJ's opinion in *R* v. *Keegstra*, [1990] 3 SCR 697, 740. For analysis of the situation in Canada, see Beatty, 'The Forms and Limits of Constitutional Interpretation'; Hogg, *Constitutional Law of Canada*, at 827. See also Pierre Legrand, 'European Legal Systems are not Converging' (1996) 45 *International Comparative Law Quarterly* 52; Mark V. Tushnet, 'Some Reflections on Method in Comparative Constitutional Law', in Sujit Choudhry (ed.), *The Migration of Constitutional Ideas* (Cambridge University Press, 2006) 67; Jacco Bomhoff, 'Balancing, the Global and the Local: Judicial Balancing as a Problematic Topic in Comparative (Constitutional) Law' (2008) 31 *Hastings International and Comparative Law Review*, 555.

[98] See Laurie Ackermann, *Human Dignity: Lodestar for Equality in South Africa* (Cape Town: Juta, 2012) 14: "[C]onstitutional Comparison is important, if not essential, for the falsification of hypotheses for ensuring that the right questions are being identified and answered, and from preventing hypotheses or arguments proceeding unchallenged down narrow, windowless corridors of the mind."

reference to international law.[99] Whether or not there is such a provision in the constitution, comparative law has great importance for understanding the national law and scrutinizing it. Needless to say, the comparative case law is not binding.[100] Nor is it a "persuasive" legal authority. It does not have the status of judgments of the Supreme Court, by which the Supreme Court is not bound. Indeed, the status of comparative law is no different than a good book or a good article. Its bearing is determined by the quality of its rationale. Comparative law is an experienced friend. It is worthwhile to take good advice from it, but it should not replace independent decision.[101]

This approach is the subject of a fierce debate in American law.[102] Supporters of the interpretive view that emphasizes the original understanding of the constitutional text are certainly of the opinion that comparative law that was not part of that understanding should not be considered.[103] It seems to me that American law has begun to lean in the direction of increasing openness to comparative law.[104] I hope that this trend continues, and that the American "exceptionalism" in this field will be replaced with cooperation with, and integration into, the international community.[105]

The basic approach to the interpretational place of comparative law in constitutional law applies to human dignity as well. Anyone who

[99] See Art. 39(1) to the Constitution of South Africa, which states that in interpreting the Bill of Rights in the constitution, the court: "(b) must consider international law; and (c) may consider foreign law." See Art. 10(2) to the Constitution of Spain: "The principles relating to the fundamental rights and liberties recognized by the Constitution shall be interpreted in conformity with the Universal Declaration of Human Rights and the international treaties and agreements thereon ratified by Spain."

[100] See Glenn H. Patrick, 'Persuasive Authority' (1987) 32 *McGill Law Journal* 261.

[101] See Iddo Porat, 'The Use of Foreign Law in Israeli Constitutional Adjudication', in Gideon Sapir, Daphne Barak-Erez and Aharon Barak (eds.), *Israeli Constitutional Law in the Making* (Oxford: Hart Publishing, 2013) 151.

[102] See Aharon Barak, *Proportionality: Constitutional Rights and their Limitations*, Doron Kalir trans. (Cambridge University Press, 2012) 68.

[103] See Jo Eric Khushal Murkens, 'Comparative Constitutional Law in the Courts: Reflections on the Originalists' Objections', Law, Society and Economics Working Papers No. 15–2008 (Department of Law, LSE, London, 2008).

[104] See Vicki C. Jackson, 'Ambivalent Resistance and Comparative Constitutionalism: Opening Up the Conversation on "Proportionality", Rights and Federalism' (1999) 1 *University of Pennsylvania Journal of Constitutional Law* 583; Waldron, 'Foreign Law and the Modern Ius Gentium'; Moshe Cohen-Eliya and Iddo Porat, 'The Hidden Foreign Law Debate in Heller: The Proportionality Approach in American Constitutional Law' (2009) 46 *San Diego Law Review* 367.

[105] See Stephen Gardbaum, 'The Myth and Reality of American Constitutional Exceptionalism' (2008) 107 *Michigan Law Review* 391, 408.

approaches human dignity according to the approach of their legal system, stands to benefit greatly from an understanding of "their" human dignity in comparison to human dignity in other legal systems. This is certainly the case if the human dignity of other legal systems influenced the framing of the local text; however, even lacking textual influence, interpretational inspiration is appropriate. It is thus only natural that the German judicial history and legal literature regarding human dignity serve as interpretational inspiration for understanding human dignity in other democratic legal systems.

However, great care should be employed when comparing laws. The historical background, the constitutional architecture and the status of human dignity in one legal system might be unique to it. Such a situation might make it difficult to compare that legal system with another legal system in which the unique characteristic does not exist.

All else being equal, the most fertile comparison is the comparison between two legal systems in which human dignity is a constitutional value but not a constitutional right. This is the case, for example, regarding comparison between human dignity in the American Bill of Rights[106] and in the Canadian Charter of Rights and Freedoms.[107] In both these legal systems, human dignity is a constitutional value and not a constitutional right. It is possible to compare the approach to human dignity in one system with the approach to it in the other. But here as well caution is necessary. The view of a person and his rights in one legal system may be different than it is in the other.

Is it useful to compare the law between a legal system in which human dignity is solely a constitutional value and a legal system in which it is a constitutional right? In my opinion the answer is yes. In a legal system in which human dignity is a constitutional right, it continues to be a constitutional value as well. That value has normative importance in various contexts, primarily in interpreting constitutional rights. Regarding this normative importance, it is possible to learn about the constitutional value of human dignity in one legal system from the constitutional value of human dignity in the other. Thus comparative law might be very useful for comparing human dignity in legal systems in which human dignity is only a constitutional value, such as the Spanish, American, Canadian and Greek law, to human dignity in German, Israeli and South African law, in which human dignity is also a constitutional right. The comparison in

[106] Constitution of the United States, Bill of Rights (1791).

[107] Canadian Charter of Rights and Freedoms (1982).

such situations will of course be at the level of constitutional values only. That comparison must, however, be carried out with great caution.

C. *Determining the ultimate purpose of the constitution*

(1) The approach of purposive interpretation

Purposive interpretation is based on the conception that all of the information regarding the purpose of the constitutional text is examined by the interpreter. There are no distinct stages of moving from one type of information to another. Indeed, a constitutional text cannot be understood without considering the intent of its framers or its original public understanding; however, the understanding of a constitutional text cannot be limited to the intent of its framers or the original understanding alone.[108] Furthermore, the purposive interpreter strives for synthesis and compatibility between the subjective and objective purpose of the constitution. The goal of the interpreter is not confrontation, but compatibility.

But what shall the interpreter do if none of these line up? Purposive constitutional interpretation's answer is that decisive consideration should be given to the objective purpose. Only thus is it possible to direct human conduct over generations of social changes; only thus can the constitution give an answer to modern needs; only thus is it possible to balance between past, present and future. True, the past has control over the present, but it does not decide it. The past directs the present, but does not enslave it. The fundamental values of the community – which draw from the past and are intertwined with social and legal history – find their modern expression in the old constitutional text.[109] Justice Brennan expressed this well:

> We current Justices read the Constitution in the only way that we can: as Twentieth Century Americans. We look to the history of the time of framing and to the intervening history of Interpretation. But the ultimate question must be, what do the words of the text mean in our time. For the genius of the Constitution rests not in any static meaning it might have had in a world that is dead and gone, but in the adaptability of its great principles to cope with current problems and current needs. What the Constitutional fundamentals meant to the wisdom of other times cannot be their measure to the vision of our times. Similarly, what those

[108] See Dorf, 'Interpretive Holism and the Structural Method', at 1788.

[109] See Bertha Wilson, 'Decision-Making in the Supreme Court' (1986) 36 *University of Toronto Law Journal* 227, 247.

> fundamentals mean for us, our descendants will learn, cannot be the measure to the vision of their time.[110]

In the same vein Justice Kirby of the Supreme Court of Australia pointed out:

> [I]n the kind of democracy which a constitution such as ours establishes, judges should make their choices by giving meaning to the words in a way that protects and advances the essential character of the polity established by the constitution. In Australia, this function is to be performed without the need constantly to look over one's shoulder and to refer to understandings of the text that were common in 1900 when the society which the Constitution addresses was so different. It is today's understanding that counts. Reference to 1900, if made at all, should be in the minor key and largely for historical interest. Not for establishing legal limitations. In my opinion, a consistent application of the view that the Constitution was set free from its founders in 1900 is the rule that we should apply. That our Constitution belongs to succeeding generations of the Australian people. That is bound to be read in changing ways as time passes and circumstances change. That it should be read so as to achieve the purposes of good government which the Constitution was designed to promote and secure. Our Constitution belongs to the 21st century, not to the 19th.[111]

(2) The subjective purpose of the constitution is not decisive

The subjective purpose that the framers of the constitution envisioned is not decisive. It should not be ignored, but it should not be given central consideration in the formulation of the ultimate constitutional purpose. This approach is accepted in comparative law. In Canada, for example, in interpreting the constitution, the Supreme Court gives only minor consideration to the intent of the framers of the constitution.[112]

[110] Brennan, 'The Constitution of the United States', at 7.

[111] See Kirby, 'Constitutional Interpretation and Original Intent', and his judgment in *Re Wakin*, (1999) 73 *AJLR* 839, 878. See also Michael Kirby, 'Australian Law – After 11 September 2001' (2001) 21 *Australian Bar Review* 253, 262 ("Given the great difficulty of securing formal constitutional change, it is just as well that the High Court has looked creatively at the document put in its charge. Had this not been done, our Constitution would have remained an instrument for giving effect to no more than the aspirations of rich white males of the nineteenth century. Fortunately, we have done better than this").

[112] See Hogg, *Constitutional Law of Canada*, at 803–4. See also *Reference re Motor Vehicle Act (British Columbia) s. 94(2)*, [1985] 2 SCR 486, 504. See also *R* v. *Therens*, (1985) 18 DLR (4th) 655, 675; *Mahe* v. *Alta*, [1990] 1 SCR 342, 369.

A similar approach was taken in a number of judgments of the Supreme Court of Australia.[113] That Court emphasized that decisive consideration should not be given to the dead hands of the constitution's framers, who reach from their graves to negate or restrict the natural implications of its provisions or fundamental doctrines. This is also the approach of the German Constitutional Court. The question arose in one case as to whether mandatory life imprisonment with no chance of parole comports with "human dignity." The court responded in the negative. It ruled that a prisoner should not be denied any shred of hope for freedom. It was argued that the intent of the framers of the constitution was to preserve life imprisonment as a mandatory sentence and that this punishment replaced the death penalty. The court rejected this "subjective" interpretation:

> Neither original history nor the ideas and intentions of the framers are of decisive importance in interpreting particular provisions of the Basic Law. Since the adoption of the Basic Law, our understanding of the content, function, and effect of basic rights has deepened. Additionally, the medical, psychological, and sociological effects of life imprisonment have become better known. Current attitudes are important in assessing the constitutionality of life imprisonment. New insights can influence and even change the evaluation of this punishment in terms of human dignity and the principles of a constitutional state.[114]

In summarizing the interpretational method accepted in Germany, Kommers pointed out:

> in Germany, original history – that is, the intentions of the framers – is seldom dispositive in resolving the meaning of the Basic Law. The Court has declared that "the original history of a particular provision of the

[113] See Haig Patapan, 'The Dead Hand of the Founders? Original Intent and the Constitutional Protection of Rights and Freedoms in Australia' (1997) 25 *Federal Law Review* 211. See *Theophenous* v. *Herald & Weekly Times Ltd.*, (1994) 182 CLR 104, 106 ("[E]ven if it could be established that it was the unexpressed intention of the framers of the Constitution that the failure to follow the United States model should preclude or impede the implication of constitutional rights, their intention in that regard would be simply irrelevant to the construction of provisions whose legitimacy lay in their acceptance by the people. Moreover, to construe the Constitution on the basis that the dead hands of those who framed it reached from their graves to negate or constrict the natural implications of its express provisions or fundamental doctrines would deprive what was intended to be a living instrument of its vitality and adaptability to serve succeeding generations") (Deane J).

[114] The Life Sentence case (BVerfGE 45, 187 (1977). The English translation is Kommers's: see Donald P. Kommers and Russell A. Miller, *The Constitutional Jurisprudence of the Federal Republic of Germany*, 3rd edn (Durham, NC: Duke University Press, 2012) 365.

> Basic Law has no decisive importance" in constitutional interpretation. Original history performs, at best, the auxiliary function of landing support to a result already arrived at by other interpretive methods. When there is conflict, however, arguments based on text, structure, or teleology will prevail over those based on history.[115]

According to purposive interpretation, the constitution should be interpreted according to its objective purpose, which reflects the modern bedrock views of society in a legal system throughout history. In this way the constitution becomes a living norm instead of a fossil. In this way the present is not indentured to the past. Indeed, constitutional interpretation is a process in which every generation expresses its fundamental values: values that were formed in light of its history.[116] This is not a process free of restrictions. The interpreter of a constitutional text acts in a given historical-social framework. Although at times he has discretion, that discretion is employed within a given system of values, tradition, history, text and structure. The modern interpreter should respect the past intentions and the past understanding. The modern constitutional purpose is formulated with a view that aspires to create a link with the past and achieve integration between it and the modern purpose. The interpreter does not remove himself from the past. The ultimate constitutional purpose is modern, but it is rooted in the past.

(3) The objective purpose and protection of the individual

It can be argued that giving a modern meaning to constitutional language does not comport with a view of the constitution as a source for protecting the individual from society.[117] According to this approach, if the constitution is interpreted according to modern views, and not according to original understanding, it will reflect the views of the modern majority. Those views will limit the rights that the majority wishes to deny to the individual. The response to this argument is, inter alia, that a modern conception of human rights does not mean a conception of rights according to the modern majority's will. According to the purposive constitutional approach, it is the fundamental values that reflect the bedrock views of modern society that give the constitution meaning, not the

[115] Donald P. Kommers, *The Constitutional Jurisprudence of the Federal Republic of Germany*, 2nd edn (Durham, NC: Duke University Press, 1997) 42. See also Friauf, 'Techniques for the Interpretation of Constitutions in German Law'.

[116] See Sandalow, 'Constitutional Interpretation', at 1068.

[117] See Antonin Scalia, 'Originalism: The Lesser Evil' (1989) 57 *University of Cincinnati Law Review* 849.

fleeting currents of opinion.[118] At times a judge will not find it easy to ignore these fleeting winds and to express society's bedrock views. It is not easy to reflect history instead of hysteria, but judges do so in all of their judicial work. They will know how to do so when interpreting the constitution.

(4) "A living constitution" and "a living tree"

The ultimate purpose of the constitution should enable it to confront a changing reality. That is the meaning of the metaphor regarding "a living constitution." Its life is not manifest merely in the application of the old constitutional principles to new circumstances.[119] The vitality of the constitution means giving modern meaning to the old constitutional principles.[120] That is also a manifestation of the constitutional metaphor of "a living tree."[121] That image indicates the limitations of metaphor. Vitality of fundamental values does not mean permitting the judge to do with them whatever he wants. The subjectivity of the constitutional framers should not be replaced with the subjectivity of its interpreters. The changing content of the values of the constitution reflects change in society's fundamental views regarding the national ethos. They are changes that reflect the history, tradition and common way of national life. They are not an expression of judicial individualism.

This vitality of the constitution is especially important regarding human dignity. This concept needs to develop not what was considered as an affront to human dignity in the past; rather it is what will be considered, based on the past, an affront to, or an enhancement of, human dignity in the future. Dupré discussed this:

> Dignity's function in this dynamic process … has become a primary tool for responding to new developments and for charting new routes across the unknown territories. [122]

[118] See Barak, *Purposive Interpretation in Law*, at 378.

[119] See Strauss, *The Living Constitution*. But see William H. Rehnquist, 'The Notion of a Living Constitution' (1976) 54 *Texas Law Review* 693; Robert Bork, *The Tempting of America: The Political Seduction of the Law* (New York: The Free Press, 1990) 163.

[120] For Justice Deane's opinion, see note 113 above.

[121] See Lord Sankey's opinion in *Edwards* v. *Attorney General of Canada*, [1930] AC 124, 136 (PC), according to which a constitution is "a living tree capable of growth and expansion within its natural limits." For this approach see Walton, 'Making Sense of Canadian Constitutional Interpretation'.

[122] Catherine Dupré, 'Dignity, Democracy, Civilisation' (2012) 33 *Liverpool Law Review* 263.

(5) Interpretation with a spacious view

A constitution should be interpreted with a spacious view.[123] Its interpretation must be generous,[124] not legalistic or pedantic.[125] A constitution determines the framework of government and individual rights. It must be interpreted in a way that expresses its character as such.[126]

Interpretation with a spacious view does not mean interpretation beyond the meaning of the language. It means giving the constitutional text an explicit or implied meaning that fulfills its purpose; a purpose that reflects historical continuity and modern fundamental views. It means an interpretation that strives for constitutional unity and harmony. Interpretation with a spacious view is not limited to the meaning of the words in the linguistic-historical context in which they were framed. It finds the meaning of the words in their historic context and according to modern fundamental views. Justice Holmes wrote:

> The provisions of the Constitution are not mathematical formulas having their essence in their form; they are organic living institutions transplanted from English soil. Their significance is vital, not formal; it is to be gathered, not simply by taking the words and a dictionary, but by considering their origin and the line of their growth.[127]

A spacious view is a view that looks at the past, the present and the future and is learned from the language and from history, culture and modern fundamental principles. It is an interpretation that includes a comprehensive view of the law at a given time in a given society. Thus, constitutional values and rights must be interpreted with a spacious view. This is also the

[123] FH 13/60 *Attorney-General* v. *Aharon Matana*, 4 IsrLR 112, 123 (1962).

[124] See Lord Wilberforce's words in *Minister of Home Affairs* v. *Fisher*, [1980] AC 319 (PC), 25 ("a generous interpretation avoiding what has been called 'the austerity of tabulated legalism' suitable to give to individuals the full measure of the fundamental rights and freedoms referred to"). See also Dickson J in *R* v. *Big M Drug Mart*, at 344 ("The interpretation should be … a generous rather than a legalistic one, aimed at fulfilling the purpose of the guarantee and securing for the individual the full benefit of the *Charter*'s protection").

[125] See the opinion of Dickson J in *Australian National Airways Pty Ltd.* v. *Commonwealth*, (1945) 71 CLR 29, 81 ("[W]e should avoid pedantic and narrow construction in dealing with [such] an instrument of government").

[126] See EA 2/84 *Moshe Neiman et al.* v. *Chairman of the Central Elections Committee for the Eleventh Knesset*, 8 IsrLR 83, 156–7 (1985) ("[W]e are dealing with the interpretation of a basic constitutional provision. Such basic provisions should be construed according to a 'spacious view' … and on the understanding that we are dealing with a provision that determines a way of life … We are concerned with a human endeavor that must adapt itself to a changing reality") (Barak J).

[127] *Gompers* v. *United States*, 233 US 604, 610 (1914).

source of the understanding that the value and right to human dignity must be interpreted with a spacious view. Human dignity, then, cannot be limited to preventing humiliation and degradation. Human dignity must be understood on the basis of the humanity of a person as such. I will discuss this further in the coming chapters. Indeed, interpretation with a spacious view looks at the constitutional provision in its general context, as part of the life of the nation throughout its entire history.

In interpreting the constitution with a spacious view the interpreter has an area of interpretational discretion.[128] That area is always limited.[129] An interpreter is not permitted to read her personal views into the constitutional text.[130] She must interpret the provisions of the constitution objectively.[131] The result does not determine the constitutional interpretation; the constitutional interpretation determines the result. That is also the meaning of the requirement that interpreters use their discretion neutrally.[132] The meaning of this neutrality is that the interpreter must reach the interpretational result by employing constitutional principles, whether she likes the result or not. However, it should be recognized that in a number of situations there is no avoiding the use of interpretational discretion.[133] Frankfurter expressed this well:

> The words of the Constitution ... are so unrestricted by their intrinsic meaning or by their history or by tradition or by prior decisions that they leave the individual justice free, if indeed they do not compel him, to gather meaning not from reading the Constitution but from reading life.[134]

128 See Beverley M. McLachlin, 'The Charter: A New Role for the Judiciary?' (1990) 29 *Alberta Law Review* 540, 546.

129 For a different approach see Mark V. Tushnet, 'Following the Rules Laid Down: A Critique of Interpretativism and Natural Principles' (1983) 96 *Harvard Law Review* 781; Mark V. Tushnet, 'Critical Legal Studies and Constitutional Law: An Essay in Deconstruction' (1984) 36 *Stanford Law Review* 623.

130 See Benjamin N. Cardozo, *The Nature of the Judicial Process* (New Haven: Yale University Press, 1921) 141.

131 See *Planned Parenthood of Southeastern Pennsylvania* v. *Casey*, 505 US 833 (1992). See also Robert W. Bennett, 'Objectivity in Constitutional Law' (1984) 132 *University of Pennsylvania Law Review* 445; David Millon, 'Objectivity and Democracy' (1992) 67 *New York University Law Review* 1.

132 See Herbert Wechsler, 'Toward Neutral Principles of Constitutional Law' (1959) 73 *Harvard Law Review* 1.

133 See Jose J. Moreso, *Legal Indeterminacy and Constitutional Interpretation* (Dordrecht and Boston: Kluwer Academic Publishers, 1998).

134 Felix Frankfurter, *On The Supreme Court – Extrajudicial Essays on the Court and the Constitution*, ed. by Philip B. Kurland (Cambridge, MA: Harvard University Press, 1970) 464.

In that situation, all that remains for the interpreter to do is to choose the solution that seems best to her. In such a situation, a pragmatic approach should be employed. Different interpreters will do so in different ways. My proposal is to strive to reach the constitutional solution that is most just. That way, law and justice converge. Can there be any better convergence than that?

6

The role of human dignity as a constitutional value

1. Three roles of human dignity as a constitutional value

The constitutional value of human dignity has a central normative role.[1] Human dignity as a constitutional value is the factor that unites the human rights into one whole. It ensures the normative unity of human rights. This normative unity is expressed in the three ways:[2] first, the value of human dignity serves as a normative basis for constitutional rights set out in the constitution; second, it serves as an interpretative principle

[1] On the role of constitutional values, see Andras Sajo and Renata Uitz (eds.), *Constitutional Topography: Values and Constitutions* (Utrecht: Eleven International Publishing, 2010). See also Stephen E. Gottlieb (ed.), *Public Values in Constitutional Law* (Ann Arbor: University of Michigan Press, 1993); Hiroshi Nishihara, 'The Significance of Constitutional Values', in Faculty of Law, Potchefstroom University for Christian Higher Education, *Constitution and Law IV: Developments in the Contemporary Constitutional State* (Johannesburg: Konrad-Adenauer-Stiftung, 2001) 11; Francois Venter, 'Utilising Constitutional Values in Constitutional Comparison', in Potchefstroom University for Christian Higher Education, Faculty of Law, *Constitution and Law IV: Developments in the Contemporary Constitutional State* (Johannesburg: Konrad-Adenauer-Stiftung, 2001) 33; Jeffrey Goldsworthy (ed.), *Interpreting Constitutions: A Comparative Study* (Oxford University Press, 2006); T. R. S, Allan, 'Constitutional Justice and the Concept of Law', in Grant Huscroft (ed.), *Expounding the Constitution: Essays in Constitutional Theory* (Cambridge University Press, 2008) 219; Mark Walters, 'Written Constitutions and Unwritten Constitutionalism', in Grant Huscroft (ed.), *Expounding the Constitution: Essays in Constitutional Theory* (Cambridge University Press, 2008) 245; Jeffrey Goldsworthy, 'Unwritten Constitutional Principles', in Grant Huscroft (ed.), *Expounding the Constitution: Essays in Constitutional Theory* (Cambridge University Press, 2008) 277.

[2] See Francois Venter, 'Human Dignity as a Constitutional Value: A South African Perspective', in Jörn Ipsen, Dietrich Rauschning and Edzard Schmidt-Jortzig (eds.), *Recht, Staat, Gemeinwohl: Festschrift für Dietrich Rauschning* (Munich: Heymann, 2001) 341, 342; Irma J. Kroeze, 'Doing Things with Values: the Role of Constitutional Values in Constitutional Interpretation' (2001) 12 *Stellenbosch Law Review* 265, 271; Henk Botha, 'Human Dignity in Comparative Perspective' (2009) 2 *Stellenbosch Law Review* 171, 177; Stuart Woolman, 'Dignity', in Stuart Woolman, Michael Bishop and Jason Brickhill (eds.), *Constitutional Law of South Africa*, 2nd edn, Revision Series 4 (Cape Town, South Africa: Juta, 2012) chapter 36, p. 19.

for determining the scope of constitutional rights, including the right to human dignity; third, the value of human dignity has an important role in determining the proportionality of a statute limiting a constitutional right. I shall briefly discuss each of these three roles.

2. Human dignity as a constitutional value that lays a foundation for all of the rights

The first role of human dignity as a constitutional value is expressed in the approach that it comprises the foundation for all of the constitutional rights.[3] Human dignity is the central argument for the existence of human rights.[4] It is the rationale for them all.[5] It is the justification for the existence of rights.[6] According to Christoph Enders, it is the constitutional

[3] See Jacques Maritain, *The Rights of Man and Natural Law* (University of Chicago Press, 1951) 65; Alan Gewirth, 'Human Dignity as the Basis of Rights', in Michael J. Meyer and William A. Parent (eds.), *The Constitution of Rights: Human Dignity and American Values* (Ithaca, NY: Cornell University Press 1992) 10; Christos Giakoumopoulos, 'Opening Speech', in European Commission for Democracy through Law, *The Principle of Respect for Human Dignity* (Strasbourg: Council of Europe, 1999) 25, 26; Paulo C. Carbonari, 'Human Dignity as a Basic Concept of Ethics and Human Rights', in Berma K. Goldewijk, Adalid C. Baspineiro and Paulo C. Carbonari (eds.), *Dignity and Human Rights: The Implementation of Economic, Social and Cultural Rights* (Antwerp: Intersentia, 2002) 35; Evadne Grant, 'Dignity and Equality' (2007) 7 *Human Rights Law Review* 299, 314; Christopher McCrudden, 'Human Dignity and Judicial Interpretation of Human Rights' (2008) 19 *European Journal of International Law* 655, 680; James Griffin, *On Human Rights* (Oxford University Press, 2008) 5, 21. See also the preamble to the International Covenant on Civil and Political Rights (1966) and the preamble to the International Covenant on Economic, Social and Cultural Rights (1966). Both preambles state that the rights in them "derive from the inherent dignity of the human person." For a critical approach to the conception that human dignity underlies all rights, see Jeremy Waldron, 'Is Human Dignity the Foundation of Human Rights?', New York University School of Law Research Paper no. 12–73 (2013).

[4] See Louis Henkin, *Human Dignity and Human Rights* (Jerusalem: The Israel Academy of Sciences and Humanities, 1995). For criticism of this approach see Doris Schroeder, 'Human Rights and Human Dignity: An Appeal to Separate the Conjoined Twins' (2012) 15 *Ethical Theory Moral Practice* 323.

[5] See Allen Buchanan, 'The Egalitarianism of Human Rights' (2010) 120 *Ethics* 679, 680.

[6] See Ronald Dworkin, *Taking Rights Seriously* (Cambridge, MA: Harvard University Press, 1978) 199 ("It makes sense to say that a man has a fundamental right against the government … if the right is necessary to protect his dignity"); Giovanni Bognetti, 'The Concept of Human Dignity in European and US Constitutionalism', in George Nolte (ed.), *European and US Constitutionalism* (Cambridge University Press, 2005) 85; Wojciech Sadurski, *Rights Before Courts: A Study of Constitutional Courts in Postcommunist States of Central and Eastern Europe* (Dordrecht: Springer, 2005) 128.

value that determines that every person has the right to have rights.[7] This does not mean that human dignity is the basic norm (*Grundnorm*) of the legal system.[8] An important and fundamental constitutional value is one thing; a basic norm is quite another.[9] The basic norm determines the binding nature of the constitution. This is unrelated to human dignity.[10] Furthermore, it should not be automatically concluded that human dignity is the most important value that serves as a key to the solution of all difficult constitutional questions.[11] Human dignity requires study and clarification, and each legal system must ultimately define its own position on this constitutional value.

3. The interpretational role of human dignity as a constitutional value

A. *General interpretational role*

The second role of human dignity as a constitutional value is to provide meaning to the norms of the legal system.[12] According to purposive interpretation,[13] all of the provisions of the constitution, and particularly all of the rights in the constitutional bill of rights, are interpreted in light

[7] See Christoph Enders, *Die Menschenwürde in der Verfassungsordnung: zur Dogmatik des Art. 1 GG* (Tübingen: Mohr Siebeck, 1997) 501; Christoph Enders, 'A Right to Have Rights – The German Constitutional Concept of Human Dignity' (2010) 3 *NUJS Law Review* 253. The idea of "a right to rights" originated in the philosophy of Hannah Arendt: see John Helis, 'Hannah Arendt and Human Dignity: Theoretical Foundations and Constitutional Protection of Human Rights' (2008) 1 *Journal of Politics and Law* 73; Samantha Besson, 'The Right to Have Rights: From Rights to Citizens and Back', in Marco Goldoni and Christopher McCorkindale (eds.), *Hannah Arendt and the Law* (Oxford and Portland, OR: Hart, 2012) 335; Alison Kesby, *The Right to Have Rights: Citizenship, Humanity, and International Law* (Oxford University Press, 2012).

[8] On basic norms see Hans Kelsen, *Pure Theory of Law*, 2nd edn, Max Knight trans. (Berkeley: California University Press, 1967).

[9] See Woolman, 'Dignity', at 22.

[10] See Laurie Ackermann, 'The Soul of Dignity: a reply to Stu Woolman', in Stuart Woolman and Michael Bishop (eds.), *Constitutional Conversations* (Cape Town: Pretoria University Law Press, 2008) 217, 228.

[11] See Botha, 'Human Dignity in Comparative Perspective', at 177.

[12] See Enders, 'A Right to Have Rights', at 256; Hugh Corder, 'Comment', in George Nolte (ed.), *European and US Constitutionalism* (Cambridge University Press, 2005) 132; Joan Small and Evadne Grant, 'Dignity Discrimination and Context: New Directions in South African and Canadian Human Rights Law' (2005) 6 *Human Rights Review* 25.

[13] See Chapter 5, section 1A.

of human dignity.[14] Thus, for example, the constitution of South Africa states that, in interpreting the Bill of Rights, the court "must promote the values that underlie an open and democratic society based on human dignity, equality and freedom."[15]

Human dignity as a constitutional value does not only influence the purposive interpretation of the constitution. It also influences the interpretation of every sub-constitutional norm in the legal system. Indeed, the constitutional value of human dignity radiates upon the entire sub-constitutional law.[16] Thus, it influences the interpretation of statutes and sub-statutory legislation. They are interpreted according to their purpose, which, through their objective purpose, includes the value of human dignity.[17]

Lastly, human dignity as a constitutional value influences the development of the common law.[18] Indeed, where common law is recognized,

[14] See Woolman, 'Dignity', at 24. See also *Dawood* v. *Minister of Home Affairs*, 2000 (3) SA 936 (CC), para. 35 ("[the value of human dignity] is a value that informs the interpretation of many, possibly all, other rights") (O'Regan J). On human dignity's role in the interpretation of social rights see Sandra Liebenberg, 'The Value of Human Dignity in Interpreting Socio-Economic Rights' (2005) 21 *South African Journal on Human Rights* 1. For a similar approach in the United States, see Chapter 11, section 3C(1). For a similar approach in Canada, see Chapter 12, section 2C(1).

[15] Art. 39(1) of the Constitution of South Africa.

[16] See the Luth case (BVerfGE 7, 198 (1958)) ("[The] Basic Law is not a value-neutral document ... Its section on basic rights establishes an objective order of values, and this order strongly reinforces the effective power of basic rights. This value system, which centers upon dignity of the human personality developing freely within the social community, must be looked upon as a fundamental constitutional decision affecting all spheres of law [public and private]. It serves as a yardstick for measuring and assessing all actions in the areas of legislation, public administration, and adjudication. Thus it is clear that basic rights also influence [the development of] private law. Every provision of private law must be compatible with this system of values, and every such provision must be interpreted in its spirit. The legal content of basic rights as objective norms is developed within private law through the medium of the legal provisions directly applicable to this area of the law. Newly enacted statutes must conform to the system of values of the basic rights. The content of existing law also must be brought into harmony with this system of values. This system infuses specific constitutional content into private law, which from that point on determines its interpretation. A dispute between private individuals concerning rights and duties emanating from provisions of private law – provisions influenced by the basic rights – remains substantively and procedurally a private-law dispute. [Courts] apply and interpret private law, but the interpretation must conform to the Constitution") (The English Translation is Kommers's – see Donald P. Kommers and Russell A. Miller, *The Constitutional Jurisprudence of the Federal Republic of Germany*, 3rd edn (Durham, NC: Duke University Press, 2012) 444).

[17] *Daniels* v. *Campbell*, 2004 (5) SA 331 (CC).

[18] *Carmichele* v. *Minister of Safety and Security*, 2001 (4) SA 938 (CC), para. 54; *NK* v. *Minister of Safety and Security*, 2005(6) SA 419 (CC). See also Woolman, 'Dignity', at 24.

judges have the duty to develop it, and if necessary modify it, so that it expresses constitutional values, including the constitutional value of human dignity. To the extent that common law determines rights and duties between individuals, it might limit the human dignity of one individual and protect the human dignity of the other. Common law is the product of a state power – the judiciary. It is thus subject to the provisions of the constitution and must be interpreted and developed according to it.[19] These ideas are all expressed in the provision of the South African Constitution that states that, in developing the common law, the court:

> must promote the spirit, purport and objects of the Bill of Rights.[20]

As expressly determined at the outset of the Bill of Rights,[21] these include the "democratic values of human dignity, equality and freedom."

Human dignity is an important constitutional value in interpreting constitutional and sub-constitutional provisions and in developing the common law. It is seen as a basic principle[22] and a supreme value.[23] At times it is seen as the most important value.[24] It has been suggested that without understanding human dignity, one cannot understand human rights.[25] However, it is not the only value to be considered. At times the value of human dignity conflicts with another constitutional value. In such a situation, constitutional balancing between the conflicting constitutional values is required. Such a balance will be struck according to the relative weight of the conflicting values.[26]

Within the interpretational role, human dignity has great importance in interpretation of constitutional rights. The scope of the various rights – the area that they cover – is influenced by the constitutional value of

[19] *New York Times* v. *Sullivan*, 376 US 254 (1964).

[20] Art. 39(2) of the Constitution of South Africa.

[21] Art. 7(2) of the Constitution of South Africa.

[22] See Stéphanie Hennette-Vauchez, 'When Ambivalent Principles Prevail: Leads for Explaining Western Legal Orders' Infatuation with the Human Dignity Principle' (2007) 10 *Legal Ethics* 193.

[23] See Sabine Michalowski and Lorna Woods, *German Constitutional Law: The Protection of Civil Liberties* (Sudbury, MA: Dartmouth Publishing, 1999).

[24] See Jackie Jones, '"Common Constitutional Traditions": Can the Meaning of Human Dignity Under German Law Guide the European Court of Justice?' (Spring 2004) *Public Law* 167, 168.

[25] See Waldron, 'Is Human Dignity the Foundation of Human Rights?', at 2.

[26] It is an interpretational balance. It does not determine the constitutionality of the sub-constitutional norm, but rather its meaning: see Aharon Barak, *Proportionality: Constitutional Rights and their Limitations*, Doron Kalir trans. (Cambridge University Press, 2012) 72.

human dignity.[27] Human dignity has this interpretational role regarding both civil rights and social rights.[28] In this context it is said of human dignity that it serves as a "radiating value."[29] It serves as a regulative,[30] organizing,[31] integrative[32] and comprehensive[33] principle. It contributes to the coherent and harmonic meaning of the text.[34] Human dignity is seen as a founding value[35] that expresses the basic concept[36] and the rationale underlying the basic right.[37] It is understood as a value that indicates that human rights are not granted by the state, and thus the state cannot take them away.[38] Indeed, human dignity stands at the foundations of democracy itself.[39] In Dworkin's well-known words, "because we honor dignity, we demand democracy."[40]

An important example is human dignity's role in interpreting the right to equality. The Constitution of South Africa[41] and the Canadian Charter[42] contain a provision defining the right to equality. Alongside the general provision on equality under the law, discrimination is prohibited

[27] See, for example, *Khosa* v. *Minister of Social Development*, 2004 (6) SA 505 (CC), para. 76. On the interpretative role of the value of human dignity in criminal law see Tatjana Hörnle and Mordechai Kremnitzer, 'Human Dignity as a Protected Interest in Criminal Law' (2011) 44 *Israel Law Review* 143; John Kleinig, 'Humiliation, Degradation and Moral Capacity' (2011) 44 *Israel Law Review* 169.

[28] See Liebenberg, 'The Value of Human Dignity in Interpreting Socio-Economic Rights'.

[29] See *Rinat* v. *Rom*, CA 6781/94, IsrSC 56(4) 72 (2002), 91.

[30] See Matthias Mahlmann, *Elemente einer ethischen Grundrechtstheorie* (Berlin: Nomos, 2008) 7.

[31] See McCrudden, 'Human Dignity and Judicial Interpretation of Human Rights', at 675; Lorraine E. Weinrib, 'Human Dignity as a Rights-Protecting Principle' (2004) 17 *National Journal of Constitutional Law* 325, 326.

[32] See David Feldman, 'Human Dignity as a Legal Value: Part 1' (Winter 1999) *Public Law* 682; David Feldman, 'Human Dignity as a Legal Value: Part 2' (Spring 2000) *Public Law* 61.

[33] See Hennette-Vauchez, 'When Ambivalent Principles Prevail', at 2.

[34] See Giakoumopoulos, 'Opening Speech'.

[35] See Botha, 'Human Dignity in Comparative Perspective'.

[36] See Henkin, *Human Dignity and Human Rights*, at 14.

[37] See Gewirth, 'Human Dignity as the Basis of Rights', at 10.

[38] See Carl J. Friedrich, 'The Political Theory of the New Democratic Constitutions' (1950) 12 *Review of Politics* 215.

[39] See William A. Parent, 'Constitutional Values and Human Dignity', in Michael J. Meyer and William A. Parent (eds.), *The Constitution of Rights: Human Dignity and American Values* (Ithaca, NY: Cornell University Press, 1992) 47.

[40] Ronald Dworkin, *Life's Dominion: An Argument About Abortion, Euthanasia, and Individual Freedom* (New York: Vintage Books, 1994) 239.

[41] See Art. 9 of the Constitution of South Africa.

[42] See Art. 15 of the Canadian Charter.

on a number of grounds,[43] including race, sex, color and sexual preference. These provisions determine that the list is not a *numerus clausus* – a determination which raises difficult interpretational problems, two of which are important to our discussion. The first question is: what is the standard by which it should be determined when differentiation between people becomes discrimination? The second question is: what is the standard by which additional grounds for discrimination, beyond those expressly determined in the constitution, should be recognized? The Supreme Court of South Africa[44] held that this standard is human dignity. Differentiation between people becomes discrimination if it violates human dignity, and additional types of differentiation are discriminatory if they violate human dignity. The Supreme Court of Canada took a similar approach in *Law* v. *Canada*.[45] Later decisions deviated from this approach.[46]

Another example is the use of the constitutional value of human dignity in criminal punishment. A number of constitutions contain a provision by which cruel, inhuman or degrading punishment is unconstitutional. The constitutional value of human dignity has been given substantial weight in interpreting this provision. Thus, for example, in South Africa it was held that the constitutional value of human dignity leads to the conclusion that whipping degrades both the person receiving the whipping

[43] See Art. 9(3) of the Constitution of South Africa: "The state may not unfairly discriminate directly or indirectly against anyone on one or more grounds, including race, gender, sex pregnancy, marital status, ethnic or social origin, colour, sexual orientation, age, disability, religion, conscience, belief, culture, language and birth." Art. 15(1) of the Canadian Charter: "Every individual is equal before and under the law and has the right to the equal protection and equal benefit of the law without discrimination and, in particular, without discrimination based on race, national or ethnic origin, colour, religion, sex, age or mental or physical disability."

[44] See *Prinsloo* v. *Van der Linde*, 1997 (3) SA 101 (CC); *President of the Republic of South Africa* v. *Hugo*, 1997 (4) SA 1 (CC). See also Albie Sachs, 'Equality Jurisprudence: The Origin of the Doctrine in the South African Constitutional Court' (1999) 5 *Review of Constitutional Studies* 76; Mark S. Kende, 'Stereotypes in South African and American Constitutional Law: Achieving Gender Equality and Transformation' (2000) 10 *Southern California Review of Law and Women's Studies* 3; Laurie W. H. Ackermann, 'Equality and the South African Constitution: The Role of Dignity' (2000) 63 *Heidelberg Journal of International Law* 537; Susie Cowen, 'Can "Dignity" Guide South Africa's Equality Jurisprudence?' (2001) 17 *South African Journal on Human Rights* 34; Arthur Chaskalson, 'Human Dignity as a Constitutional Value', in David Kretzmer and Eckart Klein (eds.), *The Concept of Human Dignity in Human Rights Discourse* (The Hague: Kluwer Law International, 2002) 133; Grant, 'Dignity and Equality'; Laurie Ackermann, *Human Dignity: Lodestar for Equality in South Africa* (Cape Town: Juta, 2012) 81.

[45] *Law* v. *Canada*, [1999] 1 SCR 497.

[46] See *R* v. *Kapp*, [2008] 2 SCR 483. On this issue see Chapter 12, section 2C(1).

and the person administering it.[47] The Supreme Court of the United States examined the question of whether or not the constitutional value of human dignity leads to the interpretational conclusion that the death penalty is a cruel and unusual punishment. Justice Brennan answered that it does.[48] His was a dissenting opinion. The majority was of the opinion that the death penalty, in and of itself, is not a cruel and inhuman punishment. However, it must be ensured that the methods of inflicting that punishment are humane.[49]

An additional example of the interpretational role of the constitutional value of human dignity can be found in the case law of the Constitutional Court of South Africa regarding social and economic rights.[50] The scope of these constitutional rights includes the requirement that the state employ "reasonable legislative and other measures, within its available resources to achieve the progressive realisation of this right."[51] It was held that in interpreting "reasonable measures," the value of human dignity should be taken into account. As Justice Yacoob wrote in *Grootboom*:

> [I]t is fundamental to an evaluation of the reasonableness of state action that account be taken of the inherent dignity of human beings. The Constitution will be worth infinitely less than its paper if the reasonableness of state action concerned with housing is determined without regard to the fundamental constitutional value of human dignity.[52]

B. Particular interpretational role: interpretation of the right to human dignity

A number of constitutions contain a constitutional right to human dignity. This is the case, for example, in the constitutions of Germany,[53] South Africa,[54] Namibia,[55] Russia,[56] Switzerland,[57] Ethiopia,[58] Colombia,[59]

[47] See *S* v. *Williams*, 1995 (3) SA 632 (CC).

[48] See *Gregg* v. *Georgia*, 428 US 153, 229 (1976) (Brennan J). See also *Furman* v. *Georgia*, 408 US 238, 270 (1972) (Brennan J).

[49] See Chapter 11, section 3B(b).

[50] See Liebenberg, 'The Value of Human Dignity in Interpreting Socio-Economic Rights'.

[51] See s. 26 of the Constitution of South Africa (1996).

[52] *Government of the Republic of South Africa and Others* v. *Grootboom*, 2001 (1) SA 46 (CC), paras. 38 and 41.

[53] See Art. 1(1) of the German Basic Law (1949).

[54] S. 10 of the Constitution of South Africa (1996).

[55] Art. 8 of the Constitution of Namibia (1990).

[56] Art. 21 of the Constitution of Russia (1993).

[57] Art. 7 of the Constitution of Switzerland (1999).

[58] Art. 24 of the Constitution of Ethiopia (1995).

[59] Art. 21 of the Constitution of Colombia (1991).

Israel,[60] Poland[61] and Hungary.[62] In these constitutions the constitutional value of human dignity plays its central role: it serves as the purpose that the right to human dignity is intended to fulfill. In light of that purpose the right itself is interpreted.

We must be sensitive to this dual function of human dignity in these legal systems: human dignity serves both as a constitutional value and as a constitutional right. As a constitutional value, its role is primarily interpretational. A statute limiting the constitutional value of human dignity is not unconstitutional for that reason alone. However, a statute that limits the constitutional right to human dignity is unconstitutional unless it is proportional.

Are the constitutional value of human dignity and the constitutional right to human dignity identical in scope? The answer to this question depends upon the general structure of the constitution and its architecture on the one hand, and the character of the constitutional right to human dignity on the other. The general structure and architecture of the constitution might lead to the conclusion that certain aspects of the constitutional value of human dignity are not included in the constitutional right to human dignity. The character of the constitutional right to human dignity as an absolute right (which is not subject to the rules of proportionality), as is the case in the German Constitution, might lead to an interpretational necessity to give the constitutional right a narrow scope that does not cover the entire scope of the constitutional value. Indeed, if *every* limitation of the constitutional value of human dignity also constitutes a limitation of the right to human dignity, then every such limitation is unconstitutional, regardless of its proportionality. No society can function under such circumstances. In that situation the legal system has two possible solutions. The first solution is to determine an identical scope for the constitutional value of human dignity and the constitutional right to human dignity, while narrowing the constitutional value. The second solution is to separate the scope of the constitutional value of human dignity from the scope of the constitutional right to human dignity, while setting a narrower scope for the right than the value. Of these two options, the second should be preferred. In light of the interpretational role of human dignity as a constitutional value in the constitution and in the entire legal system, there is no justification for giving it

[60] See Arts. 2 and 4 of Basic Law: Dignity and Liberty (1992).

[61] See Art. 30 of the Constitution of Poland (1997).

[62] See Art. 54 of the Constitution of Hungary (1989).

a narrow interpretation merely due to the unique character of the right to human dignity. The full scope of the constitutional value of human dignity should manifest itself in the entirety of the constitution, except in the interpretation of the right to human dignity. This will preserve the richness of the value on the one hand, and provide a solution for the unique character of the constitutional right to human dignity on the other.

This result – a split between the scope of the constitutional value of human dignity and the scope of the constitutional right to human dignity – is unique to legal systems in which human dignity constitutes an absolute constitutional right. In all other legal systems the identical scopes of the constitutional value of human dignity and the constitutional right of human dignity should be preserved. Indeed, this is the case in the Constitution of South Africa and in Israel's Basic Law: Human Dignity and Liberty.

4. Human dignity as a constitutional value in the limitation of constitutional rights

The third role of human dignity as a constitutional value is in the limitation of constitutional rights, and in determining the limits of such limitations.[63] Most constitutional rights are relative.[64] They may be limited; the exercise of part of their scope can be limited, such that the constitutional right will not be fulfilled in its entirety, on the condition that the limitation is proportional.[65] In determining the proportionality of the limitation, the constitutional value of human dignity plays an important role.[66] This is the case, for example, in determining the proportionality *stricto sensu*[67] of a limitation of a constitutional right in order to realize a public interest or protect another constitutional right. The purpose of the limitation, the probability that the benefit from this purpose will be realized, and the marginal benefit gained from fulfilling that purpose must be balanced against the limited right, the harm that the right will incur, and the

[63] See Enders, 'A Right to Have Rights', at 260; Robert Alexy, *A Theory of Constitutional Rights*, Julian Rivers trans. (Oxford University Press, 2002), at 192.

[64] For a definition of a relative constitutional right, see Barak, *Proportionality*, at 32.

[65] On proportionality see *ibid.*, at 19.

[66] See *Khumalo* v. *Holomisa*, 2002 (5) SA 401 (CC); *De Reuck* v. *Director of Public Prosecutions*, 2004 (1) SA 406 (CC); *Christian Education South Africa* v. *Minister of Education*, 2000 (4) SA 757 (CC); Woolman, 'Dignity', at 24. A similar approach is accepted in Canada: see Henkin, *Human Dignity and Human Rights*, at 10.

[67] On proportionality *stricto sensu*, see Barak, *Proportionality*, at 340.

probability that such harm will actually be realized.[68] This is the balancing test that is based on the marginal social importance of preventing the limitation on constitutional rights and the marginal social importance of fulfilling the public interest (such as security, public safety, or public well-being) or of protecting another constitutional right. In determining the relative weight of those considerations, the constitutional value of human dignity should be considered.[69]

[68] See *ibid.*, at 348.

[69] See Ackermann, *Human Dignity*, at 255, 267. See also R. George Wright, 'Dignity and Conflicts of Constitutional Values: The Case of Free Speech and Equal Protection' (2006) 43 *San Diego Law Review* 527.

7

Three types of model for determining the content of the constitutional value of human dignity

1. Theological models, philosophical models and constitutional models

The key question before us is: what is the content of human dignity as a constitutional value? What is the normative message that emanates from this constitutional value? The long intellectual history of the social value of human dignity[1] serves as a rich source from which we can draw two important models for understanding the constitutional value of human dignity. One model is the theological model. The other model is the philosophical model. In my opinion, these two models cannot provide a satisfactory basis for human dignity as a modern constitutional value. I would like to propose a third, distinct model, based upon a constitutional approach to human dignity.

The approach of each of the three models is different from that of the others.[2] However, at times there is no great difference in the results to which each of the three models leads. We have before us a Rawlsian phenomenon of "overlapping consensus."[3]

2. Theological models

The theological models incorporate various – and at times opposing – views of theologians dealing with human dignity. Common to all of them is the desire to grant the constitutional value of human dignity

[1] See Chapter 2, section 1A.

[2] Sensen distinguishes between a traditional paradigm, which includes the theological and philosophical models, in our terms, and a contemporary paradigm – see Oliver Sensen, 'Human Dignity in Historical Perspective: The Contemporary and Traditional Paradigms' (2011) 10 *European Journal of Political Theory* 71.

[3] See John Rawls, *Political Liberalism* (New York: Columbia University Press, 2005) 144. See also Laurie Ackermann, *Human Dignity: Lodestar for Equality in South Africa* (Cape Town: Juta, 2012) 31.

the meaning assigned to human dignity in the framework of religion.[4] Every religion has its own way of viewing human dignity.[5] Our focus here is upon Judaism and Christianity.[6] These two religions are based upon the view that man was created "in the image of God" (*imago dei*). Theologians dealing with each of these religions reach different – and at times opposing – conclusions regarding human dignity. I am not a theologian, and I am not able to contribute to this examination. This is a shame, because a great wealth of values and principles is inaccessible to me. However, I do not believe that as an interpreter of a constitutional text I must interpret it according to the views of any particular religion. I certainly am not of the opinion that I must study human dignity in the various religions in the way a theologian does. We are dealing with the understanding of a modern, constitutional text. The purposive interpretation of such a text focuses upon modern people's understanding of the constitutional value of human dignity. Indeed, a modern person is not necessarily a person whose worldview is religious. We therefore cannot assert the religious view as the basis for our understanding of the constitutional value of human dignity.

Of course, rejecting the theological models does not diminish their conclusions, to the extent that they comport with the constitutional model I support. The theological approach and the constitutional approach, despite their different points of origin – one rooted in God and the other in man – often lead to similar results. Furthermore, the constitutional model draws its lifeblood from the essence of modern man. This essence is rooted in human history, and also reflects – to some extent or another – the religious beliefs of man, the preservation and development of which are also required by the constitutional value of human dignity.

4 See Göran Collste, *Is Human Life Special? Religious and Philosophical Perspectives on the Principle of Human Dignity* (Berlin: Peter Lang, 2002). On the necessity of religion as a basis for human rights, see Michael J. Perry, *Toward a Theory of Human Rights: Religion, Law, Courts* (Cambridge University Press, 2007).

5 See Joseph Runzo, Nancy Martin and Arvind Sharma (eds.), *Human Rights and Responsibilities in the World Religions* (Oxford: Oneworld, 2003); R. Kendall Soulen and Linda Woodhead (eds.), *God and Human Dignity* (Michigan: Wm. B. Eerdmans Publishing, 2006).

6 See Chapter 2, section 1C.

3. Philosophical models

A. *Assessment of the philosophical models*

The philosophical models bring together comprehensive and important writing on human dignity by various, and conflicting, philosophers. Common to all these philosophers is the important place human dignity holds in their philosophical view.[7] The views of human dignity of Kant and Dworkin can be considered as belonging to these models. In my opinion, no one of these models can be decisive. The Israeli Supreme Court discussed this in one case, noting:

> Human dignity is a complex principle. In formulating it, one should distance oneself from the attempt to adopt one person's moral views or another person's philosophical views. Human dignity should not be turned into a Kantian concept, and it should not be seen as a manifestation of particular views of natural law.[8]

I cannot assess the philosophical basis of the philosophers mentioned above.[9] I am no philosopher. I assume that the approach of each of them regarding human dignity is well based and suitable according to its own assumptions, and that it can contribute to the modern constitutional value of human dignity. However, the underlying purposes of a constitutional text, constitutional architecture and the role of human dignity in the framework of a constitutional bill of rights, were not considerations in the formulation of the philosophical view, and they are foreign to it.

How is it possible to base a constitutional understanding of the value of human dignity upon a philosophical view that has nothing to do with the constitutional character of that value? In my opinion, the correct approach must focus upon the purpose underlying the value of human dignity in a constitution. Such a purpose should be based upon the understanding of modern society and its needs. Of course, I would be proud if it were possible to characterize my view – which is anchored in the view of a modern constitution – as a philosophical view as well; however, its relevance to

[7] See Collste, *Is Human Life Special?*

[8] HCJ 5688/92 *Wekselbaum* v. *Minister of Defense*, IsrSC 47(2) 812, 827 (1993) (Barak J) (Heb.).

[9] See Herbert Spiegelberg, 'Human Dignity: A Challenge To Contemporary Philosophy', in Rubin Gotesky and Ervin Laszlo (eds.), *Human Dignity: This Century and the Next* (New York: Gordon and Breach, 1970) 39; William T. Blackstone, 'Human Rights and Human Dignity' (1971) 9 *Philosophy Forum* 3; Ralf F. Munster, 'A Critique of Blackstone's Human Rights and Human Dignity' (1971) 9 *Philosophy Forum* 65.

understanding human dignity as a constitutional value is derived from its fundamental assumptions regarding the purpose underlying a constitutional text, not from its philosophical character.

Much like the theological models, negating any particular philosophical model cannot negate its outcomes. To the extent that these outcomes are shared by the modern constitutional model, they should be accepted. Furthermore, the contemplations of philosophers through the ages has influenced the formulation of the modern view of human dignity. Human dignity after Kant cannot be understood without relating to Kant's view. Therefore, it is appropriate to discuss their ideas. However, it should always be remembered that we must understand human dignity against the backdrop of the existing social reality and on the basis of it being a fundamental value within a modern constitution.

B. Human dignity and Kant

Human dignity plays an important role in the philosophy of Kant. Human dignity is based on a person's reason and ability to autonomously self-legislate moral rules by which she will abide. Human dignity, however, must comport with others' freedom of choice. This is every person's right to be her own master, free from the choices of other people. Human dignity means rejecting the possibility that a person will be merely a means for realizing another person's freedom of choice. This Kantian view of human dignity was placed at the foundations of the case law of the German Constitutional Court in interpreting human dignity according to the *Objektformel* (object formula).[10] Kant himself refrained from making extensive use of human dignity in his legal doctrine, where instead he focused on the just social conditions under which people can live freely and equally side by side – as derived from their humanity and morality. However, the *Objektformel* was adopted by the German Constitutional Court. Thus, for example, in the Aviation Security Case[11] it was held that a German statute that under certain conditions allowed shooting down a plane hijacked by terrorists with its passengers on board is unconstitutional. The reason for this is that the statute violated the dignity of the innocent hostages. They became merely a means for saving the lives of others.

Kant dealt with metaphysics, whereas we are dealing with the interpretation of human dignity within a modern constitutional bill of rights.

[10] See Chapter 13, section 3A. [11] BVerfGE 115, 118 (2006).

Regardless of how great Kant's contribution to human thought is, his contribution to the interpretation of a modern constitutional text is only minor. The *Objektformel* is important, and – as we shall see[12] – constitutes one of the aspects of a constitutional model of human dignity. However, it would be a mistake to limit this model to the *Objektformel* alone.

One might argue: if the Kantian *Objektformel* is enlightening and appropriate for interpreting the right to human dignity in the German Constitution, it must be enlightening and appropriate for interpreting human dignity as a value in any constitution. This argument is mistaken. Each constitution is interpreted independently; each has the purpose that lies at the foundations of its provisions; each is characterized by its own constitutional structure; each independently attributes the appropriate role to human dignity. In the German Constitution, human dignity is an absolute right. Any limitation of human dignity is unconstitutional, irrespective of its proportionality. In such a state of affairs, the constitutional right to human dignity should be given a narrow interpretation. The *Objektformel* fills this role. What about human dignity as a value in the German Constitution? This value is not interpreted solely according to the *Objektformel*. Its scope is broader, and it is in line with the constitutional model. Indeed, when the German court interprets the constitutional rights entrenched in the constitution – beyond the right to human dignity – it does so using the value of human dignity, which is broader and more comprehensive than the *Objektformel*. In legal systems in which human dignity is a relative right, there is no need to narrow the value of human dignity that lies at the foundations of that right to merely the *Objektformel*. This formula must constitute only one aspect of an entire array that reflects the constitutional value of human dignity.

C. *Human dignity and Dworkin*

Human dignity is an important concept in Dworkin's theory.[13] It appears as such in many of his writings, especially so in his book *Justice for Hedgehogs* (2011).[14] According to Dworkin, human dignity is an organizing idea, as it brings ethical principles together under the one roof of human dignity. This principle requires self-respect (which requires each person to take his own life, and the lives of others, seriously) and

[12] See Chapter 13, section 3A. [13] See Chapter 2, section 2C.

[14] Ronald Dworkin, *Justice for Hedgehogs* (Cambridge, MA: Harvard University Press, 2011).

authenticity (according to which, when relating to others, every person must express himself in his life, while finding a way of life which is good in his circumstances).

I do not have sufficient philosophical tools to assess Dworkin's view of human dignity. Intuitively, I am of the opinion that the law cannot be based upon a single principle. In my opinion, the law is based upon a number of principles, which are in a state of constant conflict and must be balanced. This conflict does not have a solution at the constitutional level, where conflict is the natural and desirable state. Conflict between the opposing principles is manifest at the sub-constitutional level (statute or common law), and is based upon the principle of proportionality. Within the framework of proportionality, balancing must be carried out.

Be that as it may, Dworkin was not interpreting the American, or any other, constitution. He did not attempt to understand human dignity as a constitutional value. His philosophical view, according to which human dignity internally unites the principles of self-respect and authenticity, cannot serve as a standard by which the constitutional value of human dignity can be understood in differently structured constitutions.

D. *Human dignity: Margalit and Statman*

Avishai Margalit examines the decent society.[15] In his view, a decent society is one whose institutions do not humiliate people.[16] It is a society that grants people self-respect. The right to human dignity is an external expression of self-respect.[17] Limiting the dignity of a person thus leads to his humiliation. I agree that humiliating a person limits his human dignity, but human dignity should not be limited merely to humiliation.

Daniel Statman takes this one step further.[18] In his opinion there are two basic approaches to understanding the value of human dignity. He calls the first approach "dignity as moral treatment." The other is "dignity as non-humiliating treatment." The first approach is that of Kant. Statman analyzes it extensively, and reaches the conclusion that "as a practical standard, the concept of dignity as moral treatment is an

[15] Avishai Margalit, *The Decent Society* (Cambridge, MA: Harvard University Press, 1996).

[16] *Ibid.*, 10. [17] *Ibid.*, 51.

[18] See Daniel Statman, 'Two Concepts of Dignity' (2001) 24 *Tel Aviv University Law Review* 541 (Heb.); Daniel Statman, 'Humiliation, Dignity, and Self Respect', in David Kretzmer and Eckart Klein (eds.), *The Concept of Human Dignity in Human Rights Discourse* (The Hague: Kluwer Law International, 2002) 209.

empty concept."[19] Statman notes: "Thus, Kant expressly recommends not using the concept of dignity in practical moral thinking."[20] In contrast, Statman's approach is "dignity as non-humiliating treatment."[21]

As noted above, human dignity in modern constitutions should not be seen as possessing the Kantian meaning. Of course, Statman's reasons are different from mine, but our conclusions are similar. In addition, I agree that dignity as non-humiliating treatment constitutes an aspect of human dignity. The difference between Statman's approach and mine is as follows: first, according to Statman, the constitutional value of human dignity as non-humiliating treatment expresses the constitutional concept of human dignity in its entirety, whereas in my opinion it is only one, very partial, aspect of human dignity.[22] Second, Statman presents only two possibilities: understanding human dignity as moral treatment (the Kantian sense) or as non-humiliating treatment (the sense defined by him). There is no third possibility. Statman writes:

> The regular sense of limitation of dignity – humiliation – provides us with a more or less clear standard for examining whether certain behavior of an individual or of the government constitutes a violation of dignity. From the moment we try to use the concept "dignity" as a normative-practical concept beyond this sense, we are left with no standard for determining whether or not behavior constitutes a limitation of dignity.[23]

I cannot agree with this approach. The constitutional model presented in this book – a model accepted in a considerable number of constitutional democracies that recognize human dignity either solely as a constitutional value or as both a constitutional value and a constitutional right – serves as a third possibility.

4. Constitutional models

A. *The characteristics of the constitutional models*

(1) An interpretational approach with a spacious view

Constitutional models are interpretational models. They interpret the structure and the architecture of the constitution as a whole. On the

[19] Statman, 'Two Concepts of Dignity', at 547. [20] *Ibid.*

[21] See also Christian Neuhäuser, 'Humiliation: The Collective Dimension', in Paulus Kaufmann, Hannes Kuch, Christian Neuhäuser and Elaine Webster (eds.), *Humiliation, Degradation, Dehumanization: Human Dignity Violated* (Dordrecht: Springer, 2010).

[22] See section 4B below. See also Martha C. Nussbaum, *Hiding from Humanity: Disgust, Shame, and the Law* (Princeton University Press, 2004) 230.

[23] Statman, 'Two Concepts of Dignity', at 552.

basis of this interpretation they determine – even without an express provision – that human dignity is a constitutional value.[24] On the basis of this very same interpretation they also determine the content of the constitutional value of human dignity. Naturally, every constitution has its own interpretation. The constitutional value of human dignity, as we have seen,[25] is not universal. It is not given the same meaning by all. Modern constitutional democracies use purposive constitutional interpretation.[26] The purposive system of interpretation on the one hand and interpretative architecture on the other determine the content of the constitutional value of human dignity within a given democracy. Indeed, the democratic nature of the constitution affects the understanding of human dignity within it.[27]

The point of departure for the constitutional models is the constitution itself. The modern constitution, which reflects the democratic nature of the regime and the society, and which has a bill of human rights at its core, recognizes human dignity as a constitutional value. It is usually one of the most important constitutional values.[28] Indeed, human dignity – alongside equality and liberty – is the basis for constitutionality itself.[29] When this is the case, there is no justification for viewing the constitutional value of human dignity with a narrow view. There is no reason to restrict the value of human dignity to "taboo cases" or to protecting people from humiliation and degradation. The constitutional value of human dignity protects all aspects of the individual and all of his aspirations. Thus, the constitutional value of human dignity should be approached with a spacious view,[30] expressing the full complexity of the human being.[31]

The German Constitution presents a unique case. In the German Constitution the right to human dignity has a unique constitutional

[24] See Chapter 6, section 1. [25] See Chapter 1, section 1A.

[26] See Chapter 5, section 1A.

[27] See Catherine Dupré, 'Dignity, Democracy, Civilisation' (2012) 33 *Liverpool Law Review* 263. See also Andrew Clapham, *Human Rights Obligations of Non-state Actors* (Oxford University Press, 2006) 535; Christoph Möllers, 'Democracy and Human Dignity: Limits of a Moralized Conception of Rights in German Constitutional Law' (2009) 42 *Israel Law Review* 416.

[28] See Chapter 12, section 2A (Canada); Chapter 14, section 1D (South Africa); Chapter 15, section 1D (Israel).

[29] See Susanne Baer, 'Dignity, Liberty, Equality: A Fundamental Rights Triangle of Constitutionalism' (2009) 59 *University of Toronto Law Journal* 417.

[30] On interpretation with a spacious view, see Chapter 5, section 4C(5) and Chapter 13, section 1F. See also *S* v. *Makwanyane*, 1995 (3) SA 391 (CC), para. 9; *Case* v. *Minister of Safety and Security*, 1996 (3) SA 617 (CC), para. 21.

[31] See Dupré, 'Dignity, Democracy, Civilisation'.

structure. It is an absolute right. It is only natural that its interpretation requires a narrow view regarding the content of the right. In order to reach this necessary conclusion, it is possible to do one of the following: give the constitutional value of human dignity a narrow meaning that fits the character of the constitutional right to human dignity; or give it a broad meaning that applies to all of the constitutional rights, except for the constitutional right to human dignity. Only a narrow aspect of the broad value will apply to the constitutional right to human dignity. It appears that the German Constitutional Court chose the second option.[32]

(2) Interpretation of the constitutional value of human dignity and the constitutional rights with a spacious view

The approach that looks upon the constitutional value of human dignity with a spacious view gives it a broad scope.[33] Every independent constitutional right has its own particular purpose that reflects its uniqueness: the particular purpose of the right to privacy is not the same as the particular purpose of the right to property. Alongside these particular purposes, there are general purposes behind all of the independent constitutional rights, including the general purpose regarding the value of human dignity. Indeed, the interpretational view derived from purposive interpretation is that human dignity is a general constitutional value at the root of all of the constitutional rights. The result is that the purposes of all of the constitutional rights partially overlap each other, as the general purpose of human dignity is common to them all.

For the most part, this overlap is of a complementary character ("complementary overlap"), as the constitutional value of human dignity common to all of the independent rights reinforces the particular purpose characterizing each separate right. At times this overlap has a conflicting character ("conflicting overlap"). The general purpose of human dignity in a particular right (e.g. the right to free speech), might oppose the particular purpose in another right (e.g. the right to privacy). Thus, when two independent constitutional rights conflict, the constitutional value of human dignity might find itself on both sides of the scales. Furthermore, at times there might be an internal conflict between different aspects of the value of human dignity within a given

[32] See Chapter 13.

[33] See Kai Möller, *The Global Model of Constitutional Rights* (Oxford University Press, 2012).

right. Thus, for example, fulfillment of one individual's free will might limit the autonomy of his will or turn him into a mere means for the satisfaction of the will of others.[34]

How should these cases of conflict be solved? Should we balance between the conflicting values at the constitutional level? Such interpretational balancing will influence the scope of the various constitutional rights. In my opinion, this approach is not correct. Conflicting overlap is a natural phenomenon in the world of constitutional values; it does not indicate a mistake in the constitution. It is a physiological phenomenon, not a pathology. It expresses the richness of the humanity of man, with all of its duplications and contradictions. Thus, the complementary or conflicting overlap should be left without a constitutional level solution: let the thousand flowers of complementary and conflicting constitutional values bloom at the constitutional level. The solution will be found at the sub-constitutional level, by the rules of proportionality.[35]

(3) The multiplicity of constitutional models

Within the constitutional interpretational approach there are a number of constitutional models. Constitutional interpretation – even within purposive constitutional interpretation – is home to different constitutional approaches regarding the content of human dignity as a constitutional value. Thus, for example, both Mahlmann[36] and Ackermann[37] support a spacious view of the constitutional value of human dignity through purposive interpretation, as I do. However, their approach is that the content of human dignity reflects the *Objektformel*, according to which the meaning of human dignity never considers a person solely as a means, and always also considers him as an end in and of himself. This formula,

[34] See the *"Peepshow"* case (BVerfGE 64, 274 (1981)), in which it was held by the Supreme Administrative Court of Germany that the petitioner was lawfully denied a license to run a business in which nude women dance before paying peeping spectators, despite the consent of the dancing women and the limitation of their right to freedom of occupation. It was held that dancing in those circumstances violates their human dignity. See also the *"Dwarf Tossing"* Case (CE, October 27, 1995, Rec. Lebon 372, Conseil d'État statuant au contentieux, n. 143578, n. 136727), in which the Conseil d'État held that a competition in which a dwarf was shot as an arrow from a bow toward a target was legally prohibited, despite the dwarf's consent and the limitation of his freedom of occupation.

[35] See Chapter 6, section 4. See also Möller, *The Global Model of Constitutional Rights*. For a different approach see Lorenzo Zucca, *Constitutional Dilemmas: Conflicts of Fundamental Legal Rights in Europe and the USA* (Oxford University Press, 2007).

[36] See Matthias Mahlmann, *Elemente einer ethischen Grundrechtstheorie* (Berlin: Nomos, 2008).

[37] See Ackermann, *Human Dignity*, at 86.

as influenced by Kant, does not sit well with me. It is too narrow. It does not reflect the full richness of human dignity as a constitutional value. Thus, for example, it is hard to reconcile the *Objektformel* with the conclusion – reached by several courts[38] – that human dignity protects a person's reputation. If human dignity is to be given a broad scope, it cannot be restricted to the *Objektformel*. A broader "formula" is needed. What is that broader framework? I now turn to that question.

B. *The content of the constitutional value of human dignity*

(1) The humanity of the person as a human being

A purposive constitutional interpretation of the constitutional value of human dignity appraises the entire scope of this value. It is a holistic approach.[39] It is intended to reflect the complexity of the person as such across the entire scope of his existence as a human being. Thus, human dignity as a constitutional value is the humanity of the person as a human being;[40] it is the protection of the humanity of a person. This view is both subjective (the internal sentiments of the individual) and objective (viewing the individual as part of a family, a group or a society).[41] Justice L'Heureux-Dubé discussed this comprehensive view in a Canadian case:

> Dignity is by its very nature a loaded and value-laden concept comprising fundamental assumptions about what it means to be a human being in society. It is an essential aspect of humanity, the absence of which is felt by all members of society.[42]

[38] See *Hill* v. *Church of Scientology of Toronto*, [1995] 2 SCR 1130; *WIC Radio Ltd.* v. *Simpson*, [2008] 2 SCR 420, para. 79; *Khumalo* v. *Holomisa*, 2002 (5) SA 401 (CC), para. 28.

[39] See Catherine Dupré, 'Unlocking Human Dignity: Towards a Theory for the 21st Century' (2009) 2 *European Human Rights Law Review* 190.

[40] See Tamar Hostovsky Brandes, 'Human Dignity as a Central Pillar in Constitutional Rights Jurisprudence in Israel: Definitions and Parameters', in Gideon Sapir, Daphne Barak-Erez & Aharon Barak (eds.), *Israeli Constitutional Law in the Making* (Oxford: Hart Publishing, 2013) 267.

[41] See Louis Henkin, *Human Dignity and Human Rights* (Jerusalem: Israel Academy of Sciences and Humanities, 1995) 59; Edward J. Eberle, *Dignity and Liberty: Constitutional Visions in Germany and the United States* (Santa Barbara: Praeger, 2002), 59; Oscar Schachter, 'Human Dignity as a Normative Concept' (1983) 77 *American Journal of International Law* 848, 849.

[42] *Nova Scotia (AG)* v. *Walsh*, [2002] 4 SCR.325, 378.

In the context of the right to equality, Justice Iacobucci of Canada wrote:

> Human dignity means that an individual or group feels self-respect and self-worth. It is concerned with physical and psychological integrity and empowerment.[43]

Justice Wilson of the Canadian Supreme Court expressed this in another case:

> [A]n aspect of the respect for human dignity on which the Charter is founded is the right to make fundamental personal decisions without interference from the state.[44]

In the same spirit, Justices Sachs and O'Regan wrote in a South African case:

> Our Constitution values human dignity which inheres in various aspects of what it means to be a human being.[45]

The Supreme Court of Israel discussed this view:

> In the center of human dignity lies the sanctity of human life and liberty. At the foundations of human dignity stand the autonomy of individual will, freedom of choice, and the freedom of action of a person as a free agent. Human dignity rests upon the recognition of the physical and spiritual wholeness of the individual, his humanity and his value as a human being, all irrespective of the extent of utility he provides for others.[46]

The approach that views the constitutional value of human dignity as the humanity of a person is accepted in constitutional literature. Mahlmann promotes a secular understanding of human dignity rather than a metaphysical one.[47] This understanding is based on the humanity of a person.[48] Ackermann also promotes the connection between human dignity and the concept of humanity. In one South African case he noted:

[43] *Law* v. *Canada (Minister of Employment and Immigration)*, [1999] 1 SCR 497, 530.

[44] *R* v. *Morgentaler*, [1988] 1 SCR 30, 164.

[45] *S* v. *Jordan* 2002 (6) SA 642 (CC), para. 74. See also *S* v. *Makwanyane*, at paras. 308, 326; *Prinsloo* v. *Van Der Linde*, 1997 (3) SA 1012 (CC), para. 31; *Government of the Republic of South Africa and Others* v. *Grootboom*, 2001 (1) SA 46 (CC), para. 83; *Minister of Home Affairs* v, *Fourie*, 2006 (1) SA 524 (CC), para. 50; *NM* v. *Smith* 2007 (5) SA 250 (CC), paras. 131–132.

[46] *The Movement for Quality Government in Israel* v. *Knesset*, HCJ 6427/02, IsrSC 61(1) 619 (2006), at 685 (Barak P.).

[47] See Mahlmann, *Elemente einer ethischen Grundrechtstheorie*, at 262.

[48] See Matthias Mahlmann, 'The Basic Law at 60 – Human Dignity and the Culture of Republicanism' (2010) 11 *German Law Journal* 9, 13 ("human dignity means the specific value of human beings derived from their humanity as such").

> Human dignity cannot be fully valued or respected unless individuals are able to develop their humanity, their "humanness", to the full extent of its potential ... An individual's human dignity cannot be fully respected or valued unless the individual is permitted to develop his or her unique talents optimally.[49]

This approach was developed by Ackermann in his book.[50] He emphasizes that human dignity is based on the individual's free will and his ability to develop his personality and fulfill his life.[51] Dupré made a valuable contribution to the understanding of human dignity as the humanity of a person. Dupré also discusses human dignity as the humanity of a person, stating:

> [D]ignity as a constitutional concept defines humanity and promotes it by acknowledging the diversity of human identities and activities.[52]

Dupré develops this approach regarding the relationship between human dignity and democracy.[53] She also made a valuable contribution to the examination of human dignity over the course of time.[54] Daly, in her extensive and in-depth analysis of human dignity, similarly emphasizes that the dignity of man is in his humanity.[55]

A contribution to the understanding of human dignity as a constitutional value was made by Charles Foster. According to him, human dignity is a necessary concept when forming a bioethical approach. He states:

> [D]ignity ... is objective human flourishing ... Dignity-enhancement is the process of humanization.[56]

Finally, Waldron made an important contribution to the modern understanding of human dignity.[57] In his article 'How Law Protects Dignity',

[49] *Ferreira* v. *Levin NO*, 1996 (1) SA 984 (CC), at para. 49.

[50] See Ackermann, *Human Dignity*. See also Henkin, *Human Dignity and Human Rights*.

[51] See Ackermann, *Human Dignity*, at 23.

[52] See Catherine Dupré, 'Human Dignity in Europe: A Foundational Constitutional Principle' (2013) 19 *European Public Law* 319, 332.

[53] See Dupré, 'Dignity, Democracy, Civilisation'.

[54] See Catherine Dupré, 'Human Dignity and the Withdrawal of Medical Treatment: A Missed Opportunity?' (2006) 6 *European Human Rights Law Review* 678; Dupré, 'Unlocking Human Dignity'.

[55] See Erin Daly, *Dignity Rights: Courts, Constitutions, and the Worth of the Human Person* (Philadelphia: University of Pennsylvania Press, 2012).

[56] Charles Foster, *Human Dignity in Bioethics and Law* (Oxford: Hart Publishing, 2011) 6.

[57] See Jeremy Waldron, *Dignity, Rank, and Rights*, ed. by Meir Dan-Cohen (Oxford University Press, 2012).

Waldron explains his understanding of the concept dignity in the following manner:

> Dignity is the status of a person predicated on the fact that she is recognized as having the ability to control and regulate her actions in accordance with her own apprehension of norms and reasons that apply to her.[58]

(2) The humanity of the person as a free being

Human dignity as a constitutional value – the humanity of man as such – means "acknowledgement that the individual is a free person, who develops his body and spirit, according to his will." The will of a human being is the manifestation of his humanity.[59] The meaning of a person as a free being is the freedom of choice granted to every person and the freedom to plan his life, and to realize himself.[60] It is his freedom of "weaving his life story."[61] From here, every person's freedom to direct his life and to develop his personality and his identity is derived. This is the freedom of the individual to design his image as he wishes, his way of life, his relationships with others, his personality and his worldview. It is the freedom of the individual "to realize his personal experience."[62] From here education

[58] Jeremy Waldron, 'How Law Protects Dignity' (2012) 71 *Cambridge Law Journal* 200, 202. Waldron's position provides the most comprehensive expression of human dignity as a constitutional value. I am uneasy, however, regarding his classification of human dignity as a status. Waldron makes it quite clear in his writing that he is not referring to the narrow, formalistic status that is associated with specific social rankings, as every person possesses the status of human dignity. Nor is he using status merely as an abbreviating concept to summarize the existing legal reality in a given society, as he states that status is a dynamic idea in law which may contain as of yet unknown circumstances. (See Jeremy Waldron, 'Does "Equal Moral Status" Add Anything to Right Reason', New York University School of Law Working Paper No. 11–52 (2011), at 3, 8.) However, the term "status" is indicative of the accepted practices of a given society at a given point in time. The content of a "status," even given the broadest interpretation, must be anchored in a specific place at a specific time and be subject to the specific justifications that that time and place provide for. The question then arises, what is the content of the status of human dignity in a society where no one, not even the king, enjoys certain fundamental dignitarian rights? For example, if in a given society no one was given the right to a fair hearing, could it be said that the right to make oneself heard is not part of the status of human dignity? I appreciate the utility of granting every person the status of a king as a rhetorical tool, but I have my doubts about Waldron's classification of human dignity as a status in the legal sense. I prefer to classify human dignity either as a constitutional value or as a constitutional right.

[59] See *Ferreira* v. *Levin*. [60] See Ackerman, *Human Dignity*, at 108.

[61] *Adalah* v. *Minister of Defense*, HCJ 8276/05, 2006-2 IsrLR 352 (2006), at 548 (Barak P.).

[62] CA 7155/96 *A.* v. *The Attorney-General* 13 IsrLR 115, 132 (1997) (Beinish J). See also *National Coalition for Gay and Lesbian Equality* v. *Minister of Justice*, 1999 (1) SA 6 (CC);

draws its importance in developing the personality of the individual. A person also has the power to design his family life according to the autonomy of his free will, and to raise his children in its framework, within the shared life of members of a family unit.

Being free means the freedom to choose where to be and where to travel to. It means that the individual has the freedom to enter into a contract and to draft a will and to determine their content. The individual also has the freedom to choose a name and to change it, to grow a beard, to have sexual relations, to eat any food she desires, and to use her desired language. This is also the freedom to choose what to think and what to want. This is the freedom to choose whether or not to incorporate. Thus the individual has the freedom to believe, or not believe, what she wants. She has freedom of expression, which "allows the individual to realize himself, to express his opinions, to express his personal traits, to refine his ideas and to develop his personality."[63] The freedom of will and of choice is the freedom of the individual "to know who his father is, who his mother is, from where he came – 'who am I', he shouts."[64] The freedom of choice is her freedom to decide how she will live her life and how she will control her destiny.

The constitution does not set a model for the human life that it deems to be good. There is no "image of man" that the constitution sets in its center. Every person creates his own image of what he deems to be a good life. There is no specific model set forth in the constitution that each person ought to strive for. As Dupré pointed out:

> [C]onstitutional humanity is its essential freedom to define itself without having to conform to a pre-determined definition imposed by the state or by public power through the constitution.[65]

It is not possible to achieve all the aspects of this self-realization if the individual does not have basic living conditions that allow his dignified human subsistence.

Dawood v. *Minister of Home Affairs*, 2000 (3) SA 936 (CC); *La Roux* v. *Dey*, 2011 (3) SA 274 (CC), para. 154.

[63] See CA 7541/10 *John Doe* v. *Dayan-Orbach* (8.2.2012), para. 17 of Justice Vogelman's opinion (Heb.).

[64] See CA 3077/90 *Jane Doe* v. *John Doe*, IsrSC 49(2) 578, 593 (1995) (Cheshin J) (Heb.).

[65] Dupré, 'Human Dignity in Europe'.

(3) The humanity of the person as autonomy of will

At the foundations of the constitutional value of human dignity stands the autonomy of individual will. The meaning of this autonomy is that the individual – she and no other individual; she, and not the state – controls her own destiny.[66]

This aspect of the humanity of the person considerably overlaps with the aspect regarding the person as a free being, because this autonomy means that the individual controls his destiny and his life story. Thus, legal provisions that limit contact between a prisoner and persons outside prison limit the autonomy of the prisoner, and entail a limitation of human dignity. There is a close association between the autonomy of individual will and his position as an equal among equals in the society in which he lives.

An important aspect of the autonomy of individual will as a reflection of the humanity of the person deals with intrusion into the boundaries of the individual's personal space. Indeed, the autonomy of individual will means that a person has rights over his own body. From this stems the recognition of the autonomy of the family: parents are autonomous in making decisions regarding their children's education, way of life, place of residence. Thus the autonomy of the individual is limited if he is taken from his home without his consent and transferred to another place. Denying a person permission to change his name limits the autonomy of his will. Preventing a person from choosing an attorney for himself limits his autonomy. Religious coercion limits the autonomy of the individual. Limitation of an ideological position might limit the autonomy of individual will, as "autonomy is not just the innate or involuntary traits of the individual, but also his ability to tell the story of his life, and to formulate ideological, conscientious, and other positions."[67]

[66] See Joseph Raz, *The Morality of Freedom* (Oxford University Press, 1986) 166 ("The ruling idea behind the ideal of personal autonomy is that people should make their own lives. The autonomous person is a (part) author of his own life. The ideal of personal autonomy is a vision of people controlling, to some degree, their own destiny, fashioning it through successive decisions throughout their lives"). For a different approach, see Conor O'Mahony, 'There is No Such Thing as a Right to Dignity' (2012) 10 *International Journal of Constitutional Law* 551; Conor O'Mahony, 'There Is No Such Thing as a Right to Dignity: A Rejoinder to Emily Kidd White' (2012) 10 *International Journal of Constitutional Law* 585.

[67] HCJ 1213/10 *Nir* v. *Speaker of the Knesset* (23.2.2012), para. 35 of Justice Jubran's opinion (Heb.).

(4) The humanity of the person as rejection of the person as a mere means

The humanity of a person includes the recognition of his value as a human being. Human beings are always an end and a value in and of themselves. This echoes the Kantian approach.[68] From this follows that human dignity means rejecting the possibility that a person will be merely a means for realizing the free will of the other person. People are equal, in the sense that no person is master over another.

At the foundations of the humanity of the person lies the view that every person is an entire world, and is an end unto himself. Of course, people often serve as means for achieving ends that are external to them; their humanity is only violated if they serve only as a means, without being an end at all. On the basis of that view, the Supreme Court of Canada decided that there should be no absolute criminal liability. Absolute liability turns the accused into a mere means, contrary to human dignity.[69] The presumption of innocence is derived from human dignity, as it expresses the view that a man is an end unto himself. In general, one could argue that the right for due process is derived from human dignity. This perspective influences criminal penalties. Criminal penalties should not turn the accused into a mere means to deter others.[70] A foreign worker should not be turned into a mere means for cheap labor.[71]

(5) The humanity of the person in the framework of a society

The various aspects of the constitutional value of human dignity that form the humanity of the person reflect humanity in the society in which she lives. It is not the humanity of a person on a desert island. It is humanity built upon relations between the individual and other individuals, and between the individual and the state.[72] It is a relational concept. A human's dignity is not simply her personal monologue; it is a dialogue between her and the other members of society. Human dignity is not only my dignity, but also the dignity of the "other" and of she who is different.[73] Human dignity is expressed in membership of a society and a community. This membership is both passive and active. It therefore includes taking part

[68] See Chapter 2, section 2B. [69] See *R* v. *Hess*, [1990] 2 SCR 906.

[70] See *S* v. *Dodo*, 2001 (3) SA 382 (CC), para. 38.

[71] See *Larbi-Odam* v. *MEC for Education*, 1998 (1) SA 745 (CC), para. 19.

[72] See *ibid*., at 781 ("autonomy is, therefore, dependent upon relationships") (Levi J). See also Ackermann, *Human Dignity*, at 75 (emphasizing the "'relationality' aspect of human dignity"); Schachter, 'Human Dignity as a Normative Concept', at 850.

[73] See *MEC for Education* v. *Pillay*, 2008 (1) SA 474 (CC), para. 53.

in and allowing the expression of the views of the community.[74] It encompasses the civil and political aspect of membership of the community, as well as the social and economic aspects of that membership;[75] hence the strong connection between human dignity and democracy. Indeed, the constitutional value of human dignity can only evolve in a democratic society.[76]

(6) The humanity of the person and the human race

The question of the influence of human dignity on the entire human race, beyond a specific democratic society, is important. Is human dignity meant to protect the human race as "*Homo sapiens*"?[77] The answer to this question is important to the field of bioethics.

In recent years there have been great advances in medical research that have raised bioethical questions, specifically in the fields of cloning, stem cell research and other methods of genetic engineering.[78] These

[74] See Ackermann, *Human Dignity*, at 103.

[75] For civil and social rights in modern constitutions, see: Asbjørn Eide, 'Realization of Social and Economic Rights and the Minimum Threshold Approach' (1989) 10 *Human Rights Law Journal* 36; Sandra Fredman, *Human Rights Transformed: Positive Rights and Positive Duties* (Oxford University Press, 2008); Varum Gauri and Daniel E. Brinks (eds.), *Courting Social Rights: Judicial Enforcement of Social and Economic Rights in the Developing World* (Cambridge University Press, 2008); Ida Elisabeth Koch, *Human Rights as Indivisible Rights: The Protection of Socio-Economic Demands under the European Convention on Human Rights* (Leiden: Martinus Nijhoff, 2009) 14; Elizabeth Ashford, 'The Alleged Dichotomy Between Positive and Negative Rights and Duties', in Charles R. Beitz and Robert E. Goodin (eds.), *Global Basic Rights* (Oxford University Press, 2009) 92; Malcolm Langford, 'Domestic Adjudication and Economic, Social and Cultural Rights: A Socio-Legal Review' (2009) 6 *Sur International Journal of Human Rights* 91; David S. Law and Mila Versteeg, 'The Evolution and Ideology of Global Constitutionalism' (2011) 99 *California Law Review* 1163, 1196; Möller, *The Global Model of Constitutional Rights*, at 5.

[76] See Lorraine E. Weinrib, 'Human Dignity as a Rights-Protecting Principle' (2004) 17 *National Journal of Constitutional Law* 325; Kai Möller, 'On Treating Persons as Ends: The German Aviation Security Act, Human Dignity, and the German Federal Constitutional Court' (Autumn 2006) *Public Law* 457; Peter Häberle, *Europäische Verfassungslehre*, 6th edition (Baden-Baden: Nomos, 2009); Möllers, 'Democracy and Human Dignity'; Catherine Dupré, 'Dignity, Democracy, Civilisation'.

[77] See Horst Dreier, *GG Grundgesetz Kommentar* (Tübingen: Mohr Siebeck, 2006), at 77.

[78] See Deryck Beyleveld and Roger Brownsword, *Human Dignity in Bioethics and Biolaw* (Oxford University Press, 2001); Leon R. Kass, *Life, Liberty and the Defense of Dignity: The Challenge for Bioethics* (New York: Encounter Books, 2002); Silja Vöneky and Rüdiger Wolfrum (eds.), *Human Dignity and Human Cloning: An Ethical Inquiry* (Leiden: Brill, 2004); President's Council on Bioethics, *Human Dignity and Bioethics: Essays Commissioned by the President's Council on Bioethics* (Washington DC: President's Council on Bioethics, 2008); Roger Brownsword, *Rights, Regulation and the*

advancements have many opponents who are concerned about the future of the human race. One of the constitutional tools used by this opposition is the right to human dignity: if protection of the human race falls within the scope of the right to human dignity, then legislation that allows for such advances in medical research limits human dignity. Insofar as the right to human dignity is absolute, any such activity would be unconstitutional. The answer to this argument is twofold: first, it is yet to be determined whether or not human dignity covers the protection of the human race; second, even if legislation allowing such research will be considered as limiting human dignity, it will not bring this research to a halt. A balance shall be struck – as in any other field – according to the rules of proportionality. This second answer, of course, does not stand its ground in German constitutional law, but it may be an appropriate answer in all other systems of law.

In my opinion – and it certainly is debatable – if the human race is within the frame of operation of the constitutional value of human dignity, then the protection of its boundaries is part of the constitutional value of human dignity. Naturally, scientific research per se does not limit the humanity of the human race. However, the practical application of such research may limit the humanity of the human race. If human dignity is also recognized as a constitutional right, such application will also infringe on the right to human dignity. This infringement will be constitutional, as long as it is proportional.

C. *Criticism of the constitutional model of humanity*

Four main arguments can be made against this view of the constitutional value of human dignity as the humanity of the person: the first argument is that this view lacks tools for assessing human dignity, and grants a free hand to anyone dealing with the concept.[79] The second argument is that this approach grants too broad a scope to the constitutional value of human dignity and, as a result, to the constitutional right of human dignity. The third argument is that this view creates internal contradictions within the scope of the constitutional value of human dignity, because it lacks a moral component. The fourth argument is that when human dignity is connected to free will and to the autonomy of the individual will,

Technological Revolution (Oxford University Press, 2008); Foster, *Human Dignity in Bioethics and Law*; Remigius N. Nwabueze, *Legal and Ethical Regulation of Biomedical Research in Developing Countries* (Farnham: Ashgate, 2013).

[79] Statman argues this – see section 3D above.

people whose mental or physical state causes them to lack autonomy of free will shall fall beyond the reach of human dignity.[80]

I cannot accept this critique. The humanity of the individual is a concept that indicates the guidelines for determining its own content. True, these guidelines do not indicate a single result; true, they grant discretion to those who deal with the concept of human dignity. However, this does not mean that this model does not provide tools of assessment. These tools are no different, in this sense, than the guidelines for determining the constitutional value of equality or liberty.

The scope of the humanity model is indeed broad. However, that is natural for a fundamental constitutional value that stands at the foundations of the entire constitution or the entire bill of rights. A solution that would grant the constitutional value of human dignity a narrow sense would in fact be at odds with such a fundamental and basic constitutional value. Human dignity is a comprehensive value that surrounds all the constitutional rights entrenched in it. It is only natural that the scope of application of this value should be broad, and cover the humanity of every single individual. It should of course be emphasized that this comprehensive humanity is not always preserved. Social life always entails limitations of the constitutional value of human dignity. That does not detract from the proposed model. The constitutional limitation of the humanity of the person does not remove the limited element from humanity. One must distinguish between the constitutional level, at which the humanity of the person reigns, and the sub-constitutional level, which recognizes the possibility of proportional limitations of the humanity of the person in order to maintain the functioning of social life.

It is noteworthy that the humanity of the individual appears in the writings of Kant as well.[81] For Kant, this humanity is associated with human rationality.[82] That is not the case according to this model. Human rationality is not a component of the proposed model. Every person, rational or irrational, has human dignity.

As to the argument about internal contradictions: indeed, the spacious view of human dignity covers human beings in all their complexity. This

[80] See O'Mahony, 'There Is No Such Thing as a Right to Dignity', at 565; Matthias Mahlmann, 'Human Dignity and Autonomy in Modern Constitutional Orders', in Michael Rosenfeld and Andras Sajo (eds.), *The Oxford Handbook of Comparative Constitutional Law* (Oxford University Press, 2012) 372.

[81] See Arthur Ripstein, *Force and Freedom: Kant's Legal and Political Philosophy* (Cambridge, MA: Harvard University Press, 2009) 30.

[82] See Ackermann, *Human Dignity* (who also bases human dignity upon human rationality).

complexity also entails internal contradictions. The individual wants one thing, as well as its opposite; the desire of one individual conflicts with the desire of another individual. Living life in society means living with these conflicts. Beyleveld and Brownsword[83] demonstrated this complexity: in different contexts, specifically those regarding bioethics, human dignity plays two roles. The first is empowerment of individual autonomy (human dignity as empowerment). The second is constraint of individual autonomy (human dignity as constraint). Beyleveld and Brownsword claim that there is tension between these two roles.[84] At times, these roles may even contradict each other. I agree. Conflicts between my will and yours are plentiful; these conflicts do not reveal weakness in the proposed model; rather they exemplify its force and the fashion in which it expresses real human experience. Humankind is a collection of all of its conflicts, and society is the product of these conflicts.

The constitutional model regarding the humanity of the person expresses this complexity in a two-stage constitutional structure: at the constitutional level are the aspects of the value of human dignity that are in conflict with one another. This conflict continues to exist with no resolution to be found here. Let a thousand flowers bloom. At the sub-constitutional level the conflicts are fully expressed and resolved. In the conflicts between the various values that express the humanity of the person, an act of interpretative balancing between the conflicting values must be conducted at the sub-constitutional level.[85] The result is as follows: at the constitutional level, the complex and contradicting world of constitutional values remains as it was – complex and full of contradictions. The world of practical life, at the sub-constitutional level, puts these values into action, while balancing between them. This balance does not affect the scope of the constitutional rights. It affects the ability to fulfill them fully.

[83] See Deryck Beyleveld and Roger Brownsword, 'Human Dignity, Human Rights, and Human Genetics' (1998) 61 *Modern Law Review* 661; Beyleveld and Brownsword, *Human Dignity in Bioethics and Biolaw*; Roger Brownsword, 'Freedom of Contract, Human Rights and Human Dignity', in Daniel Friedmann and Daphne Barak- Erez (eds.), *Human Rights in Private Law* (Oxford: Hart Publishing, 2001) 181; Roger Brownsword, 'An Interest in Human Dignity as the Basis for Genomic Torts' (2003) 42 *Washburn Law Journal* 413; Roger Brownsword, 'Bioethics Today, Bioethics Tomorrow: Stem Cell Research and the "Dignitarian Alliance"' (2003) 17 *Notre Dame Journal of Law, Ethics and Public Policy* 15; Brownsword, *Rights, Regulation and the Technological Revolution*.

[84] See Beyleveld and Brownsword, 'Human Dignity, Human Rights, and Human Genetics'.

[85] See Aharon Barak, *Proportionality: Constitutional Rights and their Limitations*, Doron Kalir trans. (Cambridge University Press, 2012) 72.

As to the argument regarding people lacking free will: these people are protected by human dignity as well. Just as human dignity shelters minors, it shelters those impaired in body or mind.

The understanding of human dignity as the humanity of a person is based on a modern-humanistic approach. This humanistic approach is not derived from a religious approach, nor is it derived from an approach that puts human rationality at its center. It is based on secular-humanism. It is based on man, rather than on God.[86] Nonetheless, many of its ideas are drawn from religious approaches, and some of its outcomes differ only slightly from those of a religious conception of human dignity.

[86] See Lorenzo Zucca, *A Secular Europe: Law and Religion in the European Constitutional Landscape* (Oxford University Press, 2012) 48.

PART III

Human dignity as a constitutional right

8

Recognition of the constitutional right to human dignity and its content

1. Constitutional recognition

A. *Express recognition of a constitutional right to human dignity*

Human dignity has a long history as a subject of theological and philosophical analysis, but a short history as a constitutional value. Its history as a constitutional right is even shorter. It appears that human dignity was first recognized as a right in the Constitution of Finland (1919).[1] Only after the Second World War did the trend of recognizing human dignity as a constitutional right begin.[2] The German Basic Law (1949) was the first to recognize an independent, express constitutional right to human dignity. After this came many constitutions, including the Constitution of Colombia (1991), Israel's Basic Law: Human Dignity and Liberty (1992), the Constitution of Russia (1993), the Constitution of South Africa (1996), the Constitution of Poland (1997), and the Constitution of Switzerland (1999). It can therefore be said that, in the second half of the twentieth century, a human dignity revolution took place. The catalyst for this revolution was the violations of human dignity that took place during the Second World War, predominantly the Holocaust of the Jewish people. In a considerable number of constitutions, human dignity is therefore both a constitutional value and a constitutional right.[3] Justice O'Regan discussed this in a South African case:

> The value of dignity in our Constitutional framework cannot therefore be doubted. The Constitution asserts dignity to contradict our past in which human dignity for black South Africans was routinely and cruelly denied. It asserts it too to inform the future, to invest in our democracy

[1] Art. 6 of the Constitution of Finland (1919): "Every Finnish citizen shall be protected by law as to life, dignity, personal liberty and property."

[2] On the parallel development in public international law, see Chapter 3, section 1.

[3] See Conor O'Mahony, 'There Is No Such Thing as a Right to Dignity' (2012) 10 *International Journal of Constitutional Law* 551.

> respect for the intrinsic worth of all human beings. Human dignity therefore informs constitutional adjudication and interpretation at a range of levels. It is a value that informs the interpretation of many, possibly all, other rights. This Court has already acknowledged the importance of the constitutional value of dignity in interpreting rights such as the right to equality, the right not to be punished in a cruel, inhuman or degrading way, and the right to life. Human dignity is also a constitutional value that is of central significance in the limitations analysis. Section 10, however, makes it plain that dignity is not only a value fundamental to our Constitution, it is a justiciable and enforceable right that must be respected and protected.[4]

The Supreme Court of Israel ruled similarly that human dignity constitutes both a constitutional value and a constitutional right. In one case it was held that:

> [T]he Basic Law does not merely declare "policy" or "ideals" (cf. art. 20(1) of the Basic Law of Germany). The Basic Law does not merely delineate a "plan of operation" or a "purpose" for the organs of government (cf. art. 27(2) of the constitution of South Africa; art. 39 of the constitution of India). It does not merely provide an "umbrella concept" with interpretive application ... Sections 2 and 4 of the Basic Law provide a right – a right that guarantees human dignity. This right corresponds with the duty of the organs of government to respect it (s. 11).[5]

At times the right to human dignity is derived, through purposive constitutional interpretation, out of one of the independent, freestanding rights, without it being recognized as an independent right. Thus, for example, the right to dignity was recognized as a constitutional right derived from the right to life in the Constitution of India.[6]

[4] *Dawood* v. *Minister of Home Affairs*, 2000 (3) SA 936 (CC), para. 35.

[5] HCJ 366/03 *Commitment to Peace and Social Justice Society* v. *Minister of Finance*, 2005-2 IsrLR 335, 347 (2005) (Barak P). See also HCJ 6427/02 *The Movement for Quality Government* v. *The Knesset*, IsrSC 61(1) 619, 680 (2006) ("However, human dignity in Israel is not just a basis and foundation for the various human rights. Human dignity in Israel is not just a social value. Human dignity is an independent right which stands on its own two feet. It exists independently, alongside the other human rights") (Barak P).

[6] See *Francis Coralie Mullin* v. *Delhi*, AIR 1981 SC 746 ("We think that the right to life includes the right to live with human dignity and all that goes along with it, namely, the bare necessaries of life such as adequate nutrition, clothing and shelter and facilities for reading, writing and expressing one-self in diverse forms, freely moving about and mixing and commingling with fellow human beings. Of course, the magnitude and content of the components of this right would depend upon the extent of the economic development of the country, but it must, in any view of the mutter, include the right to the basic necessities of life and also the right to carry on such functions and activities as constitute the bare minimum expression of the human") (Bhagwati J).

It is interesting to note that courts rarely make use of the option of deriving a daughter-right to human dignity from independent, express constitutional rights. Thus for example, in Canada human dignity could have been derived as a daughter-right of the right to life, liberty and security of the person.[7] The Supreme Court of Canada refused to do so.[8] Similarly, in the United States human dignity could have been derived as a daughter-right of the independent right to liberty.[9] The US Supreme Court refused to do so.[10]

B. *Recognition of a constitutional right to human dignity by implication*

Could a constitutional right to human dignity be implied by the structure and architecture of the constitution?[11] The constitutional value of human dignity can be implied by the constitutional structure and architecture. Can an additional step be taken, recognizing the right to human dignity from the same process of implication? The answer of course depends upon the structure of each constitution and the ways in which it is interpreted. Thus, for example, the High Court of Australia recognized an implied constitutional right to political expression.[12] Elsewhere I proposed that within the Israeli Constitutional Bill of Rights, the constitutional right to access to justice should be recognized by implication.[13] With that in mind, I would argue that in light of the centrality of the constitutional

[7] Art. 7 of the Canadian Charter of Rights and Freedoms.

[8] See Chapter 12, section 1A.

[9] The 14th Amendment of the US Constitution. See *Griswold* v. *Connecticut*, 381 US 479 (1965).

[10] See Chapter 11, section 1B.

[11] On constitutional implications, see Chapter 5, section 2D.

[12] See *Nationwide News Pty Limited* v. *Wills*, (1992) 177 CLR 1; *Australian Capital Television Pty Limited* v. *Commonwealth*, (1992) 177 CLR 106; *Theophanous* v. *Herald & Weekly Times Limited*, (1994) 182 CLR 104; *Stephens* v. *West Australian Newspapers Limited*, (1994) 182 CLR 211; *Cunliffe* v. *Commonwealth*, (1994) 182 CLR 272; *McGinty* v. *Western Australia*, (1996) 186 CLR 140; *Lange* v. *Australian Broadcasting Corporation*, (1997) 189 CLR 520; *Kruger* v. *Commonwealth*, (1997) 190 CLR 1; *Levy* v. *Victoria*, (1997) 189 CLR 579. See also Suri Ratnapala, *Australian Constitutional Law: Foundations and Theory*, 2nd edition (South Melbourne: Oxford University Press, 2007) 299; Maryam Minai, Helen Conrad and Philip Lynch, 'The Right to a Fair Hearing and Access to Justice: Australia's Obligations', Human Right's Law Resource Centre Ltd. (Submission to the Senate Legal and Constitutional Affairs Committee: Inquiry into Australia's Judicial System, the Role of Judges and Access to Justice, 2009).

[13] Aharon Barak, 'The Right to Access to the Justice System', in Asher Grunis, Eliezer Rivlin, and Michael Karayanni (eds.) *Shlomo Levin Book* (Jerusalem: Nevo, 2013) 31 (Heb.).

value of human dignity, legal systems that do not have an independent freestanding right to human dignity should seriously consider recognition of human dignity by implication.

C. *Recognition of human dignity as a constitutional right by filling a lacuna in a constitution*

(1) The lacuna

Where human dignity as a constitutional right is derived from an independent, express right, as is the case in India,[14] the recognition is of an express constitutional right to human dignity. We have also discussed the possibility of recognizing human dignity by implication.[15] But if it is not possible to recognize human dignity as a constitutional right either expressly or through implication, can the lack of a provision regarding the right to human dignity be a lacuna (gap) in the constitution, which the court has the power to fill?[16]

Before answering this question, we must distinguish between recognizing a constitutional right by implication from the constitutional structure, and a lacuna in the constitution. Constitutional implication is based on the constitutional language and the implications entailed within that language. A lacuna assumes a lack of any language, be it express or implied, relevant to the particular issue, creating an incomplete constitutional text striving for completion. A constitutional lacuna is an incompleteness of the constitutional text that contradicts its purpose. The constitutional text can be compared to a wall missing a forgotten brick.[17] A lacuna is filled by extra-interpretational activity. "In interpreting a text, the judge grants meaning to what there 'is'. In filling a *lacuna*, the judge adds to what 'is not'."[18] Such activity is recognized in continental systems, although not in common law systems, regarding lacunae in statutes.[19]

[14] See section 1A above.

[15] See section 1B above.

[16] See Aharon Barak, *Proportionality: Constitutional Rights and their Limitations*, Doron Kalir trans. (Cambridge University Press, 2012) 56.

[17] See Aharon Barak, *Purposive Interpretation in Law* (Princeton University Press, 2005) 68.

[18] See John Henry Merryman, 'The Italian Legal Style III: Interpretation' (1966) 18 *Stanford Law Review* 583, 593.

[19] See Art. 12 of the Italian Civil Codex: "If a controversy cannot be decided by a precise provision, consideration is given to provisions that regulate similar cases or analogous matters; if the case still remains in doubt, it is decided according to the general principles of the legal order of the state." See also Mario Beltramo, Giovanni E. Longo and John

There is no lacuna when the constitution's silence is interpreted as a negative implication.[20] A negative implication exists when the silence "speaks." It is based on the conception that the language exhausted the purpose; that the silence was a conscious one. It is silence with a message. However, at times the silence is interpreted as a truncated arrangement that needs completion. The doctrine of lacuna applies to this type of silence.[21]

(2) A lacuna in a constitution?

The question of whether or not the idea of filling a lacuna also applies to a constitution raises several problems. First, should it not be said that in any case where the constitution is "silent" it has established a negative implication, and there is therefore no lacuna? Second, even assuming that there is a lacuna in the constitution, are judges authorized to fill it? Did the High Court of Australia, which recognized an implied constitutional right to political free speech, fill a lacuna in the Australian constitution regarding human rights? Is the decision of Justice Douglas, who recognized the constitutional right to privacy within the penumbra of several rights in the American Bill of Rights, an example of filling lacunae in the US Constitution? Third, what are the rules of gap-filling in a constitution?

An affirmative answer to the question whether a constitutional lacuna can be filled by a court was given by the Federal Supreme Court of Switzerland.[22] The Court recognized the existence of constitutional lacunae (*Lücken*), and their authority to fill them. A lacuna exists when the constitution lacks a right that comprises either a vital component of a democratic state based upon the rule of law, or a precondition to the exercise of express constitutional rights.[23] Through this method, the Federal

Henry Merryman (trans.), *The Italian Civil Code* (Dobbs Ferry: Oceana Publications 1969).

[20] For the distinction between a lacuna and a negative implication, see Barak, *Proportionality*, at 94.

[21] On the doctrine of lacuna see Merryman, 'The Italian Legal Style III', at 593; Chaim Perelman, *Le Problème des Lacunes en Droit* (Brussels: Émile Bruylant, 1968); Alfred E. Von Overbeck, 'Some Observations on the Role of the Judge under the Swiss Civil Code' (1977) 37 *Louisiana Law Review* 681; Claus-Wilhelm Canaris, *Die Feststellung von Lücken im Gesetz: Eine Methodologische Studie über Voraussetzungen und Grenzen der Rechtsfortbildung Praeter Legem*, 2nd edn (Berlin: Duncker & Humblot, 1983).

[22] Jean François Aubert, *Traite de Droit Constitutionnel Suisse* (Neuchâtel: Ides et Calendes, 1967) 126; Jörg Paul Müller and Stefan Müller, *Grundrechte: Besonderer Teil* (Bern: Stämpfli & Cie, 1985) 287; Ulrich Häfelin, Walter Haller and Helen Keller, *Schweizerisches Bundesstaatsrecht*, 8th edn (Zurich: Schulthess, 2012) 44.

[23] Luzius Wildhaber, 'Limitations on Human Rights in Times of Peace, War and Emergency: A Report on Swiss Law', in Armand L. C. De Mestral *et al.* (eds.), *The Limitation of Human Rights in Comparative Constitutional Law* (Cowansville: Yvon Blais, 1986) 41, 44.

Supreme Court recognized the right to property, the right to life and liberty, the right to freedom of expression and the right to assembly.

When a constitutional problem can be solved within the framework of the language of the constitutional text, there is no lacuna. Therefore, daughter-rights are not lacunae that have been filled, as they are derived from the express meaning of the language of the constitutional right. Thus Australian decisions regarding the freedom of political expression will not be considered as filling lacunae if they can be based on implication from the Australian constitution regarding the structure of Australian democracy and elections.

The distinction between express or implied meaning on the one hand and the filling of a lacuna on the other is of great importance for two main reasons. First, judicial determination of the implied meaning of the language of a constitutional right is included within the legitimate judicial interpretational activity. In contrast, the judicial legitimacy of filling a lacuna in a constitution cannot be based on interpretational activity. It requires special legitimacy, which does not exist in many legal systems.[24] Second, the express or implied meaning of the language of a constitutional right is derived according to the rules of interpretation of the legal system. Rules for filling lacuna are extra-interpretational. Every legal system that recognizes the lacuna doctrine has its own extra-interpretational rules. These rules are usually based on analogy and reference to the fundamental principles of the system.[25]

2. The content of the constitutional right: the realization of the constitutional value

A. *The general approach*

According to purposive interpretation, the content of a right is determined by its underlying purpose. The purpose of the constitutional right to human dignity is to realize the constitutional value of human dignity. Thus its purpose is to realize a person's humanity.[26] The dignity of a human being is his free will; the freedom to shape his life and fulfill himself. It is a person's freedom to write his life story.

At the core of a person's humanity stands the autonomy of her will, which means that the person herself – she, and no one else – determines her destiny. The state does not intervene in the affairs of the individual

[24] See Barak, *Proportionality*, at 57. [25] *Ibid.*, at 58.

[26] See Chapter 7, section 4B(1).

and in his relations with others. Indeed, a person's humanity is her free will. This free will is denied if her choices are dictated by another person. A person must not be treated merely as a means for satisfying the desire of another person. Human dignity reflects the humanity of a person as a member of society. It is not the humanity of a person on a desert island.

The unique purpose that characterizes each constitutional right is distinguished from the general purpose of that right: realization of the constitutional value of human dignity. Within the constitutional right to human dignity the general purpose and the unique purpose are combined. The two are one: the realization of the constitutional value of human dignity.

Is having a variety of rights not superfluous according to this view? Does it not follow that the constitutional right to human dignity, which will realize the constitutional value of human dignity, is sufficient? No. Every constitutional right has its own unique purpose. That purpose can overlap complementarily with the constitutional value of human dignity.[27] It can be in conflict with the constitutional value of human dignity.[28] Alongside these particular rights stands the constitutional right to human dignity, which in part overlaps complementarily with them, and in part conflicts with them. The complement and conflict do not alter the boundaries of the various rights. The resolution to the conflict will not be found at the constitutional level. At this level, the conflict remains as it was. The resolution will be found at the sub-constitutional level. Sub-constitutional norms (statutes or common law) may limit conflicting constitutional rights, and this limitation will be constitutional so long as it is proportional.

B. *The unique case of the German Basic Law*

The direct relationship between the constitutional right to human dignity and the constitutional value of human dignity is the product of the constitutional model, and must be adapted to specific constitutional structures. Ultimately, we are dealing with the interpretation of the right to human dignity in a given constitution, and this interpretation must be in harmony with the general constitutional architecture. When it does not fit, the relationship between the right and the value must be adapted so that it fits the comprehensive conception of the constitution. This sort of adaptation is required for the German Constitution.

[27] See Chapter 9, section 2E(1). [28] See Chapter 9, section 2E(4).

In German constitutional law, as in other constitutions, the meaning of the constitutional value of human dignity is the humanity of the person.[29] The constitutional value of human dignity is seen as the constitution's supreme value.[30] The case law and literature see in human dignity the spirit and essence of the entire constitution.[31] It is the center of the constitutional structure[32] and the value that controls all other parts of the constitution. This supreme status reflects the understanding that Germany rejects its Nazi past and the severe violations of human dignity that characterized it,[33] and enshrines the very human dignity so desecrated by the Nazis as its topmost value.

In Germany, the constitutional right to human dignity is absolute.[34] The rules of proportionality do not apply to it. It is eternal. The rules of constitutional amendment do not apply to it. The result is that the scope of human dignity as a constitutional right is inherently narrow and limited. If human dignity is an absolute right, and any limitation of it is unconstitutional, the right to human dignity cannot cover all aspects of the peoples' humanity. This is the source of the approach of German constitutional law that human dignity as a constitutional right covers only extreme situations in which taboos of human existence are violated.[35] This includes the prohibition of torture, the prohibition of degradation and the duty to ensure the minimal subsistence of the individual in society. The baseline for understanding human dignity as a constitutional right is the approach that human dignity is limited where a person is seen as a mere means for the realization of another person's ends. Human dignity in German constitutional law is restricted to always seeing a person as an end and not only as an object. This is the source of the focus

[29] See Chapter 13, section 2B.

[30] See Horst Dreier, *GG Grundgesetz Kommentar* (Tübingen: Mohr Siebeck, 2006) 162; Bodo Pieroth and Bernhard Schlink, *Grundrechte, Staatsrecht II* (Heidelberg: C. F. Müller Verlag, 2006) 80; Matthias Mahlmann, *Elemente einer ethischen Grundrechtstheorie* (Berlin: Nomos, 2008) 179.

[31] See BVerfGE 12, 45 (1960); BVerfGE 27, 1 (1969); BVerfGE 30, 173 (1971); BVerfGE 45, 187 (1977); BVerfGE 82, 60 (1990). See also Donald P. Kommers and Russell A. Miller, *The Constitutional Jurisprudence of the Federal Republic of Germany*, 3rd edn (Durham, NC: Duke University Press, 2012) 355.

[32] BVerfGE 7, 198 (1958); BVerfGE 35, 202 (1973); BVerfGE 39, 1 (1975).

[33] See Pieroth and Schlink, *Grundrechte, Staatsrecht II*, at 80; Dreier, *GG Grundgesetz Kommentar*, at 154.

[34] See Chapter 13, section 1B.

[35] See Michael Sachs, *Grundgesetz Kommentar* (Berlin: Springer, 2003) 82.

on the *Objektformel* ("object formula"), which is influenced by Kantian philosophy.[36]

This understanding of the right to human dignity is narrower than the understanding of human dignity as the humanity of the person.[37] The external interpretative context, regarding the historic and social background, could have led to the constitutional value of human dignity being identical to the constitutional right to human dignity – as the humanity of the person. However, the internal interpretative context regarding the constitutional architecture, which sees human dignity as an absolute and eternal right, forces the scope of the constitutional value of human dignity (the humanity of a person) to be detached from the scope of the constitutional right to human dignity (rejection of a person as a mere means). Only those aspects of the constitutional value of human dignity that are related to appreciating a person as an end and not merely a means determine the scope of the right to human dignity. Therefore, only cases similar to those violating a "taboo" such as torture and minimum human subsistence fall within the boundaries of the constitutional right to human dignity.

3. Purposive constitutional interpretation and human dignity

A. *Interpretation with a spacious view*

This volume is based on the assumption that purposive interpretation is the basis for the constitutional model of understanding human dignity as a constitutional value.[38] According to this interpretation, the constitutional

[36] The *Objektformel*, according to Dürig's definition, determines: "Human dignity as such is affected when a concrete human being is reduced to an object, to a mere means, to a dispensable quantity. [Violations of dignity involve] the degradation of the person to a thing, which can, in its entirety, be grasped, disposed of, registered, brainwashed, replaced, used and expelled." See Günter Dürig, 'Der Grundrechtssatz von der Menschenwürde' (1956) *Archiv des öffentlichen Rechts* 81, 125. The translation is Botha's: see Henk Botha, 'Human Dignity in Comparative Perspective' (2009) 2 *Stellenbosch Law Review* 171, 183. See also Mahlmann, *Elemente einer ethischen Grundrechtstheorie*, at 190; Dreier, *GG Grundgesetz Kommentar*, at 168; Laurie Ackermann, *Human Dignity: Lodestar for Equality in South Africa* (Cape Town: Juta, 2012) 117; David P. Currie, *The Constitution of the Federal Republic of Germany* (University of Chicago Press, 1994) 314; Eckart Klein, 'Human Dignity in German Law', in David Kretzmer and Eckart Klein (eds.), *The Concept of Human Dignity in Human Rights Discourse* (The Hague: Kluwer Law International, 2002) 145, 150.

[37] See Ariel L. Bendor and Michael Sachs, 'Human Dignity as a Constitutional Concept in Germany and in Israel' (2011) 44 *Israel Law Review* 26.

[38] See Chapter 5, section 1A.

value of human dignity is interpreted with a spacious view.[39] The constitutional model is based upon the understanding of the constitutional right to human dignity in light of the constitutional value of human dignity. The conclusion, therefore, is that the constitutional right to human dignity is also interpreted with a spacious view. This interpretation is based upon the constitutional text's unique character. The Supreme Court of Israel discussed this in *Bank Mizrahi*:

> The scope of a right is determined by its interpretation. This is constitutional interpretation. It is sensitive to the unique character of the document under examination ... The constitution is interpreted in accordance with the constitutional purpose ... The constitutional purpose may be discerned from language, history, culture and basic principles. A constitutional provision is not enacted in a vacuum and it does not develop in a constitutional incubator. It constitutes part of life itself ... Constitutional interpretation must be based upon constitutional unity, and not upon constitutional disharmony. It reflects the role of the constitutional text in the structure of government and society. It endows it with the meaning that enables it to fulfill its role in the present and future in the most suitable manner.[40]

This was written regarding all of the constitutional rights. It fully applies to the right to human dignity. The interpreter must "consider the circumstances of time and place, the basic values of society and its way of life, the social and political consensus and the normative reality. These are all tools that the judge has at his disposal for interpreting the legal concept of human dignity."[41]

B. *A spacious view is not a limitless view*

The purpose of the constitutional right to human dignity is to realize the constitutional value of human dignity. This constitutional value is not restricted solely to preventing torture and degradation.[42] However, purposive interpretation is not limitless interpretation. The limits of

[39] On constitutional interpretation with a "spacious view," see Chapter 4, section 4C(5).

[40] CA 6821/93 *Bank Mizrahi* v. *Migdal Cooperative Village*, 1995-2 IsrLR 1, 234–6 (1995) (Barak P).

[41] HCJ 366/06 *Commitment to Peace and Social Justice Society* v. *Minister of Finance*, at 358 (Barak P).

[42] See HCJ 4128/02 *Man, Nature and Law* v. *Prime Minister of Israel*, IsrSC 58(3) 503, 513 (2004) ("Constitutional interpretation of the right to human dignity must determine its constitutional traits. It is not to be restricted merely to torture and degradation because this would miss its underlying purpose") (Barak P).

the constitutional right are determined by its language's express and implied meaning – what can be "inserted" into the term human dignity – and by its purpose – the realization of the constitutional value of human dignity. Thus, for example, the rights of a corporation cannot be included within the framework of human dignity. Corporations have no humanity.

C. *Purposive interpretation of human dignity and limitation of a different right*

The constitutional value of human dignity may conflict with general or particular values underlying constitutional rights. As far as the constitutional values are concerned, this conflict ought not to affect their scope. Each constitutional value expresses its own ideals; each constitutional value stands on its own, and its scope is unchanged by other values that reflect different ideals. But what happens to the constitutional right? Is the scope of a constitutional right realizing one of these conflicting ideals affected by the conflict? For example, the constitutional value of human dignity includes the value of a person's reputation. This value might conflict with the independent freestanding value of freedom of expression underlying the constitutional right to freedom of expression. Can this conflict affect the scope of the constitutional right to human dignity? Should we say that the particular value overcomes the general value?

The answer is that this conflict will have no outcome on the constitutional level. The constitutional value of human dignity is not narrowed as a result of the conflict, and the constitutional right to human dignity is not narrowed as a result. This is the case regarding any particular value and any particular right. The results of the conflict will be felt in the sub-constitutional level. A statute that limits freedom of expression in order to protect a person's reputation will be constitutional only if it is proportionate.

A similar conclusion will be reached if we look at this situation as a conflict between two constitutional rights. Assume, for example, that the constitutional right to human dignity covers a person's reputation as well. Assume further that the independent freestanding right to freedom of expression covers statements that damage another's reputation. There is now a conflict between the right to human dignity and the right to freedom of expression. What is the result of this conflict? Should it not be said that the particular constitutional right (to freedom of expression) overcomes the general constitutional right (to human dignity)? My answer is that this conflict will not be solved at the constitutional level. This conflict is not indicative of a constitutional pathology. It reflects the richness of rights in a democracy. The conflict remains as it was at the constitutional level, and is resolved only at the sub-constitutional level through the application of the rules of proportionality.[43]

D. Purposive interpretation of human dignity and limitation of the public interest

The constitutional value of human dignity might conflict with the public interests, for example the security of the state and public order. These interests might also exist at the constitutional level, expressly or by implication. Can this conflict affect the scope of the constitutional right to human dignity? Are we to say that the public interest prevails over the constitutional value of human dignity at the constitutional level?

This question arose in Israel. For security reasons, a statute[44] temporarily prohibited Israelis' foreign spouses from the West Bank and the Gaza Strip from entering Israel to fulfill their and their children's right to family life in Israel. The question was whether or not the statute was constitutional. In order to answer this question, an additional question was asked: does the statute limit the constitutional right to human dignity? The court held that the right to human dignity includes the right to family life. The question that arose in this context was as follows: what is the scope of the Israeli spouse's right to marry? Does the right to human dignity include the right of the Israeli spouse to live his family life with the foreign spouse in Israel?

It was argued before the court that public interest dictates that the key to entrance into Israel be in the hands of the state, and not subject to the decision of the Israeli to marry a foreign citizen. In light of this public interest, the question arose whether the public interest in the state retaining the key to entrance into Israel (and not placing it in the hands of the Israeli spouse) narrows the constitutional right of the Israeli spouse to family life, in the sense that the constitutional right does not include living as a family in Israel. The opinions were split on this question. The majority was of the opinion that considerations of public interest are important, and they should be taken into account when assessing the proportionality

[43] See HCJ 1435/03 *Jane Doe* v. *The Disciplinary Tribunal of the Civil Service*, IsrSC 58(1) 529 (2003).

[44] The Citizenship and Entry into Israel Law (Temporary Provision), 5753-2003 SH 544.

of the limitation of the constitutional right to family life in Israel. The public good, however, cannot narrow the constitutional right to family life and remove from it the fulfillment of the right in Israel. The dissenting opinion was that the consideration of the public good narrows the scope of the constitutional right. The majority stated in its decision:

> [T]aking the public interest into account – no matter how important it may be – must be done within the framework of examining the conditions of the limitation clause (the second stage of the constitutional scrutiny) and not within the framework of determining the scope of the constitutional right itself (the first stage of the constitutional scrutiny). This is the case with regard to the right to family life and it is also the case with regard to every other constitutional right … The methodology adopted by my colleague will eventually reduce the constitutional protection given to human rights to a significant degree. It is likely to lead, for example, to an approach that taking into account the public interest, such as national security or public safety, with regard to the right to freedom of expression, should find its place in determining the scope of freedom of expression and not in determining the constitutional possibility of limiting it. Changing the "place" of the public interest is not a mere technical or methodological matter. It is a matter with deep implications for human rights in Israel. It involves a drastic reduction in the scope of human rights … It involves a dilution of the constitutional protection of human rights in Israel … Our role as judges, at this stage of our national life, is to recognize in full the scope of human rights, while giving full strength to the power of the limitation clause to allow a limitation of those rights, when necessary, without restricting their scope.[45]

Underlying this approach is an in-depth view of the constitutional right. It presents a constitutional right as an ideal that society must aspire to realize. This ideal may of course conflict with other ideals or interests that society must aspire to realize. This conflict will not be solved by restricting the ideals, but rather by limiting the ways in which they are exercised. A constitutional right continues to stand, complete and pure, as an aspiration that traverses boundaries and time. It is in constant conflict with other aspirations. This conflict is solved at the sub-constitutional level. It is governed by the rules of proportionality in the limitation clause. The rules of proportionality, which balance the ways that the constitutional right and the conflicting aspirations are exercised, do not affect, and do not restrict, the significance of the constitutional right or its scope. Proportionality affects the exercise of the right at the sub-constitutional level in a given society at a given time.

[45] HCJ 7052/03 *Adalah* v. *Minister of Interior*, 2006-1 IsrLR 443, 548–549 (2006) (Barak P).

This approach grants a society the ideals to which it should aspire, and reinforces their position, even if they are not fully realized de facto. Thus the boundaries and vigor of the constitutional right are preserved even in times of emergency or other difficult situations. The necessary limitations of constitutional rights in times of emergency or moments of crisis should be limitations on the exercise of the constitutional right, and must not narrow the scope of the right from within. Limiting the ways in which the constitutional right may be exercised at a given time remains temporary, and does not influence its scope. In addition, a clear distinction between a constitutional right and the public good will enrich the public and constitutional discourse. The demarcation between law and politics will be drawn in a clearer and more precise fashion. The various considerations taken into account will be demonstrated in their clear and appropriate form, and the importance attributed to them will be transparent and subject to assessment and critique.[46] This approach is also accepted in comparative law.[47]

[46] See Barak, *Proportionality*, at 79.

[47] See Nicholas Emiliou, *The Principle of Proportionality in European Law* (Cambridge, MA: Kluwer Law International, 1996) 53 ("The doctrinal separation between the constituent elements of basic rights and their limits avoids the inclusion of public interest and welfare considerations directly in the elements of basic rights themselves. In this way, the danger of arbitrarily restricting freedom by way of an ad hoc definition of basic rights is also avoided, ultimately ensuring optimal freedom"); Stuart Woolman and Henk Botha, 'Limitations', in Stuart Woolman, Michael Bishop and Jason Brickhill (eds.), *Constitutional Law of South Africa*, 2nd edn, Revision Series 4 (Cape Town: Juta, 2012) chapter 34, p. 20 ("The first stage of analysis is generally understood to require the judge to determine the ambit of the right. The determination is made by asking what values underlie the right and then, in turn, what practices serve those values. The judge is not required to compare the importance of the values underlying the right allegedly being infringed with the values said to underlie the policy or right or interest said to support the alleged infringement. This comparison is left for the second stage of analysis under the limitations clause. It is under the limitations clause that we ask whether a party's interest in having a challenged law upheld is of sufficient import to justify the infringement of a right … [T]he determination made here is one of definition or demarcation, not balancing. We are asking what counts as protected assembly activity, not whether this kind of protected activity, when offset against some competing set of public or private interests, still merits protection. We are deciding what values animate and what practices are protected by a particular right. The problem of value conflict between a right and a law that limits the exercise of that right is played out at the next stage of inquiry – the limitations clause"). See also *De Reuck* v. *Director of Public Prosecutions*, 2004 (1) SA 406 (CC), para. 48 ("The respondents dispute that child pornography, as defined by the Act, is expression.

E. *Criticism of this view and response*

This approach may be criticized as leading to a "cheapening of the constitutional right."[48] Can it be said that the autonomy of individual will, which underlies human dignity, also includes the autonomy to commit a criminal offense? Is it correct to think that free will, which underlies human dignity, covers the freedom to commit a tort? Does such an approach not trivialize human dignity?[49]

My answer to these arguments is that they reflect but a first impression. Everyone understands that an entire system of statutes justifiably limits rights and enables functional social life. The question of the constitutionality of that system is examined within the framework of proportionality.[50] This approach reflects the complexity of human life, which is full of contradicting values and rights. These contradictions should not be resolved by negating one of the constitutional values or rights. They should be resolved by balancing the competing constitutional values and rights. This balance is carried out according to the rules of proportionality. The act of balancing occurs at the sub-constitutional level, rather than at the constitutional level.[51] Justice Ackermann of the Constitutional Court of South Africa discussed this in response to an argument regarding the trivialization of the constitutional right to liberty:

Relying on the approach of the United States Supreme Court where certain categories of expression are unprotected forms of speech, the respondents argued such materials do not serve any of the values traditionally considered as underlying freedom of expression, namely, truth-seeking, free political activity and self-fulfillment. This argument must fail. In this respect, our Constitution is different from that of the United States of America. Limitations of rights are dealt with under section 36 of the Constitution and not at the threshold level. Section 16(1) expressly protects the freedom of expression in a manner that does not warrant a narrow reading. Any restriction upon artistic creativity must satisfy the rigours of the limitation analysis") (Langa DCJ); SC 58/2005 *Hansen* v. *The Queen*, [2007] NZSC 7, para. 22 (NZ) ("The first question is the interpretation of the right. In ascertaining the meaning of the right, the criteria for justification are not relevant. The meaning of the right is ascertained from the 'cardinal values' it embodies. Collapsing the interpretation of the right and the s1 justification is insufficiently protective of the right. The later justification is according to a stringent standard, in which a party seeking to justify must show that the limit on a fundamental right is 'demonstrably justified' in a free and democratic society. The context for the application of s1 is then the violation of a constitutionally guaranteed right or freedom") (Elias CJ).

[48] CrimA 4424/98 *Silgado* v. *The State of Israel*, IsrSC 56(5) 529, 556 (2002) (Strasberg-Cohen J).

[49] See Barak, *Proportionality*, at 43.

[50] See Kai Möller, *The Global Model of Constitutional Rights* (Oxford University Press, 2012).

[51] See Barak, *Proportionality*, at 87.

> I cannot comprehend why an extensive construction of freedom would "trivialize" the Charter, either in theory or in practice, or, more relevantly for our purposes, our present Constitution. It might trivialise a constitution (it would indeed cause chaos) if it resulted in the regulating measures being struck down. But that is not the consequence. An extensive construction merely requires the party relying thereon to justify it in terms of a limitation clause. It does not trivialise a constitution in theory; in fact it has the reverse effect by emphasising the necessity for justifying intrusion into freedom. It does not trivialise a constitution in practice because in the vast majority of cases dealing with regulatory matters, the justification is so obviously incontestable that it is taken for granted and never becomes a live issue. In the borderline cases (and even in mundane regulatory statutes such cases may arise) there is no pragmatic reason why the person relying on the measure ought not to justify it.[52]

Another argument is that my approach to understanding the constitutional right has a negative effect on constitutional discourse. According to this argument, this is manifest, inter alia, in diminishing the status of the legislature, as every piece of legislation ultimately limits various human rights according to their broad definition. If the court is the arbiter of every such limitation – what will become of the legislature? Indeed, the argument that "human dignity should not displace the dignity of the statute"[53] is an important argument. The dignity of the legislature is precious for everyone to whom democracy and human rights are important.[54] There is no contradiction between my approach regarding the scope of human rights and respecting the legislature, just as there is no contradiction between judicial review of the constitutionality of a statute and respecting the statute. The dignity of the statute and the legislature is found in the respect for the constitution. The dignity of the law is not affronted if a judge deems it to be in violation of the constitution, just as the dignity of a judge is not affronted if the legislature amends a law to negate the interpretive effects of a decision.[55]

An additional argument is that my position overburdens the second stage of constitutional analysis (the proportionality stage), and results in the diluted protection of human rights. According to this argument,

[52] *Ferreira* v. *Levin NO* 1996 (1) SA 984 (CC), para. 82 (Ackermann J).

[53] HCJ 7111/95 *Local Government Center* v. *The Knesset*, IsrSC 50(3) 485, 496 (1996) (Zamir J).

[54] See Jeremy Waldron, *The Dignity of Legislation* (Cambridge University Press, 1999).

[55] On the dialogue between the legislative and judicial branches see Peter W. Hogg and Alison A. Bushell, 'The Charter Dialogue between Courts and Legislatures' (1997) 35 *Osgoode Hall Law Journal* 75; Aharon Barak, *The Judge in a Democracy* (Princeton University Press, 2006) 236.

strengthening the limitation clause in order to grant proper protection to human rights should actually lead to a narrowing of the scope of those rights. Considering the common good or the rights of others within the definition of the scope of rights will lead to a narrower definition of that scope. Hogg made this argument regarding the analysis of human rights in Canada.[56] I am of the opinion that the concern raised by Hogg is not substantial, certainly not when the limitation clause is employed in a way that takes into consideration the uniqueness of each right and the particular circumstances of its limitation.

Finally, it is argued that my approach will ultimately overburden the court's case load. This argument lacks factual substance. It is unsupported by past experience. In any case, if the flood this argument predicts does come, the court will need to find the means to deal with it. Moving the "location" in which the common good is considered is certainly not the only means. In my opinion, it is the method of last resort, and should only be employed if there is truly no other option.

[56] See Peter W. Hogg, 'Interpreting the Charter of Rights: Generosity and Justification' (1990) 28 *Osgoode Hall Law Journal* 817.

9

Human dignity as a framework right (mother-right)

1. Human dignity as a framework right

A. *Framework rights*

Constitutional rights designed as principles[1] – such as property, liberty and privacy – are, inherently, framework rights.[2] On the other hand, constitutional rights designed as rules – such as the right of a citizen to vote or to enter his country[3] – are particular rights. A framework right is based upon generality. It has an open range of application. The framers of the constitution did not include the particular factual and legal elements for the application of the right from its underlying constitutional value in the constitutional language. Inherently, framework rights do not focus upon a particular type of act, nor do they protect particular human conduct.

1 On the distinction between principles and rules, see Humberto Bergmann Avila (ed.), *Theory of Legal Principles* (Dordrecht: Springer, 2007). For Alexy's approach, see Robert Alexy, *A Theory of Constitutional Rights*, Julian Rivers trans. (Oxford University Press, 2002); Frederick Schauer, *Thinking Like a Lawyer: A New Introduction to Legal Reasoning* (Cambridge, MA: Harvard University Press, 2009) 188. See also Pierre J. Schlag, 'Rules and Standards' (1985) 33 *UCLA Law Review* 379; Kathleen M. Sullivan, 'The Supreme Court 1991 Term – Forward: The Justices of Rules and Standards' (1992) 106 *Harvard Law Review* 22; Louis Kaplow, 'Rules Versus Standards: An Economic Analysis' (1992) 42 *Duke Law Journal* 557; Joseph Grodin, 'Are Rules Really Better than Standards' (1993) 45 *Hastings Law Journal* 569; Frederick Schauer, 'The Convergence of Rules and Standards' (2003) 3 *New Zealand Law Review* 303; Larry Alexander and Ken Kress, 'Against Legal Principles', in Andrei Marmor (ed.), *Law and Interpretation: Essays in Legal Philosophy* (Oxford: Clarendon Press, 2007) 279; Martin Borowski (ed.), *On the Nature of Legal Principles* (Stuttgart: Franz Steiner Verlag, 2010).

2 They are also called "generic rights" or "matrix rights." See Michel Melchior, 'Rights Not Covered by the Convention', in R. Macdonald, F. Matscher and H. Petzold (eds.), *The European System for the Protection of Human Rights* (Dordrecht: Martinus Nijhoff, 1993) 593.

3 See Art. 6(b) of Basic Law: Human Dignity and Liberty ("Every Israeli national has the right of entry into Israel from abroad").

A constitutional right formulated as a principle serves as a "common roof,"[4] under which a wide variety of situations crowd together. Common to all of them is that they are expressions of the general principle that shapes the right. For the sake of convenience, these situations can be cataloged and grouped into categories, all of which fall within the general principle. Under the canopy of the constitutional framework right, constitutional rights derived from it or that radiate[5] from it crowd together. These rights are inherently of a lower level of generality than the framework right.[6] Most of these rights are themselves framework rights at a lower level of generality. They too provide a platform for deriving daughter-rights. At the lowest level of generality there will be a number of particular rights that focus upon a specific type of act and particular human conduct. They reflect legal norms that are rules.[7] For example, the right to liberty in the US Constitution is a framework right. The right to privacy is derived from it at a lower level of generality.[8] A woman's right to have an abortion is derived from that right at an even lower level of generality. At the lowest level of generality the rule granting a specific woman the right to an abortion will be derived.

A framework right is therefore a mother-right.[9] From it are derived daughter-rights. If the daughter-rights themselves are framework rights at a lower level of generality, granddaughter-rights are to be derived from them. Other imagery expressing this concept views the mother-right as a tree and the daughter-rights as branches growing out from it.

4 LCA 10520/03 *Ben Gvir* v. *Dankner* (12.11.2006), para. 3 of Justice Arbel's opinion ("In the case before us there are two basic rights lying on the scales – freedom of expression versus the right to dignity and good name. These freedoms share a common roof; it is the roof of the constitutional value of human dignity").

5 See Andrew R. Simmonds, 'Measure for Measure: Two Misunderstood Principles of Damages, Exodus 21:22–25, "Life for Life, Eye for Eye," and Matthew 5:38–39, "Turn the Other Cheek"' (2004) 17 *Saint Thomas Law Review* 123; Robert Leckey, 'Embodied Dignity' (2005) 5 *Oxford University Commonwealth Law Journal* 63.

6 See Lawrence H. Tribe, *The Invisible Constitution* (New York: Oxford University Press, 2008); Mark Walters, 'Written Constitution and Unwritten Constitutionalism', in Grant Huscroft (ed.), *Expounding the Constitution: Essays in Constitutional Theory* (Cambridge University Press, 2008) 245. See also Mark V. Tushnet, 'Can You Watch Unenumerated Rights Drift' (2006) 9 *University of Pennsylvania Journal of Constitutional Law* 209.

7 On legal rules, see note 1 above.

8 See Chapter 11, section 1B.

9 On the use of the term "mother-right" (*Muttergrundrecht*), see Catherine Dupré, *Importing Law in Post-Communist Transitions: The Hungarian Constitutional Court and the Right to Human Dignity* (Oxford and Portland, OR: Hart Publishing, 2003) 67. The Constitutional Court of Hungary also used a similar term (*anyajog*).

Daughter-rights are derived from mother-rights through an act of interpretation. The number of daughter-rights and their categorization must not be predetermined. The categories of daughter-rights are open. Social changes might cause changes in the understanding of the mother-right, and along with it changes in the daughter-rights derived from it. The interpretation of the mother-right determines the boundaries of possible derivations of daughter-rights. These boundaries have been demarcated by the language of the mother-right and by its purpose.

When a constitutional daughter-right is derived from a mother-right recognized as an independent freestanding right in the constitution, the daughter-right, like the mother-right, is an express constitutional right. It is not an implied constitutional right. Although it does not have its own name, its name is that of the mother-right. It is an enumerated right, as it is part of the enumerated mother right.[10] The difference between the mother-right and the daughter-right is in the level of generality. Just as the independent mother-right to freedom of speech entails the daughter-right to burn the flag,[11] the mother-right to human dignity entails the right to reputation. Both of these daughter-rights are express constitutional rights as they are part of the mother-rights.[12]

The constitutional right to human dignity is formulated as a principle. It constitutes a framework right, or a mother-right. Daughter-rights at a lower level of generality are derived from it, and they too are generally framework rights from which granddaughter-rights can be derived. When the derived right determines the factual and legal elements of its application, it constitutes a particular daughter-right formulated as a rule.

B. *A bundle of rights*

This conception of a framework right or mother-right indicates that constitutional rights designed as principles are essentially bundles of rights. They all have a common framework; they are all included within the meaning of the constitutional text; and they all fulfill a common principle that serves as a roof under which they are all gathered into a unified whole. The rope that binds the bundle is not external to it, but is rather its very

[10] On this issue, see section 1C below.

[11] See *Texas* v. *Johnson*, 491 US 397 (1989).

[12] See Laurence Tribe and Michael Dorf, 'Levels of Generality in the Definition of Rights' (1990) 57 *University of Chicago Law Review* 1057; Mark V. Tushnet, 'Justification in Constitutional Adjudication: A Comment on Constitutional Interpretation' (1994) 72 *Texas Law Review* 1707.

essence. The character of the bundle is determined by the values underlying the mother-right. This is the internal logic of the right. However, each component in the bundle has its own legal and factual elements at various levels of generality. The content of the mother-right determines the components of the bundle. The framework right – the mother-right – is therefore a family of rights, with separate factual and legal elements at various levels of generality (some are framework rights and some are particular rights) that have gathered together into one family framework. The family framework determines the "genetic code" of the mother-right. This code determines the character of each of the daughter-rights derived from the mother-right.

Human dignity – like other rights formulated as principles – constitutes a bundle of rights. The term "human dignity" does not detail the factual and legal elements for determining the scope of the constitutional right to human dignity. Human dignity is based upon a generality. Its content is the constitutional value of human dignity. Its daughter-rights realize – under the canopy of human dignity – the purpose underlying the constitutional right to human dignity.

C. *Framework rights and rights with no special name*

The mother-right is a right with a family name. And what are the names of the daughter-rights derived from this right? The constitution gave a family name to the framework right or to the mother-right. It did not give a name to the daughter-right, and should not do so, as the daughter-rights are part of the mother-right. Their name is the name of the mother-right. They have no names of their own. This status does not turn the daughter-rights into implied or unwritten rights.[13] They are express rights, and they are among the express rights established in the constitution.

At times the daughter-rights are called "unenumerated rights."[14] To the extent that this term expresses the idea that these rights are not independent, freestanding rights, I can accept it. However, if this term expresses the

[13] On implied rights, see Chapter 5, section 2D.

[14] Dworkin criticized the use of the term "unenumerated rights" in American law: see Ronald Dworkin, 'Unenumerated Rights: Whether and How Roe Should Be Overruled' (1992) 59 *University of Chicago Law Review* 381. Dworkin notes that "the distinction between enumerated and unenumerated constitutional rights … is bogus." He proposes that "the distinction between enumerated and unenumerated rights is safely shut up with other legal concepts dishonorably discharged for bad philosophy." See also Richard Posner, 'Legal Reasoning from the Top Down and from the Bottom Up: The Question of Unenumerated Constitutional Rights', in Geoffrey R. Stone, Richard A. Epstein and Cass

idea that these rights were not expressly determined in the constitution, I object to this term. The daughter-rights are expressly determined in the constitution. They are part of the framework rights, or the mother-rights, at a lower level of generality.[15] Their name is the name of the framework right. The name of the daughter-right is the name of the mother-right.

The scope of the daughter-right is delineated by the scope of the mother-right. The daughter-right cannot deviate from the framework of the mother-right. The "genes" of the mother-right act from within the daughter-right. Therefore, if the daughter-right were to stand on its own as an independent right, its scope would be different than the scope it received as a daughter-right.

2. Daughter-rights of human dignity

A. *Daughter-rights fulfill the mother-right's purpose*

The independent constitutional right is the mother-right of human dignity. Derived, or radiating, from it are daughter-rights reflecting, at different levels of generality, the various civil and social aspects of human dignity. They reflect different categories of acts or omissions that can affect human dignity. Aggregated together, these categories are part of the whole, but they never exhaust it. "[T]his categorization will never reflect the full scope of the right to human dignity, nor does it intend to do so. It is intended to assist in understanding of the framework provision concerning human dignity."[16] The Supreme Court of Israel derived a long list of daughter-rights from human dignity as a mother-right.[17]

B. *The various aspects of the humanity of a person*

The framework right to human dignity is complex and multifaceted. It can be protected and limited in many different ways. Each of those ways reflects means by which the humanity of a person is realized. Regarding the framework right of human dignity, the Supreme Court of Israel noted in *Adalah*:

R. Sunstein (eds.), *The Bill of Rights in the Modern State* (University Of Chicago Press, 1992) 433.

[15] See section 1A above.

[16] HCJ 7052/03 *Adalah* v. *Minister of Interior*, 2006-1 IsrLR 443, 487 (2006) (Barak P).

[17] See Chapter 15, section 2A.

> The nature of such a right is that, according to its wording, it does not give explicit details of the particular types of activity to which it applies. It is open-ended … The situations to which it applies are derived from the interpretation of the open language of the Basic Law against the background of its purpose. These situations can be classified, for convenience, into categories and types, such as the right to a dignified human existence … the right to physical and emotional integrity … the right to a name … the right of an adult to be adopted … and similar "specific" rights that are derived from the general right. In constitutional literature they are called derivative constitutional rights norms … Naturally the scope of application of the derivative rights raises difficult questions of interpretation. As long as they have not been separated by the Knesset from human dignity and stated independently, there is no alternative to interpretational activity that focuses on human dignity and seeks to determine the scope of this right, while attempting to formulate the types of cases included in it.[18]

There is a great deal of vagueness as to the boundaries of the mother-right to human dignity. It appears that these boundaries will never be fully delineated. The vagueness will never disappear; it will only evolve. What in the past was vague might become clear over the course of time. What seemed clear in the past might, years later, turn out to be vague. This is the fate of a legal norm formulated as a principle. This is the case in private law regarding principles like good faith. This holds true in public law, regarding constitutional rights and constitutional values. This applies to the constitutional right of human dignity with full force.

C. *Deriving a daughter-right from the mother-right of human dignity*

What are the guidelines for deriving a daughter-right from the mother-right of human dignity? The answer is that the daughter-right will be recognized under the following two conditions. First, the description of the daughter-right is included in one of the linguistic meanings of the term human dignity. The question of whether this meaning is natural or exceptional, regular or special, or primary or secondary is unimportant. Second, the underlying purpose of the daughter-right must be included in the underlying purposes of the mother-right to human dignity. Here the question of whether this purpose is central or peripheral to the humanity of the person is unimportant.

The many linguistic meanings of human dignity on the one hand, and the many elements or aspects comprising the purpose underlying human

[18] *Adalah* v. *Minister of Interior*, at 486–7 (Barak P).

dignity as a constitutional value on the other hand, naturally lead to the recognition of a considerable number of constitutional daughter-rights. Some of them are located in the core of human dignity, and some in its periphery. They all constitute parts of the whole. One can therefore speak of different categories at different levels of generality of daughter-rights derived from human dignity. A *numerus clausus* of these daughter-rights should not be drawn up.

It should be emphasized that the core of the daughter-right will not always be the same as the core of the mother-right. Situations may arise where the core of the daughter-right is to be found in the penumbra of the mother-right. Of course, everything that can be found at the core of the mother-right regarding a specific daughter-right will also be found at the core of the daughter-right. It seems to me as though, in principle, there could be a daughter-right whose core and penumbra could be found in the penumbra of the mother-right.

D. *Daughter-rights and those same rights as independent rights*

Assume that a constitutional bill of rights includes, alongside the express independent freestanding right to human dignity, a considerable number of other express independent freestanding rights. Many of them may also constitute daughter-rights of human dignity. This raises a question regarding the relationship between the daughter-rights (such as the daughter-rights to reputation or equality) and those same rights as independent rights. Does the nominal equivalence determine equivalence of content?

These constitutional rights are not identical in content. Common to them is the humanity of a person as a human being. What differentiates between them is the part of the independent right that does not express only the humanity of a person. Take freedom of expression, for example. The right to freedom of expression as an independent right is based on a number of rationales.[19] Only those aspects that are linked to the humanity of a person will be recognized as part of the daughter-right to freedom of expression. Thus the daughter-right to freedom of expression will not apply to corporations since human dignity is the dignity of human beings, not corporations. Of course, the independent right to freedom of expression applies to corporations as well.

[19] See for example Frederick Schauer, *Free Speech: A Philosophical Inquiry* (Cambridge University Press, 1982); Lee C. Bollinger, *The Tolerant Society* (Oxford: Clarendon Press, 1986); Eric Barendt, *Freedom of Speech*, 2nd edn (Oxford University Press, 2005).

E. *The relationship between the daughter-rights of human dignity*

(1) Lack of overlap, complementary overlap and conflicting overlap

The constitutional right to human dignity covers the entire array of aspects through which the humanity of a person may be expressed. The various aspects are put into action by the daughter-rights. These daughter-rights reflect, each in its own field, the comprehensive expression of the humanity of a person. At times there is no connection between daughter-rights. Each daughter-right stands alone, without overlapping any other daughter-right. At times there is overlap between a number of daughter-rights. Overlap occurs where a given aspect of human dignity is found within the scope of a number of daughter-rights. This overlap can be complementary or conflicting. What is the law in such situations? In all of these cases, the result is the same: the relationship between one daughter-right and other daughter-rights is irrelevant to the interpretation of the mother- and daughter-right's scope of application. This relationship is predominantly important at the sub-constitutional level, and it is mainly manifested in the rules of proportionality.

(2) Lack of overlap

The humanity of a person is complex. It has elements that reflect a certain aspect of human dignity without overlapping another aspect of the humanity of a person. Thus, for example, both the daughter-right to parenthood and family and the daughter-right to basic human subsistence reflect aspects of human dignity. Most of the time, the different elements of the humanity of a person found in these two constitutional daughter-rights do not overlap each other. Of course, when interpreting the provisions regarding human dignity in the constitutional bill of rights, each one of the two daughter-rights is to be taken into account. They reflect different aspects of the whole. A statute limiting one of these daughter-rights will usually not limit the other daughter-right, nor will it protect it. When examining the proportionality of the limitation of one daughter-right, the other daughter-right will not be relevant.

(3) Complementary overlap

Overlap between different daughter-rights of human dignity is complementary where a certain aspect of that right is entitled to protection by a number of daughter-rights. Thus, for example, the daughter-right to equality and the daughter-right to family overlap each other where the limitation of family life is achieved in a discriminatory way. The same can be said regarding the daughter-right to equality and the daughter-right to education. They overlap where equality in education has been limited. This limitation might limit both the daughter-right to equality and the daughter-right to education. What is the result of this complementary overlap?

The complementary overlap does not affect the boundaries of the overlapping daughter-rights. They each retain their previous boundaries. Complementary overlap is not a constitutional failure to be prevented. It is a welcome normative reality. It reflects the humanity of a person. It is important at the sub-constitutional level, especially regarding the rules of proportionality. The component of proportionality *stricto sensu* (balance) within the rules of proportionality examines the marginal social importance of preventing the limitation of human dignity by a sub-constitutional norm, as compared to the marginal social importance of realizing the worthy purpose of the sub-constitutional norm.[20] In determining the marginal social importance of preventing the limitation of human dignity, consideration is given to the fact that the norm limits a number of constitutional daughter-rights. This limitation of multiple daughter-rights might lead to the conclusion that their integration brings greater force to bear. At times the recognition that a statute limits a number of daughter-rights leads to the conclusion that the statute has limited the core of the constitutional right, not its periphery.

Where a statute limits an aspect of human dignity found in a number of constitutional daughter-rights, the constitutionality of the statute must be examined according to the proportionality of the limitation of each of the daughter-rights. It is not sufficient to examine the limitation of only one of the daughter-rights. Indeed, it may be that the limitation of one daughter-right is proportional, but the limitation of another daughter-right is disproportionate.

(4) Conflicting overlap

(a) Conflicting overlap between two principles Daughter-rights of human dignity are in a state of conflicting overlap when a certain aspect of human dignity that is or should be protected from limitation by one daughter-right of human dignity conflicts with another aspect that is or should be protected from limitation in another daughter-right. One

[20] See Aharon Barak, *Proportionality: Constitutional Rights and their Limitations*, Doron Kalir trans. (Cambridge University Press, 2012) 340.

daughter-right may empower a person, while the other daughter-right may constrain her. Human dignity, as a constitutional value, might appear on both sides of the scales.[21]

Thus, for example, the daughter-right to reputation conflicts with the daughter-right to freedom of expression where the protection of reputation limits freedom of expression. Similarly, the daughter-right to freedom of movement might conflict with the daughter-right to freedom of worship where freedom of movement is limited in order to protect freedom of worship. It may also conflict with the daughter-right to freedom of demonstration and protest, where the right to freedom of movement is limited due to the existence of a demonstration. In addition, the protection of the daughter-right to freedom from religion might limit the daughter-right to freedom of religion. The daughter-right to freedom of expression might conflict with the daughter-right to freedom of religion. The daughter-right to be a parent may collide with the daughter-right not to be a parent. The distinctive characteristic of this conflict is that it occurs within the framework of the constitutional mother-right to human dignity.

How is this conflict resolved? The resolution is not found in one daughter-right's victory over another. Nor is the solution found in redelineation of the boundaries between the conflicting daughter-rights, so that the conflict is avoided. At the constitutional level – that is at the level of the mother-right and the daughter-right – the conflict remains as it was. The constitutional right reflects the multiplicity of aspects that characterize human dignity. The conflict does not indicate an error or a constitutional pathology. We do not expect that one of the daughter-rights – the vanquished one – will (completely or partially) cease to be a daughter-right of human dignity. Conflicting overlap indicates the richness of human dignity, and the constant conflict between its components.[22]

The conflict between the daughter-rights does not alter the scope of the bundle of rights that is the whole of human dignity. Indeed, the solution to the conflict is found at the sub-constitutional level. At this level

[21] See LCA 4740/00 *Amar* v. *Yoseph*, IsrLR 401, 410 (2001) ("[O]ne's reputation and freedom of expression are derived from the same 'mother' right itself, from human dignity. These two twins – one's reputation and freedom of expression – toss about in the bowels of democracy. At times they complete each other. At times they clash with each other. The freedom of expression of one damages the reputation of the other … the liberty of the citizen stands against the right of the citizen, meaning, his liberty to sound out what is in his heart and to hear what others have to express, against his right not to be injured in his dignity and reputation") (Barak P).

[22] HCJ 1435/03 *Jane Doe* v. *The Disciplinary Tribunal of the Civil Service*, IsrSC 58(1) 529, 538 (2003) (Barak P).

it will be determined whether a sub-constitutional (statute or common law) norm that limited one daughter-right in order to protect another daughter-right is constitutional. The standard for determining that constitutionality is the rules of proportionality.[23] The question, therefore, is whether limitation of one daughter-right or the protection of another daughter-right is proportional. In the framework of proportionality, the key question will usually be whether the sub-constitutional norm is balanced correctly between the social importance of preventing additional limitation of one daughter-right and the social importance of additional benefit from protection of the conflicting daughter-right.[24] The solution to the conflict is found in the proper balancing between the limitation of one aspect of human dignity (reflected in one constitutional daughter-right) and the protection of another aspect of human dignity (reflected in another daughter-right). Both constitutional daughter-rights are expressions of the complexity of the mother-right to human dignity.[25]

In executing this balance, the point of view at the outset should be that both conflicting daughter-rights are of constitutional status. They are both derived from the mother-right of human dignity, which is a constitutional mother-right. However, the social importance of each of the daughter-rights at the point of conflict is not identical.[26] On the one hand, one must consider the social importance of protection of the first of the daughter-rights. For this, one must consider the social importance of this daughter-right, the level of protection it has received in the past, and the additional protection that the sub-constitutional norm grants it. One must also consider the extent of the chance that the additional protection will materialize. On the other hand, one must consider the social importance of the limited right, and the social importance of preventing

[23] *Ibid.*, at 537–9. [24] See Barak, *Proportionality*, at 362.

[25] See HCJ 10907/04 *Soloduch* v. *City of Rehovot* (1.8.2010), para. 74 of Justice Proccacia's opinion ("[At] times, the right to freedom of religion on the one hand and the right to freedom from religion on the other, collide head-on in a certain set of circumstances. Such a collision is characteristic of a pluralistic society in which people with different views and beliefs live together and when it occurs a proper balance is needed between these two basic rights, which flow from the very same source – human dignity. From the value of human dignity flows the right of every person to shape his beliefs and lifestyle according to his free will. Both a religious person and a secular person have this right to the same extent. When a religious reality leads to a possible conflict between religious and secular lifestyles, an act of balancing is needed in order to mediate and find the balancing point that will allow people with different lifestyles and beliefs to live together with mutual respect").

[26] See Barak, *Proportionality*, at 359.

its limitation. One must also consider the chances that the limitation will materialize.

What happens when the scales are balanced? I wrote elsewhere[27] that in such a situation – wherein constitutional human rights lie on both sides of the balanced scales – there is no reason not to leave the sub-constitutional norm standing. In such a state of affairs, the function of the court as protector of human rights has been carried out, and the sub-constitutional norm should not be determined to be unconstitutional.

(b) Conflicting overlap between a principle and a rule Most constitutional rights are formulated as principles. Some are formulated as rules.[28] When a right is formulated as a principle, the principle reflects an ideal that can be attained at different levels of intensity without the constitution taking any stand whatsoever on the issue. With a right formulated as a rule, the right itself determines the factual and legal conditions determining how the ideal shall be implemented.

What if there is conflicting overlap between the daughter-right of human dignity (formulated as a principle) and an independent constitutional right formulated as a rule? In this conflict, the constitutional right formulated as a rule prevails. This is due to the application of the interpretational rule according to which, in a conflict between a specific norm and a general norm, the specific norm prevails (*lex specialis derogat legi generali*).

F. The relationship between daughter-rights and independent constitutional rights

In many cases a statute's limitation of human dignity also limits another independent freestanding right enshrined in the constitution. The reason for this is as follows: the constitutional value of human dignity underlies the right to human dignity. It is not limited to that right. The constitutional value of human dignity covers most of the constitutional rights enshrined in the constitution. Each of these independent constitutional rights is intended, inter alia, to realize a certain aspect of human dignity. Thus, for example, freedom of occupation is an expression of the autonomy of individual will. Through freedom of occupation, a person shapes his personality. Similarly, the right to property allows a person to express his personality. This is also the case regarding the right to personal liberty,

[27] *Ibid.*, at 366. [28] For this distinction, see section 1A above.

which realizes the autonomy of individual will. The right to privacy delineates an area in which the individual can be left alone.

How is the daughter-right of human dignity different than these independent rights? The answer is that the daughter-right of human dignity is intended only to fulfill a specific aspect of human dignity. The other constitutional rights, however, are intended to fulfill, alongside the aspect of human dignity, other constitutional values as well. The result is that there is not a full overlap between the constitutional right to human dignity and the other constitutional rights.

There is no full overlap; but a partial overlap does exist. The question therefore arises: what is the relationship between the overlapping daughter-rights and an independent constitutional right? The answer is that, at the constitutional level, the overlap will remain without any attempt being made to alter the scope of the daughter-rights or the overlapping independent freestanding right. The solution regarding this overlap is found at the sub-constitutional level.

I shall begin with complementary overlap. In that situation, human dignity (via a daughter-right) and an aspect of human dignity within an independent right strengthen each other. This is a natural phenomenon. Thus a statute that limits both the right to human dignity (by limiting a daughter-right) as well as the aspect of human dignity in an independent right will need to withstand the test of proportionality regarding the limitation of each of those two rights. This is also the case with a statute that protects these aspects of human dignity and limits another constitutional right. Take for example a statute intended to fulfill the public interest, which discriminates between citizens regarding their freedom of occupation. The constitutionality of such a statute – which may limit human dignity by limiting the daughter-right to equality and the independent mother-right to freedom of occupation – will be examined according to the rules of proportionality. These rules are usually the same for limitations of human dignity (the daughter-right to equality) and limitations of freedom of occupation. Similarly, a statute might limit the daughter-right to equality and the mother-right to property or the mother-right to privacy.

What about conflicting overlap? The conflict can be between a daughter-right of human dignity that complements a certain aspect of an independent right and the other aspects of that independent right. Thus, for example, the autonomy of individual will – which underlies both the daughter-right of human dignity and the aspect of human dignity in the right to property – might conflict with the other values that underlie the rights to property. This is a conflict between two constitutional mother-rights: the right to human dignity and the right to property. The solution to this conflict will not be at the constitutional level. It will be determined at the sub-constitutional level by the rules of proportionality.

10

The area covered by the right to human dignity

1. The area covered and the overlap problem

As a result of the broad scope of the constitutional value of human dignity in most legal systems, excluding Germany, the constitutional right to human dignity also has a broad scope. This situation raises many questions. I shall discuss four methodological questions. The first is the question of whether or not there is an area of human existence that is exclusively (or uniquely) covered by the constitutional right to human dignity. Second, what is the role of the constitutional right to human dignity in areas where there is complementary overlap between the right to human dignity and the other constitutional rights? Third, what is the relationship between the constitutional right to human dignity and the constitutional right to personal liberty? Fourth, should the right to human dignity be considered a "residual right"?

2. The area covered exclusively by the right to human dignity in a comprehensive bill of rights

The answer to the question whether human dignity has an exclusive zone of application – an exclusive normative territory – is to be found in the structure of the constitutional bill of rights.[1] The more extensive the bill of rights, and rich in constitutional rights that have human dignity as a purpose, so the exclusive zone – the exclusive normative territory – of human

[1] See, Charles L. Black, *Structure and Relationship in Constitutional Law* (Baton Rouge: Louisiana State University Press, 1969); Akhil Reed Amar, 'Intratextualism' (1999) 112 *Harvard Law Review* 747; Ashok Desai, 'Constitutional Amendments and the "Basic Structure" Doctrine', in Venkat Lyer (ed.), *Democracy, Human Rights and the Rule of Law: Essays in Honour of Nani Palkhivala* (New Delhi: Butterworths India, 2000) 90; Michael Dorf, 'Interpretive Holism and the Structural Method, or How Charles Black Might Have Thought about Campaign Finance Reform and Congressional Timidity' (2003) 92 *Georgetown Law Journal* 833; Laurence Tribe, *The Invisible Constitution* (New York: Oxford University Press, 2008).

dignity as a constitutional right narrows. Take for example the Bill of Rights in the Constitution of South Africa.[2] This bill of rights includes most of the civil and social constitutional rights recognized in comparative law. As a result, most of the situations that fall within the right to human dignity also fall within one of the other constitutional rights. Thus, for example, one of the purposes underlying the right to freedom of expression in the Constitution of South Africa is dignity.[3] This purpose also underlies the constitutional right to human dignity. The result is that this "zone" of human dignity is no longer exclusive to the constitutional right of human dignity; it overlaps with the constitutional right to freedom of expression. An additional example is the constitutional right to equality. Underlying this right is an important component of human dignity.[4] To the extent that discrimination limits that component, that discrimination will be prohibited both by the constitutional right to equality and by the constitutional right to human dignity. The need to refer exclusively to the right to human dignity in this area is thus avoided.

If so, what is the exclusive zone of the constitutional right to human dignity in the Constitution of South Africa? The answer is that the exclusive zone includes only those areas that are part of the constitutional right of human dignity and do not fall within other constitutional rights. Thus, for example, protection of a person's reputation[5] and his right to family life[6] are not recognized in the Constitution of South Africa as independent freestanding constitutional rights. This zone in the Constitution of South Africa therefore remains the exclusive domain of the constitutional right of human dignity.

[2] Another example is the Constitution of Colombia, as interpreted by its Constitutional Court; see Erin Daly, *Dignity Rights: Courts, Constitutions and the Worth of the Human Person* (Philadelphia: University of Pennsylvania Press, 2012) 26, 40.

[3] See *Khumalo* v. *Holomisa* 2002 (5) SA 401 (CC), paras. 21, 25; Dario Milo, Glenn Penfold and Anthony Stein, 'Freedom of Expression', in Stuart Woolman, Michael Bishop and Jason Brickhill (eds.), *Constitutional Law of South Africa*, 2nd edn, Revision Series 4 (Cape Town: Juta, 2012) chapter 42, p. 25.

[4] See *Ferreira* v. *Levin NO*, 1996 (1) SA 984 (CC), para. 145; *National Coalition for Gay and Lesbian Equality* v. *Minister of Justice* 1999 (1) SA 6 (CC), para. 125; Stuart Woolman, 'Dignity', in Stuart Woolman, Michael Bishop and Jason Brickhill (eds.), *Constitutional Law of South Africa*, 2nd edn, Revision Series 4 (Cape Town: Juta, 2012) chapter 36, p. 25; Laurie Ackermann, *Human Dignity: Lodestar for Equality in South Africa* (Cape Town: Juta, 2012) 86, 181.

[5] See *Khumalo* v. *Holomisa*, at paras. 23–27. See also Woolman, 'Dignity', at 55.

[6] See *Dawood* v. *Minister of Home Affairs*, 2000 (3) SA 936 (CC), para. 36; *Booysen* v. *Minister of Home Affairs and Another*, 2001 (4) SA 485 (CC), para. 10; *Islamic Unity Convention* v. *Independent Broadcasting Authority*, 2002 (4) SA 294 (CC), para. 10.

Social developments may cause the exclusive zone of human dignity in a comprehensive bill of rights to expand or contract as time passes. According to the rules of purposive interpretation, scientific developments might justify altering our understanding of the scope of the right to human dignity. Thus, for example, scientific development in the areas of genetic engineering, cloning and stem cell research are at the center of bioethics. Certain aspects of this normative zone might be influenced by the right to human dignity, especially if this right is interpreted as protecting not only the dignity of the individual person, but also the dignity of the human race.[7] On the other hand, there may be no other provision in the constitution regarding these issues.

According to this interpretational approach, there can theoretically be a situation in which the bill of rights is so comprehensive that its spectrum of rights would cover all conduct that limits human dignity, even without the right to human dignity. That might be the result in a bill of rights where there is a "catch-all provision" alongside the right to human dignity. This provision determines that all conduct limiting the free will and autonomy of the individual that is not covered by the other particular constitutional rights falls within the catch-all right. In principle, in this sort of situation the right to human dignity does not have an exclusive zone, as any conduct that limits human dignity and is not included in the particular rights will fall within the "catch-all right."

It appears that this may be the situation regarding the constitutional Bill of Rights in the German Constitution. Thus, for example, this constitution recognizes the right to develop one's personality.[8] This right has been interpreted as a catch-all right (*Auffanggrundrecht*). Every governmental act that limits the free will of the individual and does not fall within one of the particular constitutional rights recognized in the

[7] On human dignity and bioethics see: Deryck Beyleveld and Roger Brownsword, 'Human Dignity, Human Rights, and Human Genetics' (1998) 61 *Modern Law Review* 661; Leon R. Kass, 'Defending Human Dignity', in President's Council on Bioethics, *Human Dignity and Bioethics* (Washington DC: President's Council on Bioethics, 2008) 297; Roger Brownsword, *Rights, Regulation and the Technological Revolution* (Oxford University Press, 2008); Charles Foster, *Choosing Life, Choosing Death: The Tyranny of Autonomy in Medical Ethics and Law* (Oxford: Hart Publishing, 2009); Charles Foster, *Human Dignity in Bioethics and Law* (Oxford: Hart Publishing, 2011). See also Daly, *Dignity Rights*, at 119.

[8] See Art. 2(1) of the German Basic Law. On the interpretation of this provision, see Matthias Mahlmann, *Elemente einer ethischen Grundrechtstheorie* (Berlin: Nomos, 2008) 337. See also Werner Heun, *The Constitution of Germany: A Contextual Analysis* (Oxford University Press, 2011) 204.

German Constitution is considered to limit the right to develop one's personality.[9] It thus appears that there remains a narrow zone in the German Constitution for the exclusive application of the right to human dignity.[10] Its "normative territory" is largely non-exclusive. Indeed, the right to human dignity in the German Constitution is seen as predominantly protecting the other constitutional rights from the type of limitation that entails limitation of human dignity. Thus, human dignity usually joins one of the other rights recognized in the constitution, and prevents its limitation absolutely: that is, the prevention of limitation is not subject to proportionality[11] when the limitation of that right turns the injured party into a mere means for realizing a public interest ("the object formula").

In all of those cases, the existence of a separate constitutional right to human dignity is important for three reasons: first, we cannot know the future. Developments might occur that do not fall under the catch-all right but do fall under the right to human dignity. Second, even lacking a zone exclusive to the constitutional right to human dignity, the fact that government action limits not only a specific constitutional right but also the right to human dignity has legal importance. The existence of the constitutional right to human dignity grants human dignity special bearing. It is not solely a constitutional value, but also a freestanding constitutional right. For example, take legislation that limits a certain right in order to protect human dignity. If human dignity is solely a constitutional value, the protection of human dignity falls within the framework of the state's authority to protect the common good; however, if human dignity is a constitutional right, it is protected through the constitutional duty of the state – a duty that is not merely authority – to protect the positive constitutional right. The difference between authority and duty might be

[9] Including limitations such as feeding pigeons in the town square (see BVerfGE 54, 143 (1980)) or prohibition of riding in certain forests (see BVerfGE 80, 137 (1989)), which influence the development of personality only slightly.

[10] An example of this is the right to minimum human subsistence derived from human dignity, together with the constitutional provision according to which Germany is a social state (*Sozialer Bundesstaat*); see Hartz IV, BVerfGE 125, 175 (2010): "The direct constitutional benefit claim to a guarantee of a subsistence minimum that is in line with human dignity only covers those means which are vital to maintain an existence that is in line with human dignity. It guarantees the whole subsistence minimum by a uniform fundamental right guarantee which encompasses both the physical existence of the individual, that is food, clothing, household goods, housing, heating, hygiene, and health … and ensuring the possibility to maintain inter-human relationships and a minimum of participation in social, cultural and political life, given that humans as persons of necessity exist in social relationships."

[11] See Horst Dreier, *GG Grundgesetz Kommentar* (Tübingen: Mohr Siebeck, 2006) 162.

expressed within the rules of proportionality. Third, in a number of constitutions each constitutional right is characterized by its own limitations clause. The elements of these limitations clauses are derived from, and adapted to, the various rights. A situation could arise in which a limitations clause belonging to a particular right sets conditions that are less severe, from the standpoint of a statute limiting that right, than the conditions in the limitations clause on the right to human dignity. In such a situation, even if the statute limiting that right withstands its limitations, it might fail because it does not withstand the limitations clause on the right to human dignity.

3. The constitutional right to human dignity and the complementary overlap with independent constitutional rights in a partial bill of rights

In contrast to the bounty of constitutional rights in some constitutions, the bill of rights in others is only partial; the reasons for this are mainly historical. Let us now assume that among the rights recognized in a partial bill of rights is the constitutional right to human dignity. Let us further assume that this right is not absolute, but merely of a relative character that is subject to the rules of proportionality. In this situation the constitutional right to human dignity will apply to a broad range of areas. Its exclusive normative territory is expansive, because it fully or partially covers areas that are covered in other constitutions by independent rights that do not appear in the partial constitution. In such a state of affairs, the right to human dignity has a central role in the bill of rights.

This is the normative reality in Israel. For historical reasons, the constitutional Bill of Rights enshrined in Basic Law: Human Dignity and Liberty and in Basic Law: Freedom of Occupation is slim.[12] The Bill of Rights expressly includes only a small number of rights.[13] Many rights recognized in comparative law did not receive constitutional status as an independent right. These include, inter alia, the rights to: equality,

[12] On this history, see Amnon Rubinstein, 'The Story of the Basic Laws' (2012) 13 *Law and Business* 79 (Heb.). See also Orit Kamir, *Israeli Honor and Dignity: Social Norms, Gender Politics and the Law*, 2nd edition (Jerusalem: Carmel, 2004) 126 (Heb.); Amnon Rubenstien, 'The Israeli Law of Return – its Justification and Pitfalls', Lecture Given at the Israeli Democracy Institute (2013).

[13] See Chapter 15, section 1E.

reputation, freedom of expression, freedom of conscience and religion, education, family (including marriage and parenthood), labor rights, health care, freedom of movement within the state and due process. The Supreme Court of Israel found that: first, the rights that were not included in the express Bill of Rights could not be recognized as independent rights through interpretation; second, there is no negative implication against recognizing the dignitary aspects of these rights within the framework of the mother-right to human dignity through one or more of its daughter-rights.[14] Of course, human dignity and its daughter-rights, being only one of the constitutional rights in the bill of rights, cannot fill the entire void left by a partial bill of rights.

4. Architectural difficulty: the right to human dignity and the right to personal liberty

A. Presenting the problem

Purposive constitutional interpretation with a spacious view grants the constitutional right to human dignity a broad scope. This situation raises the question of what is the relationship between the right to human dignity and the right to personal liberty.[15] This question has arisen in a number of constitutions. The answer to it is important, as it touches on a structural aspect of a constitutional bill of rights, and the architectural structure's influence on the scope of the right to human dignity. I shall discuss the answer given to this question in South African, Canadian and Israeli constitutional law.

[14] See Chapter 15, section 1E.

[15] For this question in American and German constitutional law, see Edward J. Eberle, *Dignity and Liberty: Constitutional Visions in Germany and the United States* (Santa Barbara: Praeger, 2002). Professor Whitman wrote that continental constitutional law is based on human dignity, whereas American constitutional law is based on liberty. See James Q. Whitman, 'The Two Western Cultures of Privacy: Dignity Versus Liberty' (2004) 113 *Yale Law Journal* 1151; James Q. Whitman, '"Human Dignity" in Europe and the United States: the Social Foundations', in Georg Nolte (ed.), *European and US Constitutionalism* (Cambridge University Press 2005) 108. See also Guy E. Carmi, 'Dignity versus Liberty: The Two Western Cultures of Free Speech' (2008) 26 *Boston University International Law Journal* 277; Daniel McGirr, 'Liberty in an American and German Constitutional Context Through the Lens of Isaiah Berlin and Lord Acton' (Forthcoming, available on SSRN).

B. *South Africa*

Section 12(1) of the Constitution of South Africa, which is part of the Bill of Rights, states:

> 12. Freedom and Security of the Person:
>
> (1) Everyone has the right to freedom and security of the person, which includes the right-
> (a) not to be deprived of freedom arbitrarily or without just cause;
> (b) not to be detained without trial;
> (c) to be free from all forms of violence from either public or private sources;
> (d) not to be tortured in any way; and
> (e) not to be treated or punished in a cruel, inhuman or degrading way.

Interpretation of this provision was discussed in *Ferreira*.[16] That case discussed the constitutionality of a section in the South African Companies Act that required persons being examined in winding-up proceedings to answer incriminating questions. The answers to the questions could be used against the examinee in future criminal proceedings. It was argued that the provision in the Companies Act contradicts the right to due process; however, the constitutional due process provisions would not apply as the examinees did not have the status of accused. The question then arose: does the Act limit the constitutional right to freedom and security of the person?

Opinions in the Constitutional Court of South Africa were split: the dissenting Justice Ackermann held that the constitutional provision on freedom applies to the applicants. According to his view, the right to freedom is an independent right that is separate from the right to personal security. The right to freedom is a general right regarding a person's right to develop his personality. A person's right to freedom is a right to an area in which:

> a person ... is or should be left to do or be what he is able to do or be, without interference by other persons.[17]

[16] *Ferreira* v. *Levin NO*. See also Michael Bishop and Stuart Woolman, 'Freedom and Security of the Person', in Stuart Woolman, Michael Bishop and Jason Brickhill (eds.), *Constitutional Law of South Africa*, 2nd edn, Revision Series 4 (Cape Town: Juta, 2012) chapter 40.

[17] *Ferreira* v. *Levin NO*, at para. 52.

According to Ackermann, the right to freedom means:

> [T]he right of individuals not to have "obstacles to possible choices and activities" placed in their way by … the State.[18]

Justice Ackermann noted that this wide area overlaps with many of the other individual rights enshrined in the Bill of Rights. His approach, therefore, is that the individual freedom rights should be seen as "residual freedom rights."[19] In the opinion of Justice Ackermann, the Companies Act limited the residual right to freedom.

The majority concurred with the result reached by Justice Ackermann. In their opinion, the provision of the Companies Act limited the constitutional right against self-incrimination. However, these Justices did not agree with Justice Ackermann's interpretation of the section regarding the right to freedom. In the opinion of President Chaskalson, the main purpose of the right to freedom is to protect the individual from physical acts by the state. The provision is not restricted only to that, but it should not be interpreted as a general provision protecting any kind of liberty.

C. *Canada*

The Canadian Charter includes the following provision:

> 7. Life, Liberty and Security of Person
> Everyone has the right to life, liberty and security of the person and the right not to be deprived thereof except in accordance with the principles of fundamental justice.[20]

The Supreme Court of Canada has dealt with the interpretation of the word "liberty" in this provision.[21] The accepted approach is that underlying this provision is liberty from physical restrictions. It was held, however, that liberty is not confined merely to physical restrictions. In *Blencoe*[22] a complaint was submitted against the respondent for sexual harassment. The British Columbia Human Rights Commission delayed its handling of the complaint for a long period of time, causing the respondent various kinds of damages. He argued that this violated his right to liberty. The Supreme

[18] *Ibid.*, at para. 54. [19] *Ibid.*, at para. 57.

[20] Art. 7 of the Canadian Charter of Rights and Freedoms. On the interpretation of this provision, see Peter W. Hogg, *Constitutional Law of Canada*, 5th edn (Toronto: Thomson Carswell, 2007), vol. II, 365; Tanya Lee, 'Section 7 of the Charter: an Overview' (1985) 43 *University of Toronto Faculty Law Review* 1.

[21] See Hogg, *Constitutional Law of Canada*, at 371.

[22] *Blencoe* v. *British Columbia (Human Rights Commission)*, [2000] 2 SCR 307.

Court was split on the issue. The majority opinion was that the right to liberty is not confined to liberty from physical restraint. It also applies where a person is prevented from making fundamental personal choices.[23] It was held that the delay in handling the complaint against the respondent did not violate his ability to make fundamental personal choices. The minority opinion refused to take a position regarding the scope of the right to liberty. It would have ordered the expedition of the complaint at the administrative level. In additional decisions it was emphasized that the right to liberty is found in the chapter on "legal rights," and is thus confined mainly to criminal proceedings.[24] It therefore does not cover economic[25] or political[26] liberty.

D. *Israel*

Article 5 of Basic Law: Human Dignity and Liberty states:

> 5. Personal Liberty
> There shall be no deprivation or restriction of the liberty of a person by imprisonment, arrest, extradition or otherwise.

What is the scope of the right to personal liberty? Is there a difference between the scope of the right to human dignity and that of the right to personal liberty, or is everything found in one of the rights also found in the other? If the latter is correct, what justification is there for two different rights with identical content? Does that not justify a narrow interpretation of the constitutional right to human dignity?

In order to answer these questions, we must examine the scope of the right to personal liberty. What is included in it? What purpose is it intended to fulfill? Does it grant constitutional status to a general right to personal liberty, or is it restricted to certain aspects of liberty only? And if it is so restricted, what aspects of liberty is it restricted to? The right to personal liberty has not enjoyed a thorough examination in the case law. It has not undergone a process similar to that which the right to human dignity underwent.[27] Nonetheless, there are many *obiter dicta* regarding

[23] See *ibid.*, at paras. 49, 54.

[24] Re ss. 193 and 195.1 of Criminal Code (Prostitution Reference) [1990] 1 SCR 1123, 1173 ("[T]he restrictions on liberty and security of the person that s. 7 is concerned with are those that occur as a result of an individual interaction with the justice system, and its administration") (Lamer J).

[25] See Hogg, *Constitutional Law of Canada*, at 374.

[26] See *ibid.*, at 375.

[27] See Chapter 15, section 1E.

the scope of the right.[28] The question before us is whether these *obiter dicta* can provide a basis for the scope of the right to personal liberty.

The first part of Article 5 of Basic Law: Human Dignity and Liberty focuses on three situations in which the personal liberty of an individual is limited: imprisonment, arrest and extradition. Interpretation of each of these terms raises difficult interpretational questions that are beyond the scope of this volume. Were Article 5 to cover only these situations, it would be seen as a particular constitutional right with a restricted scope regarding the physical limitation of personal liberty stemming from imprisonment, arrest or extradition. No difficulty would arise even if the three situations that form that right were only intended to protect the humanity of a person. If that were the case, I would say that personal liberty is a particular right, and human dignity is a general right.

In the second part of Article 5 of Basic Law: Human Dignity and Liberty, the term "otherwise" is the source of the difficulty regarding the right to personal liberty. What does that provision cover? Does it provide a general right to liberty, or is it confined to certain types of limitation of liberty? Three different interpretational answers can be provided for this question.

According to the first interpretation, "otherwise" means any restriction that limits the physical liberty of a person. According to this interpretational approach, the provision in Article 5 is to be interpreted such that "otherwise" will apply to forms of limitation that share features common to the three forms listed at the beginning of the Article (*ejusdem generis*). It appears that the common feature is the limitation of a person's physical liberty. Thus, included in "otherwise" are the taking or limitation of a person's liberty through detention (which does not amount to arrest) and restriction of the freedom of movement (in ways other than

[28] Thus, for example, it has been held that a worker's right to choose an employer is part of the right to liberty (see HCJ 8111/96 *New Federation of Workers* v. *Israel Aerospace Industries Ltd.*, IsrSC 58(6) 481 (2004) (Heb.)). The same is so regarding the protection of a person's reputation (LCA 10520/03 *Ben Gvir* v. *Dankner* (12.11.2006) (Heb.)) and the protection of their right to create family life (*Adalah* v. *Minister of Interior*, at 476; HCJ 466/07 *MK Zahava Galon* v. *The Attorney General*, para. 26 of Deputy President Rivlin's opinion (11.1.2012) (Heb.)). It has further been held that the refusal to grant a divorce limits a woman's liberty (HCJ 2123/08 *John Doe* v. *Jane Doe* (6.7.2008) (Heb.)). It has further been held that the freedom of religion and conscience (LPPA 4201/09 *Raik* v. *Prison Services* (24.3.2010) (Heb.)) and the freedom of expression (CA 7541/10 *John Doe* v. *Dayan-Orbach*, para. 76 of Deputy President Rivlin's opinion (8.2.2012) (Heb.)) are derived from both liberty and human dignity.

imprisonment). In contrast, taking or restricting liberty "otherwise" will not include denying the freedom of marriage, the right to due process, the right to vote and run for office or the right to reputation.

The second interpretation contradicts the first interpretation head-on. According to this second interpretation, "otherwise" means any way that removes or limits personal liberty. According to this interpretation, the provision of Article 5 of Basic Law: Human Dignity and Liberty protects the general right to personal liberty. It thus grants protection to a person's ability to fulfill his individual will and his autonomy. It is a person's ability to write his life story. Thus, a person's personal liberty is limited not only when his physical liberty is limited, but also in any case of limitation of free will or autonomy. For example, according to this interpretation, the denial of the freedom to marry and the freedom of parenthood, limitation of the right to a fair trial, denial of the right to vote and run for office, and denial of protection of reputation all constitute limitation of personal liberty.

The third interpretation is found between these two extremes. According to it, the regular and typical case is one found within the first interpretation, that is limitations of a person's physical liberty. However, it is possible to add situations that do not entail limitation of physical liberty, but are related to it, such as the right of a defendant to a fair trial.

It appears to me that the two extreme interpretations should be rejected. Personal liberty is not only a person's physical freedom. It is true that the impression one receives from the language is that "otherwise" is any type of physical limitation other than imprisonment, arrest and extradition, which are expressly stated in Article 5 of Basic Law: Human Dignity and Liberty.[29] However, that impression is based on a linguistic reading of the article, rather than a rule of purposive interpretation. Nonetheless, personal liberty is not any limitation of free will and the autonomous exercise of will. Were we to interpret Article 5 of Basic Law: Human Dignity and Liberty in this way, we would turn the right to personal liberty into a general right with a scope similar to that of human dignity. This result would impair the structure of Basic Law: Human Dignity and Liberty. It does not comport with the architecture of the Basic Law. There is no justification for recognizing two general rights with scopes that nearly fully overlap complementarily.

[29] This is the interpretational rule known as *ejusdem generis*. On this rule see Antonin Scalia and Bryan A. Garner, *Reading Law: The Interpretation of Legal Texts* (St. Paul: West Publishing, 2012) 199; Francis Bennion, *Statutory Interpretation*, 3rd edn (London: LexisNexis Butterworths, 1997) 954.

It seems as though the term "otherwise" should be interpreted as any limitation entailing physical restriction of a person's liberty, or other similar restriction (whether physical or otherwise). Thus the right to personal liberty is formulated as a particular right that exists alongside the right to human dignity, which is a general right.

It can of course be argued that the constitutional architecture of Basic Law: Human Dignity and Liberty can be preserved if personal liberty is turned into a general constitutional right and human dignity is turned into a particular right that will apply, for example, only in cases of humiliation and degradation or similar cases. In my opinion, this solution is not a good one, for four reasons. First, that would require a comprehensive revamping of the understanding of human dignity and all of its daughter-rights in Israel. I see no interpretational justification for such a revolution. Second, in legal systems in which human dignity and liberty are constitutional rights, such as in South Africa, the general right is the right to human dignity, not the right to liberty. Third, from the standpoint of the structure of the constitutional rights, it is natural to interpret the term "human dignity" such that it is granted application as a general right. In contrast, the structure of the right to personal liberty, which focuses upon taking a person's liberty by imprisonment, arrest or extradition, and which adds "otherwise" almost as an afterthought, makes it difficult to justify an interpretational view by which the character of a general right can be extracted from the term "otherwise." Fourth, this overlap between human dignity and liberty might lead to a narrowing of the protection of human rights, as the right to human dignity is both a positive and a negative right. In contrast, the right to personal liberty seems to be a negative right only.

5. Human dignity is not a "residual right"

Some aspects of the constitutional value of human dignity are protected by various independent constitutional rights, both in a full constitutional bill of rights and in a partial one. Should it not be said that when there is complementary overlap the particular independent freestanding constitutional right will be applied and not the general right to human dignity, regardless of whether there is a full or partial bill of rights? Such an approach can be found in the decisions of the Constitutional Court of South Africa.[30]

[30] See Woolman, 'Dignity', at 24. See also Chapter 14, section 1F(2).

This approach is problematic. The better view is that in any case of complementary overlap between the constitutional right to human dignity and other constitutional rights, each of them must be examined separately. The constitutional right to human dignity should not be seen as a residual right; that would be at odds with the centrality of the value and the right to human dignity in the constitution. It is inappropriate from a methodological standpoint. The particular right does not detract from the general right to human dignity. They both apply to the limiting conduct, each from its own viewpoint. The normative solution to the complementary overlap is not in constitutional law, but rather in sub-constitutional law. The statute limiting a constitutional right in an area of complementary overlap will be constitutional only if it is proportional. This proportionality is examined separately for each of the constitutional rights. This is certainly the case if the proportionality requirements are different for each constitutional right; however, even when there is one general limitations clause applying to all the constitutional rights, the limitation of each of the constitutional rights should be examined separately. This is for two reasons. First, a public interest may require a different level of importance to justify limiting the right to human dignity than to justify limiting the particular independent right. Second, the importance of preventing the limitation of the particular right might be different than the importance of preventing the limitation of the independent right to human dignity.

PART IV

Human dignity in comparative law

11

Human dignity in American constitutional law

1. A constitutional right to human dignity is not recognized in the federal constitution

A. *The lack of a special express provision on human dignity in the federal constitution*

The Constitution of the United States and the Bill of Rights within it were drafted at the end of the eighteenth century. It is therefore no wonder that no express, special provision regarding human dignity was included in it. Although the concept of human dignity was discussed in the religious and philosophical literature of that period, it did not make its way into the law at that time. The Declaration of the Rights of Man and of the Citizen (1789), a product of the French revolution, is the same age as the US Constitution, and mentions only the honor (*dignités*) of man, and not the richer sense of dignity which we are discussing. The appearance of human dignity in constitutions began in earnest only after the Second World War.[1] That term was not formally expressed in the US Constitution.

B. *Human dignity is not part of a framework right in the federal constitution*

The US Constitution recognizes a number of constitutional rights designed as framework rights or mother-rights.[2] This is the case regarding the Fifth Amendment to the Constitution, which determines:

> No person shall be … deprived of life, liberty or property, without due process of law.[3]

[1] See Chapter 4, section 2A. [2] See Chapter 9, section 1A.
[3] US Constitution, amend. V (1791).

The Fourteenth Amendment to the Constitution determines:

> Nor shall any state deprive any person of life, liberty, or property, without due process of law nor deny to any person within its jurisdiction the equal protection of the laws.[4]

Should it not be said that the framework (or mother-) rights to life and liberty also include a derivative (or daughter-) right to human dignity at a lower level of generality? Can the constitutional right to human dignity not be found in the constitutional right to due process of law, which is interpreted as including not only procedural aspects of due process, but also the substantive aspects? The US Supreme Court decided that the constitutional right to liberty includes the constitutional right to privacy.[5] Why should the constitutional right to liberty not include the constitutional right to human dignity as well? In the case of *Francis Coralie Mullin* v. *Delhi* (1981)[6] the Supreme Court of India found that the right to life[7] includes the right to human dignity. Is the option of deriving human dignity from the right to life not at the disposal of the US Supreme Court?

The answer to these questions is that, theoretically, those options are open to American law. Similar proposals have also been discussed (both positively and negatively) in the legal literature;[8] however, they have not been adopted by the Supreme Court.[9] Even Justices Brennan[10] and

[4] US Constitution, amend. XIV (1868).

[5] See *Roe* v. *Wade*, 410 US 113 (1973). See also the Judgment of Justice Harlen in *Griswold* v. *Connecticut*, 381 US 479 (1965).

[6] *Francis Coralie Mullin* v. *Delhi*, AIR 1981 SC 746.

[7] Art. 21 of the Constitution of India determines: "No person shall be deprived of his life or personal liberty except according to procedure established by law."

[8] See William A. Parent, 'Constitutional Values and Human Dignity', in Michael J. Meyer and William A. Parent (eds.), *The Constitution of Rights: Human Dignity and American Values* (Ithaca, NY: Cornell University Press, 1992) 49; Edward J. Eberle, *Dignity and Liberty: Constitutional Visions in Germany and the United States* (Santa Barbara: Praeger, 2002) 47; Neomi Rao, 'On the Use and Abuse of Dignity in Constitutional Law' (2008) 14 *Columbia Journal of European Law* 201, 245.

[9] See Erin Daly, 'Constitutional Dignity: Lessons from Home and Abroad', Widener Law School Legal Studies Research Paper 08-07 (2007); Erin Daly, 'Human Dignity in the Roberts Court: A Story of Inchoate Institutions, Autonomous Individuals, and the Reluctant Recognition of a Right' (2011) 37 *Ohio Northern University Law Review* 381.

[10] See Jeremy Rabkin, 'What We Can Learn about Human Dignity from International Law' (2003) 27 *Harvard Journal of Law and Public Policy* 145, 156. See also Michael J. Meyer, 'The Constitution of Rights: Human Dignity and American Values – Introduction', in Michael J. Meyer and William A. Parent (eds.), *The Constitution of Rights: Human Dignity and American Values* (Ithaca, NY: Cornell University Press, 1992) 6; Parent, 'Constitutional Values and Human Dignity', at 69. Both of these authors refer to Hamilton. In defending the constitution, Hamilton pointed out that a constitution is "the safest course for your

Kennedy,[11] whose decisions emphasize the value of human dignity, did not hold that the value of human dignity also constitutes a constitutional right derived from one of the constitutional rights expressly enshrined in the federal Bill of Rights.

This can be explained in a number of ways. First, the rules of constitutional interpretation accepted in the US Supreme Court make it difficult to derive a constitutional daughter-right from one of the express rights in the constitution. Constitutional interpretation based on the original public understanding at the time the constitution was framed (originalism) prevents recognition of human dignity as a constitutional daughter-right, as at the time the constitution was framed, human dignity was not part of legal discourse and was not considered a value worthy of protection. The concept of dignity at that time dealt with the honor of institutions or officials. Constitutional interpretation based on the intent of the founding fathers also makes it difficult to recognize a constitutional right to human dignity. Even Justice Brennan, who advocates for interpretation of the constitution as a living document,[12] did not suggest that human dignity ought to be recognized as a constitutional right. It is true that the constitutional right to privacy, which was not recognized at the time of framing, has been recognized. However, considering the stark differences of opinion in the Supreme Court regarding privacy and women's right to abort, it is doubtful that the Court will recognize a constitutional right to human dignity in a similar manner.

Second, all the importance the American jurisprudence sees in human dignity notwithstanding, that importance is with respect to the constitutional value of human dignity, and is not strong enough to lead to recognition of a constitutional right as well.

Third, there is concern that recognition of a derived constitutional right to human dignity as part of an express constitutional right in the federal constitution will upset the constitutional balance that the Bill of Rights is built upon, and will weaken the protection of human rights.[13] Thus, for example, it has been argued that the American Bill of Rights is based upon the individual's liberty vis-à-vis the government, and not upon dignity.[14] This concern was raised regarding recognition of the constitutional value

liberty, your dignity, and your happiness" – Alexander Hamilton, *The Federalist Papers* (New York: The Modern Library, 1937) No. 84, 6.

11 See section 3B(3) below.

12 See Chapter 5, section 4C(1).

13 See Rao, 'On the Use and Abuse of Dignity in Constitutional Law'.

14 See Marc C. McAllister, 'Human Dignity and Individual Liberty in Germany and the United States as Examined through Each Country's Leading Abortion Cases' (2004) 11 *Tulsa Journal of Comparative & International Law* 491.

of human dignity.[15] Such concern would of course intensify if human dignity were to be recognized not only as a constitutional value but as a constitutional daughter-right as well.

Fourth, some think that human dignity is foreign to the culture of American society, and certainly to the accepted understanding of law in the United States.[16] As we shall see, although human dignity is recognized as a social value, it has not been sufficiently developed in American law and has not reached the stage at which it can be recognized as a constitutional right.[17] It is usually recognized as a constitutional value sporadically, by one judge or another, but not by the Court as a whole. It appears mainly in dissenting opinions. The content and scope of the social and constitutional value of human dignity have not been sufficiently clarified, and it has not reached the level of importance that would allow it to be recognized as a constitutional right derived from one of the existing constitutional rights.[18]

[15] See Rao, 'On the Use and Abuse of Dignity in Constitutional Law'; Neomi Rao, 'Three Concepts of Dignity in Constitutional Law' (2011) 86 *Notre Dame Law Review* 183.

[16] See James Q. Whitman, 'Enforcing Civility and Respect: Three Societies' (2000) 109 *Yale Law Journal* 1279; James Q. Whitman, 'On Nazi "Honour" and the New European "Dignity"', in Christian Joerges and Navraj S. Ghaleigh (eds.), *Darker Legacies of Law in Europe: The Shadow of National Socialism* (Oxford: Hart Publishing, 2003), 243; Gabrielle S. Friedman and James Q. Whitman, 'The European Transformation of Harassment Law: Discrimination versus Dignity' (2003) 9 *Columbia Journal of European Law* 241; James Q. Whitman, 'The Two Western Cultures of Privacy: Dignity Versus Liberty' (2004) 113 *Yale Law Journal* 1151; Giovanni Bognetti, 'The Concept of Human Dignity in European and US Constitutionalism', in George Nolte (ed.), *European and US Constitutionalism* (Cambridge University Press, 2005) 85; James Q. Whitman '"Human Dignity" in Europe and the United States: the Social Foundations', in George Nolte (ed.), *European and US Constitutionalism* (Cambridge University Press, 2005) 108.

[17] See Jordan J. Paust, 'Human Dignity as a Constitutional Right: A Jurisprudentially Based Inquiry into Criteria and Content' (1984) 27 *Howard Law Journal* 145, 150; Gerald Neuman, 'Human Dignity in United States Constitutional Law', in Dieter Simon and Manfred Weiss (eds.), *Zur Autonomie des Individuums: Liber Amicorum Spiros Simitis* (Baden-Baden: Nomos, 2000), 249; Vicki C. Jackson, 'Constitutional Dialogue and Human Dignity: States and Transnational Constitutional Discourse' (2004) 65 *Montana Law Review* 15, 17; Rao, 'On the Use and Abuse of Dignity in Constitutional Law', at 239; Johanna Kalb, 'Litigating Dignity: A Human Rights Framework' (2011) 74 *Albany Law Review* 1725.

[18] See Eberle, *Dignity and Liberty*, at 47.

C. *Human dignity and* Griswold *v.* Connecticut

Griswold[19] dealt with the constitutionality of a Connecticut statute that prohibited the use of any drug or article to prevent conception. The majority held that that law was unconstitutional. One of the Justices in the majority was Justice Douglas. According to his approach, the various rights in the American Bill of Rights have penumbras derived from the rights themselves, which grant them life and substance. These penumbras contain peripheral rights, without which the rights would be less protected. One of those peripheral rights found in the penumbras of the expressly entrenched rights is the right to privacy. Justice Douglas wrote:

> specific guarantees in the Bill of Rights have penumbras, formed by emanation from those guarantees that help give them life and substance ... Various guarantees create zones of privacy.[20]

The Connecticut statute violated the zone of privacy, and was thus unconstitutional.

According to this approach, it can be argued that one of the peripheral rights located in the penumbras of the express constitutional rights is the right to human dignity. The analysis of Justice Douglas, who viewed privacy as a recognized right in the periphery of various constitutional rights, can be applied *a fortiori* to the right to human dignity. As we shall see,[21] in a long list of decisions the Supreme Court has recognized human dignity as a value underlying many constitutional rights. Why then should a zone of human dignity not be recognized as a constitutional right?

The question has been raised in the legal literature.[22] The accepted approach is that Justice Douglas' approach in *Griswold* was incorrect. According to this criticism, recognition of privacy as a constitutional right rested upon the mother-right to liberty, and it was not recognized as a separate, freestanding right. That was the approach of Justice Harlan in *Griswold*, and it is the accepted approach today. It is interesting to ponder whether Justice Douglas' penumbras approach could be used to recognize an implied right to privacy. Such a right – were it to be recognized – would not be derived from the right to liberty, but rather from the structure of

[19] *Griswold* v. *Connecticut*, 381 US 479 (1965). [20] *Ibid.*, at 484.

[21] See section 3B(1) below.

[22] See Morris D. Forkosch, 'Privacy, Human Dignity, Euthanasia – Are These Independent Constitutional Rights?' (1974) 3 *University of San Fernando Valley Law Review* 1; Maxine D. Goodman, 'Human Dignity in Supreme Court Constitutional Jurisprudence' (2006) 84 *Nebraska Law Review* 740, 743.

the American Bill of Rights.[23] This line of thought has not been adopted in American judgments.

2. Human dignity as a constitutional right in the state constitutions

The federal constitution does not include a constitutional right to human dignity. Is such a right recognized in the constitutions of the states comprising the American federation? The answer is that in most of the state constitutions there is no provision on human dignity. The constitutions of three states – Montana, Illinois and Louisiana – as well as that of the territory of Puerto Rico, refer to human dignity.[24]

The 1972 Constitution of Montana includes a provision on human dignity. It states:

> The dignity of the human being is inviolable, No person shall be denied the equal protection of the laws. Neither the state nor any person, firm, corporation, or institution shall discriminate against any person in the exercise of his civil or political rights on account of race, color, sex, culture, social origin or condition, or political or religious ideas.[25]

Examination of the process that led to the enactment of this constitution reveals that this provision was apparently influenced by a parallel provision appearing in the constitution of Puerto Rico.[26] The provision is seldom used with regard to dignity.[27]

In the 1971 Illinois Constitution the term "individual dignity" can be found. It appears in the heading and body of Article 1(20) of the constitution, stating:

> Individual Dignity
> To promote individual dignity, communications that portray criminality, depravity or lack of virtue in, or that incite violence, hatred, abuse or hos-

[23] See Chapter 5, section 2D.

[24] See Kalb, 'Litigating Dignity'; Jackson, 'Constitutional Dialogue and Human Dignity'.

[25] Art. II, §4. See Tia R. Robbin, 'Untouched Protection From Discrimination: Private Action in Montana's Individual Dignity Clause' (1990) 51 *Montana Law Review* 553, 555.

[26] See Matthew O. Clifford and Thomas P. Huff, 'Some Thoughts on the Meaning and Scope of the Montana Constitution's Dignity Clause with Possible Applications' (2000) 61 *Montana Law Review* 301, 321.

[27] See Robbin, 'Untouched Protection from Discrimination'; Clifford and Huff, 'Some Thoughts on the Meaning and Scope of the Montana Constitution's Dignity Clause'; Heinz Klug, 'The Dignity Clause of the Montana Constitution: May Foreign Jurisprudence Lead the Way to an Expanded Interpretation?' (2003) 64 *Montana Law Review* 133; Amanda K. Eklund, 'The Death Penalty in Montana: A Violation of the Constitutional

> tility toward, a person or group of persons by reason of or by reference to religious, racial, ethnic, national or regional affiliation are condemned.

The provision is intended to promote the human dignity of the individual by rejecting the various types of negative conduct determined in it. Beyond that, there is no reference to human dignity in this constitution. The section is the product of a proposal of one of the members of the constitutional convention, Mr. Victor Arrigo.[28] It was clarified in the explanatory notes of the Bill of Rights Committee that the objective of the section is not to restrict or alter the freedom of expression. It was emphasized that the provision does not recognize any constitutional right or cause of action, and cannot place any restriction upon the state. The provision has been called a "constitutional sermon." Seldom has it been put to use, and even when it is referred to, it is noted that it does not determine a constitutional right.

Louisiana's constitution from 1974 of contains a section with the heading "Right to Individual Dignity." The body of the section does not mention individual dignity. The section reads:

> Right to Individual Dignity
> No person shall be denied the equal protection of the laws. No law shall discriminate against a person because of race or religious ideas, beliefs, or affiliations. No law shall arbitrarily capriciously, or unreasonably discriminate against a person because of birth, age, sex, culture, physical condition, or political ideas or affiliations. Slavery and involuntary servitude are prohibited, except in the latter case as punishment for crime.[29]

This provision is a reiteration of the Thirteenth and Fourteenth Amendments to the federal constitution, with added detail.[30] The heading of the section, which is dedicated to the right to individual dignity, associates human dignity with the right to equality and the prohibition of slavery. The judicial history has not found particular importance in the heading of the section, and has not recognized human dignity as a special concept requiring discussion.

Right to Individual Dignity' (2004) 65 *Montana Law Review* 135; James E. Dallner and D. Scott Manning, 'Death with Dignity in Montana' (2004) 65 *Montana Law Review* 309.

28 See Elmer Gertz, *For the First Hours of Tomorrow: The New Illinois Bill of Rights* (Urbana: University of Illinois Press, 1972) 107.

29 Art. I, §3.

30 See Lee Hargrave, *The Louisiana State Constitution: A Reference Guide* (Westport: Greenwood Publishing Group, 1991) 23.

Puerto Rico is a self-governed territory of the United States. It has its own constitution, adopted in 1952. The second article of the constitution contains the Bill of Rights. Section 1 of this article states:

> The dignity of the human being is inviolable. All men are equal before the law. No discrimination shall be made on account of race, color, sex, birth, social origin or condition, or political or religious ideas. Both the laws and the system of education shall embody these principles of essential human equality.

3. Human dignity as a constitutional value in the federal constitution

A. *Human dignity and the dignity of the state*

According to research conducted in 2003, since the establishment of the US Constitution in 1789 the term "dignity" has appeared in approximately nine hundred judgments.[31] In the eighteenth and nineteenth centuries the term was used in the context of the dignitary status of one who must be respected. The primary possessor of dignity was the state itself. In contrast, in the twentieth century, during which approximately two-thirds of all of the judgments referring to dignity were handed down, dignity is the dignity of a person.[32]

Comprehensive literature in the United States has dealt with the dignity of the state and the immunity that dignity grants it.[33] That subject is beyond the framework of this volume. Some think that there is a relevant

[31] See Judith Resnik and Julie Chi-Hye Suk, 'Adding Insult to Injury: Questioning the Role of Dignity in Conceptions of Sovereignty' (2003) 55 *Stanford Law Review* 1921, 1933. See also Goodman, 'Human Dignity in Supreme Court Constitutional Jurisprudence'; Daly, 'Human Dignity in the Roberts Court'; Stephen J. Wermiel, 'Law and Human Dignity: The Judicial Soul of Justice Brennan' (1998) 7 *William & Mary Bill of Rights Journal* 223, 224. On the use of human dignity by other federal courts, see Paust, 'Human Dignity as a Constitutional Right', at 161.

[32] Resnik and Suk, 'Adding Insult to Injury', at 1934; McAllister, 'Human Dignity and Individual Liberty', at 501.

[33] See Evan H. Caminker, 'Judicial Solicitude for State Dignity' (2001) 574 *Annals of the American Academy of Political and Social Science* 81; Resnik and Suk, 'Adding Insult to Injury'; Dodson Scott, 'Dignity: The New Frontier of State Sovereignty' (2003) 56 *Oklahoma Law Review* 777; Jeremy M. Sher, 'A Question of Dignity: The Renewed Significance of James Wilson's Writings on Popular Sovereignty in the Wake of Alden v. Maine' (2005) 61 *New York University Annual Survey of American Law* 591; Erin Daly, *Dignity Rights: Courts, Constitutions and the Worth of the Human Person* (Philadelphia: University of Pennsylvania Press, 2012).

internal association between the dignity of the state and the dignity of the individual, and that it is possible to learn about one from the other.[34] I have serious doubts in this regard. The dignity of the state and the dignity of the individual are two different things. I shall turn, therefore, to the judicial history dealing with the dignity of the individual.

B. *The history of human dignity as a constitutional value*

(1) Pre-Second World War

The American Declaration of Independence and the preamble to the US Constitution do not contain express reference to the terms "dignity" or "human dignity." As we have seen,[35] the American Bill of Rights does not include any express mention of dignity either. In *Chisholm* v. *Georgia*,[36] Justice Wilson discussed the dignity of the state and the dignity of a person together:

> A state, useful and valuable as the contrivance is, is the inferior contrivance of man; and from his native dignity derives all its acquired importance.[37]

More than a hundred years later, the term "dignity" appears in a judgment of Justice Field.[38] In his dissenting opinion dealing with the right against abortion, the Justice referred to:

> The sentiment of personal self-respect, liberty, independence and dignity which has inhabited the breasts of English speaking peoples for centuries.[39]

Only since the 1940s has the term "dignity" been used frequently. Justices such as Harlan, Holmes and Brandeis did not make any reference in their opinions to dignity.

(2) The 1940s and 1950s

The substantial change in reliance upon human dignity in the US Supreme Court's decisions took place in the early 1940s.[40] Some see the outbreak of

[34] Resnik and Suk, 'Adding Insult to Injury'; Daly, 'Human Dignity in the Roberts Court'; Daly, *Dignity Rights*.

[35] See section 1A above.

[36] *Chisholm* v. *Georgia*, 2 US 419, 455 (1793).

[37] *Chisholm* v. *Georgia*, at 455.

[38] *Brown* v. *Walker*, 161 US 591 (1896).

[39] *Ibid*., at 632.

[40] See Wermiel, 'Law and Human Dignity'; Goodman, 'Human Dignity in Supreme Court Constitutional Jurisprudence'; Neuman, 'Human Dignity in United States Constitutional

the Second World War and the atrocities committed by the Nazis, which became widely known in the USA, as an explanation for this.[41] The post-war jurisprudence is attributed to the recognition of human dignity in the preamble to the Charter of the United Nations (1945), the Universal Declaration of Human Rights (1948) and the enactment of the German Basic Law (1949).[42]

The first judgment that referred to human dignity was *Glasser* v. *United States*,[43] which was handed down in 1942. In his dissenting opinion, Justice Frankfurter wrote:

> The guarantees of the Bill of Rights are not abstractions. Whether their safeguards of liberty and dignity have been infringed in a particular case depends upon particular circumstances.[44]

A number of months later, in June 1942, the decision in *Skinner* v. *Oklahoma*[45] was handed down. In that case Justice Jackson noted:

> There are limits to the extent to which a legislatively represented majority may conduct biological experiments at the expense of the dignity and personality and natural powers of a minority – even those who have been guilty of what the majority define as crimes.[46]

The next judgment was handed down in March 1943 in *McNabb* v. *United States*.[47] In his opinion, Justice Frankfurter wrote:

> A democratic society, in which respect for the dignity of all men is central, naturally guards against the misuse of the law enforcement process.[48]

The principle decisions in this era that relied on dignity were written by Justice Murphy. On December 18, 1944, he gave two decisions on human

Law'; Paust, 'Human Dignity as a Constitutional Right'; Daly, 'Human Dignity in the Roberts Court'; Daly, 'Constitutional Dignity'; Resnik and Suk, 'Adding Insult to Injury'.

41 See Neuman, 'Human Dignity in United States Constitutional Law', at 255; Resnik and Suk, 'Adding Insult to Injury', at 1926.

42 See Neuman, 'Human Dignity in United States Constitutional Law', at 255; Wermiel, 'Law and Human Dignity', at 227.

43 *Glasser* v. *United States*, 315 US 60 (1942). The judgment dealt with interpretation of the Sixth Amendment to the Constitution.

44 *Ibid.*, at 89.

45 *Skinner* v. *Oklahoma*, 316 US 535 (1942). The judgment dealt with the constitutionality of a statute that required sterilization of criminals under certain conditions.

46 *Ibid.*, at 546.

47 *McNabb* v. *United States*, 318 US 332 (1943). The case dealt with the admissibility of evidence elicited by the police contrary to procedure.

48 *Ibid.*, at 343.

dignity. The first case[49] dealt with the interpretation of a statute. Justice Murphy wrote:

> The utter disregard for the dignity and well-being of colored citizens shown by this record is so pronounced as to demand the invocation of constitutional condemnation.[50]

The second case dealt with the interpretation of the American Bill of Rights. It was a case dealing with the constitutionality of an order prohibiting the presence of American citizens of Japanese descent on the West Coast of the United States and concentrating them in set locations. This was a result of the Japanese bombing of Pearl Harbor, the American declaration of war against Japan and the fear of a Japanese invasion of the United States. In *Korematsu* v. *United States*[51] the Supreme Court held that the orders were constitutional despite their discriminatory character due to security needs, as a number of American citizens of Japanese descent had assisted the enemy. Justice Murphy was one of the dissenting justices. In his opinion he wrote:

> To give constitutional sanction to that inference in this case, however well-intentioned may have been the military command on the Pacific Coast, is to adopt one of the cruelest of the rationales used by our enemies to destroy the dignity of the individual and to encourage and open the door to discriminatory actions against other minority groups in the passions of tomorrow.[52]

The following year, in 1945, judgment was given in *Screws* v. *United States.*[53] This case examined the results of the conduct of police who arrested a man, using force that led to his death. Justice Murphy opened his dissenting opinion with the following words:

> Robert Hall, a Negro citizen, has been deprived not only of the right to be tried by a court, rather than by ordeal. He has been deprived of the right to life itself. That right belonged to him not because he was a Negro or a member of any particular race or creed. That right was his because he was an American citizen, because he was a human being. As such, he was entitled to all the respect and fair treatment that befits the dignity of man, a dignity that is recognized and guaranteed by the constitution.[54]

[49] *Steele* v. *Louisville & Nashville Railroad Co. et al.*, 323 US 192 (1944).
[50] *Ibid.*, at 208.
[51] *Korematsu* v. *United States*, 323 US 214 (1944).
[52] *Ibid.*, at 240.
[53] *Screws* v. *United States*, 325 US 91 (1945).
[54] *Ibid.*, at 134.

At the end of the Second World War, the commanders of the Japanese Army were tried in courts-martial. Petitions against these proceedings were heard in the Supreme Court and rejected. In the two judgments Justice Murphy found himself in the minority. In both he relied upon the human dignity of the commanders of the Japanese army to support his decision. The first case was *In re Yamashita.*[55] Yamashita had been the commander of the Japanese Army in the Philippines. He was captured by the US Army. He was tried before a military court for violation of the laws of war. He argued in the Supreme Court against the constitutionality of the proceedings. His arguments were rejected by the majority. In the dissenting opinion, Justice Murphy wrote:

> If we are ever to develop an orderly international community based upon a recognition of human dignity, it is of the utmost importance that the necessary punishment of those guilty of atrocities be as free as possible from the ugly stigma of revenge and vindictiveness.[56]

The second case was *Homma* v. *Patterson.*[57] It raised questions similar to those that had been examined in *Yamashita*, and thus the writ for habeas corpus was rejected with no special reasoning, on the basis of that previous case. In his dissenting opinion, Justice Murphy wrote:

> Today the lives of Yamashita and Homma, leaders of the enemy forces vanquished in the field of battle, are taken without regard to due process of law. There will be few to protest. But tomorrow the precedent here established can be turned against others. A procession of judicial lynching without due process of law may now follow. No one can foresee the end of this failure of objective thinking and of adherence to our high hopes of a new world. The time for effective vigilance and protest, however, is when the abandonment of legal procedure is first attempted. A nation must not perish because, in the natural frenzy of the aftermath of war, it abandoned its central theme of the dignity of the human personality and due process of law.[58]

A third case,[59] which was decided in that same year, also dealt with military adjudication. The petitioner claimed that his case should be tried before a civilian court. The Supreme Court accepted the petition. In his judgment, Justice Murphy wrote that the decision not to try the petitioner before a regular court was based on racist considerations:

> Racism has no place whatever in our civilization. The constitution as well as the conscience of mankind disclaims its use for any purpose, military

[55] *In re Yamashita*, 327 US 1 (1946). [56] *Ibid.*, at 29.
[57] *Homma* v. *Patterson, Secretary of War*, 327 US 759 (1946).
[58] *Ibid.*, at 760. [59] *Duncan* v. *Kahanamoku*, 327 US 304 (1946).

> or otherwise. It can only result, as it does in this instance, in striking down individual rights and in aggravating rather than solving the problems toward which it is directed. It renders impotent the ideal of the dignity of the human personality, destroying something of what is noble in our way of life. We must therefore reject it completely whenever it arises in the course of a legal proceeding.[60]

This trend of invoking human dignity continued throughout the 1940s[61] and until the mid 1950s.[62]

(3) Continued use of human dignity in the Supreme Court

(a) Expanding the application of human dignity to most of the Bill of Rights The use of dignity continued to intensify from the mid 1950s

[60] *Ibid.*, at 334.

[61] *Carter* v. *Illinois*, 329 US 173, 175 (1946) ("It is for them, therefore, to choose the methods and practices by which crime is brought to book, so long as they observe those ultimate dignities of man which the United States Constitution assures") (Frankfurter J); *Louisiana ex. rel. Francis* v. *Resweber*, 329 US 459, 468 (1947) ("The fourteenth amendment … did mean to withdraw from the states the right to act in ways that are offensive to a decent respect for the dignity of man, and heedless to his freedom") (Frankfurter J); *Harris* v. *United States*, 331 US 145, 198 (1947) ("this, like each of our constitutional guaranties, often may afford a shelter for criminals. But the forefathers thought this was not too great a price to pay for that decent privacy of home, papers and effects which is indispensable to individual dignity and self-respect") (Jackson J); *Adamson* v. *California*, 332 US 46, 65 (1947) ("If the basis of selection is merely that these provisions of the first eight amendments are incorporated which commend themselves to individual justices as indispensable to the dignity and happiness of a free man, we are thrown back to a merely subjective test") (Frankfurter J); *Oyama* v. *California*, 332 US 633, 663 (1948) ("The constitution of the United States, as I read it, embodies the highest political ideals of which man is capable. It insists that our government, whether state or federal, shall respect and observe the dignity of each individual, whatever may be the name of his race, the color of his skin or the nature of his beliefs") (Murphy J); *Brinegar* v. *United States*, 338 US 160, 180 (1949) ("the human personality deteriorates and dignity and self-reliance disappear where homes, persons and possessions are subject at any hour to unheralded search and seizure by the police") (Jackson J).

[62] *Johnson* v. *Eisentrager*, 339 US 763, 798 (1950) ("Our nation proclaims a belief in the dignity of human beings as such, no matter what their nationality or where they happen to live") (Black J); *United States* v. *Carignan*, 342 US 36, 47 (1951) ("We in this country early made the choice – that the dignity and privacy of the individual were worth more to society than an all-powerful police") (Douglas J); *Rochin* v. *California*, 342 US 165, 174 (1952) ("It does not fairly represent these decisions to suggest that they legalize force so brutal and so offensive to human dignity in securing evidence from a suspect as is revealed by this record") (Frankfurter J); *Stein* v. *New York*, 346 US 156, 207 (1953) ("That rule is the product of a civilization which, by respecting the dignity even of the least worthy citizen, raises the stature of all of us and builds an atmosphere of trust and confidence in government") (Douglas J); *Irvine* v. *California*, 347 US 128, 146 (1954) ("The cases in which coercive or physical infringements of the dignity and privacy of the individual were involved were not deemed sports in our constitutional law but applications of a general

onward. In many cases – too many to quote[63] – generations of Supreme Court Justices, in both majority and minority opinions, wrote that human dignity is a constitutional value taken into consideration in the interpretation of the various rights enshrined in the Bill of Rights. An expression of that can be found in the following words of Justice Stewart, in a case dealing with the right to reputation:

> The right of man to the protection of his own reputation from unjustified invasion and wrongful hurt reflects no more than our basic concept of the essential dignity and worth of every human being – a concept at the root of any decent system of ordered liberty.[64]

Justice Harlan similarly noted that the freedom of expression is based upon the belief:

> [T]hat no other approach would comport with the premise of individual dignity and choice upon which our political system rests.[65]

If human dignity was invoked in the 1940s predominantly to protect the individual from the police powers of the state, since the 1950s human dignity has served as a value underlying the great majority of the rights enshrined in the American Bill of Rights. Extensive judicial history has recognized human dignity as the value underlying the First Amendment,[66] the Fourth Amendment,[67] the Fifth

principle. They are only instances of the general requirement that states in their prosecutions respect certain decencies of civilized conduct") (Frankfurter J); *Ullman* v. *United States*, 350 US 422, 449 (1956) ("The fifth Amendment protects the conscience and the dignity of the individual, as well as his safety and security, against the compulsion of government") (Douglas J); *Frank* v. *Maryland*, 359 US 360, 376 (1959) ("The Commands of our First Amendment (as well as the prohibitions of the Fourth and the Fifth) are indeed closely related, safeguarding not only privacy and protection against self-incrimination but conscience and human dignity and freedom of expression as well") (Douglas J).

63 See Goodman, 'Human Dignity in Supreme Court Constitutional Jurisprudence'; Neuman, 'Human Dignity in United States Constitutional Law'; Paust, 'Human Dignity as a Constitutional Right'; Daly, 'Human Dignity in the Roberts Court'; Daly, 'Constitutional Dignity'; Resnik and Suk, 'Adding Insult to Injury'.

64 *Rosenblatt* v. *Baer*, 383 US 75, 92 (1966).

65 *Cohen* v. *California*, 403 US 15, 24 (1971).

66 See *Gertz* v. *Robert G. Welch*, 418 US 323 (1974); *Beard* v. *Banks*, 548 US 521, 553 (2006); *Citizens United* v. *FEC*, 130 S. CT. 876, 972 (2010).

67 *Osborn* v. *United States*, 385 US 323, 343 (1966); *Wainwright* v. *New Orleans*, 392 US 598, 607 (1968); *Segura* v. *United States*, 468 US 796, 839 (1984); *Skinner* v. *Railway Labor Executives' Association*, 489 US 602, 644 (1989); *National Treasury Employees Union* v. *Von Raab*, 489 US 656, 681 (1989); *Hudson* v. *Michigan*, 547 US 586, 594 (2006); *Florence* v. *Board of Chosen Freeholders of the County of Burlington*, 566 US 132 S. Ct. 1510 (2012) (Breyer J dissenting). See also John D. Castiglione, 'Hudson and Samson: The Roberts

Amendment,[68] the Sixth Amendment,[69] the Seventh Amendment,[70] the Eighth Amendment,[71] and all aspects of the Fourteenth Amendment.[72]

(b) The contribution of Justice Brennan Justice Brennan had a central role in recognizing human dignity as a constitutional value in American law.[73] In articles he wrote[74] and in judgments he gave during his thirty-

Court Confronts Privacy, Dignity, and the Fourth Amendment' (2007) 68 *Louisiana Law Review* 63; John D. Castiglione, 'Human Dignity under the Fourth Amendment' (2008) *Wisconsin Law Review* 655.

[68] *Miranda* v. *Arizona*, 384 US 436, 457, 460, 537 (1966); *Doe* v. *United States*, 487 US 201, 219 (1988); *United States* v. *Balysis*, 524 US 666, 713 (1998).

[69] *McKaskle* v. *Wiggins*, 465 US 168, 178 (1984); *Portuondo* v. *Agard*, 529 US 61, 76 (2000); *Indiana* v. *Edwards*, 554 US 164 (2008).

[70] *Irvin* v. *Dowd*, 366 US 717, 721 (1961).

[71] *Trop* v. *Dulles*, 356 US 86, 100 (1958); *Estelle* v. *Gamble*, 429 US 97, 102 (1976); *Hewitt* v. *Helms*, 459 US 460 (1983); *Hudson* v. *Palmer*, 468 US 517, 553 (1984); *Hope* v. *Pelzer*, 536 US 730, 738, 745 (2002); *Roper* v. *Simmons*, 543 US 551, 560, 589 (2005); *Woodford* v. *Ngo*, 548 US 81, 123 (2006); *Kennedy* v. *Louisiana*, 554 US 407 (2008); *Brown* v. *Plata*, 131 S. Ct. 1910, 1928 (2011). See also Hugo A. Bedau, 'The Eighth Amendment, Human Dignity, and the Death Penalty', in Michael J. Meyer and William A. Parent (eds.), *The Constitution of Rights: Human Dignity and American Values* (Ithaca, NY: Cornell University Press, 1992), at 145.

[72] *Heart of Atlanta Motel Inc.* v. *United States*, 379 US 241 (1964); *California* v. *Goldfarb*, 430 US 199, 205, 210 (1977): *NAACP* v. *Clorborne Hardware Co.*, 458 US 886, 918 (1982); *Thornburgh* v. *American College of Obstetricians & Gynecologists*, 476 US 747, 772 (1986); *Ohio* v. *Akron Center for Reproductive Health*, 497 US 502, 520 (1990); *Washington* v. *Glucksberg*, 521 US 702 (1997); *Vacco* v. *Quill*, 521 US 793 (1997); *Planned Parenthood of Southeastern Pennsylvania* v. *Casey*, 505 US 833, 851, 916, 920, 983 (1992); *Miller* v. *Johnson*, 515 US 900, 911 (1995); *Adarand Construction* v. *Pena*, 515 US 200, 218 (1995); *J.E.B.* v. *Alabama ex. rel. T.B.*, 511 US 127, 142 (1994); *United States* v. *Virginia*, 518 US 515 (1996); *Cruzan* v. *Director, Missouri Department of Health*, 497 US 261, 289, 344 (1990); *Rice* v. *Cayetano*, 528 US 495, 517 (2000); *Stenberg* v. *Carhart*, 530 US 914 (2000); *Lawrence* v. *Texas*, 539 US 558, 567, 575 (2003); *Gonzales* v. *Carhart*, 550 US 124 (2007); *Parents Involved in Community Schools* v. *Seattle School District No. 1*, 551 US 701, 746 (2007); *McDonald* v. *City of Chicago*, 561 US 3025 (2010). See also Barbara Herman, 'Mutual Aid and Respect for Persons' (1984) 94 *Ethics* 577; Christopher A. Bracey, 'Dignity in Race Jurisprudence' (2005) 7 *University of Pennsylvania Journal of Constitutional Law* 669; Reva B. Siegel, 'Dignity and the Politics of Protection: Abortion Restrictions Under Casey/Carhart' (2008) 117 *Yale Law Journal* 1694; Reva B. Siegel, 'Dignity and Sexuality: Claims on Dignity in Transnational Debates over Abortion and Same-Sex Marriage' (2012) 10 *International Journal of Constitutional Law* 355.

[73] See Wermiel, 'Law and Human Dignity'; Parent, 'Constitutional Values and Human Dignity'.

[74] William J. Brennan Jr., 'Rededication Address: The American Bar Association's Memorial to the Magna Carta' (1986) 19 *Loyola of Los Angeles Law Review* 55; William J. Brennan Jr., 'The Constitution of the United States: Contemporary Ratification' (1986) 27 *South Texas Law Review* 433; William J. Brennan Jr., 'The Bill of Rights and the States: The Revival of State Constitutions as Guardians of Individual Rights' (1986) 61 *New York*

four year term for the Supreme Court,[75] Justice Brennan emphasized the centrality of human dignity as a value underlying the American Bill of Rights. In one of his articles (from 1984), he wrote:

> [T]he constitution is a sublime oration on the dignity of man, a bold commitment by a people to the ideal of libertarian dignity protected through law.[76]

In *Paul* v. *Davis* (1976) he wrote:

> I have always thought that one of this court's most important roles is to provide a formidable bulwark against governmental violation of the constitutional safeguards securing in our free society the legitimate expectations of every person to innate human dignity and sense of worth.[77]

This approach is a unifying theme throughout Justice Brennan's judgments.[78] It is especially expressed in his decisions regarding the Eighth Amendment to the Constitution. According to that Amendment, cruel and unusual punishment is not to be inflicted.[79] In his opinion in *Furman* v. *Georgia*[80] (1972) he wrote:

University Law Review 535; William J. Brennan Jr., 'Color-Blind, Creed-Blind, Status-Blind, Sex-Blind' (1987) 14 *Human Rights* 30.

75 See Wermiel, 'Law and Human Dignity'.

76 Brennan, 'The Constitution of the United States', at 438.

77 *Paul* v. *Davis*, 424 US 693, 734 (1978).

78 See *Schmerber* v. *California*, 384 US 757, 767 (1966) ("The overriding function of the Fourth Amendment is to protect personal privacy and dignity against unwarranted intrusion by the state"); *Goldberg* v. *Kelly*, 397 US 254, 265 (1970) ("From its founding the basic commitment of this Nation has been to foster the dignity and well-being of all persons within its borders"); *Hampton* v. *Mow Sun Wong*, 426 US 88, 107 (1976); *United States* v. *Martinez-Fuerte*, 428 US 543, 573 (1976); *Roberts* v. *United States Jaycees*, 468 US 609, 625 (1984): ("In the context of renewing state actions under the Equal Protection Clause, this Court has frequently noted that Discrimination based on archaic and overbroad assumptions about the relative needs and capacities of the sexes forces individuals to labor under stereotypical notions that often bear no relationship to their actual abilities. It thereby both deprives persons of their individual dignity and denies society benefits of wide participation in political, economic, and cultural life"); *Winston* v. *Lee*, 470 US 753, 760 (1985); *O'Lone* v. *Estate of Shabazz*, 482 US 342, 368 (1987): ("to deny the opportunity to affirm membership in a spiritual community, however, may extinguish an inmate's last source of hope for dignity and redemption"); *United States* v. *Stanley*, 483 US 669, 708 (1987) ("Soldiers ought not to be asked to defend a constitution indifferent to their essential human dignity"); *Cruzan* v. *Director, Missouri Department of Health*, at 302 (1990) ("Nancy Cruzan is entitled to choose to die with dignity").

79 See Roderick Oxford, 'Eighth Amendment ETS Claims: A Matter of Human Dignity' (1993) 18 *Oklahoma City University Law Review* 505.

80 *Furman* v. *Georgia*, 408 US 238, 270 (1972).

> At bottom, then, the Cruel and Unusual Punishment clause prohibits the infliction of uncivilized and inhuman punishments. The state, even as it punishes, must treat its members with respect for their intrinsic worth as human beings. A punishment is "cruel and unusual," therefore, if it does not comport with human dignity.[81]

In *Gregg* v. *Georgia* (1976)[82] he added, regarding the Eighth Amendment:

> [F]oremost among the "moral concepts" recognized in our case and inherent in the clause is the primary moral principle that the state even as it punishes must treat its citizens in a manner consistent with their intrinsic worth as human beings – a punishment must not be so severe as to be degrading to human dignity. A judicial determination whether the punishment of death comports with human dignity is therefore not only permitted but compelled by the clause.[83]

He reiterated this approach in additional opinions.[84]

(c) The contribution of Justice Kennedy In some of his most important decisions, Justice Kennedy cast the deciding vote while invoking the constitutional value of human dignity.[85] The first and most central case is *Planned Parenthood of Southeastern Pennsylvania* v. *Casey* (1992).[86] In this case, the Supreme Court was asked to overrule *Roe* v. *Wade* (1973). In *Casey*, Justices O'Connor, Souter and Kennedy write:

> These matters, involving the most intimate and personal choices a person may make in a lifetime, choices central to personal dignity and autonomy, are central to the liberty protected by the Fourteenth Amendment.[87]

81 *Ibid.*, at 270. 82 *Gregg* v. *Georgia*, 428 US 153 (1976).

83 *Ibid.*, at 229.

84 *Jones* v. *Barnes*, 463 US 745, 759, 763 (1983); *Autry* v. *McKaskie*, 465 US 1090, 1091 (1984); *Glass* v. *Louisiana*, 471 US 1080, 1085 (1985) ("[t]he 'physical and mental suffering' inherent in any method of execution is so 'uniquely degrading to human dignity' that, when combined with the arbitrariness by which capital punishment is imposed, the trend of enlightened opinion, and the availability of less severe penological alternatives, the death penalty is always unconstitutional"); *DeGarmo* v. *Texas*, 474 US 973, 974 (1985); *Roach* v. *Aiken*, 474 US 1039, 1042 (1986); *Davidson* v. *Cannon*, 474 US 344, 356 (1986); *Walton* v. *Arizona*, 497 US 639, 655 (1990) ("[T]he concern for human dignity, lying at the core of the Eighth Amendment requires that a decision to impose the death penalty be made only after an assessment of its propriety in each individual case").

85 See Daly, 'Constitutional Dignity'.

86 *Planned Parenthood of Southeastern Pennsylvania* v. *Casey*, 505 US 833 (1992).

87 *Planned Parenthood of Southeastern Pennsylvania* v. *Casey*, at 851.

This was the first time that constitutional questions regarding abortion were decided based the human dignity of the woman, as derived from the liberty protected in the Fourteenth Amendment to the Constitution.

In *J.E.B.* v. *Alabama* (1994)[88] the constitutionality of a statute on jury selection that discriminated against women was examined. In his opinion, Justice Kennedy stated[89] that this discrimination injures a woman's human dignity.

In *Rice* v. *Cayetano* (2000)[90] the question was whether the petitioner was discriminated against on the basis of race when prevented from voting in state elections. In his judgment, Justice Kennedy answered this question in the affirmative. Regarding racial discrimination, Justice Kennedy wrote:

> One of the principle reasons race is treated as a forbidden classification is that it demeans the dignity and worth of a person to be judged by ancestry instead of by his or her own merit and essential qualities.[91]

Stenberg v. *Carhart* (2000)[92] examined the constitutionality of a Nebraska statute that absolutely prohibited partial-birth abortion. The statute was found unconstitutional. In his dissenting opinion, Justice Kennedy relied upon the human dignity of the fetus as a basis for denying the right to an abortion:

> A State may take measures to ensure the medical profession and its members are viewed as healers, sustained by a compassionate and rigorous ethic and cognizant of the dignity and value of human life, even life which cannot survive without the assistance of others.[93]

Lawrence v. *Texas* (2003)[94] is another landmark judgment based upon human dignity. In that case it was decided that the Texas statute prohibiting homosexual relations between adults is unconstitutional. The judgment was written by Justice Kennedy, and it is based upon human dignity. He wrote:

> [A]dults may choose to enter upon this relationship in the confines of their homes and their own private lives and still retain their dignity as free persons.[95]

[88] *J.E.B.* v. *Alabama ex. rel. T.B.*, 511 US 127 (1994).
[89] *Ibid.*, at 152. [90] *Rice* v. *Cayetano*, 528 US 495 (2000).
[91] *Ibid.*, at 517. [92] *Stenberg* v. *Carhart*, 530 US 914 (2000).
[93] *Ibid.*, at 962. [94] *Lawrence* v. *Texas*, 539 US 558 (2003).
[95] *Ibid.*, at 567.

Further on in his opinion he writes:

> The stigma this criminal statute imposes, moreover, is not trivial. The offense, to be sure, is but a class C misdemeanor, a minor offence in the Texas legal system. Still, it remains a criminal offence with all that imports for the dignity of the persons charged.[96]

Another judgment written by Justice Kennedy dealt with the death penalty. The question was whether inflicting the death penalty upon a 17-year-old minor is unconstitutional, as cruel and unusual punishment. Justice Kennedy wrote the opinion for the Supreme Court in *Roper* v. *Simmons* (2005),[97] determining that the statute is unconstitutional:

> By protecting even those convicted of heinous crimes, the Eighth Amendment reaffirms the duty of the government to respect the dignity of all persons.[98]

Justice Kennedy returned to the problem of the constitutionality of laws prohibiting abortion in *Gonzales* v. *Carhart* (2007).[99] In this case as well, a federal statute prohibiting partial-birth abortions was discussed. The Supreme Court found the statute constitutional. Justice Kennedy wrote the opinion of the court. As in *Casey*,[100] Justice Kennedy relied upon the human dignity of the woman. Whereas in *Casey* human dignity provided the basis for a woman's free will to decide whether or not to have an abortion, in *Carhart* human dignity served as the basis for denying the right to have an abortion. It was held that the statute "expresses respect for the dignity of human life."[101] This human dignity is the human dignity of the fetus and of the woman having an abortion, who might suffer trauma due to the abortion.[102]

In *Parents Involved in Community Schools* v. *Seattle School District No. 1* (2007)[103] at issue was a high-school acceptance policy that incorporated considerations of racial diversity. Justice Kennedy wrote:

> When the government classifies an individual by race, it must first define what it means to be of a race. Who exactly is white and who is nonwhite? To be forced to live under a state-mandated racial label is inconsistent with the dignity of individuals in our society.[104]

96 *Ibid.*, at 572. 97 *Roper* v. *Simmons*, 543 US 551 (2005).
98 *Ibid.*, at 6. 99 *Gonzales* v. *Carhart*, 550 US 124 (2007).
100 *Planned Parenthood of Southeastern Pennsylvania* v. *Casey*.
101 *Stenberg* v. *Carhart*, at 157.
102 See Siegel, 'Dignity and the Politics of Protection'; Siegel, 'Dignity and Sexuality'.
103 *Parents Involved in Community Schools* v. *Seattle School District No. 1*, 551 US 701 (2007).
104 *Ibid.*, at 797.

In *Brown, Governor of California* v. *Plata* (2011)[105] the crowding in the prisons of California was discussed. The Federal District Court held that prisoners were unable to receive suitable medical treatment.[106] The attempts to ameliorate the situation were not successful. The court ordered a restriction on the number of prisoners held in the prisons, which was upheld by the US Court of Appeals for the Ninth Circuit. An appeal to the Supreme Court failed as well. The judgment was written by Justice Kennedy, and it is based upon the prisoners' right to human dignity:

> Prisoners retain the essence of human dignity inherent in all persons. Respect for that dignity animates the Eighth Amendment prohibition against cruel and unusual punishment.[107]

In *United States* v. *Windsor* (2013)[108] the constitutionality of the Defense of Marriage Act (DOMA) was examined.[109] This statute determined that:

> In determining the meaning of any Act of Congress, or of any ruling, regulation, or interpretation of the various administrative bureaus and agencies of the United States, the word "marriage" means only a legal union between one man and one woman as husband and wife, and the word "spouse" refers only to a person of the opposite sex who is a husband or a wife.[110]

Ms. Windsor and her female partner married in Canada. The marriage was recognized in New York. The partner died, and bequeathed all her property to Ms. Windsor, who wished to benefit from the exemption from federal inheritance tax for a remaining spouse. This exemption was denied to her pursuant to DOMA. She argued that the provision was unconstitutional.

A majority of the Supreme Court accepted the argument. Justice Kennedy wrote for the court. He determined that DOMA violated the human dignity of the married couple:

> The federal statute is invalid, for no legitimate purpose overcomes the purpose and effect to disparage and to injure those whom the State, by its marriage laws, sought to protect in personhood and dignity. By seeking to displace this protection and treating those persons as living in marriages less respected than others, the federal statute is in violation of the Fifth Amendment.[111]

105 *Brown, Governor of California* v. *Plata*, 131 S. Ct. 1910 (2011).
106 *Coleman* v. *Schwarzenegger*, 922 F. Supp. 2d 882 (ED Cal. 2009).
107 *Brown* v. *Plata*, at 12.
108 *United States* v. *Windsor*, 133 S. Ct. 2675 (2013).
109 1 USC §7 (1996). 110 Art. 3 of the DOMA.
111 *United States* v. *Windsor*, at 25–26.

C. *The assessment of human dignity as a constitutional value in the US Constitution*

(1) The status of human dignity as a constitutional value

Examination of the American federal case law reveals that it has constantly and consistently recognized human dignity as a constitutional value. From the 1940s to recent decisions (2013), human dignity has been recognized as the value underlying a number of rights in the Bill of Rights.[112] What is the status of this constitutional value? According to Murphy, it is the most important value in the US Constitution:

> [H]uman dignity is not merely one of the fundamental values of the American constitutional system, it is the fundamental value.[113]

Maxine Goodman claims that:

> [H]uman dignity ... is a core value underlying express and un-enumerated constitutional rights and guarantees.[114]

It seems to me that a more balanced view of the normative reality in the American case law[115] is that human dignity is indeed a recognized constitutional value, and that since the Second World War it has played an important role in the interpretation of a number of rights in the American Bill of Rights.[116] The importance of this constitutional value is growing

[112] Louis Henkin, 'Human Dignity and Constitutional Rights', in Michael J. Meyer and William A. Parent (eds.), *The Constitution of Rights: Human Dignity and American Values* (Ithaca, NY: Cornell University Press, 1992), at 228.

[113] Walter Murphy, 'The Art of Constitutional Interpretation: A Preliminary Showing', in Mont J. Harmon (ed.), *Essays on the Constitution of the United States* (Port Washington, NY: Kennikat Press, 1978), 130, 157; Walter F. Murphy, 'An Ordering of Constitutional Values' (1979–1980) 53 *Southern California Law Review* 703, 745 ("The basic value in the United States Constitution, broadly conceived, has become a concern for human dignity").

[114] See Goodman, 'Human Dignity in Supreme Court Constitutional Jurisprudence', at 743, 748.

[115] These statements may contain an element of exaggeration. In five central judgments of the Supreme Court on human rights associated with human dignity, human dignity is not mentioned at all: see *Brown* v. *Board of Education*, 347 US 483 (1954); *Griswold* v. *Connecticut*; *Roe* v. *Wade*; *Atkins* v. *Virginia*, 536 US 304 (2002); *Virginia* v. *Black*, 538 US 343 (2003).

[116] See Neuman, 'Human Dignity in United States Constitutional Law', at 270 ("[T]he concept of human dignity has played a significant role in the interpretation of U.S. constitutional rights in the latter half of the twentieth century"); Louis Henkin, *Human Dignity and Human Rights* (Jerusalem: The Israel Academy of Sciences and Humanities, 1995), 20 ("[S]ome conception of human dignity – of human dignity prime – was no doubt implicit").

in American constitutional law,[117] but it has not yet attained across-the-board recognition.

(2) The essence of human dignity in American common law

Examination of the judgments of the US Supreme Court in which human dignity appears as the decisive reason for the decision reveals that treatment of human dignity is fragmented and undeveloped.[118] The Justices point out that their decisions are an attempt to realize human dignity, but they do not explain what human dignity is, what it covers, and what are the elements that comprise it.[119] There is no discussion of the relationship between dignity on the one hand, and a person's freedom of expression[120] and privacy[121] on the other. Justice Brennan recognized this limitation in the American case law, explaining in an article he authored:

> I do not mean to suggest that we have in the last quarter century achieved a comprehensive definition of the constitutional idea of human dignity ... the demands of human dignity will never cease to evolve.[122]

It seems that Neomi Rao is correct in saying that the use of human dignity in American case law is intuitive[123] and lacks an attempt to understand the concept. While legal scholars in America, including Dworkin, Waldron and Gewirth, are making an important effort and a substantial contribution to understanding the doctrinal concept of human dignity,

[117] See Rao, 'Three Concepts of Dignity in Constitutional Law', at 270; Daly, 'Constitutional Dignity', at 2.

[118] See Jackson, 'Constitutional Dialogue and Human Dignity', at 17 ("The role of the concept of 'human dignity' in the court's jurisprudence is episodic and underdeveloped"; Rao, 'On the Use and Abuse of Dignity in Constitutional Law', at 202 ("In the United States, the Supreme Court has also invoked the concept of human dignity, but more tentatively"); Neuman, 'Human Dignity in United States Constitutional Law', at 249 ("[T]he principle of human dignity is recognized in US law, but it is under developed").

[119] See McAllister, 'Human Dignity and Individual Liberty', at 561; Rao, 'On the Use and Abuse of Dignity in Constitutional Law', at 202; Daly, 'Constitutional Dignity'.

[120] See Ronald J. Krotoszynski, 'A Comparative Perspective on the First Amendment: Free Speech, Militant Democracy, and the Primacy of Dignity as a Preferred Constitutional Value in Germany' (2004) 78 *Tulane Law Review* 1549, 1563.

[121] See Bognetti, 'The Concept of Human Dignity in European and US Constitutionalism'; Whitman, 'Enforcing Civility and Respect'; Whitman, 'On Nazi "Honour" and the New European "Dignity"'; Friedman and Whitman, 'The European Transformation of Harassment Law'; Whitman, 'The Two Western Cultures of Privacy'; Jeremy M. Miller, 'Dignity as a New Framework, Replacing the Right to Privacy' (2007) 30 *Thomas Jefferson Law Review* 1.

[122] Brennan, 'The Constitution of the United States', at 443.

[123] See Rao, 'On the Use and Abuse of Dignity in Constitutional Law', at 208.

no real attempt has been made to link that understanding with the Bill of Rights. A constitutional discussion regarding the question of whether protection of human rights in America will increase or decrease if human dignity is in the Bill of Rights has only recently begun,[124] mainly in the writing of Whitman,[125] Daly[126] and Siegel.[127]

How will human dignity, which appears on both sides of the question, affect a woman's right to have an abortion?[128] How will human dignity influence the recognition of positive rights in American constitutional law?[129] Discussion of these and other issues[130] raises the question of whether Rao is correct in saying that recognition of human dignity will insert communitarian and socialist factors into the constitution, which is based on the autonomy of the individual.[131] Is she correct in saying that the American Bill of Rights is based on the liberty of the individual vis-à-vis the state, and that any other approach that might stem from human dignity, such as social aspects of protecting the individual from himself or from his bad luck, might upset the internal structure of the Bill of Rights?[132] Or maybe Daly is right that recognition of human dignity will actually reinforce the liberty expressly and particularly enshrined in

[124] *Ibid.*; Rao, 'Three Concepts of Dignity in Constitutional Law'; Resnik and Suk, 'Adding Insult to Injury', at 1938.

[125] See Whitman, 'Enforcing Civility and Respect'; Whitman, 'On Nazi "Honour" and the New European "Dignity"'; Friedman and Whitman, 'The European Transformation of Harassment Law'; Whitman, 'The Two Western Cultures of Privacy'; Whitman, '"Human Dignity" in Europe and the United States'.

[126] See Erin Daly, 'The New Liberty' (2005) 11 *Widener Law Review* 221; Daly, 'Human Dignity in the Roberts Court'; Daly, 'Constitutional Dignity'.

[127] See Siegel, 'Dignity and the Politics of Protection'; Siegel, 'Dignity and Sexuality'.

[128] See Siegel, 'Dignity and the Politics of Protection'; Siegel, 'Dignity and Sexuality'; McAllister, 'Human Dignity and Individual Liberty'; Rao, 'Three Concepts of Dignity in Constitutional Law'.

[129] See Rao, 'On the Use and Abuse of Dignity in Constitutional Law', at 220; Rao, 'Three Concepts of Dignity in Constitutional Law', at 222; Hillel Sommer, 'Background Paper on: Human Dignity as a Constitutional Right', submitted to the Knesset's Constitution, Law and Justice Committee (The Interdisciplinary Center, Herzliya, 2005).

[130] An additional question regarding the influence of human dignity on substantive criminal law – see Michal Buchhandler-Raphael, 'Drugs, Dignity and Danger: Human Dignity as a Constitutional Constraint to Limit Overcriminalization' (2013) 80 *Tennessee Law Review* 291; Lois Shepherd, 'Dignity and Autonomy after Washington v. Gluckberg: An Essay about Abortion, Death and Crime' (1998) 7 *Cornell Journal of Law and Public Policy* 431.

[131] Rao, 'Three Concepts of Dignity in Constitutional Law'.

[132] Daly, 'The New Liberty'.

the Bill of Rights;[133] and that human dignity should be granted stronger recognition in American law?[134]

It seems that American constitutional law is in the opening stages of use of the concept of human dignity. The more fundamental discussion of whether that concept should be used in understanding the Bill of Rights in the US Constitution has only just begun.[135]

[133] Daly, *Dignity Rights.* [134] Daly, 'Constitutional Dignity', at 2.

[135] Rao, 'On the Use and Abuse of Dignity in Constitutional Law'; Erin Daly, 'Dignity in the Service of Democracy', Widener Law School Research Paper 11-07 (2010); Daly, *Dignity Rights*; Daly, 'Human Dignity in the Roberts Court'; Rao, 'Three Concepts of Dignity in Constitutional Law'; Siegel, 'Dignity and Sexuality'; Siegel, 'Dignity and the Politics of Protection'.

12

Human dignity in Canadian constitutional law

1. The Canadian Charter does not recognize a constitutional right to human dignity

A. *The lack of an independent right to human dignity*

The term "human dignity" is not expressly mentioned in the Canadian Charter of Rights and Freedoms[1] or in any other part of the constitution. The preamble to the Charter states:

> Whereas Canada is founded upon principles that recognize the supremacy of God and the rule of law.

The preamble does not expand on this, nor does it determine anything regarding human dignity.[2] Thus human dignity does not constitute an independent, freestanding right.

B. *Rejection of human dignity as a derived (daughter) constitutional right*

Does the Canadian Charter recognize human dignity as a constitutional right derived from one of the independent rights it has enshrined within? Is human dignity recognized as a daughter-right[3] of the mother (framework)-right set out in section 7 of the Canadian Charter? That right determines:

[1] Canadian Charter of Rights and Freedoms, Part I of the Constitution Act, 1982, being Schedule B to the Canada Act, 1982, c. 11 (UK).

[2] See Lorne Sossin, 'The "Supremacy of God", Human Dignity and the Charter of Rights and Freedoms' (2003) 52 *University of New Brunswick Law Journal* 227. The author proposes seeing human dignity as a bridge connecting the supremacy of God to the rule of law. Note that in the preamble to the Canadian Bill of Rights and Freedoms, which was a "regular" statute lacking constitutional status, human dignity was mentioned. See section 1C below.

[3] See Chapter 9, section 2A.

> Everyone has the right to life, liberty and security of the person and the right not to be deprived thereof except in accordance with the principles of fundamental justice.[4]

Should a daughter-right to human dignity not be derived from the right to life, liberty or security of the person? As we shall see,[5] human dignity is a central constitutional value in the Canadian Charter. Should it not be said that fulfillment of that value in the framework of the constitutional right to life, liberty or security of the person establishes a daughter-right to human dignity?

This question arose before the Supreme Court of Canada in *Blencoe*.[6] In that case, Mr. Blencoe argued that his liberty had been limited due to unreasonable delays in the British Columbia Human Rights Commission's handling of sexual harassment complaints against him. A majority of the appeals court determined that:

> s. 7, under the rubric of liberty and security of the person, operates to protect both the privacy and dignity of citizens against the stigma of undue, prolonged humiliation and public degradation of the kind suffered by [Blencoe] here.[7]

That approach was rejected by the Supreme Court. Justice Bastarache wrote:

> Respect for the inherent dignity of persons is clearly an essential value in our free and democratic society which must guide the courts in interpreting the *Charter*. This does not mean, however, that dignity is elevated to a free-standing constitutional right protected by s. 7 of the *Charter*. Dignity has never been recognized by this Court as an independent right but has rather been viewed as finding expression in rights, such as equality, privacy or protection from state compulsion … [T]he notion of "dignity" in the decisions of this court is better understood not as an autonomous *Charter* right, but rather, as an underlying value … Respect for a person's reputation, like respect for dignity of the person, is a value that underlies the *Charter*. These two values do not support the respondent's proposition that protection of reputation or freedom from the stigma associated with human rights complaints are independent constitutional s. 7 rights … Dignity and reputation are not self-standing rights. Neither is freedom from stigma.[8]

4 On the analysis of this right, see Peter W. Hogg, *Constitutional Law of Canada*, 5th edn (Toronto: Thomson Carswell, 2007) vol. I, 366.

5 See section 2A(1) below.

6 *Blencoe* v. *British Columbia (Human Rights Commission)*, [2000] 2 SCR 307.

7 *Ibid.*, at para. 26.

8 *Ibid.*, at para. 77.

In Justice Bastarache's opinion, in order for the respondent's constitutional right to be limited, the state act must have had a serious and profound effect on his psychological integrity. Not every limitation of human dignity will lead to violation of section 7 of the Canadian Charter. Justice Bastarache quotes another case, in which Justice Lamer wrote:

> If liberty or security of the person under s. 7 of the *Charter* were defined in terms of attributes such as dignity, self worth and emotional well-being, it seems that liberty under s. 7 would be all inclusive. In such a state of affairs there would be serious reason to question the independent existence in the *Charter* of other rights and freedoms such as freedom of religion and conscience or freedom of expression.[9]

It seems that the real question that Justice Bastarache confronted was the question of the scope of the right enshrined in section 7 of the Canadian Charter.[10] He held that it should not be said that section 7 is limited in every case in which human dignity is limited. The limitation must have a serious and deep effect upon the psychological integrity of a person. Balancing with other values underlying section 7 of the *Canadian Charter* is also needed. It seems that there cannot be any doubt that a daughter-right of human dignity is not recognized in the Canadian Charter.

C. *Human dignity as a sub-constitutional value*

The Canadian Charter does not contain any express provision stating that human dignity is a constitutional value. However, a provision to that effect exists in a number of sub-constitutional sources. Thus, for example, the preamble to the Canadian Bill of Rights,[11] which is a "regular" statute of the Parliament of Canada, states:

> The Parliament of Canada, affirming that the Canadian Nation is founded upon principles that acknowledge the supremacy of God, the dignity and worth of the human person and the position of the family in a society of free men and free institutions.

A similar provision is found in the preamble to the legislation of the provinces regarding human rights. Thus, for example, the preambles of the Ontario Human Rights Code[12] and the Quebec Charter of Human

[9] *Reference re ss. 193 and 195.1(1)(c) of the Criminal Code (Man.)*, [1990] 1 SCR 1123, 1170.
[10] See Hogg, *Constitutional Law of Canada*, at 371.
[11] Canadian Bill of Rights, SC 1960 (RSC 1970).
[12] Province of Ontario Human Rights Code, RSO 1990.

Rights and Freedoms[13] include reference to the value of human dignity. The Canadian common law also recognized the value of human dignity. Justice Cory discussed that in one case:

> Traditionally, the common law and Canadian society have recognized the fundamental importance of the innate dignity of the individual.[14]

But is human dignity recognized as a constitutional value? Is it recognized as an implied constitutional value in the Canadian Charter?

2. Human dignity as a constitutional value in the Canadian Charter

A. *The centrality of human dignity as a constitutional value*

(1) In the Canadian Charter in general

In a long line of judgments[15] generations of Justices of the Supreme Court of Canada have recognized human dignity[16] as a constitutional value. It has been held that human dignity underlies the social[17] and political[18] structure of Canada and the Canadian legal system.[19] It has been noted that there is a close association between human dignity and the Canadian Charter.[20] This charter does not protect rights and freedoms of economic nature, but it does protect rights and freedoms associated

[13] Quebec Charter of Human Rights and Freedoms, SQ 1975.

[14] *R* v. *Stillman*, [1997] 1 SCR 607, 658. See also *R* v. *S (R.J.)*, [1995] 1 SCR 451, 605 in which Justice L'Heureux-Dubé pointed out that "dignity of the individual is a fundamental value underlying both the common law and the Charter."

[15] My research located more than 80 judgments of the Supreme Court (between 1985 and 2011) in which the Justices based their opinions upon the value of human dignity when interpreting the Canadian Charter.

[16] The reference is to dignity and self-worth; inherent dignity; human dignity; innate dignity – see Dierk Ullrich, 'Concurring Visions: Human Dignity in the Canadian Charter of Rights and Freedoms and the Basic Law of the Federal Republic of Germany' (2003) 3 *Global Jurist Frontiers* 1, 17.

[17] See *Rodriguez* v. *British Columbia (Attorney General)*, [1993] 3 SCR 519, 585 ("As members of a society based upon respect for the intrinsic value of human dignity of every human being") (Sopinka J).

[18] See *R* v. *Zundel*, [1992] 2 SCR 731, 806 ("A democratic society capable of giving effect to the Charter's guarantees is one which strives toward creating a community committed to equality, liberty and human dignity") (Cory and Iaccboucci JJ).

[19] See *R* v. *Swain*, [1991] 1 SCR 933, 970 ("the basic principles underlying our legal system are built on respect for the autonomy and intrinsic value of all individuals") (Lamer J).

[20] See *R* v. *Morgentaler*, [1988] 1 SCR 30, 164 ("The Charter and the right to individual liberty guaranteed under it are inextricably tied to the concept of human dignity") (Wilson J).

with the dignity of a person. The economic aspect is protected only to the extent that human dignity necessitates.[21] Indeed, the approach is that the Canadian Charter is based upon human dignity.[22] It has been emphasized that human dignity is an important value[23] underlying each of the rights enshrined in the Canadian Charter,[24] and at the heart of all human rights.[25] Chief Justice Dickson, regarding the limitations on charter rights – which must be demonstrably justified in a free and democratic society – noted that:

> The Court must be guided by the values and principles essential to a free and democratic society which I believe embody ... respect for the inherent dignity of the human person.[26]

Despite the centrality of human dignity as a constitutional value in the Canadian Charter, it is not the supreme value, and not even the most important value. It is one of the fundamental and important values upon which the Canadian Charter is based.

(2) In certain constitutional rights

(a) The right to equality Alongside the general statements about the centrality of human dignity in the Canadian Charter as a whole, special emphasis has been placed upon its centrality to certain constitutional rights. In this context, it has been emphasized in a long line of judgments that there is close association between the right to equality[27] set out in the

[21] See *Egan* v. *Canada*, [1995] 2 SCR 513 (L'Heureux-Dubé J). See also Martha Jackman, 'Poor Rights: Using the Charter to Support Social Welfare Claims' (1993–1994) 19 *Queen's Law Journal* 65.

[22] See *Blencoe* v. *British Columbia (Human Rights Commission)*, at 352 ("The Charter and the rights it guarantees are inextricably bound to concepts of human dignity") (Bastarache J.); *M. (A)* v. *Ryan*, [1997] 1 SCR 157, 199 ("human dignity, a basic value underlying the charter") (McLachlin J).

[23] See *WIC Radio Ltd.* v. *Simpson*, [2008] 2 SCR 420, 429 ("the worth and dignity of each individual ... is an important value underlying the Charter") (Binnie J).

[24] See *R* v. *Morgentaler*, at 166 ("The idea of human dignity finds expression in almost every right and freedom guaranteed in the Charter") (Wilson J); *Hill* v. *Church of Scientology of Toronto*, [1995] 2 SCR 1130, 1179 ("the innate dignity of the individual, a concept which underlies all the Charter rights") (Cory J); *R* v. *Kapp*, [2008] 2 SCR 483, 504 ("the protection of all of the rights guaranteed by the Charter has as its lodestar the promotion of human dignity") (McLachlin CJ and Abella J).

[25] See *Egan* v. *Canada*, at 543 ("This Court has recognized that inherent human dignity is the heart of individual rights in a free and democratic society") (L'Heureux-Dubé J).

[26] *R* v. *Oakes* [1986] 1 SCR 103, 136 (Dickson CJ).

[27] See s. 15 of the Canadian Charter. For analysis of this provision, see section 2B(2)(a) below.

Canadian Charter and human dignity.[28] It has been noted that the objective underlying the right to equality is to respect human dignity,[29] to protect it,[30] to prevent it being violated[31] and to promote it.[32]

(b) The right to freedom of expression The jurisprudence of the Supreme Court of Canada has seen an important association between the right to freedom of expression and the value of human dignity.[33] It has been stated that the underlying justification of human dignity regarding self-fulfillment also underlies the right to freedom of expression.[34] Justices McLachlin and LeBel expressed this in one case:

[28] See *Granovsky* v. *Canada (Minister of Employment and Immigration)*, [2000] 1 SCR 703, 736 ("The concept of 'human dignity' has been present in s. 15 since the beginning") (Binnie J). But see *R* v. *Kapp*, in which the court addressed difficulties in applying the dignity test to equality.

[29] See *Gosselin* v. *Quebec (Attorney General)*, [2002] 4 SCR 429, 551 ("a purposive approach to this right must take into consideration a concern for individual human dignity of all those subject to law ... disrespect for human dignity lies at the heart of discrimination") (L'Heureux-Dubé and Bastarache JJ).

[30] See *Stoffman* v. *Vancouver General Hospital*, [1990] 3 SCR 483, 546 ("The interests which the guarantee of equality embodied in s. 15 were meant to protect; i.e., human dignity and the sense of self-worth and self-esteem, were thus violated") (Wilson J); *Thibaudeau* v. *Canada*, [1995] 2 SCR 627, 701 ("the purpose of s. 15 is to protect human dignity by ensuring that all individuals are recognized at law as being equally deserving of concern, respect and consideration") (Cory and Iacobucci JJ); *Law* v. *Canada (Minister of Employment and Immigration)*, [1999] 1 SCR 497, 529 ("the purpose of s. 15(1) is to prevent the violation of essential human dignity") (Iacobucci J); *Winko* v. *British Columbia (Forensic Psychiatric Institute)*, [1999] 2 SCR 625, 674 ("The central purpose of the guarantee in s. 15 is to protect an individual's right to be treated with dignity") (McLachlin J); *Lovelace* v. *Ontario*, [2000] 1 SCR 950, 984 ("The central purpose of the guarantee in s. 15(1) is to protect against the violation of essential human dignity") (Iacobucci J).

[31] See *Corbiere* v. *Canada (Minister of Indian and Northern Affairs)*, [1999] 2 SCR 203, 216 ("the general purpose of s. 15(1) to prevent the violation of human dignity") (McLachlin and Bastrarche JJ).

[32] See *McKinney* v. *University of Guelph*, [1990] 3 SCR 229, 399 ("The purpose of the equality guarantee is the promotion of human dignity") (Wilson J); *M.* v. *H.*, [1999] 2 SCR 3, 125 ("the central purpose of the s. 15(1) equality guarantee is to protect and promote human dignity") (Gunthier J).

[33] See *Reference re ss. 193 and 195.1(1)(c) of the Criminal Code (Man.)*, [1990] 1 SCR 1123, 1183 ("language is, indeed, an expression of one's culture and often of one's sense of dignity and self-worth") (Lamer J).

[34] See *R* v. *Keegstra*, [1990] 3 SCR 697, 811 ("the emphasis which this Court has placed upon the inherent dignity of the individual in interpreting Charter guarantees suggests that the rationale of self-actualization should also play an important part in decisions under s. 2(b) of the Charter ... Freedom of expression protects certain values which we consider fundamental – democracy, a vital, vibrant and creative culture, the dignity of the individual") (McLachlin J).

> The core values which free expression promotes include self fulfillment, participation in social and political decision making, and the communal exchange of ideas. Free speech protects human dignity and the right to think and reflect freely on one's circumstances and condition. It allows a person to speak not only for the sake of expression itself, but also to advocate change, attempting to persuade others in the hope of improving one's life and perhaps the wider social, political, and economic environment.[35]

(c) The right to life, liberty and security of the person A central right in the Canadian Charter is the right determined in section 7.[36] According to section 7, every person has a right to life, liberty and security of the person, and the right not to be deprived thereof except in accordance with the principles of fundamental justice. The scope of the right to liberty is unclear.[37] Limitation of the value of human dignity can, in exceptional cases, constitute a limitation of liberty. This could occur in a situation where it detracts from a person's ability to make basic choices that go to the core of human dignity.[38] It has been held that security of the person includes certain situations that limit the value of human dignity,[39] and that some aspects of human dignity are included in it.[40]

(d) Legal rights It is broadly accepted that principles of fundamental justice are limited when the dignitary aspects of the rights of the accused are limited. These principles are based upon the recognition of human dignity, its importance and the rule of law.[41] It has been determined as part of this view that an absolute criminal liability offense is unconstitutional,[42]

35 *R.W.D.S.U., Local 558* v. *Pepsi-Cola Canada Beverages (West) Ltd.*, [2002] 1 SCR 156, 172.

36 See section 1B above.

37 See Chapter 10, section 4C. See also, Hogg, *Constitutional Law of Canada*, at 365; Margot Young, 'Section 7 and the Politics of Social Justice' (2005) 38 *University of British Columbia Law Review* 539.

38 See *Godbout* v. *Longueuil (City)*, [1997] 3 SCR 844, para. 66 ("the autonomy protected by the s. 7 right to liberty encompasses only those matters that can properly be characterized as fundamentally or inherently personal such that, by their very nature, they implicate basic choices going to the core of what it means to enjoy individual dignity and independence") (La Forest J).

39 See *Rodriguez* v. *British Columbia (Attorney General)*, at 634 ("s. 241(b) infringes the right in s. 7 of the Charter to security of the person, a concept which encompasses the notions of dignity and the right to privacy") (McLachlin J).

40 See *R* v. *Daviault*, [1994] 3 SCR 63, 126 ("The Charter calls for a similar response. Central to its values are the integrity and dignity of the human person. These serve to define the principles of fundamental justice") (Sopinka J).

41 See *Reference re Motor Vehicle Act (British Columbia) s. 94(2)*, [1985] 2 SCR 486, 503.

42 *Ibid*. See also *R* v. *Seaboyer*, [1991] 2 SCR 577, 606.

and that criminal liability must be based upon *mens rea*.[43] The rules of search and seizure[44] are based on "the integrity of the body,"[45] limitation of which is a limitation of human dignity.[46] This protection also covers "biographic information" received from searches of computers.[47] The law regarding the right to remain silent ("not to be compelled to be a witness")[48] is also influenced by human dignity.[49]

The situation is the same regarding the provision according to which everyone has the right not to be subjected to any cruel and unusual treatment or punishment.[50] The Supreme Court determined that in deciding whether treatment is cruel or unusual, the value of human dignity should be considered.[51] The death penalty is prohibited in Canada. The question arose whether accused persons can be extradited from Canada to the USA without demanding a guarantee that they will not be executed in the USA. In *Kindler*[52] the majority decided that a fugitive can be extradited without requiring a guarantee from the USA that he will not be executed. That approach was changed in *Burns*,[53] in which it was held that such

43 See *R* v. *Hess*, [1990] 2 SCR 906, 918.

44 See s. 8 of the Canadian Charter.

45 *R* v. *Dyment*, [1988] 2 SCR 417, 429.

46 *Ibid.*, at para. 27 ("the use of a person's body without his consent to obtain information about him, invades an area of personal privacy essential to the maintenance of his human dignity") (La Forest J); *R* v. *Greffe*, [1990] 1 SCR 755, 795 ("it is the intrusive nature of the rectal search and considerations of human dignity and bodily integrity that demand the high standard of justification before such a search will be reasonable" (Lamer J); *R* v. *Golden*, [2001] 3 SCR 679, 737 ("a strip search is a much more intrusive search and accordingly, a higher degree of justification is required in order to support the higher degree of interference with individual freedom and dignity (Iacobucci and Arbour JJ); *R* v. *Stillman*, at 642.

47 See *R* v. *Plant*, [1993] 3 SCR 281, 293 ("In fostering the underlying values of dignity, integrity and autonomy, it is fitting that s. 8 of the Charter should seek to protect a biographical core of personal information which individuals in a free and democratic society would wish to maintain and control from dissemination to the state") (Sopinka J).

48 See s. 11(c) of the Canadian Charter.

49 See *R* v. *Amway Corp.*, [1989] 1 SCR 21, 40 ("Applying a purposive interpretation to s. 11(c), I am of the opinion that it was intended to protect the individual against the affront to dignity and privacy inherent in a practice which enables the prosecution to force the person charged to supply the evidence out of his or her own mouth") (Sopinka J).

50 See s. 12 of the Canadian Charter.

51 See *R* v. *Smith*, [1987] 1 SCR 1045, para. 98 ("A punishment will be cruel and unusual if … [t]he punishment is of such character or duration as to outrage the public conscience or to be degrading to human dignity") (Lamer J).

52 *Kindler* v. *Canada (Minister of Justice)*, [1991] 2 SCR 779. See also *Reference Re Ng Extradition*, [1991] 2 SCR 858.

53 *United States* v. *Burns*, [2001] 1 SCR 283.

extradition violates principles of fundamental justice. In his dissent in *Kindler*, Justice Cory wrote:

> Although any form of punishment may be a blow to human dignity, some form of punishment is essential for the orderly functioning of society. However, when a punishment becomes so demanding that all human dignity is lost, then the punishment must be considered cruel and unusual.[54]

The minority opinion in *Kindler* became the majority opinion in *Burns*. However, the basis for the decision is not section 12 of the Canadian Charter, where cruel and unusual punishment is prohibited, but rather section 7.

B. *The content of human dignity*

(1) Human dignity as the humanity of the person

The Justices of the Supreme Court of Canada have attempted, each in their own way, to express their conception of the value of human dignity. It has been emphasized that the value of human dignity is an "abstract and subjective,"[55] elusive[56] and value-ridden[57] concept. It has been noted that there may be different conceptions of the concept of human dignity. Nonetheless, an attempt has been made to understand the essence of human dignity in the Canadian Charter. That essence is unrelated to the rank and status of a person.[58] It is inherent in a person and his relations with others. A principled expression of this was provided by Justice L'Heureux-Dubé:

> Dignity is [a] concept comprising fundamental assumptions about what it means to be a human being in a society. It is an essential aspect of humanity, the absence of which is felt by all members of society.[59]

Human dignity is the humanity of a person. That humanity is expressed in various acts that promote it, and in other acts that limit it. It is therefore

[54] *Kindler* v. *Canada (Minister of Justice)*, at 814.

[55] *R* v. *Kapp*, at 511 ("Human dignity is an abstract and subjective notion") (McLachlin CJ, Abella J)

[56] *Canadian Foundation for Children, Youth and the Law* v. *Canada (Attorney General)*, [2004] 1 SCR 76, 132 ("The concept of 'human dignity' is somewhat elusive") (Binnie J).

[57] *Nova Scotia (Attorney General)* v. *Walsh*, [2002] 4 SCR 325, 370 ("Dignity is by its very nature a loaded and value-ridden concept") (L'Heureux-Dubé J).

[58] See *Law* v. *Canada (Minister of Employment and Immigration)*, at 530.

[59] See *Nova Scotia (Attorney General)* v. *Walsh*, at 370.

examined by judges in the framework of their discussion of the various rights.

(2) The various expressions of human dignity

(a) Human dignity in *Law* The most comprehensive analysis of human dignity was performed by Justice Iacobucci in *Law*.[60] This case dealt with the right to equality. The constitutionality of a statute granting pensions following the death of a spouse was examined. The statute determined that a spouse younger than 30 would receive lower benefits than a spouse over 30 would receive. The question was whether this provision violates the right to equality. Justice Iacobucci determined that the purpose underlying the right to equality is preventing violation of human dignity:

> The purpose of s. 15(1) is to prevent the violation of essential human dignity and freedom through the imposition of disadvantage, stereotyping, or political or social prejudice, and to promote a society in which all persons enjoy equal recognition at law as human beings or as members of Canadian society, equally capable and equally deserving of concern, respect and consideration.[61]

Further on in the judgment Justice Iacobucci asks: "What is human dignity?"[62] He answers in the context of the right to equality enshrined in the Canadian Charter (section 15(1)):

> Human dignity means that an individual or group feels self-respect and self-worth. It is concerned with physical and psychological integrity and empowerment. Human dignity is harmed by unfair treatment premised upon personal traits or circumstances which do not relate to individual needs, capacities, or merit. It is enhanced by laws which are sensitive to the needs, capacities, and merits of different individuals, taking into account the context underlying their differences. Human dignity is harmed when individuals and groups are marginalized, ignored, or devalued, and is enhanced when laws recognize the full place of all individuals and groups within Canadian society. Human dignity within the meaning of the equality guarantee does not relate to the status or position of an individual in society per se, but rather concerns the manner in which a person legitimately feels when confronted with a particular law. Does the law treat him or her unfairly, taking into account all of the circumstances regarding the individuals affected and excluded by the law?[63]

[60] *Law* v. *Canada (Minister of Employment and Immigration)*.
[61] *Ibid.*, at 529. [62] *Ibid.*, at 530. [63] *Ibid.*

This view of human dignity, although determined in the context of the right to equality, could of course inform an understanding of human dignity in other contexts.

(b) Human dignity in *Morgentaler* An additional point of view on human dignity can be found in Justice Wilson's judgment in *Morgentaler*.[64] That case examined a statutory criminal provision prohibiting abortion.[65] The majority opinion, delivered by Chief Justice Dickson,[66] decided that the provision infringes upon pregnant women's right to liberty and security of the person,[67] and cannot be saved by the provisions of the limitations clause.[68] Justice Wilson wrote a concurring opinion in which she explained that the criminal provision limits the woman's liberty and security of the person because it limits her human dignity:

> The *Charter* and the right to individual liberty guaranteed under it are inextricably tied to the concept of human dignity.[69]

In Justice Wilson's opinion, underlying the Canadian Charter is a theory according to which:

> The state will respect choices made by individuals and, to the greatest extent possible will avoid subordinating these choices to any one conception of the good life ... Thus, an aspect of the respect for human dignity on which the *Charter* is founded is the right to make fundamental personal decisions without interference from the state ... The right to reproduce or not to reproduce which is in issue in this case ... is properly perceived as an integral part of modern woman's struggle to assert *her* dignity and worth as a human being.[70]

Regarding the statute prohibiting abortions, Justice Wilson writes:

> She is truly being treated as a means – a means to an end which she does not desire but over which she has no control. She is the passive recipient of a decision made by others as to whether her body is to be used to nurture new life. Can there be anything that comports less with human dignity and self-respect?[71]

The two foundations upon which Justice Wilson bases her opinion – the right to make basic, personal decisions and not be a mere means in the

[64] *R* v. *Morgentaler*, [1988] 1 SCR 30.
[65] See s. 251 of the Canadian Criminal Code, RSC 1970, c. C-34.
[66] *R* v. *Morgentaler*, at 35.
[67] See s. 7 of the Canadian Charter.
[68] See s. 1 of the Canadian Charter.
[69] *R* v. *Morgentaler*, at 164.
[70] *Ibid.*, at 166–72 (emphasis in original).
[71] *Ibid.*, at 173.

decisions of others – are consistent themes in the jurisprudence of the Supreme Court of Canada.

(c) Human dignity, free will and individual autonomy The view that human dignity means, inter alia, a person's free will to develop his body and spirit as he desires[72] by using his own autonomy of free will[73] is a consistent theme in the Canadian Supreme Court's jurisprudence. Human dignity is limited if an accused is extradited to a country where he may face the death penalty,[74] if the right to participate in elections is limited,[75] if a prisoner is denied the right to vote,[76] if a person is required to incriminate himself,[77] if the possibility of ending his life is taken from him,[78] if he is subjected to sexual relations against his will,[79] if he is discriminated against due to stereotyping and social prejudice in appointments or in any other way that harms his self-respect,[80] and if he is degraded and dehumanized.[81] Human dignity requires protection of a person's reputation,[82] his

[72] *Ibid.* See also *Miron* v. *Trudel*, [1995] 2 SCR 418, para. LXV ("the principle of equality … recognizes the dignity of each human being and each person's freedom to develop his body and spirit as he or she desires") (McLachlin J).

[73] See *R* v. *Morgentaler*, at 166; *Rodriguez* v. *British Columbia (Attorney General)*, at 560; *R* v. *Ewanchuk*, [1999] 1 SCR 330, 348 ("Having control over who touches one's body, and how, lies at the core of human dignity and autonomy") (Major J).

[74] See *Kindler* v. *Canada (Minister of Justice)*.

[75] See *Reference re Prov. Electoral Boundaries (Sask.)*, [1991] 2 SCR 158.

[76] See *Sauvé* v. *Canada (Chief Electoral Officer)*, [2002] 3 SCR 519.

[77] See *R* v. *White*, [1999] 2 SCR 417; *R* v. *Stillman*.

[78] See *Rodriguez* v. *British Columbia (Attorney General)*.

[79] See *R* v. *Mabior*, 2012 SCC 47, [2012] 2 SCR 584, para. 45 ("sexual assault is wrong because it denies the victim's dignity as a human being") (McLachlin CJ).

[80] See *Miron* v. *Trudel*; *Law* v. *Canada (Minister of Employment and Immigration)*; *M. (A)* v. *Ryan*.

[81] See *R* v. *Butler*, [1992] 1 SCR 452, 479 ("degrading or dehumanizing materials place women (and sometimes men) in positions of subordination, servile submission or humiliation. They run against the principles of equality and dignity of all human beings") (Sopinka J).

[82] See *Hill* v. *Church of Scientology of Toronto*; *R* v. *Lucas*, [1998] 1 SCR 439, 463 ("The protection of an individual's reputation from willful and false attack recognizes … the innate dignity of the individual") (Cory J); *WIC Radio Ltd.* v. *Simpson*, at 429 ("the worth and dignity of each individual, including reputation, is an important value underlying the Charter") (Binnie J); *Bou Malhab* v. *Diffusion Métromédia CMR Inc.* [2011] 1 SCR 214, 229 ("Since good reputation is related to dignity … it is also tied to the rights protected by the Canadian Charter. Reputation is a fundamental feature of personality that makes it possible for an individual to develop in society") (Deschamps J).

privacy,[83] his full participation in society as an equal member,[84] and his freedom of expression.[85]

(d) Human dignity and viewing a person as an end unto himself Human dignity is limited when a person is seen as a means for attaining the ends of another person or of society, and not as an end in and of himself. A person's dignity is limited when he is seen as an object and not a human being, his own identity and will are irrelevant, and he is controlled by the will of another. Thus, a woman's dignity is limited if she is prohibited from having an abortion;[86] the human dignity of a defendant is limited if he is found criminally liable and sentenced to prison without *mens rea* or negligence;[87] his dignity is limited when he is subject to a sexual act against his will.[88]

(e) Human dignity within a society Human dignity is the dignity of a person within the society in which he lives. A person's dignity is promoted where his full place in the society in which he lives is recognized;[89] human dignity is protected where he is allowed to participate fully in his society as an equal[90] and take responsibility for what is happening in society.[91]

[83] See *M. (A)* v. *Ryan*, at para. 80 ("That privacy is essential to human dignity, a basic value underlying the Charter, has also been recognized") (L'Heureux-Dubé J).

[84] See *Gosselin* v. *Quebec (Attorney General)*, at 462 ("The aspect of human dignity targeted by s. 15(1) is the right of each person to participate fully in society and to be treated as an equal member") (McLachlin CJ).

[85] See *R.W.D.S.U., Local 558* v. *Pepsi-Cola Canada Beverages (West) Ltd.*, at 176 ("Free speech protects human dignity and the right to think and reflect freely on one's circumstances and condition") (McLachlin CJ and LeBel J).

[86] See *R* v. *Morgentaler*.

[87] See *R* v. *Hess*, at 924 ("to imprison a 'mentally innocent' person is to inflict grave injury on that person's dignity and sense of worth … that person is treated as little more than a means to an end. That person is in essence told that because of an overriding social or moral objective he must lose his freedom even though he took all reasonable precautions to ensure that no offence was committed") (Wilson J).

[88] See *R* v. *Mabior*, at para. 48 ("To engage in sexual acts without the consent of another person is to treat him or her as an object and negate his or her human dignity") (McLachlin CJ).

[89] See *Law* v. *Canada (Minister of Employment and Immigration)*, at 530 ("Human dignity … is enhanced when laws recognize the full place of all individuals and groups within Canadian society") (Iacobucci J).

[90] See *Gosselin* v. *Quebec (Attorney General)*, at 462 ("The aspect of human dignity targeted by s. 15(1) is the right of each person to participate fully in society and to be treated as an equal member") (McLachlin CJ).

[91] See *R* v. *Salituro*, [1991] 3 SCR 654, 682 ("The dignity of the person arises not only from the exercise of rights such as freedom to choose, but also, and just as importantly, from

Therefore, fulfillment of human dignity requires that a person's vote in elections not be unduly debased or diluted[92] and that he be granted the right to vote.[93] Freedom of expression promotes human dignity because it allows a person to express himself and persuade others of hope for positive change.[94]

C. *The role of human dignity as a constitutional value*

(1) Human dignity as an interpretational standard for determining the scope of a constitutional right

Human dignity as a constitutional value has an interpretational role. Human dignity is seen as a constitutional value that is fulfilled by the various constitutional rights. The rights have been interpreted in a way that fulfills that value.[95] Chief Justice Dickson writes:

> The court must be guided by the values essential to a free and democratic society which I believe embody … respect for the inherent dignity of the human person.[96]

Justice Bastarache has repeated that same approach:

> Respect for the inherent dignity of persons is clearly an essential value in our free and democratic society which must guide the courts in interpreting the Charter.[97]

the assumption of the responsibility that naturally flows from participation in the life of the community") (Iacobucci J).

92 See *Reference re Prov. Electoral Boundaries (Sask.)*, at 196 ("Respect for individual dignity and social equality mandate that citizen's votes not be unduly debased or diluted") (McLachlin J).

93 See *Sauvé* v. *Canada (Chief Electoral Officer)*, at para. 35 ("Denying citizens the right to vote runs counter to our constitutional commitment to the inherent worth and dignity of every individual") (McLachlin CJ).

94 See *R.W.D.S.U., Local 558* v. *Pepsi-Cola Canada Beverages (West) Ltd.*, at 172 ("Free speech protects human dignity and the right to think and reflect freely, on one's circumstances and conditions. It allows a person to speak not only for the sake of expression itself, but also to advocate change, attempting to persuade others in the hope of improving one's life and perhaps the wider social, political, and economic environment") (McLachlin CJ and LeBel J).

95 See *Gosselin* v. *Quebec (Attorney General)*, at 546 ("[R]espect for the dignity of all human beings is an important, if not fundamental, value of this or any society, and that the interpretation of the Charter may be aided by taking such values into account") (L'Heureux-Dubé J). See also *R* v. *Mabior*, at para. 45 ("The Charter values of equality, autonomy, liberty, privacy and human dignity are particularly relevant to … interpretation") (McLachlin CJ).

96 *R* v. *Oakes*, at para. 64.

97 *Blencoe* v. *British Columbia (Human Rights Commission)*, at 363.

Human dignity is not the only value that a given particular right is intended to fulfill. Indeed, human dignity is only one of the values that must be fulfilled, and the Court must balance between it and other values that a given right fulfills. Furthermore, even where human dignity has been recognized as a goal of a certain right, it is not the entire scope of human dignity that is the goal of the right, but rather a certain aspect of human dignity. Nonetheless, and subject to those caveats, human dignity has had great influence on the interpretation of the various rights and on the determination of their scope.

In a long line of cases it has been noted that among other values, the value of human dignity underlies the right to equality.[98] This jurisprudence reached its peak in *Law*,[99] in which it was determined that the central purpose underlying the right to equality is human dignity. A few years later the approach changed. In *Kapp*[100] the Court indicated the difficulties in adopting human dignity as an organizing principle for equality, and proposed other tests.[101]

(2) Human dignity in the limitation of constitutional rights

The constitutional rights enshrined in the Canadian Charter are relative. They can be limited. These limitations themselves have limitations. This is determined in section 1 of the Canadian Charter:

> The Canadian Charter of Rights and Freedoms guarantees the rights and freedoms set out in it subject only to such reasonable limits prescribed by law as can be demonstrably justified in a free and democratic society.

This provision was interpreted as reflecting proportionality.[102] It determines the principles that must be fulfilled in order to justify the limitation of a constitutional right in a free and democratic society. As the Court held

[98] See section 2A(2)(a) above.

[99] See *Law* v. *Canada (Minister of Employment and Immigration)*. See also Errol P. Mendes, 'Taking Equality into the 21st Century: Establishing the Concept of Equal Human Dignity' (2000) 12 *National Journal of Constitutional Law* 3; Robert Leckey, 'Embodied Dignity' (2005) 5 *Oxford University Commonwealth Law Journal* 63.

[100] See *R.* v. *Kapp*.

[101] Ackermann criticized this decision – see Laurie Ackermann, *Human Dignity: Lodestar for Equality in South Africa* (Cape Town: Juta, 2012) 241. See also Christopher Essert, 'Dignity and Membership, Equality and Egalitarianism: Economic Rights and Section 15' (2006) 19 *Canadian Journal of Law and Jurisprudence* 507; Rory O'Connell, 'The Role of Dignity in Equality Law: Lessons from Canada and South Africa' (2008) 6 *International Journal of Constitutional Law* 267.

[102] See *R* v. *Oakes*, at 143. See also Aharon Barak, *Proportionality: Constitutional Rights and their Limitations*, Doron Kalir trans. (Cambridge University Press, 2012) 161, 166.

in *Oakes*, these principles include human dignity. Chief Justice Dickson wrote about these principles, including human dignity, in *Oakes*:

> The underlying values and principles of a free and democratic society are the genesis of the rights and freedoms guaranteed by the *Charter* and the ultimate standard against which a limit on a right or freedom must be shown, despite its effect, to be reasonable and demonstrably justified.[103]

Human dignity has an important role in the rules of proportionality. First, a statute limiting a right enshrined in the Canadian Charter has a suitable purpose if its purpose is to promote human dignity. Second, in the framework of the *stricto sensu* proportionality (balancing) component, substantial consideration will be given to the side of the scales upon which human dignity lies. Thus, if a statute limits a right enshrined in the Charter, and the limitation is of an aspect regarding human dignity, that will be given substantial consideration in the balancing between prevention of that limitation and the fulfillment of the public objective that the statute is intended to fulfill.

[103] *R* v. *Oakes*, at para. 64.

13

Human dignity in German constitutional law

1. The normative traits of human dignity

A. *The provisions of Article 1(1) of the German Basic Law*

Human dignity is enshrined in the first article of the German Basic Law – which is the German Constitution. The Article reads:

(1) Human dignity shall be inviolable. To respect and protect it shall be the duty of all state authority.
(2) The German people therefore acknowledge inviolable and inalienable human rights as the basis of every community, of peace and of justice in the world.
(3) The following basic rights shall bind the legislature, the executive and the judiciary as directly applicable law.[1]

Extensive legal literature has dealt with this provision.[2] Its wording has influenced the drafting of provisions on human dignity in many

[1] The original wording: "(1) Die Würde des Menschen ist unantastbar. Sie zu achten und zu schützen ist Verpflichtung aller staatlichen Gewalt. (2) Das Deutsche Volk bekennt sich darum zu unverletzlichen und unveräußerlichen Menschenrechten als Grundlage jeder menschlichen Gemeinschaft, des Friedens und der Gerechtigkeit in der Welt. (3) Die nachfolgenden Grundrechte binden Gesetzgebung, vollziehende Gewalt und Rechtsprechung als unmittelbar geltendes Recht." The official translation of *unantastbar* is inaccurate.

[2] For German literature, see Christoph Enders, *Die Menschenwürde in der Verfassungsordnung: zur Dogmatik des Art. 1 GG* (Tübingen: Mohr Siebck, 1997); Michael Sachs, *GG Verfassungsrecht II. Grundrechte* (Berlin: Springer, 2003); Horst Dreier, *GG Grundgesetz Kommentar* (Tübingen: Mohr Siebeck, 2006); Bodo Pieroth and Bernhard Schlink, *Grundrechte Staatsrecht II* (Heidelberg: C. F. Müller Verlag, 2006); Matthias Mahlmann, *Elemente einer ethischen Grundrechtstheorie* (Berlin: Nomos, 2008). In addition to literature in German, there is extensive literature on human dignity in the German Constitution in other languages. See, inter alia, Mordechai Kremnitzer and Michal Kramer, *Human Dignity as a Supreme and Absolute Constitutional Value in German Law – In Israel Too?* (Jerusalem: The Israel Democracy Institute, 2011) (Heb.); Kurt Sontheimer, 'Principles of Human Dignity in the Federal Republic', in Paul Kirchhof and Donald P. Kommers and American Institute for Contemporary German Studies (eds.), *Germany*

constitutions.[3] A discussion on human dignity in comparative law usually begins with this provision.[4] It is characterized by three main normative traits: human dignity is an absolute right; it is an eternal right; and it

and its Basic Law: Past, Present, and Future: A German–American Symposium Dräger-Stiftung Publication (Baden-Baden: Nomos, 1993) 213; David P. Currie, *The Constitution of the Federal Republic of Germany* (University of Chicago Press, 1994) 315; Christian Walter, 'Human Dignity in German Constitutional Law', in European Commission for Democracy through Law, Venice Commission, CDL-STD 26, *The Principle of Respect for Human Dignity* (Strasbourg: Council of Europe, 1999) 25; Ernst Benda, 'The Protection of Human Dignity (Article 1 of the Basic Law)' (2000) 53 *SMU Law Review* 443; Winfried Brugger, 'May Government Ever Use Torture – Two Responses from German Law' (2000) 48 *American Journal of Comparative Law* 661; Eckart Klein, 'Human Dignity in German Law', in David Kretzmer and Eckart Klein (eds.), *The Concept of Human Dignity in Human Rights Discourse* (The Hague: Kluwer Law International, 2002) 145; Jackie Jones, '"Common Constitutional Traditions": Can the Meaning of Human Dignity under German Law Guide the European Court of Justice?' (Spring 2004) *Public Law* 167; Susanne Baer, 'Dignity, Liberty, Equality: A Fundamental Rights Triangle of Constitutionalism' (2009) 59 *University of Toronto Law Journal* 417; Henk Botha, 'Human Dignity in Comparative Perspective' (2009) 2 *Stellenbosch Law Review* 171; Christoph Möllers, 'Democracy and Human Dignity: Limits of a Moralized Conception of Rights in German Constitutional Law' (2009) 42 *Israel Law Review* 416; Matthias Mahlmann, 'The Basic Law at 60 – Human Dignity and the Culture of Republicanism' (2010) 11 *German Law Journal* 9; Christoph Enders, 'A Right to Have Rights – The German Constitutional Concept of Human Dignity' (2010) 3 *NUJS Law Review* 253; Mattias Mehlmann, 'Human Dignity and Autonomy in Modern Constitutional Orders', in Michael Rosenfeld and Andras Sajo (eds.), *The Oxford Handbook on Comparative Constitutional Law* (Oxford University Press, 2012) 370; Laurie Ackermann, *Human Dignity: Lodestar for Equality in South Africa* (Cape Town: Juta, 2012); Donald P. Kommers and Russell A. Miller, *The Constitutional Jurisprudence of the Federal Republic of Germany*, 3rd edn (Durham, NC: Duke University Press, 2012).

3 See Chapter 3, section 1.

4 See William A. Parent, 'Constitutional Commands of Human Dignity: A Bicentennial Essay in Honor of Mr. Justice William J. Brennan, Jr.' (1992) 5 *Canadian Journal of Law and Jurisprudence* 237; Edward J. Eberle, 'Human Dignity, Privacy and Personality in German and American Constitutional Law' (1997) *Utah Law Review* 963; Luis Aníbal Avilés Pagán, 'Human Dignity, Privacy and Personality Rights in the Constitutional Jurisprudence of Germany, The United States and The Commonwealth of Puerto Rico' (1998) 67 *Revista Juridica Universidad de Puerto Rico* 343; Edward J. Eberle, *Dignity and Liberty: Constitutional Visions in Germany and the United States* (Santa Barbara: Praeger, 2002); Dierk Ullrich, 'Concurring Visions: Human Dignity in the Canadian Charter of Rights and Freedoms and the Basic Law of the Federal Republic of Germany' (2003) 3 *Global Jurist Frontiers* 1; Lorne Sossin, 'The "Supremacy of God", Human Dignity and the Charter of Rights and Freedoms' (2003) 52 *University of New Brunswick Law Journal* 227; Catherine Dupré, *Importing Law in Post-Communist Transitions: The Hungarian Constitutional Court and the Right to Human Dignity* (Oxford and Portland, OR: Hart Publishing, 2003); Marc C. McAllister, 'Human Dignity and Individual Liberty in Germany and the United States as Examined through Each Country's Leading Abortion Cases' (2004) 11 *Tulsa Journal of Comparative & International Law* 491; Jones, 'Common Constitutional Traditions'; Ronald J. Krotoszynski, 'A Comparative Perspective on the First Amendment: Free Speech, Militant Democracy, and the Primacy of Dignity as a

constitutes the supreme value in the entire constitution. A fourth trait is attributed to human dignity, regarding the area it covers. I shall discuss all four traits in turn.

B. *Human dignity as an absolute right*

Article 1(1) of the German Basic Law states that human dignity is untouchable (*unantastbar*). This expression has been translated into English in the official publication as "inviolable." That is an incorrect translation. The term "inviolable" in the official translation translates correctly into German as "*unverletzlich*" (see Article 4(1) of the Constitution of Germany, which determines that the right to freedom of faith and conscience is " *unverletzlich*"). The term "*unantastbar*" means "untouchable": an absolute prohibition of limitation. That provision has been interpreted as stating that human dignity is an absolute right.[5] A right is absolute if its entire scope is protected. Thus an absolute right cannot be limited;[6] the limitations clause does not apply to it; the rules of proportionality do not apply to it; it cannot be balanced in order to protect other constitutional rights or to fulfill a public interest.[7] Any limitation of human dignity constitutes a violation of the right. Any limitation of the right to human dignity is unconstitutional.

This approach raises complicated questions. Is it jurisprudentially possible to recognize absolute rights? There are different and conflicting opinions on the matter.[8] Some think that even in German constitutional

Preferred Constitutional Value in Germany' (2004) 78 *Tulsa Law Review* 1549; Giovanni Bognetti, 'The Concept of Human Dignity in European and US Constitutionalism', in George Nolte (ed.), *European and US Constitutionalism* (Cambridge University Press, 2005) 85; Erin Daly, 'Constitutional Dignity: Lessons from Home and Abroad', Widener Law School Legal Studies Research Paper 08-07 (2007); James Fyfe, 'Dignity as Theory: Competing Conceptions of Human Dignity at the Supreme Court of Canada' (2007) 70 *Saskatchewan Law Review* 1; Ariel L. Bendor and Michael Sachs, 'Human Dignity as a Constitutional Concept in Germany and in Israel' (2011) 44 *Israel Law Review* 26; Botha, 'Human Dignity in Comparative Perspective'.

5 On absolute rights see Aharon Barak, *Proportionality: Constitutional Rights and their Limitations*, Doron Kalir trans. (Cambridge University Press, 2012) 27. See also Nils Teifke, 'Human Dignity as an "Absolute Principle"?', in Martin Borowski (ed.), *On the Nature of Legal Principles* (Stuttgart: Franz Steiner Verlag, 2010) 93.

6 See Mahlmann, *Elemente einer ethischen Grundrechtstheorie*, at 228; Klein, 'Human Dignity in German Law', at 148; Pieroth and Schlink, *Grundrechte Staatsrecht II*, at 80.

7 See Sachs, *GG Verfassungsrecht II*, at 83.

8 See Alan Gewirth, 'Are There Any Absolute Rights?' (1981) 31 *Philosophical Quarterly* 1; Robert Alexy, *A Theory of Constitutional Rights*, Julian Rivers trans. (Oxford University Press, 2002) 64.

law, human dignity is a relative right.[9] Therefore, torture, which limits human dignity, can be justified in extreme cases.[10] This opinion is not accepted in the German literature,[11] and it was expressly rejected in the *Aviation Security Case*.[12] That case examined a statute authorizing use of military force against an airplane hijacked by terrorists with hostages on board. The statute authorized shooting the plane down if there is no other way to prevent harm to innocent people outside the plane. It was held that the statute is unconstitutional because it limits the hostages' right to life in a way that violates their human dignity. Their death is merely a means to the end of saving others. The absolute character of the right to human dignity prevented an examination of the proportionality of the limitation of the hostages' right.

A troubling question is whether human dignity can be limited in order to protect human dignity. That question arises in the case of abortion. The human dignity of the fetus opposes the human dignity of the pregnant woman.[13] Some have expressed the opinion that a limitation in such circumstances is constitutional, as human dignity is found on both sides of the scales.[14] The accepted opinion is that even in such a situation the absolute character of the right to human dignity is preserved,[15] and

[9] See Alexy, *A Theory of Constitutional Rights*, at 64. See also Michael Klopfer, 'Leben und Würde des Menschen', in Peter Badura and Horst Dreier (eds.), *Festschrift 50 Jahre Bundesverfassungsgericht* (Tübingen: Mohr Siebeck, 2001) 82; Roman Herzog, Rupert Scholz, Matthias Herdegen and Hans H. Klein, *Maunz & Dürig Grundgesetz Kommentar* (Munich: C. H. Beck'sche Verlagsbuchhandlung, 2007) 12.

[10] See Gay Moon and Robin Allen, 'Dignity Discourse in Discrimination Law: A Better Route to Equality?' (2006) 11 *European Human Rights Law Review* 610.

[11] See Pieroth and Schlink, *Grundrechte Staatsrecht II*, at 84.

[12] BVerfGE 115, 118 (2006). On this judgment see Oliver Lepsius, 'Human Dignity and the Downing of Aircraft: The German Federal Constitutional Court Strikes Down a Prominent Anti-terrorism Provision in the New Air-transport Security Act' (2006) 7 *German Law Journal* 761; Kai Möller, 'On Treating Persons as Ends: The German Aviation Security Act, Human Dignity, and the German Federal Constitutional Court' (Autumn 2006) *Public Law* 457; Nina Naske and Georg Nolte, 'Legislative Authorization to Shoot Down Aircraft Abducted by Terrorists if Innocent Passengers Are on Board – Incompatibility with Human Dignity as Guaranteed by Article 1(1) of the German Constitution'(2007) 101 *American Journal of International Law* 466; Raymond Youngs, 'Germany: Shooting Aircraft and Analyzing Computer Data' (2008) 6 *International Journal of Constitutional Law* 331.

[13] See Mahlmann, *Elemente einer ethischen Grundrechtstheorie*, at 228.

[14] See Fabian Wittreck, 'Menschenwürde und Folterverbot' (2003) 56 *Die Öffentliche Verwaltung* 873.

[15] See Mahlmann, *Elemente einer ethischen Grundrechtstheorie*, at 198; Pieroth and Schlink, *Grundrechte Staatsrecht II*, at 84.

even when human dignity lies on both sides of the scales, no balancing is carried out.

There are those who hold that the absolute protection of human dignity applies only to activities that fall within the core of the right to human dignity. Acts that fall in the periphery of human dignity receive only relative protection.[16] That approach was not accepted in the German literature,[17] and it seems superfluous, as the general provision of the Basic Law determines that the essence (core) of each right cannot be affected.[18]

C. *Human dignity as an eternal right*

Article 79(3) of the German Basic Law determines that a number of issues, including the principles in Article 1 of the German Basic Law, cannot be constitutionally amended. The part of the provision dealing with human dignity states:

> Amendments to this Basic Law affecting ... the principles laid down in [Article] 1 ... shall be inadmissible.[19]

Thus it was determined that the principles enshrined in Article 1 of the German Basic Law, including the principles underlying human dignity, are eternal.[20] A constitutional amendment purporting to limit them is unconstitutional[21] whether it directly amends Article 1 of the Basic Law or whether, while amending other articles, it limits the aspect of human dignity protected in other constitutional rights.[22] In order to amend those principles, a new constitution must be enacted. The mechanism for

16 See Mattias Herdegen, 'Die Garantie der Menschenwürde: absolut und doch differenziert?," in Rolf Gröschner and Oliver W. Lembcke (eds.), *Das Dogma der Unantastbarkeit* (Tübingen: Mohr Siebeck, 2009) 93.

17 See Dreier, *GG Grundgesetz Kommentar*, at 226.

18 Art. 19(2) of the German Basic Law: "In no case may the essence of a basic right be affected."

19 The original wording is: "Eine Änderung dieses Grundgesetzes, durch welche die Gliederung des Bundes in Länder, die grundsätzliche Mitwirkung der Länder bei der Gesetzgebung oder die in den Artikeln 1 und 20 niedergelegten Grundsatze berührt würden, ist unzulässig."

20 See Dreier, *GG Grundgesetz Kommentar*, at 209; Kremnitzer and Kramer, *Human Dignity as a Supreme and Absolute Constitutional Value.*

21 On the unconstitutional constitutional amendment see Aharon Barak, 'Unconstitutional Constitutional Amendment' (2011) 44 *Israel Law Review* 321.

22 See Pieroth and Schlink, *Grundrechte Staatsrecht II*, at 80.

amending the existing constitution – constitutional amendment – is not a possibility.[23]

Eternity clauses in constitutions are rare,[24] and usually determine the basic structure of government, such as the eternity of its republican and democratic nature, and its secular character.[25] In a federative state, that character is eternalized in the constitution. What sets the German Constitution apart is the granting of eternal character to human dignity.[26]

D. *Human dignity as the supreme value in the German constitution*

The absolute and eternal character of human dignity is an expression of the approach of the judgments and literature in Germany, which see human dignity as the supreme constitutional value.[27] The spirit and essence of the entire constitution are learned from this value.[28] This value is the center of the constitutional structure;[29] it is the constitutional principle controlling all parts of the constitution.[30] This supreme status reflects the objective underlying the human dignity provision: reinforcing the lessons of the Second World War and the Holocaust.[31] The supreme status of the constitution reflects Germany's rejection of its Nazi past and the severe violations of human dignity that characterized it.[32] It places the value of

[23] Some believe that only a revolution can bring about amendment of the eternity provision in the German Constitution – see Benda, 'The Protection of Human Dignity', at 445.

[24] See Richard Albert, 'Constitutional Handcuffs' (2010) 42 *Arizona State Law Journal* 663; Yaniv Roznai, 'Unconstitutional Constitutional Amendment – The Migration and Success of a Constitutional Idea' (2013) 61 *American Journal of Comparative Law* 657.

[25] See, for example, Article 4 of the Turkish Constitution.

[26] An exception to this is the Constitution of Brazil of 1988, which recognized the absolute character of the constitutional provision regarding the federative aspect, equality in elections, separation of powers and human rights.

[27] See Mahlmann, *Elemente einer ethischen Grundrechtstheorie*, at 195; Dreier, *GG Grundgesetz Kommentar*, at 162–234; Pieroth and Schlink, *Grundrechte Staatsrecht II*, at 80; Kremnitzer and Kramer, *Human Dignity as a Supreme and Absolute Constitutional Value*, at 19.

[28] See BVerfGE 12, 45 (1960); BVerfGE 27, 1 (1969); BVerfGE 30, 173 (1971); BVerfGE 45, 187 (1977); BVerfGE 82, 60 (1990). See also Kommers and Miller, *The Constitutional Jurisprudence of the Federal Republic of Germany*, at 355.

[29] See BVerfGE 7, 198 (1958); BVerfGE 35, 202 (1973); BVerfGE 39, 1 (1975).

[30] See BVerfGE 6, 32 (1957); BVerfGE 87, 209 (1992).

[31] Pieroth and Schlink, *Grundrechte Staatsrecht II*, at 80; Dreier, *GG Grundgesetz Kommentar*, at 154.

[32] Dreier, *GG Grundgesetz Kommentar*, at 161; James Q. Whitman, 'On Nazi "Honour" and the New European "Dignity"', in Christian Joerges and Navraj S. Ghaleigh (eds.), *Darker*

human dignity, which the Nazis desecrated, at the topmost rung of their ladder of values.

There is no other constitution in which human dignity has such a central role. Thus, for example, in the Constitution of South Africa (1996) human dignity has a central place, but it stands alongside two additional values – equality and liberty – that are identical to human dignity in their constitutional status.[33] That is not the case in the German Constitution. Human dignity is peerless; it is the supreme value upon which the entire constitutional structure is based.

E. *The area covered by human dignity as a constitutional right*

These three traits of human dignity – its absolute, eternal and supreme character – distinguish human dignity in the German Basic Law. They grant it unique normative status. With this in mind, an additional trait of human dignity in German constitutional law that distinguishes it in comparison to human dignity in other constitutions should be pointed out. The Bill of Rights in the German Basic Law is comprehensive. Even without a constitutional right to human dignity, the existing framework of rights contains every individual interest or will limited by the state or unprotected by it. This is made possible primarily by the constitutional right enshrined in Article 2(1) of the German Basic Law:

> Every person shall have the right to free development of his personality insofar as he does not violate the rights of others or offend against the constitutional order or the moral law.[34]

The right to develop one's personality has been interpreted by the Constitutional Court as a sort of "catch-all right." Human conduct that is not included in the framework of the other rights are caught in the net of a person's right to develop his personality, regardless of the importance of the act or its centrality to the development of a person's personality. Thus, for example, a statute regulating riding in the forest[35] or prohibiting feeding pigeons in the town square[36] limits the constitutional right to the free

Legacies of Law in Europe: The Shadow of National Socialism (Oxford: Hart Publishing, 2003) 243.

[33] See Arts. 1, 7(1), 36 and 39 of the Constitution of South Africa.

[34] The original wording is: "(1) Jeder hat das Recht auf die freie Entfaltung seiner Persönlichkeit, soweit er nicht die Rechte anderer verletzt und nicht gegen verfassungsmäßige Ordnung oder das Sittengesetz verstößt."

[35] BVerfGE 80, 137 (1989). [36] BVerfGE 54, 143 (1980).

development of the personality of a person wishing to ride a horse in the forest or to feed pigeons in the town square. Of course, the limitation will be constitutional if it is proportionate.

This raises a question that is unique to German constitutional law: what is the area covered by the constitutional right to human dignity? If everything is covered by the other constitutional rights, what is left for human dignity? What act or omission of the state is protected by Article 1(1) of the German Basic Law that is not protected by other sections of the German Bill of Rights? Comprehensive and conflicting answers have been given to this question in German legal scholarship. The result of this debate is reflected, inter alia, in the approach that grants human dignity, as a separate and independent right, a most narrow scope that is exclusively its own and is not shared with other constitutional rights.

F. *The uniqueness of human dignity in German constitutional law*

The traits that characterize human dignity grant it a unique status in German constitutional law.[37] It is only natural that the interpretation of a right that is absolute will lead to results that narrow the area covered by the right.[38] The scope of the right must be narrow in order to prevent a situation in which many state actions – including socially important actions – will be prevented, as they will be held unconstitutional even if they are proportionate. Such a restricted breadth of limitation sits well with the narrow scope that human dignity has in the framework of the German Bill of Rights.

This uniqueness of human dignity in German constitutional law raises a number of questions. The first question is whether human dignity in German constitutional law is a constitutional right, or merely a constitutional value. The second question is: how can the elements of human dignity be defined? The third question is: what is the scope of human dignity in the Basic Law. The fourth question is: what influence does the uniqueness of human dignity in German law have on its applicability in comparative constitutional law? I shall discuss these questions below.

[37] See Sontheimer, 'Principles of Human Dignity', at 214.

[38] See Dreier, *GG Grundgesetz Kommentar*, at 162; Botha, 'Human Dignity in Comparative Perspective', at 218.

2. Human dignity as a constitutional value and a constitutional right

A. *Human dignity solely as a constitutional value*

There is consensus that human dignity is a constitutional value in German constitutional law. The question is whether it is solely a constitutional value, or also a constitutional right. In the German legal literature the opinion has been expressed that human dignity is solely a constitutional value. That approach has a textual anchor in Article 1(3) of the Basic Law, which determines that "[t]he following basic rights shall bind the legislature, the executive and the judiciary." This excludes the obligation of Article 1(1) itself, which enshrines human dignity.[39] Professor Dürig supported that view.[40] According to his approach, human dignity is an objective constitutional value, but does not constitute a subjective right as well.[41]

According to that approach, the objective constitutional value of human dignity is of great importance, especially in interpreting the constitution in general, and particularly the constitutional rights. However, in light of its uniqueness, human dignity is not a constitutional right. Dreier indicates that in all the cases in which the Constitutional Court has invoked human dignity, it has done so together with (*in Verbindung mit*) a specific constitutional right. Dreier also notes that it cannot be said that human dignity underlies the core of every constitutional right.[42] If that were so, the eternity clause would apply to that core, and that certainly is not the case. However, limitation of any constitutional right through a limitation of human dignity is unconstitutional, and that prohibition is absolute, even if the right itself is of relative value. I shall discuss this aspect in the discussion of human dignity as a constitutional right.

Professor Enders expressed the view that human dignity is a constitutional value and that its content is the right to have rights.[43] I shall discuss that approach in the discussion of human dignity as a constitutional right.

[39] See Walter, 'Human Dignity in German Constitutional Law', at 3.

[40] See Herzog *et al.*, *Maunz & Dürig Grundgesetz Kommentar*, at 33; Sachs, *GG Verfassungsrecht II*, at 82.

[41] See Dreier, *GG Grundgesetz Kommentar*, 209.

[42] *Ibid.*, at 226.

[43] Enders, *Die Menschenwürde in der Verfassungsordnung*. See also Enders, 'A Right to Have Rights'.

Opposing these approaches is the view that human dignity is both an objective constitutional value and a subjective constitutional right.[44] It appears that this latter is the accepted approach.[45]

B. *Human dignity as a constitutional right*

In contrast to the approach that sees human dignity as solely a constitutional value is the approach that sees it also as a constitutional right. Assuming that it is also a right, what does that right determine? There are a number of approaches to that issue. I shall discuss three of them in this context.

The first approach sees human dignity as a right to constitutional rights. The point of departure for this approach is that, fundamentally, human dignity is a constitutional value. The content of this value is "a right to have rights."[46] In my opinion, to the extent that the state has a duty pursuant to this value, it should be seen as a value that also constitutes a right, the content of which is the right to have rights.

A different approach, which seems to be that of Dreier,[47] is that human dignity is a constitutional value that determines the actions through which constitutional rights can be fulfilled. Thus, for example, every person has a right to life. That is a relative right. It can be limited if the limitation is proportional. However, limitation of the right to life is prohibited – prohibited absolutely – if it is done in a way that limits human dignity, such as by way of torture. That approach, which in my opinion reflects human dignity in German law well, cannot be satisfied with the determination that human dignity is solely a constitutional value. By imposing a state duty, it also creates a constitutional right. However, this right does not

[44] Mahlmann, *Elemente einer ethischen Grundrechtstheorie*, at 219; Sachs, *GG Verfassungsrecht II*, at 42; Benda, 'The Protection of Human Dignity', at 35; Klein, 'Human Dignity in German Law', at 147; Pieroth and Schlink, *Grundrechte Staatsrecht II*, at 80. See also BVerfGE 109, 133, 181 (2004).

[45] See Juliane Kokott, 'From Reception and Transplantation to Convergence of Constitutional Models in the Age of Globalization – With Particular Reference to the German Basic Law', in Christian Starck (ed.,) *Constitutionalism, Universalism and Democracy: A Comparative Analysis* (Baden-Baden: Nomos, 1999) 71, 81.

[46] See Enders, *Die Menschenwürde in der Verfassungsordnung*, at 501; Enders, 'A Right to Have Rights', at 255. As support for his view (on p. 501) Enders quotes Hannah Arendt, who noted that human dignity is "the right to have rights" – see Hannah Arendt, *The Origins of Totalitarianism* (New York: Harcourt, Brace & Co., 1951). For analysis of her approach, see John Helis, 'Hannah Arendt and Human Dignity: Theoretical Foundations and Constitutional Protection of Human Rights' (2008) 1 *Journal of Politics and Law* 73.

[47] See Dreier, *GG Grundgesetz Kommentar*, at 226.

have "its own normative zone," and it has no exclusive area of influence without reliance on the other constitutional rights. This right should be seen as a way to exercise the other constitutional rights. Thus human dignity always joins another constitutional right. What makes it unique is that it prohibits limitation of the various constitutional rights when they limit human dignity. The conclusion is that regarding any relative constitutional right there are a number of ways of limiting it that are prohibited absolutely: in other words, regardless of the proportionality of the limitation. These are limitations of a (relative) constitutional right that entail limitation of human dignity or an infringement upon the core of the right as per Article 19(2) of the Basic Law.

A third approach, which is accepted by most of those dealing with the question in Germany, is that human dignity is not only a (objective) constitutional value, but also a (subjective) constitutional right.[48] The definition of this right and its scope are controversial.

3. The definition of human dignity

A. Negative and positive definitions

German constitutional law has experienced difficulty in defining human dignity. This is an obvious difficulty, considering the debate regarding the question of whether human dignity is solely a constitutional value or also a constitutional right, and in light of the lack of clarity regarding the area covered by human dignity. It is only natural that the answers to the question of whether human dignity is a value or a right and to the question of its scope directly affect the answer to the question of definition.

A way out of the definitional difficulty can be found by defining human dignity in a negative fashion. Human dignity is limited if a person is subjected to torture, degradation, discrimination or cruel punishment. But can human dignity be given a positive definition? An attempt at an affirmative answer to this question was made by Dürig. According to his approach, human dignity is limited where a person is seen merely as a means for achieving someone else's ends. Human dignity is always seeing a person as an end and not as a mere means or an object. That is the object formula (*Objektformel*). Extensive literature discusses the advantages and disadvantages of this approach. It was recently adopted in the

[48] See Pieroth and Schlink, *Grundrechte Staatsrecht II*, at 80.

Aviation Security Case.[49] The human dignity of the hostages was limited, because in their deaths they would become mere means for saving the lives of others.

Mahlmann[50] tried to give human dignity a positive definition that is detached from religious views and mainly adopts the object formula. According to his definition, a person is an intellectual-moral being, who develops himself within society. Human dignity is derived from his humanity. The content of human dignity is based upon his being a rational and free being, capable of moral action. This explanation is not metaphysical or Kantian. Underlying it is an empirical view. A person sees himself as an end, with no person being preferred over another. According to measures of justice and humanity, a person is not merely a means, but is an end in and of himself.

A number of authors point out the association between human dignity and democracy.[51] Thus, for example, for Möllers democracy and human rights are grounded in human dignity.[52] They are both based on peoples' ability to make rational decisions and to be free.[53] Human dignity protects what makes a person human: not life itself, but rather human nature. What distinguishes human beings is their ability to make decisions by giving reason to their actions. A person should not be seen as mere flesh and blood. Thus torture is prohibited. By the same token, a woman should not be prevented from dancing nude in a glass cell as men pay to watch her (peep show) of her own volition to make a living,[54] and the decision in the *Aviation Security Case* is incorrect.[55]

Most approaches focus upon human dignity in the framework of society. Human dignity is not the human dignity of a person on a desert island.

B. *Shared and conflicting elements of the various definitions*

Despite the substantive difference between the various definitions, they are likely to lead to identical conclusions in a number of situations. Naturally, these are extreme situations – situations in which a universal

[49] BVerfGE 115, 118 (2006).

[50] See Mahlmann, *Elemente einer ethischen Grundrechtstheorie*, at 195; Mahlmann, 'The Basic Law at 60', at 23.

[51] See Botha, 'Human Dignity in Comparative Perspective'.

[52] See Möllers, 'Democracy and Human Dignity'.

[53] See *ibid.*, at 433.

[54] See BVerfGE 64, 274, 279 (1981).

[55] See Möllers, 'Democracy and Human Dignity', at 434.

taboo has been broken. Sachs lists four of these situations.[56] The first is protection and ensuring bodily integrity. Included in this are the prohibition of torture, severe punishments, brainwashing, systematic rape and degradation. The second is ensuring basic equality between people. The third is protection of the personal identity of the individual, and protection of a person's psychological integrity and intellectual fulfillment. The fourth is ensuring the minimal subsistence of the individual in society.

Beyond the common core there is debate. An example is the ruling of the Federal Administrative Court that determined that a statute prohibiting peep shows is unconstitutional.[57] This ruling comports with the object formula. It does not comport with the fulfillment of a person's personal identity.

4. The scope of human dignity

A. *The dignity of every person as a human being*

Human dignity – as a constitutional value or a constitutional right – is the dignity of every person. Citizenship, residency, age, sex, health condition and personal traits are not relevant to human dignity. The only necessary condition is being a human being. Thus a person who is illegally within the state's borders has a constitutional right to dignity. In contrast, a corporation does not have human dignity. Human dignity cannot be waived, lost or expunged. Detainees and prisoners are entitled to human dignity. Minors are entitled to human dignity.

Human dignity, whether as a value or as a right – has both a negative and a positive aspect. This is expressly determined in Article 1(1) of the German Basic Law, which states:

> To respect and protect [human dignity] shall be the duty of all state authority.

The duty to *respect* reflects the negative aspect. The state is not permitted to limit human dignity. The duty to *protect* reflects the positive aspect. The state must protect human dignity from acts by third parties. The provision of Article 1(1) of the German Basic Law is exclusively dedicated to human dignity. It does not apply to the other rights. The positive aspect of

[56] See Sachs, *GG Verfassungsrecht II*, at 42.
[57] See note 54 above.

those rights was established by the German Constitutional Court by way of interpretation.[58]

B. *Human dignity's beginning and end*

(1) Human dignity's beginning

Human dignity begins at the beginning of life. Therefore, according to the accepted approach, a fetus also possesses human dignity.[59] "[W]here there is human life it is accompanied by human dignity."[60] According to the case law, life begins at the time that the ovum is implanted in the uterus (approximately twelve days after fertilization).[61] Is legislation decriminalizing abortions as a general rule, rather than in extreme circumstances, always unconstitutional as it limits the life of a fetus in a way that limits its human dignity? The *First Abortion Case* answered that question in the affirmative.[62] This view was changed in the *Second Abortion Case*.[63] The Court held that an abortion fundamentally limits the unborn fetus' right to life, and the state is duty-bound to protect the life of the fetus by force of Article 1(1) of the Basic Law. However, not every abortion limits human dignity, and the fetus' right to life must be balanced against the rights of the mother. Legislation allowing an abortion after medical consultation is constitutional, in certain circumstances, as the injury to the life of the fetus is carried out in a way that does not limit human dignity. In addition, the court held that abortions performed by the twelfth week of pregnancy need not be criminalized.[64]

The decisions in both abortion cases received sharp criticism. Both assume that the fetus is protected by human dignity. According to the critics – chiefly Dreier[65] – the proper "location" of the question of abortions is not in Article 1(1) of the German Basic Law (dealing with human dignity), but rather in Article 2 (dealing with the right to life). In this

[58] See BVerfGE 7, 198 (1958).

[59] See Dreier, *GG Grundgesetz Kommentar*, at 173; Mahlmann, *Elemente einer ethischen Grundrechtstheorie*, at 198.

[60] BVerfGE 39, 1 (1975) (the *First Abortion Case*). See also Walter, 'Human Dignity in German Constitutional Law'.

[61] See Mahlmann, *Elemente einer ethischen Grundrechtstheorie*, at 224.

[62] See BVerfGE 39, 1 (1975). See also Mahlmann, *Elemente einer ethischen Grundrechtstheorie*, at 198.

[63] See BVerfGE 88, 203 (1993).

[64] See Kommers and Miller, *The Constitutional Jurisprudence of the Federal Republic of Germany*, at 392.

[65] See Dreier, *GG Grundgesetz Kommentar*, at 175.

framework, both the right of the mother and the right of the fetus must be considered. This consideration occurs within the normative framework of proportionality, which is based, inter alia, upon balancing between the right of the mother and the right of the fetus. From the point of view of the fetus, "locating" the abortion problem within human dignity prevents any balancing due to the absolute character of human dignity. It also prevents any possibility of differentiating between an abortion performed in the first twelve weeks of pregnancy and an abortion performed after that. In both cases, the abortion will be unconstitutional. This result is undesirable, as it precludes any consideration of the human dignity of the pregnant mother.

(2) Human dignity's end

Human dignity does not come to an end at a person's death. The dead are also entitled to human dignity.[66] This is true of the body of the deceased, and the dignity of his memory. Therefore, the body is not to be used as a source for organs for the benefit of others without advance consent, or the consent of relatives. Nor can we extend the life of organs in the body of a pregnant woman who has died in order to enable the birth of a live baby.[67] A body is not to be shown in public for commercial ends.[68] The memory of the dead is not to be tarnished. The right to human dignity belongs to the deceased. It is exercised by his relatives.[69] The right of the deceased is not in force forever. Its application is temporally limited. As the memory of the deceased fades, so fades his right to human dignity.[70] Thus there is nothing preventing evacuation of cemeteries after the passage of time, and there is nothing preventing presentation of skeletons of those who died long ago.

C. *Human dignity and bioethics*

In recent years, and with the development of new technologies, new ways of creating life have been discovered. From in vitro fertilization to

[66] See *ibid.*, at 176; Mahlmann, *Elemente einer ethischen Grundrechtstheorie*, at 226.

[67] See Kremnitzer and Kramer, *Human Dignity as a Supreme and Absolute Constitutional Value*, at 62; Walter, 'Human Dignity in German Constitutional Law'; Alexander Jooss, 'Life After Death? Post Mortem Protection of Name, Image and Likeness under German Law with Specific Reference to "Marlene Dietrich"' (2001) 12 *Entertainment Law Review* 141.

[68] See Kremnitzer and Kramer, *Human Dignity as a Supreme and Absolute Constitutional Value*, at 62; Dreier, *GG Grundgesetz Kommentar*, at 177.

[69] See Mahlmann, *Elemente einer ethischen Grundrechtstheorie*, at 228.

[70] *Ibid.*

cloning, bioethics has developed while attempting to outline a normative framework for examining the constitutionality of the new technologies. In Germany, one of the important sources for determining normative standards for bioethics is human dignity.[71] Thus, for example, some believe that life begins when an ovum is fertilized outside the uterus, and from that stage forward human dignity determines what is permissible. Others believe that cloning harms the human race, and that the human race – and not only each person as an individual – is protected by human dignity.

5. Human dignity in German constitutional law and comparative law

Human dignity as a constitutional value and as a constitutional right has been the subject of impressive and unprecedented development in the Constitutional Court of Germany and in German legal scholarship.[72] Only the tip of the iceberg has been revealed in this chapter.[73] It is only natural that other legal systems turn to German constitutional law for interpretational inspiration when dealing with problems that arise regarding human dignity. At times, legal scholarship in a given country is criticized for not turning sufficiently to German law for interpretational inspiration.[74] However, the uniqueness of human dignity in the German constitutional law greatly limits the relevance of the German approach to human dignity for other legal systems that recognize human dignity as a constitutional right.

Indeed, comparative law can make use of the legal questions dealt with by German constitutional jurisprudence and legal scholarship, and from the way those questions are treated. However, the German answers to those questions are much less useful. This is because those answers are

[71] See Dreier, *GG Grundgesetz Kommentar*.

[72] For an assessment of the contribution of German legal scholarship and of the case law of the Constitutional Court of Germany to the understanding of human dignity, see Stuart Woolman, 'Dignity' in Stuart Woolman, Michael Bishop and Jason Brickhill (eds.), *Constitutional Law of South Africa*, 2nd edn, Revision Series 4 (Cape Town: Juta, 2012) chapter 36; Ackermann, *Human Dignity*, at 115; Botha, 'Human Dignity in Comparative Perspective', at 173 ("The scope and sophistication of the dignity jurisprudence of German courts – in particular the Federal Constitutional Court – and the depth of academic comment by German constitutional law scholars on the concept and uses of dignity are unparalleled in any other country").

[73] See Dupré, *Importing Law in Post-Communist Transitions*.

[74] See Botha, 'Human Dignity in Comparative Perspective'.

directly influenced by the unique character of the right to human dignity in the German constitution. The absolute and eternal character of the right to human dignity, the conception of human dignity as the supreme constitutional value, and the fact that all human conduct that is not included in a specific constitutional right is granted constitutional protection by the catch-all right to personality, rather than by human dignity, influence the understanding of the right to human dignity in the German Constitution, and serve as the factors that grant that right a narrow sense in German constitutional law. That uniqueness and its results do not exist in constitutions that do not grant the constitutional right to human dignity the narrow scope it has in German constitutional law.[75]

The absolute character of the right to human dignity is unique to German law. There is nothing comparable in other constitutions. That character is naturally a factor in the narrow interpretation of the constitutional right to human dignity. Such an interpretation is not necessary in the other legal systems, in which human dignity is a relative constitutional right. The same is true regarding the eternal character of the right to human dignity. It also is a factor in the narrow interpretation of human dignity, and it too is unique to German constitutional law. In other constitutions the right to human dignity is not eternal. The understanding of human dignity as the supreme constitutional value reflects German history and the violations of human dignity under the Third Reich. Other states have different histories. Even if they recognize the importance of human dignity, they do not grant it supremacy over all other values. Lastly, the area covered by the constitutional right to human dignity in German law raises questions that are unique to that legal system, and stem from the structure of the Bill of Rights, which includes the catch-all right of development of personality. That raises the difficult question of whether human dignity as a freestanding right possesses an exclusive normative zone, and if there is such a zone, what is its scope? Those who hold that there is indeed a normative zone exclusive to human dignity must come to the conclusion that this zone is so narrow that it is almost limited to the breaking of taboo. These questions do not arise in other legal systems, in which there is no catch-all right to development of personality and there is no special reason for a narrow sense of the right to human dignity.

It therefore seems that the right to human dignity in the German jurisprudence and legal scholarship reflects its unique character in German

[75] See Kokott, 'From Reception and Transplantation to Convergence of Constitutional Models', at 81.

constitutional law. It is an exceptional and unusual character that leads to a narrow interpretation of the right. Reference to it in the interpretation of other constitutions is worthwhile, but it must be carried out with great caution: such reference is worthwhile, despite its uniqueness, to the extent that it deepens our understanding of our own legal systems. The difference between the right to human dignity in the German Constitution and the right to human dignity in other legal systems allows the other legal systems to understand themselves in a deeper and more comprehensive way.[76] Indeed, this is the role of comparative law. When we look at comparative law, we look into a mirror, and the reflection we see is the reflection of the image of our own legal system. But we must glance cautiously, in light of the uniqueness of the right to human dignity in the German Basic Law.

It appears that comparing human dignity in German law to other legal systems is less restricted when the basis for the comparison is not the constitutional right, but rather the constitutional value of human dignity. When the basis is the constitutional value, the unique constitutional architecture of each constitution has less influence, while values shared by democratic societies have greater influence. It thus seems to me that the German constitutional law's view of the constitutional value of human dignity can provide us with greater assistance than its view of the constitutional right to human dignity. Nonetheless, great caution should be employed even in comparing the values.[77] We have seen the uniqueness of German law, which sees human dignity as the single supreme constitutional value. In other constitutions human dignity is either not the sole supreme value or it is not an elevated value at all. The difference in the status of the values in the legal systems influences the lessons that one legal system can learn from another. However, similar to the comparison of the constitutional right, comparison of the constitutional value of human dignity in the different legal systems holds up a mirror, in which a legal system can come to know itself in a deeper and more comprehensive way.

[76] See Eberle, 'Human Dignity, Privacy and Personality', at 1055; McAllister, 'Human Dignity and Individual Liberty', at 520; Krotoszynski, 'A Comparative Perspective on the First Amendment', at 608; Ullrich, 'Concurring Visions', at 101.

[77] Mathias Reimann, 'Prurient Interest and Human Dignity: Pornography Regulation in West Germany and the United States' (1987) 21 *University of Michigan Journal of Law Reform* 201.

14

Human dignity in South African constitutional law

1. The normative traits of human dignity

A. *The provisions of section 10 of the South African Constitution*

Section 10 of the Constitution of South Africa determines that human dignity is a constitutional right. It states:

> Human Dignity
> Everyone has inherent dignity and the right to have their dignity respected and protected.[1]

Extensive judgments have interpreted this provision.[2] Legal literature has studied the constitutional right and constitutional value of human dignity. It appears that Woolman is correct in stating that the South African jurisprudence regarding human dignity is the most developed, following that of the Constitutional Court of Germany.[3] I should add that next to the German literature, the South African legal literature regarding its provision on human dignity is the most developed.[4]

[1] All references are to the provisions of the Final Constitution of 1996.

[2] For analysis of the case law, see Stuart Woolman, 'Dignity', in Stuart Woolman, Michael Bishop and Jason Brickhill (eds.), *Constitutional Law of South Africa*, 2nd edn, Revision Series 4 (Cape Town: Juta, 2012) chapter 36, p. 1.

[3] *Ibid.*

[4] *Ibid.* See also, mainly, Irma J. Kroeze, 'Human Dignity in Constitutional Law in South Africa', in European Commission for Democracy through Law, *The Principle of Respect for Human Dignity* (Strasbourg: Council of Europe, 1999); G. E. Devenish, *A Commentary on the South African Bill of Rights* (Durban: Butterworths 1999) chapter 5: 'Respect for Human Dignity', p. 79; Arthur Chaskalson, 'Human Dignity as a Foundational Value of Our Constitutional Order' (2000) 16 *South African Journal on Human Rights* 193; Nicholas Haysom, 'Dignity', in Halton Cheadle, Dennis Davis and Nicholas Haysom (eds.), *South African Constitutional Law: The Bill of Rights* (Durban: Butterworths, 2002); Arthur Chaskalson, 'Human Dignity as a Constitutional Value', in David Kretzmer and Eckart Klein (eds.), *The Concept of Human Dignity in Human Rights Discourse* (The Hague: Kluwer Law International, 2002), 133; Henk Botha, 'Equality, Dignity and the Politics of Interpretation' (2004) 19 *South African Public Law* 724; Lourens Ackermann,

Human dignity in the Constitution of South Africa is characterized by four normative traits. First, human dignity is a relative right. Second, human dignity is not an eternal right; it can be amended. Third, human dignity is a supreme value, but is not the only supreme value. Fourth, the constitutional right to human dignity covers acts and omissions that at times overlap other constitutional rights, but it also covers acts and omissions that fall in its exclusive domain and are not included within the scope of other rights. I shall discuss each of these four traits in turn.

B. *Human dignity as a relative right*

Is the constitutional right to human dignity, as it is formulated in section 10 of the Constitution of South Africa, a relative or absolute right?[5] As we have seen, a right is absolute if its entire scope is protected such that it cannot be limited. Any limitation constitutes a violation.[6] In contrast, a right is relative if its protection does not necessarily extend to the entirety of its scope. It can be limited. The limitation will be constitutional if it fulfills the conditions of the limitations clause. In most legal systems the requirement is that the limitation must be proportional.[7] Thus, only a disproportional limitation of a relative right constitutes a violation. What is the nature of the right to human dignity in the Constitution of South Africa?

The accepted view is that the rights in the Constitution of South Africa are relative.[8] This is the case regarding all the rights in the Constitution of South Africa,[9] including the right to human dignity.[10] The reason for

'The Significance of Human Dignity for Constitutional Jurisprudence', Lecture Before Stellenbosch Law Faculty (August 15, 2005); Sandra Liebenberg, 'The Value of Human Dignity in Interpreting Socio-Economic Rights' (2005) 21 *South African Journal on Human Rights* 1; Henk Botha, 'Human Dignity in Comparative Perspective' (2009) 2 *Stellenbosch Law Review* 171.

5 For definition of the terms relative right and absolute right, see Aharon Barak, *Proportionality: Constitutional Rights and their Limitations*, Doron Kalir trans. (Cambridge University Press, 2012) 32.

6 For the distinction between a limitation and a violation, see *ibid.*, at 101–2.

7 On proportionality, see *ibid.*

8 See Stuart Woolman and Henk Botha, 'Limitations', in Stuart Woolman, Michael Bishop and Jason Brickhill (eds.), *Constitutional Law of South Africa*, 2nd edn, Revision Series 4 (Cape Town: Juta, 2012) chapter 34, p. 1; Botha, 'Human Dignity in Comparative Perspective', at 196; Devenish, *A Commentary on the South African Bill of Rights*, at 84.

9 See *S* v. *Mamaboto*, 2001 (3) SA 409 (CC), para. 72; *De Reuck* v. *Director of Public Prosecutions*, 2004 (1) SA 406 (CC), para. 89.

10 See *Minister of Home Affairs* v. *NICRO*, 2005 (3) SA 280 (CC), para. 23 ("The rights entrenched in the Bill of Rights include equality, dignity, and various other human rights and freedoms. These rights give effect to the founding values and must be construed

this is that the general limitations clause applies to all of the rights in the Bill of Rights.[11] Thus this general limitations clause also applies to human dignity. Indeed, in a number of judgments holding that a statute limited the right to human dignity, the Constitutional Court went on to examine whether or not the limitation was proportional.[12] Of course, in the framework of that examination substantial consideration will be given to the importance of the right to human dignity and the constitutional value of human dignity. Any limitation of any constitutional right, including the constitutional right to human dignity, must be reasonable and justifiable in an open and democratic society based on the values of human dignity, equality and liberty.[13]

Opposing this accepted view, Venter[14] pointed out that the right to human dignity in section 10 of the Constitution of South Africa contains two parts.[15] The first part determines that everyone has inherent

consistently with them. They are, however, not absolute and in principle are subject to limitation in terms of section 36(1) of the Constitution") (Chaskalson CJ). See also Haysom, 'Dignity'; David Leibowitz and Derek Spitz, 'Human Dignity', in Stuart Woolman, Michael Bishop and Jason Brickhill (eds.), *Constitutional Law of South Africa*, 2nd edn, Revision Series 4 (Cape Town: Juta, 2012) chapter 12, p. 17.

[11] See s. 36(1) of the South African Constitution: "The rights in the Bill of Rights may be limited only in terms of law of general application to the extent that the limitation is reasonable and justifiable in an open and democratic society based on human dignity, equality and freedom, taking into account all relevant factors, including (a) the nature of the rights; (b) the importance of the purpose of the limitation; (c) the nature and extent of the limitation; (d) the relation between the limitation and its purpose; and (e) less restrictive means to achieve the purpose."

[12] *Minister of Home Affairs* v. *NICRO*; *Dawood* v. *Minister of Home Affairs*, 2000 (3) SA 936 (CC), para. 57 ("there can be no doubt that there will be circumstances when the constitutional right to dignity that protects the rights of spouses to cohabit may justifiably be limited by refusing the spouses the right to cohabit in South Africa even pending a decision upon an application for an immigration permit") (O'Regan J); *Booysen* v. *Minister of Home Affairs and Another*, 2001 (4) SA 485 (CC), para. 10; *Islamic Unity Convention* v. *Independent Broadcasting Authority*, 2002 (4) SA 294 (CC), para. 30; *Bhe* v. *Magistrate*, 2005 (1) SA 580 (CC), paras. 72–73.

[13] See s. 36(1), note 11 above; *Khumalo* v. *Holomisa*, 2002 (5) SA 401 (CC), para. 41; *Khosa* v. *Minister of Social Development*, 2004 (6) SA 505 (CC).

[14] See Francois Venter, 'Human Dignity as a Constitutional Value: A South African Perspective', in Jörn Ipsen, Dietrich Rauschning and Edzard Schmidt-Jortzig (eds.), *Recht, Staat, Gemeinwohl: Festschrift für Dietrich Rauschning* (Munich: Heymann 2001).

[15] On the distinction between the two parts of the provision, see *S* v. *Dodo*, 2001 (3) SA 382 (CC), para. 35 ("The human dignity of all persons is independently recognized as both an attribute and a right in section 10 of the Constitution, which proclaims that '[e]veryone has inherent dignity and the right to have their dignity respected and protected.' It is also one of the foundational values of the Constitution and is woven, in a variety of other ways, into the fabric of our Bill of Rights") (Ackermann J).

dignity. The second part determines everyone's right to have their dignity respected and protected. In Venter's opinion, the first part of the provision indicates that the dignity of a person is not *ex lege*, but rather is inherent in each person as a human being.[16] This provision does not define a constitutional right, but rather declares the natural, inalienable state that exists independently of the constitution. It is the second part of the provision that determines the right. That right is not the right to human dignity. It is merely the right to have human dignity respected and protected. Venter writes:

> The statement that "everyone has inherent dignity" can hardly be understood to be a constitutional creation of human dignity as a phenomenon of law. Nor can the phrase be read as the establishment of a right to human dignity. The relevant *right* continued to be one to the enjoyment of respect and to the protection of a pre-existing human attribute, human dignity. The purport of the phrase is again that human dignity is an inalienable, inborn characteristic of each individual person.[17]

Botha relies upon Venter's approach and points out that it can be argued that the first part of section 10 of the Constitution of South Africa, which determines that everyone has inherent dignity, grants absolute protection to the internal core of human dignity. Botha writes:

> It could even be argued that the reference to the "inherent dignity" of every person has a similar meaning to the declaration in the German Basic Law that dignity is "inviolable," and that it serves to give absolute protection to an inner core of dignity. On this interpretation, section 10 does not simply confer a subjective right which, like all rights, is subject to limitation. In addition to conferring a right, it also declares the belief of the founders of the Constitution that the dignity of the person exists prior to its recognition in a constitution and that, accordingly, the negation of the inherent dignity of the person – in distinction to limitations of the rights to have one's dignity respected and protected – cannot be justified in the name of countervailing interests.[18]

[16] See Lourens Ackermann, 'The Legal Nature of the South African Constitutional Revolution' (2004) 4 *New Zealand Law Review* 633, 647: "It is significant that s. 10 first proclaims that 'everyone *has* inherent dignity' before entrenching the right of 'everyone … to have their dignity respected and protected.' This underscores, in my view, the recognition by the constitution that human dignity is not merely a protected and entrenched right, but that the concept of human dignity is definitional to what it means to be a human – that all humans have inherent dignity as an attribute independent of and antecedent to any constitutional protection thereof. It is, I would argue, expected as a categorical constitutional imperative."

[17] Venter, 'Human Dignity as a Constitutional Value', at 340 (emphasis in original).

[18] Botha, 'Human Dignity in Comparative Perspective', at 197.

True, the structure of section 10 of the Constitution of South Africa raises a considerable interpretational problem. The parallel provision in the Interim Constitution of South Africa (of 1993) determined that "[e]very person shall have the right to respect and protection of his or her dignity."[19] The permanent constitution repeats that provision, exchanging the term "every person" with "everyone," and adding the term "inherent dignity." What is the significance of that addition?

In my opinion, the addition indicates the particular importance of the right to human dignity as a constitutional right[20] and its status as the basis for all the other rights. The addition does not grant absolute character to this right or to its core aspect. The term "inherent dignity" should not be seen as similar to the provision in the German Constitution that human dignity is "*unantastbar*."[21] There is no similar term in the Constitution of South Africa, and in my opinion it is not possible to conclude, from the term "inherent dignity," that human dignity cannot be limited. This is mainly due to the fact that human dignity is included within the purview of the general limitations clause, and can thus be limited like any other right.[22]

The conclusion is that the right to human dignity in the Constitution of South Africa is relative. There is no formal distinction between the limitation of the core of the right and the limitation of the zone outside the core.[23] All aspects of the right to human dignity can be limited, and the conditions set out in the limitations clause apply to all of them. Of course, in order to justify limitation of the right to human dignity, all the provisions of the limitations clause must be fulfilled. This includes the provision according to which the limitation must be reasonable and justifiable in a free and democratic society based on human dignity, liberty and freedom.[24] A particularly strong justification is required to limit human dignity in a free and democratic society based on human dignity. Nonetheless, a distinction should be made between the question of whether the right to human dignity can theoretically be limited (and my

[19] S. 10 of the Interim Constitution of South Africa (1993).

[20] It thus adopts the approach of the Constitutional Court in *S* v. *Makwanyane*, 1995 (3) SA 391 (CC).

[21] Art. 1(1) of the German Basic Law. See Chapter 13, section 1B.

[22] S. 36 of the South African Constitution.

[23] The limitations clause of the Interim Constitution of South Africa stated in Art. 33(1)(b) that limitation of a right in the Bill of Rights "shall not negate the essential content of the right in question." That provision did not appear in the Final Constitution of South Africa (of 1996).

[24] S. 36(1), note 11 above.

answer is that it can) and the question of whether the limitation is proportional (and that answer will depend upon the specific circumstances). The first question examines the character of the right as absolute or relative. The second question examines the possible limitations on the relative right.

If my approach to section 10 of the Constitution of South Africa is correct, then the conclusion is that in South Africa, as in Israel,[25] the right to human dignity is a relative right. In this way it is conspicuously different from the right to human dignity in the German Constitution, in which human dignity is seen as an absolute right.

C. *Human dignity as a constitutionally amendable constitutional right*

It is uncontroversial that, according to the express language of the Constitution of South Africa, human dignity, both as a constitutional right and as a constitutional value, is not eternal. The constitutional value of human dignity is enshrined, inter alia, in section 1(a) of the constitution, which states:

> The Republic of South Africa is one, sovereign, democratic state founded on the following values:
>
> (a) Human dignity, the achievement of equality and the advancement of human rights and freedoms.

That provision is amendable.[26]

The constitutional right to human dignity is enshrined in section 10 of the Constitution of South Africa. It is one of the sections included in the Second Chapter of the constitution, which is the Bill of Rights. The rights included in that chapter are amendable as well.[27]

Thus both the constitutional value of human dignity and the constitutional right to human dignity are amendable.[28] From this standpoint, there is no similarity between the value of human dignity in the Constitution of South Africa and human dignity in the German Constitution. The German Constitution eternalizes human dignity,[29] whereas the Constitution of

[25] See Chapter 15, section 1B.

[26] See s. 74(1) of the Constitution of South Africa.

[27] See s. 74(2) of the Constitution of South Africa

[28] See Venter, 'Human Dignity as a Constitutional Value', at 346; Botha, 'Human Dignity in Comparative Perspective', at 198.

[29] See *Du Plessis* v. *De Klerk*, 1996 (3) SA 850 (CC), para. 92 ("I do believe that the German Basic Law (GBL) was conceived in dire circumstances bearing sufficient resemblance to

South Africa allows amendment of the constitutional value of human dignity. It is interesting to note in this context that the constitutional value of human dignity enjoys a stronger entrenchment than the constitutional right to human dignity. Whereas a majority of 75 percent of the members of the legislative body are needed to amend a constitutional value, amendment of the constitutional right to human dignity requires, inter alia, only two-thirds of the members of the legislative body.

Despite the fact that the express provisions of the Constitution of South Africa do not grant an eternal character to the constitutional right and the constitutional value of human dignity, can such eternality be recognized by implication? This question raises the problem of the unconstitutional constitutional amendment.[30] The question is whether a constitutional amendment that fulfills the procedural provisions regarding constitutional amendments might be unconstitutional because it contradicts the basic structure upon which the constitution is based. On this issue, the Supreme Court of India developed the approach according to which an amendment to the constitution is unconstitutional if it changes the basic structure of the constitution. Such an amendment would be so fundamental that it could not be achieved by way of constitutional amendment.[31]

our own to make critical study and cautious application of its lessons to our situation and Constitution warranted. The GBL was no less powerful a response to totalitarianism, the degradation of human dignity and the denial of freedom and equality than our Constitution. Few things make this clearer than Art. 1(1) of the GBL, 2 particularly when it is borne in mind that the principles laid down in Art. 1 are entrenched against amendment of any kind by Art. 79(3)") (Ackermann J).

30 For this question see Aharon Barak, 'Unconstitutional Constitutional Amendment' (2011) 44 *Israel Law Review* 321; Richard Albert, 'Nonconstitutional Amendments' (2009) 22 *Canadian Journal of Law and Jurisprudence* 5, 28; Richard Albert, 'Constitutional Handcuffs' (2010) 42 *Arizona State Law Journal* 663; Yaniv Roznai, 'Unconstitutional Constitutional Amendment – The Migration and Success of a Constitutional Idea' (2013) 61 *American Journal of Comparative Law* 657.

31 See P. A. Sathe, 'Amendability of Fundamental Rights: Golaknath and the Proposed Constitutional Amendment' (1969) 33 *Supreme Court Cases Journal* 42; Nani A. Palkhivala, 'Fundamental Rights Case: Comment' (1973) 4 *Supreme Court Cases Journal* 57; Ramesh D. Garg, 'Phantom of Basic Structure of the Constitution: A Critical Appraisal of the Kesavananda Case' (1974) 16 *Journal of Indian Law Institute* 243; Upendra Baxi, 'The Constitutional Quicksands of Kesavananda Bharati and the Twenty Fifth Amendment' (1974) 1 *Supreme Court Cases Journal* 45; P. K. Tripathi, 'Kesavananda Bharati v. State of Kerata: Who Wins?' (1974) 1 *Supreme Court Cases Journal* 3; Ashok Desai, 'Constitutional Amendments and the "Basic Structure" Doctrine', in Venkat Lyer (ed.), *Democracy, Human Rights and the Rule of Law: Essays in Honour of Nani Palkhivala* (New Delhi: Butterworths India, 2000) 90; Pavani P. Rao, 'Basic Features of the Constitution' (2002) 2 *Supreme Court Cases Journal* 463; Sudhir Krishnaswamy, *Democracy and Constitutionalism in India: A Study of the Basic Structure Doctrine*

Does this Indian ruling apply to the Constitution of South Africa as well? Section 167(4)(d) of the constitution authorizes the Constitutional Court to decide on the constitutionality of any constitutional amendment.[32] Is that jurisdiction restricted solely to examination of the procedural aspect of constitutional amendment, or does it also apply to examination of the content of the constitutional amendment? And if such examination were included in that jurisdiction, by what standards would it be executed?

These questions arose in *Premier of Kwazulu-Natal*.[33] Deputy President Mahomed determined that the rule is that if the constitutional amendment was enacted according to procedure, the amendment is constitutional. He added, however:

> It may perhaps be that a purported amendment to the Constitution, following the formal procedure prescribed by the Constitution, but radically and fundamentally restructuring and re-organizing the fundamental premise of the Constitution, might not qualify as an "amendment" at all. That problem has engaged the Indian Supreme Court for some years and it has been held that the power of amendment of the Constitution, vested in the Legislature, could not be employed – "to the extent of destroying the basic features and structure of the Constitution."[34]

The Court held that there was no need to come to a decision regarding this approach as in the case before it the amendments to the constitution were not fundamental to the extent of abrogating or destroying it. The question arose again in *United Democratic Movement*.[35] The Constitutional Court reiterated the approach of Deputy President Mahomed in *Premier of*

(Oxford University Press, 2009). See especially the following cases: *Kesavananda Bharati* v. *State of Kerala* (1973) 4 SCC 225 at 366; *Indira Gandhi* v. *Raj Narain*, AIR 1975 SC 229; *Minerva Mills* v. *Union of India*, AIR 1980 SC 1789. For literature outside India see David G. Morgan, 'The Indian "Essential Features" Case' (1981) 30 *International and Comparative Law Quarterly* 307; Rory O'Connell, 'Guardians of the Constitution: Unconstitutional Constitutional Norms' (1999) 4 *Journal of Civil Liberties* 48; Mathew Abraham, 'Judicial Role in Constitutional Amendments in India: The Basic Structure Doctrine', in Mads Andenas (ed.), *The Creation and Amendment of Constitutional Norms* (British Institute of International and Comparative Law, 2000) 195; Gary J. Jacobsohn, 'An Unconstitutional Constitution? A Comparative Perspective' (2006) 4 *International Journal of Constitutional Law* 460.

[32] S. 167(4)(d) determines that only the Constitutional Court is authorized to "decide on the constitutionality of any amendment to the Constitution."

[33] *Premier of Kwazulu-Natal* v. *President of the Republic*, 1996 (1) SA 769 (CC).

[34] *Ibid.*, at para. 47.

[35] *United Democratic Movement* v. *President of the Republic of South Africa*, 2003 (1) SA 488 (CC).

Kwazulu-Natal[36] and determined that, in that case also, the constitutional amendment did not abrogate or destroy the constitution.

The question of whether a constitutional amendment is unconstitutional if it violates the basic structure of the constitution is therefore an open question in the constitutional law of South Africa.[37] It is to be assumed that the theoretical basis of the basic structure doctrine is also open to new examination in South Africa, as its discussion was *obiter dictum*. In this context, it will be appropriate to examine whether to accept the approach of Deputy President Mahomed in *Premier Kwazulu-Natal*, according to which alteration of the basic structure of the constitution is unconstitutional because it cannot be categorized as an "amendment." That was the approach underlying the judgments of a number of Justices of the Supreme Court of India at the beginning of the development of the doctrine regarding alteration of the basic structure of the constitution.[38] The legislature wished to overcome the doctrine by expressly determining, by way of constitutional amendment, that constitutional amendment shall not be limited due to its content, even if the amendment changes or repeals provisions of the constitution. The Supreme Court of India found that this constitutional amendment was itself unconstitutional.[39] It was held that the basic structure doctrine is not based upon the term "amendment," but rather the interpretation of the constitution as a whole. Those wishing to alter the basic structure of the constitution must achieve their goal by way of enacting a new constitution. Are there restrictions upon the content of a new constitution? That is a question that is beyond the subject matter of this volume.

Now let us assume that the basic structure doctrine is adopted in South Africa.[40] Can that turn the constitutional right to human dignity into an eternal right? Does narrowing the scope of the right to human dignity or annulling that right fall within that doctrine? What about amendment or annulment of the constitutional value of human dignity?

[36] See note 33.

[37] See Christopher Roederer, 'Founding Provisions', in Stuart Woolman, Michael Bishop and Jason Brickhill (eds.), *Constitutional Law of South Africa*, 2nd edn, Revision Series 4 (Cape Town: Juta, 2012) chapter 15. In *Merafrong Demarcation Forum* v. *President of the Republic of South Africa*, (2008) 5 SA 171 (CC) it was held that a constitutional amendment of the borders of the provinces of the entire Republic must be rational. That is a substantive requirement that has been recognized by the Constitutional Court. Can it be said that alteration of the basic structure of the constitution is not rational?

[38] See *Kesavananda Bharati* v. *State of Kerala*.

[39] See *Minerva Mills* v. *Union of India*.

[40] See Albert, 'Nonconstitutional Amendments', at 28.

The answers to these questions depend on the way the Constitutional Court fleshes out the basic structure doctrine. It seems to me that if its content would be similar to the approach accepted by the Supreme Court of India, the annulment of the constitutional right to human dignity or the constitutional value of human dignity would be interpreted as altering the basic structure of the constitution. These are, of course, extreme cases. Difficult questions are likely to arise if the constitutional amendment does not annul the right to human dignity but only narrows its scope. Would that also be viewed as an alteration of the basic structure of the constitution? Similarly, what if the constitutional amendment does not annul all of the provisions granting constitutional status to the constitutional value of human dignity, but only some of them? And what if the constitutional amendment does not lead to the annulment of the constitutional value in a specific context, but only narrows it? All of these are questions that have yet to be answered.

It appears, however, that there are significant differences between the eternality of human dignity in German constitutional law and its eternality in South African constitutional law. Whereas in the German Constitution there is an express provision stating that human dignity is eternal, there is no such provision in the Constitution of South Africa. Even if it is held that the eternality of human dignity, whether as a constitutional value or a constitutional right, is derived from the basic structure of the constitution, the protection of that basic structure in South Africa is different than the protection of human dignity in the Constitution of Germany.

D. *Human dignity as a supreme value*

Many titles have been bestowed upon human dignity as a constitutional value in South African judgments. It has been called a supreme value;[41] a value of the highest order;[42] that it is its cornerstone;[43] and that it is a

[41] See *S* v. *Makwanyane*, at para. 111. See also Kroeze, 'Human Dignity in Constitutional Law in South Africa'; Nazeem M. I. Goolam, 'Human Dignity – Our Supreme Constitutional Value' (2001) 4 *Potchefstroom Electronic Law Journal* 1.

[42] See Chaskalson, 'Human Dignity as a Foundational Value'; Goolam, 'Human Dignity'.

[43] See *S* v. *Makwanyane*, at para. 329; *Khosa* v. *Minister of Social Development*, at para. 114; *De Reuck* v. *Director of Public Prosecutions*, at para. 61. See also *Christian Education South Africa* v. *Minister of Education*, 2000 (4) SA 757 (CC), para. 36; *Daniels* v. *Campbell*, 2004 (5) SA 331 (CC), para. 54; Haysom, 'Dignity'.

founding[44] and foundational[45] value that serves as an inspiration[46] and motif that runs right through the rights in the Bill of Rights.[47] The value of human dignity has been described as a value that lies at the heart of human rights,[48] is their source[49] and grants them a moral basis.[50]

This approach to the value of human dignity is important. However, it does not make the value of human dignity into the sole supreme value. It must be remembered that the Interim Constitution of South Africa did not include any special reference to the constitutional value of human dignity. The Interim Constitution only recognized the right to human dignity.[51] The change took place in the final Constitution of South Africa of 1996.[52] That constitution refers to the value of human dignity in four sections.[53] The First Chapter of the constitution arranges the founding provisions, and the first section of that chapter states:

> The Republic of South Africa is one, sovereign, democratic state founded on the following values:
> (a) Human dignity, the achievement of equality and the advancement of human rights and freedoms.
> (b) Non racialism and non-sexism.
> (c) Supremacy of the constitution and the rule of law.
> (d) Universal adult suffrage, a national common voters roll, regular elections and a multi-party system of democratic government, to ensure accountability, responsiveness and openness.[54]

[44] See *S* v. *Makwanyane*, at para. 328; *S* v. *Dodo*, at para. 35; *Khumalo* v. *Holomisa*, at para. 26; *Khosa* v. *Minister of Social Development*, at para. 85; *Daniels* v. *Campbell*, at para. 54. See also *Government of the Republic of South Africa and Others* v. *Grootboom*, 2001 (1) SA 46 (CC).

[45] See *S* v. *Makwanyane*, at para. 328; *Dawood* v. *Minister of Home Affairs*, at para. 35; *S* v. *Dodo*, at para. 35; *Khumalo* v. *Holomisa*, at para. 28; *De Reuck* v. *Director of Public Prosecutions*, at para. 62; *Minister of Home Affairs* v. *NICRO*, at para. 21. See also *National Coalition for Gay and Lesbian Equality* v. *Minister of Home Affairs*, 2000 (2) SA 1 (CC), para. 58; *Minister of Home Affairs* v. *Watchenuka*, 2004 (4) SA 326 (SCA) para. 26.

[46] See *Minister of Home Affairs* v. *Watchenuka*, at para. 26.

[47] See *National Coalition for Gay and Lesbian Equality* v. *Minister of Justice*, 1999 (1) SA 6 (CC), para. 120. See also Botha, 'Human Dignity in Comparative Perspective', at 171.

[48] See *Prinsloo* v. *Van der Linde*, 1997 (3) SA 1012, para. 32.

[49] See *S* v. *Makwanyane*, at para. 144.

[50] See Haysom, 'Dignity', at 126.

[51] S. 10 of the Interim Constitution.

[52] That is surely influenced by the judgment in *S* v. *Makwanyane*.

[53] A number of sections include references to dignity, but not to human dignity, rather the dignity of government institutions (see ss. 165(4), 181 and 196).

[54] See s. 1 of the Constitution of South Africa.

The Second Chapter of the constitution is the Bill of Rights. This chapter opens with section 7, and the language of the first paragraph of subsection (1) is relevant to our discussion:

> This Bill of Rights is the cornerstone of democracy in South Africa. It enshrines the rights of all people in our country and affirms the democratic values of human dignity, equality and freedom.

The Bill of Rights chapter includes two additional sections that refer to human dignity. One is the limitations clause ("Limitation of Rights"). It states:

> The rights in the Bill of Rights may be limited only in terms of law of general application to the extent that the limitation is reasonable and justifiable in an open and democratic society based on human dignity, equality and freedom.[55]

The other section deals with "Interpretation of the Bill of Rights." The relevant part of this section determines:

> When interpreting the Bill of Rights, a court, tribunal or forum –
> (a) must promote the values that underlie an open and democratic society based on dignity, equality and freedom.[56]

The conclusion arising from these four sections is that human dignity is certainly a value of supreme and foundational importance, as determined in the decisions of the Constitutional Court. However, it is not the only supreme value, and it is not the most foundational value. The basic provisions (in section 1 of the constitution) emphasize equality alongside dignity.[57] The provisions regarding limitations of rights (in section 36 of the constitution) and interpretation (section 39) determine human dignity, equality and freedom as the supreme constitutional values.

The conclusion that arises from the language of the constitution is that these three values – human dignity, equality and freedom – are the foundational[58] and supreme values of the Constitution of South Africa.[59] They express the essence of the constitution, which is intended to create a

[55] S. 36(1) of the Constitution of South Africa.

[56] S. 39(1)(a) of the Constitution of South Africa.

[57] *Minister of Home Affairs* v. *NICRO*, at para. 21.

[58] *Khosa* v. *Minister of Social Development*, at para. 85; *Daniels* v. *Campbell*, at para. 54; *Minister of Home Affairs* v. *NICRO*, at para. 96.

[59] *S* v. *Makwanyane*, at para. 111; *Government of the Republic of South Africa and Others* v. *Grootboom*, at para. 23; *Islamic Unity Convention* v. *Independent Broadcasting Authority*, at para. 33; *Bhe* v. *Magistrate*, at para. 48; *Minister of Home Affairs* v. *NICRO*, at para. 21.

new social order rejecting apartheid.[60] The apartheid regime violated the human dignity of non-whites, discriminated against them and infringed upon their freedom. The constitution is a detachment from that regime. It is based upon the constitutional values of human dignity, equality and freedom that were severely violated during apartheid.[61] These, therefore, are the supreme values of the constitution, and in the words of Justice Sachs:

> As with all determination about the reach of constitutionally protected rights, the starting and ending point of the analysis must be to affirm the values of human dignity, equality and freedom.[62]

And in the words of Justice Ngcobo:

> This history serves to remind us where we have come from as a nation and where we are going. Indeed it serves to remind us of the goal that we have fashioned for ourselves in the Constitution, namely, to establish a new society founded on human dignity, equality and fundamental freedoms. It also helps us to understand the plight of millions of people living in deplorable conditions and in great poverty. It reminds us that at the heart of our constitutional democracy lies the commitment to address these conditions and to transform our society into one in which there will be human dignity, freedom and equality.[63]

Indeed, there is great similarity between the apartheid past that the Constitution of South Africa was intended to reject[64] and the Nazi past that the Constitution of Germany was intended to reject.[65] There is also similarity between the two constitutions regarding the way they detach

See also *Ferreira* v. *Levin NO*, 1996 (1) SA 984 (CC), para. 49. Some add the value of life (see *S* v. *Makwanyane*, at para. 214, 326; *Minister of Home Affairs* v. *Watchenuka*, at para. 26) and the value of democracy (see Haysom, 'Dignity', at 124).

60 *S* v. *Makwanyane*, at para. 262. See also Devenish, *A Commentary on the South African Bill of Rights*, at 83; Chaskalson, 'Human Dignity as a Foundational Value'; Ackermann, 'The Legal Nature of the South African Constitutional Revolution', at 650; Arthur Chaskalson, 'Dignity and Justice for All' (2009) 24 *Maryland Journal of International Law* 24.

61 *S* v. *Makwanyane*, at para. 329; *Dawood* v. *Minister of Home Affairs*, at para. 35; *Jaftha* v. *Schoeman*, 2005 (2) SA 140 (CC), para. 27; *Port Elizabeth Municipality* v. *Various Occupiers*, 2005 (1) SA 217 (CC), para. 15; *Minister of Home Affairs* v. *Fourie*, 2006 (1) SA 524 (CC), para. 59; *NM* v. *Smith*, 2007 (5) SA 250 (CC), paras. 49, 133.

62 *Port Elizabeth Municipality* v. *Various Occupiers*, at para. 15.

63 *Residents of Joe Slovo Community, Western Cape* v. *Thubelisha Homes* 2010 (3) SA 454 (CC), para. 191.

64 See *S* v. *Makwanyane*, at para. 262; *Minister of Home Affairs* v. *Fourie*, at para. 59; *Residents of Joe Slovo Community, Western Cape* v. *Thubelisha Homes*, at para. 191.

65 See *Du Plessis* v. *De Klerk*, at para. 92; Haysom, 'Dignity', at 127.

from the past.[66] However, the Constitution of South Africa did not adopt three important legal institutions adopted in the German Constitution: the absolute, eternal and supreme character of human dignity. According to the Constitution of South Africa, human dignity is relative, amendable and one of three supreme values.

E. *The area covered by human dignity as a constitutional right*

(1) A zone of exclusive application of human dignity

The Bill of Rights in the Constitution of South Africa is a masterpiece. It is the product of highly developed constitutional thinking informed by the experience of other constitutions and the research of the best legal scholars within South Africa and beyond. It is a most impressive legal architectural structure. In my opinion, the Bill of Rights in the Constitution of South Africa approaches constitutional perfection more than any other modern bill of rights. The legal problems with which many constitutional states struggle were meticulously examined in preparing the Bill of Rights in South Africa, and they were given good, express solutions.[67] The Constitutional Court of South Africa and legal scholarship in South Africa interpreted the provisions of the Bill of Rights in a manner that fulfills its underlying purpose.[68] Despite the difficult and complex social conditions in South Africa, it appears that the constitutional law in general, and human rights in particular, have benefitted from development and have blossomed in a way that is unparalleled in democratic constitutional states.

The Bill of Rights is comprehensive. It includes civil and political rights alongside social and economic rights. What is the "normative zone" covered by the constitutional right to human dignity? This zone is certainly determined mainly by the constitutional value of human dignity. The purpose underlying the constitutional right is the fulfillment of the

[66] See Chaskalson, 'Human Dignity as a Foundational Value'.

[67] See for example the provision on the founding provisions of the Constitution (s. 1); the provision regarding the state duty to respect, protect, promote and fulfill the various rights (s. 7(2)); the application of the Constitution to corporations (s. 8(4)); the solution to the problem of direct or indirect constitutional application (s. 8(2)–(3)); the treatment of social rights (ss. 22–30); the recognition of a constitutional right to just administrative action (s. 33); the liberal rules of *locus standi* (s. 38); and the comprehensive and fundamental provision on interpretation of the constitutional bill of rights (s. 39).

[68] Particularly deserving of praise is the comprehensive and thorough commentary on the constitution of South Africa: Stuart Woolman, Michael Bishop and Jason Brickhill (eds.), *Constitutional Law of South Africa*, 2nd edn, Revision Series 4 (Cape Town: Juta, 2012).

constitutional value. However, it is accepted that the constitutional value of human dignity is not limited merely to the constitutional right to human dignity. Human dignity as a constitutional value underlies many of the constitutional rights.[69] Thus, for example, the value of human dignity is counted among the purposes underlying the right to freedom,[70] freedom of expression,[71] privacy,[72] equality,[73] and the social rights.[74] The case law has emphasized that human dignity is a motif that runs right through all the constitutional rights. In the words of Justice Ackermann:

> The human dignity of all persons ... is also one of the fundamental values of the Constitution and is woven, in a variety of other ways, into the fabric of our Bill of Rights.[75]

As a result, the normative zone covered by the constitutional right to human dignity overlaps with the normative zone covered by the other constitutional rights appearing in the constitutional Bill of Rights.[76] The zones are not identical, as the value of human dignity is the only constitutional value underlying the constitutional right to human dignity; but human dignity is not the only value, nor is it the main value, underlying the other constitutional rights. I shall discuss the results of this overlap separately. The question that is currently posed is whether there is a zone of human conduct that is covered exclusively by the right to human dignity. Is there an interest or will of the individual that does not fall into the zones of the other rights and for which the only vessel is human dignity? Can it not be said that all parts of the normative zone that would be covered by the right to human dignity, if it were to stand alone as the only right in the constitutional Bill of Rights, are within the normative

[69] See Woolman, 'Dignity', at 22; *De Reuck* v. *Director of Public Prosecutions*, at para. 62: "Dignity is a founding value of our Constitution. It informs most if not all of the rights in the Bill of Rights and for that reason is of central significance in the limitations analysis" (Langa DP).

[70] See *Ferreira* v. *Levin NO*, at para. 49, 52; *Prince* v. *President of the Law Society of the Cape of Good Hope*, 2002 (2) SA 794 at para. 49.

[71] See *Khumalo* v. *Holomisa*, at paras. 21, 25.

[72] See *ibid.*, at para. 27; *NM* v. *Smith*, at para. 131.

[73] See *Ferreira* v. *Levin NO*, at para. 251; *National Coalition for Gay and Lesbian Equality* v. *Minister of Justice*, at para. 125.

[74] See *Khosa* v. *Minister of Social Development*, at para. 44; *Government of the Republic of South Africa and Others* v. *Grootboom*, at para. 23; *Jaftha* v. *Schoeman*, at para. 21.

[75] *S* v. *Dodo*, at para. 35.

[76] *Dawood* v. *Minister of Home Affairs*, at para. 35; *Jaftha* v. *Schoeman*, at para. 21. See also Haysom, 'Dignity', at 134, 138; Woolman, 'Dignity', at 25.

zones of the other constitutional rights, such that the constitutional right to human dignity has no exclusive domain?

The accepted approach in South African jurisprudence and literature is that although human dignity as a constitutional right overlaps other constitutional rights to a great extent, there is a zone of human conduct that is exclusive to it and that does not overlap other constitutional rights. Thus, for example, *Dawood*[77] discussed the constitutionality of a statute restricting the ability of a non-resident spouse who is married to a resident of South Africa to attain South African resident status. It was argued that the statue limits the right to human dignity and is disproportional. In accepting that argument, Justice O'Regan wrote:

> In this case, however, it cannot be said that there is a more specific right that protects individuals who wish to enter into and sustain permanent intimate relationships than the right to dignity in section 10. There is no specific provision protecting family life as there is in other constitutions and in many international human rights instruments. The applicants argued that legislation interfering with the right to enter into such relationships infringed the rights to freedom of movement and the rights of citizens to reside in South Africa. It may well be that such legislation will have an incidental and limiting effect on these rights, but the primary right implicated is, in my view, the right to dignity. As it is the primary right concerned, it is the right upon which we should focus.[78]

Woolman describes the accepted approach in South African jurisprudence as follows:

> [D]ignity has operated as a first order rule in a number of intimate association matters because the Constitutional Court could identify no other specific right that would protect the interests of the married couples or life partners in question. High Courts have extended the protection that FC [Final Constitution] s. 10 affords intimate associations beyond the confines of marriage or life partnerships to relationships between grandparents and grandchildren. High Courts have also deployed dignity as an operational rule when no other right would protect the linguistic interests of a party before the court.[79]

Similarly, the right to reputation – which is not recognized as an independent, freestanding right in the South African Constitution – is derived

[77] *Dawood* v. *Minister of Home Affairs*. See also *Booysen* v. *Minister of Home Affairs and Another*, at para. 10.

[78] *Dawood* v. *Minister of Home Affairs*, at para. 36.

[79] Woolman, 'Dignity', at 20.

from the right to human dignity. Thus, in the terminology of this volume, reputation is a daughter-right of human dignity.

(2) Human dignity and the residual right to freedom

Should it not be said that those components that in Woolman's opinion are included in the right to human dignity, in lieu of any other relevant constitutional right, belong to a catch-all right to freedom? That is the situation in German constitutional law. The constitutional right to the freedom to develop one's personality covers, inter alia, any will or interest that a person has. It is a "catch-all right." In any case, human dignity in the German Constitution has no exclusive "zone." What is the situation regarding this issue in the Constitution of South Africa?

The right to freedom is enshrined in section 12 of the Constitution of South Africa:

> Freedom and Security of the Person
>
> (1) Everyone has the right to freedom and security of the person, which includes the right –
> (a) not to be deprived of freedom arbitrarily or without just cause;
> (b) not to be detained without trial;
> (c) to be free from all forms of violence from either public or private sources;
> (d) not to be tortured in any way; and
> (e) not to be treated or punished in a cruel, inhuman or degrading way.
> (2) Everyone has the right to bodily and psychological integrity, which includes the right –
> (a) to make decisions concerning reproduction;
> (b) to security in and control over their body; and
> (c) not to be subjected to medical or scientific experiments without their informed consent.

There is consensus that this provision protects freedom from use of force. But does it protect freedom from non-forceful limitation? Does it protect the right to marry?

Are we dealing with two separate rights – one to freedom and the other to security of the person – or are we dealing with one right, which is the freedom from limitation of security of the person?[80] This question arose

[80] See Michael Bishop and Stuart Woolman, 'Freedom and Security of the Person', in Stuart Woolman, Michael Bishop and Jason Brickhill (eds.), *Constitutional Law of South Africa*, 2nd edn, Revision Series 4 (Cape Town: Juta, 2012) chapter 40, p. 1.

in *Coetzee*[81] but was left for future decision. It arose again and was decided in *Ferreira*.[82] In a dissenting opinion, Justice Ackermann opined that the provision of section 12(1) of the Constitution of South Africa distinguishes between two constitutional rights. One is the right to freedom and the other is the right to security of the person. In his opinion, the right to freedom is:

> the right of individuals not to have "obstacles to possible choices and activities" placed in their way by ... the state.[83]

Justice Ackermann calls this the "residual freedom right."[84] The majority did not accept that approach. President Chaskalson,[85] with the concurrence of the other Justices on the panel, held that the main goal of that provision is to ensure the physical integrity of the individual. Nonetheless, he noted that it is not the only goal. There might be exceptional cases in which the term "freedom" will be given a broader meaning than ensuring physical integrity. In discussing such cases, President Chaskalson wrote:

> This does not mean that we must necessarily confine the application of section 11(1) to the protection of physical integrity. Freedom involves much more than that, and we should not hesitate to say so if the occasion demands it. But, because of the detailed provisions of Chapter 3, such occasions are likely to be rare. If despite the detailed provisions of Chapter 3 a freedom of a fundamental nature which calls for protection is identified, and if it cannot find adequate protection under any of the other provisions in Chapter 3, there may be a reason to look to section 11(1) to protect such a right. But to secure such protection, the otherwise unprotected freedom should at least be fundamental and of a character appropriate to the strict scrutiny to which all limitations of section 11 are subjected.[86]

The conclusion is that the right to freedom in the Constitution of South Africa for the most part – and subject to exceptions – is not a catch-all right. That does not pull the rug out from under the constitutional right to human dignity. President Chaskalson wrote in *Ferreira*:

> In the context of the multiplicity of rights with which it is associated in Chapter 3, human dignity can and will flourish without such an extensive interpretation being given to section 11(1).[87]

81 *Coetzee* v. *Government of the Republic of South Africa*, 1995 (4) SA 631 (CC), para. 44.

82 *Ferreira* v. *Levin NO*.

83 *Ibid.*, at para. 54.

84 *Ibid.*, at para. 57.

85 *Ibid.*, at para. 170.

86 *Ibid.*, at para. 184. See also the judgment of Justice Sachs in that case, at para. 254. See also the judgment of Justice O'Regan in *Bernstein* v. *Bester NO*, 1996 (2) SA 751 (CC).

87 *Ferreira* v. *Levin NO*, at para. 173.

A review of the judicial history and literature in South Africa indicates that in rare cases, human dignity is invoked as the sole relevant right for solving a problem. Woolman discusses this:

> Dignity is rarely a first order rule. That is, the right to dignity *alone* is rarely dispositive of a constitutional matter.[88]

The reason for this is that the normative zone in which only dignity applies is most narrow. In the great majority of cases, certainly in the great majority of cases that have come before the courts of South Africa, the conduct limiting the right to human dignity also limited other constitutional rights. However, it should be emphasized that the significant overlap between the various constitutional rights and human dignity has not led to a narrowing of the scope of human dignity. The overlap has not led to an alteration of the boundaries of the right to human dignity. I shall discuss the results of this overlap separately.

F. *The uniqueness of the right to human dignity in South African constitutional law*

(1) Human dignity as a constitutional right that covers all conduct that falls within human dignity as a constitutional value

Human dignity in the Constitution of South Africa is a relative right. It can be proportionately limited. It is not an eternal right. It constitutes one of the supreme values of the Bill of Rights. It is part of the constitutional Bill of Rights that for the most part does not include a "catch-all right." Is there anything unique about human dignity in the Constitution of South Africa? As we have seen, human dignity as a constitutional right in Germany is unique.[89] It is an absolute, eternal and supreme right. It acts within a constitutional Bill of Rights characterized by a catch-all right to develop one's personality. These traits have led to the narrowing of the zone covered by the constitutional right to human dignity. Does such a narrowing also characterize the right to human dignity in the Constitution of South Africa? Human dignity as a constitutional right in Israel has a unique character.[90] It is a relative right. It is not eternal. It reflects one of the supreme values of the Bill of Rights. The other constitutional rights cover narrow zones of human rights. These traits have led

[88] Woolman, 'Dignity', at 19 (emphasis in original).

[89] See Chapter 13, section 1A. [90] See Chapter 15, section 1E.

to an expansion of the scope of human dignity to also include daughter-rights and granddaughter-rights that in other constitutions are freestanding rights but in Israel are parts of human dignity. Should there be such an expansion in South Africa as well?

The uniqueness of the right to human dignity in South Africa does not warrant a narrowing of the scope it covers. That normative zone should cover all human activity that the constitutional value of human dignity is intended to fulfill. The reasons that led to the narrowing of human dignity as a right in the Constitution of Germany do not apply to South Africa. From this standpoint there is great similarity between the zone covered by the constitutional right to human dignity in South Africa and the zone covered by the right to human dignity in Israel. The difference between the two legal systems is manifest in the fact that many of the daughter-rights or granddaughter-rights that in Israel are included only in the right to human dignity, constitute independent, freestanding rights in South Africa.

(2) The overlap between the right to human dignity and the other constitutional rights

How should one examine situations in which both the constitutional right to human dignity and another right in the constitutional Bill of Rights are limited? In South Africa the constitutional value of human dignity applies to many of the constitutional rights.[91] Thus the zone covered by those rights – to the extent that the specific aspect of the right also fulfills the value of human dignity – is also included within the right to human dignity. What is the effect of such a complementary overlap? The overlap does not alter the scope of the rights. Quite the opposite: each right is reinforced due to its overlap with the other right.[92] In that situation, what should the court do? In *Dawood* Justice O'Regan wrote:

[91] See *S* v. *Makwanyane*, at para. 328; *Ferreira* v. *Levin NO*, at para. 49; *National Coalition for Gay and Lesbian Equality* v. *Minister of Justice*, at para. 114; *Prince* v. *President of the Law Society of the Cape of Good Hope*, at para. 49; *Khumalo* v. *Holomisa*, at paras. 21, 27; *NM* v. *Smith*, at para. 131. See also *S* v. *Jordan* 2002 (6) SA 642 (CC), para. 53.

[92] See *National Coalition for Gay and Lesbian Equality* v. *Minister of Justice*, at para. 114; *National Coalition for Gay and Lesbian Equality* v. *Minister of Home Affairs*, at para. 31; *Government of the Republic of South Africa and Others* v. *Grootboom*, at para. 83; *Islamic Unity Convention* v. *Independent Broadcasting Authority*, at para. 26 ("freedom of expression is one of a 'web of mutually supporting rights' in the Constitution. It is closely related to freedom of religion, belief and opinion (s. 15), the right to dignity (s. 10)") (Langa DP); *S* v. *Jordan*, at para. 52; *Minister of Home Affairs* v. *Watchenuka*, at para. 25; *Khosa* v. *Minister of Social Development*, at paras. 40–41, 104; *NM* v. *Smith*, at para. 131.

> In many cases ... where the value of human dignity is offended, the primary constitutional breach accessioned may be of a more specific right such as the right to equality or the right not to be subject to slavery, servitude or forced labour.[93]

It should be emphasized that Justice O'Regan did not state that the question of the application of human dignity should not be examined where the primary constitutional breach is of a right with a specific character, such as the right to equality or the right not to be subject to slavery, servitude or forced labor. Nonetheless it appears that the accepted approach is that where there has been a limitation of human dignity and a specific right, the limitation of the right to human dignity adds nothing.[94] Woolman writes:

> [The] ubiquity of dignity has led the Court to adhere to a relatively restrictive rule regarding the use of dignity as a first order rule: where a court can identify the infringement of a more specific right, FC s 10 should not be added to the enquiry.[95]

This leads to the small number of cases in which the court examines human dignity as a constitutional right.[96] De facto, the right to human dignity has become a residual right and applies only in such cases where no other applicable right can be found.[97]

It seems to me that a better approach would be to examine each right separately in every case of complementary overlap between constitutional rights. Human dignity should not be seen as a residual right. The

[93] *Dawood* v. *Minister of Home Affairs*, at para. 35.

[94] Woolman, 'Dignity', at 20 ("[W]here a court can identify an infringement of a more specific right, FC s. 10 will (ostensibly) not add to the enquiry"). See also Botha, 'Human Dignity in Comparative Perspective', at 198.

[95] Woolman, 'Dignity', at 24.

[96] *Ibid.* ("Because some rights are understood, immediately, to be expressions of the commitment to dignity – say, the prohibitions on torture (FC s. 12), slavery, servitude or forced labour (FC s. 13) – and many other rights, once refracted through the value of dignity, become expressions of the more basic (non-justiciable) commitment to dignity – say the right to equality and the right not to be subject to cruel, inhuman or degrading punishment – the need for dignity to function as a rule that disposes of cases directly is less pronounced than it might otherwise be").

[97] See Botha, 'Human Dignity in Comparative Perspective', at 198 ("dignity thus assumes the role of a residual right which is used to interpret and give shape to more specific rights, and which is relied upon directly only in cases in which no more specific right is available"). The author notes, however, that the Court has not been consistent in this approach: at times it examines whether the right to human dignity has been limited even when the limitation also limits other rights. See also Iain Currie, Johan de Waal and Cora Hoexter, *The New Constitutional and Administrative Law* (Landsdowne: Juta, 2001) vol. I, 362.

residuality of human dignity does not comport with the centrality of the right in the Bill of Rights. It would prevent it from fulfilling its role in the Bill of Rights, and might lead to a weakening of human dignity within the constitution. An example of just such an undesirable result can be found in the South African Constitutional Court's jurisprudence regarding the "minimum core" issue.

(3) The minimum core problem

In interpreting the sections in the constitutional Bill of Rights dealing with social rights, the Constitutional Court of South Africa held that these rights do not protect the minimum core of subsistence.[98] The minimal core question should be examined in the framework of the reasonable measures the state must take in order to ensure the fulfillment of those rights within its available resources.[99] If protecting the minimum core of a right exceeds the state's available resources, the state is under a constitutional obligation to do so. This approach of the Constitutional Court is controversial.[100] I shall not analyze the criticism; but I will note, regarding the subject of our discussion, that the minimum ensured subsistence should have also been examined within the framework of the right to human dignity. A similar examination was carried out by the German Constitutional Court[101] and by the Supreme Court of Israel.[102] Both courts held that human dignity protects minimum dignified subsistence. In Germany that minimum is an absolute minimum. In Israel it is a relative minimum, which can be limited in the framework of the limitations clause. In other words, the limitation must be proportional.

The argument that the right to human dignity stands alongside the social and economic rights was raised in the Constitutional Court of South Africa.[103] The court determined, in the general spirit of its common law, that where there are specific rights (for our purposes – the relevant social rights), human dignity should not be discussed. Justice Mokgoro writes:

> This Court has made it clear that any claim based on socio-economic rights must necessarily engage the right to dignity. The lack of adequate

[98] See *Government of the Republic of South Africa and Others* v. *Grootboom*; *Minister of Health* v. *Treatment Action Campaign (No. 2)*, 2002 (5) SA 721 (CC).

[99] See for example s. 26 of the Constitution of South Africa dealing with the constitutional right to housing: "(1) Everyone has the right to have access to adequate housing. (2) The state must take reasonable legislative and other measures, within its available resources, to achieve the progressive realisation of this right."

[100] See Sandra Liebenberg, *Socio-Economic Rights: Adjudication under a Transformative Constitution* (Claremont: Juta, 2010).

[101] See Chapter 13, section 3B. [102] See Chapter 15, section 2B.

[103] See *Jaftha* v. *Schoeman*, at para. 21.

> food, housing and health care is the unfortunate lot of too many people in this country and is a blight on their dignity. Each time an applicant approaches the courts claiming that his or her socio-economic rights have been infringed the right to dignity is invariably implicated. The appellants' reliance on section 10 as a self-standing right therefore does not add anything to this matter making it unnecessary to consider the attempted amplification of their case in this regard.[104]

Indeed, the Justice is right that limiting social rights involves the right to dignity. In the case at hand she found the solution within the social rights themselves. But what if the social rights do not solve the problem? As we have seen, the Constitutional Court decided that the provisions on social rights do not include the minimum core of human dignity. The right is not a right to minimum human subsistence, but rather to reasonable measures, within the state's available resources, to ensure fulfillment of the social and economic rights.

In this state of affairs, the court should examine whether the constitutional right to human dignity has been limited. If it has been, the examination must proceed in order to ascertain whether the limitation is proportionate. The result could well be that the limitation of the right to human dignity is indeed proportionate. This possible conclusion cannot render the need to examine the right to human dignity unnecessary. If the value of human dignity is relevant to minimum human subsistence, what justification can there be to negate the examination of whether the right to human dignity has been limited?

There is apparently no controversy that the social and economic rights should not be interpreted as a negative implication regarding the right to minimum human subsistence. All that the Constitutional Court of South Africa determined – and that too is the subject of debate – is that the social and economic rights do not recognize a separate right to minimal human subsistence. It was not held that the entire constitutional Bill of Rights does not contain such a right. In this situation it is appropriate to examine whether the constitutional right to human dignity has been limited. If the answer is affirmative, the examination must progress to the question of whether the limitation is proportional. The outcome of that examination might of course be that the limitation of the right to human dignity is proportional. That possible conclusion does not preclude the need to examine the right to human dignity. If the value of human dignity

[104] *Ibid.*

is relevant to a minimum human subsistence, how can there be no need to examine whether the right to human dignity has been limited?

2. Human dignity as a constitutional value and a constitutional right in South African constitutional law

A. *Human dignity as one of the human rights*

The Constitution of South Africa recognizes human dignity both as a constitutional value and as a constitutional right.[105] Justice O'Regan discussed this in *Dawood*:

> The value of dignity in our Constitutional framework cannot therefore be doubted. The Constitution asserts dignity to contradict our past in which human dignity for black South Africans was routinely and cruelly denied. It asserts it too to inform the future, to invest in our democracy respect for the intrinsic worth of all human beings. Human dignity therefore informs constitutional adjudication and interpretation at a range of levels. It is a value that informs the interpretation of many, possibly all, other rights. This Court has already acknowledged the importance of the constitutional value of dignity in interpreting rights such as the right to equality, the right not to be punished in a cruel, inhuman or degrading way, and the right to life. Human dignity is also a constitutional value that is of central significance in the limitations analysis. Section 10, however, makes it plain that dignity is not only a value fundamental to our Constitution, it is a justiciable and enforceable right that must be respected and protected. In many cases, however, where the value of human dignity is offended, the primary constitutional breach occasioned may be of a more specific right such as the right to bodily integrity, the right to equality or the right not to be subjected to slavery, servitude or forced labour.[106]

As Justice O'Regan pointed out, the constitutional value of human dignity is of great importance. It provides a moral basis for the other rights,[107] and is at times a part of the purpose underlying the rights. However, the constitutional value of human dignity does not, in and of itself, establish a constitutional right to human dignity.[108] Human dignity as a constitutional right is enshrined in Section 10 of the Constitution of South Africa.

[105] See Susie Cowen, 'Can "Dignity" Guide South Africa's Equality Jurisprudence?' (2001) 17 *South African Journal on Human Rights* 34, 46.

[106] *Dawood* v. *Minister of Home Affairs*, at para. 35. See also *Bhe* v. *Magistrate*, at para. 48.

[107] See Devenish, *A Commentary on the South African Bill of Rights*, at 81.

[108] See *Minister of Home Affairs* v. *NICRO*, at para. 21 ("The values enunciated in section 1 of the Constitution are of fundamental importance. They inform and give substance to all the provisions of the Constitution. They do not, however, give rise to discrete and

B. The relationship between the constitutional value of human dignity and the constitutional right to human dignity

What is the relationship between the constitutional value of human dignity and the constitutional right to human dignity in the Constitution of South Africa? The answer is that the constitutional value of human dignity constitutes the main purpose underlying the constitutional right to human dignity. The main purpose underlying the constitutional right to human dignity is to fulfill the constitutional value of human dignity. I now turn to examine the value of human dignity that underlies the constitutional right to human dignity.

3. The scope of the constitutional value of human dignity

A. Definitional difficulties

The constitutional value of human dignity determines the scope of the constitutional right to human dignity. What is the definition of the constitutional value of human dignity in the South African Constitution? There is no accepted answer to this question. The constitution itself does not define the value. Judges[109] and scholars[110] have emphasized the difficulty in defining the constitutional value of human dignity. However, there is no escaping the need to determine – at least as an initial determination – what human dignity means as a constitutional value. Without doing so, this constitutional value cannot fulfill its function. Haysom correctly noted that:

> It is not enough to show that human dignity is a beacon which illuminates a path for human-rights interpretation. The direction in which the beacon lies must be described.[111]

enforceable rights in themselves. This is clear not only from the language of section 1 itself, but also from the way the Constitution is structured and in particular the provisions of Chapter 2 which contains the Bill of Rights") (Chaskalson CJ).

109 See *Harksen* v. *Lane NO*, 1998 (1) SA 300 (CC), para. 50. Justice Goldstone quotes Justice L'Heureux-Dubé: "Dignity [is] a notoriously elusive concept." (*Egan* v. *Canada*, [1995] 2 SCR 513). See also Justice Ackermann's decision in *National Coalition for Gay and Lesbian Equality* v. *Minister of Justice*, at para. 28: "Dignity is a difficult concept to capture in precise terms."

110 See Haysom, 'Dignity', at 131; Botha, 'Human Dignity in Comparative Perspective', at 201.

111 Haysom, 'Dignity', at 131.

A reading of the judgments of the Constitutional Court reveals a rich jurisprudence regarding certain aspects of the value of human dignity, without an attempt to define it as a whole. The reason for this may be the Court's desire, at this initial stage of constitutional development, not to lay a comprehensive theoretical basis for human dignity.[112] That cannot exempt the legal scholarship of South Africa from trying to define its conceptualization of the value of human dignity as it is reflected in the decisions of the courts. Indeed, such an attempt appears in the writing of some of the authors[113] – including the legal scholarship of Justice Ackermann.[114]

B. *Human dignity as seeing a person as an end and not a mere means*

Common to many of the South African judgments is the Kantian conception[115] that human dignity as a constitutional value means viewing a person as an end in and of herself, and rejecting the view of her as a mere means for attaining the ends of others.[116] Underlying this view is

112 Woolman, 'Dignity', at 7, footnote 1.

113 See Haysom, 'Dignity'; Woolman, 'Dignity'; Botha, 'Human Dignity in Comparative Perspective'.

114 Ackermann, 'The Significance of Human Dignity for Constitutional Jurisprudence', at 4. See also Laurie Ackermann, 'Equality and Non-Discrimination: Some Analytical Thoughts' (2006) 22 *South African Journal on Human Rights* 597, 602; Laurie Ackermann, 'The Soul of Dignity: A Reply to Stu Woolman', in Stuart Woolman and Michael Bishop (eds.) *Constitutional Conversations* (Cape Town: Pretoria University Law Press, 2008) 217, 223; Laurie Ackermann, *Human Dignity: Lodestar for Equality in South Africa* (Cape Town: Juta, 2012).

115 Justice Ackermann bases his definition of human dignity on the Kantian view – see Ackermann, 'The Soul of Dignity'; Ackermann, 'The Legal Nature of the South African Constitutional Revolution', at 650. Woolman's approach is similar – see Woolman, 'Dignity', at 7: "Individual as an end-in-herself." For criticism of this approach, see Drucilla Cornell, 'Bridging the Span toward Justice: Laurie Ackermann and the Ongoing Architectonic of Dignity Jurisprudence' (2008) *Acta Juridica* 18.

116 See *S* v. *Dodo*, at paras. 35–38. In this case the Court held that inflicting disproportional punishment means seeing the criminal as a mere means. That means "to ignore, if not to deny, that which lies at the very heart of human dignity. Human beings are not commodities to which a price can be attached; they are creatures with inherent and infinite worth; they ought to be treated as ends in themselves, never merely as means to an end" (Ackermann J). See also *S v. Jordan*, at para. 74: "To the extent that the dignity of prostitutes is diminished, the diminution arises from the character of prostitution itself. The very nature of prostitution is the commodification of one's body. Even though we accept that prostitutes may have few alternatives to prostitution, the dignity of prostitutes is diminished not by section 20(1)(aA) but by their engaging in commercial sex work. The very character of the work they undertake devalues the respect that the Constitution regards as inherent in the human body. This is not to say that as prostitutes they are

not only a philosophical view based on Kant,[117] but also the bitter experience of apartheid, which, at its foundations, viewed non-whites as a mere means to serve whites, and not as ends in and of themselves.[118] Justices Ackermann, O'Regan and Sachs discussed this in *Prinsloo*:

> We are emerging from a period of our history during which the humanity of the majority of the inhabitants of this country was denied. They were treated as not having inherent worth; as objects whose identities could be arbitrarily defined by those in power rather than as persons of infinite worth. In short, they were denied recognition of their inherent dignity.[119]

The view that a person should not be seen as a mere means for satisfying the will of others means recognition of people's equality in human dignity.[120] That approach also leads to recognition that the humanity of a person is what underlies her dignity as a human being[121] and to the recognition of her ability to exercise her autonomy[122] in order to develop her personality.[123] That recognition is the recognition of the intrinsic worth,[124] inherent worth[125] and self-worth[126] of every person, of her free

stripped of the right to be treated with respect by law enforcement officers. All arrested and accused persons must be treated with dignity by the police. But any invasion of dignity, going beyond that ordinarily implied by an arrest or charge, that occurs in the course of arrest or incarceration cannot be attributed to section 20(1)(aA), but rather to the manner in which it is being enforced" (Ngcobo J).

117 For Kant's approach, see Chapter 2, section 2B.

118 See the words of President Chaskalson in *S* v. *Makwanyane*, at para. 26, according to which the death penalty is unconstitutional, inter alia, because "it strips the convicted person of all dignity and treats him or her as an object to be eliminated by the state."

119 *Prinsloo* v. *Van der Linde*, at para. 31.

120 See Woolman, 'Dignity', at 10; Botha, 'Human Dignity in Comparative Perspective', at 203.

121 *S* v. *Makwanyane*, at para. 308, 326; *Prinsloo* v. *Van der Linde*, at para. 31; *National Coalition for Gay and Lesbian Equality* v. *Minister of Home Affairs*, at para. 54; *Minister of Home Affairs* v. *Fourie*, at para. 50.

122 See *National Coalition for Gay and Lesbian Equality* v. *Minister of Justice*, at para. 117; Haysom, 'Dignity', at 131–2; Botha, 'Human Dignity in Comparative Perspective', at 204.

123 See *Ferreira* v. *Levin NO*, at para. 49.

124 See *S* v. *Makwanyane*, at para. 328; *Ferreira* v. *Levin NO*, at para. 250; *Khumalo* v. *Holomisa*, at para. 27.

125 See *S* v. *Makwanyane*, at para. 328; *Prinsloo* v. *Van der Linde*, at para. 31; *Harksen* v. *Lane*, at para. 49; *National Coalition for Gay and Lesbian Equality* v. *Minister of Home Affairs*, at para. 42; *Minister of Home Affairs* v. *Fourie*, at para. 50.

126 See *National Coalition for Gay and Lesbian Equality* v. *Minister of Home Affairs*, at para. 42 ("The sting of past and continuing discrimination against both gays and lesbians is the clear message that it conveys, namely, that they, whether viewed as individuals or in their same-sex relationships, do not have the inherent dignity and are not worthy of the human respect possessed by and accorded to heterosexuals and their relationships. This

will,[127] and of what it means to be a human being.[128] Limitation of the human dignity of an individual limits the human dignity of all members of society.[129] From this stems the close association between human dignity of the individual and the society in which she lives.[130] A person is a part of society. In the words of Justice Ackermann, the constitution does not relate to the individual:

> as being in heroic and atomistic isolation from the rest of humanity.[131]

The constitution relates to the individual as a part of society. Justice Sachs discussed this in one case:

> While recognising the unique worth of each person, the Constitution does not presuppose that a holder of rights is as an isolated, lonely and abstract figure possessing a disembodied and socially disconnected self.

discrimination occurs at a deeply intimate level of human existence and relationality. It denies to gays and lesbians that which is foundational to our Constitution and the concepts of equality and dignity, which at this point are closely intertwined, namely that all persons have the same inherent worth and dignity as human beings, whatever their other differences may be. The denial of equal dignity and worth all too quickly and insidiously degenerates into a denial of humanity and leads to inhuman treatment by the rest of society in many other ways. This is deeply demeaning and frequently has the cruel effect of undermining the confidence and sense of self-worth and self-respect of lesbians and gays") (Ackermann J). See also *National Coalition for Gay and Lesbian Equality* v. *Minister of Justice*, at paras. 120, 124–125, 127; *Khumalo* v. *Holomisa*, at para. 27; *Minister of Home Affairs* v. *Watchenuka*, at para. 27.

127 See *National Coalition for Gay and Lesbian Equality* v. *Minister of Justice*, at para. 117.

128 See *S v. Jordan*, at para. 74 (O'Regan and Sachs JJ): "Our Constitution values human dignity which inheres in various aspects of what it means to be a human being. One of these aspects is the fundamental dignity of the human body which is not simply organic. Neither is it something to be commodified." See also *NM* v. *Smith*, at paras. 131–132; *S* v. *Makwanyane*, at para. 326 ("to share in the experience of humanity") (O'Regan J); *Government of the Republic of South Africa and Others* v. *Grootboom*, at para. 83 ("human beings are required to be treated as human beings") (Yacoob J).

129 See *Government of the Republic of South Africa and Others* v. *Grootboom*, at para. 83. See also *Port Elizabeth Municipality* v. *Various Occupiers*, at para. 18 ("It is not only the dignity of the poor that is assailed when homeless people are driven from pillar to post in a desperate quest for a place where they and their families can rest their heads. Our society as a whole is demeaned when state action intensifies rather than mitigates their marginalisation. The integrity of the rights-based vision of the Constitution is punctured when governmental action augments rather than reduces denial of the claims of the desperately poor to the basic elements of a decent existence. Hence the need for special judicial control of a process that is both socially stressful and potentially conflictual") (Sachs J).

130 In this light the principle of *ubuntu*, based on solidarity between the individuals in society, was emphasized. See Botha, 'Human Dignity in Comparative Perspective', at 204.

131 *Ferreira* v. *Levin NO*, at para. 52.

> It acknowledges that people live in their bodies, their communities, their cultures, their places and their times.[132]

From this stems the interdependence of the members of society. In *Bernstein*, Justice O'Regan discussed this interdependence in the context of liberty. Her explanation also applies to the value of human dignity:

> [T]he democratic society contemplated by the Constitution is not one in which freedom would be interpreted as license, in the sense that any invasion of the capacity of an individual to act is necessarily and inevitably a breach of that person's constitutionally entrenched freedom. Such a conception of freedom fails to recognise that human beings live within a society and are dependent upon one another. The conception of freedom underlying the Constitution must embrace that interdependence without denying the value of individual autonomy. It must recognise the important role that the state, and others, will play in seeking to enhance individual autonomy and dignity and the enjoyment of rights and freedoms.[133]

4. The scope of the constitutional right to human dignity

A. *Overlap and conflict between human dignity and other constitutional rights*

The constitutional right to human dignity in the Constitution of South Africa is intended to fulfill the constitutional value of human dignity. The constitutional right is interpreted according to the accepted rules for constitutional interpretation in South Africa.[134] It has already been noted that at times the right to human dignity overlaps complimentarily other constitutional rights.[135] This is because the other constitutional rights are also intended to fulfill the value of human dignity, alongside other constitutional values and social objectives. In this state of affairs, the rights reinforce one another.[136]

132 *National Coalition for Gay and Lesbian Equality* v. *Minister of Justice*, at para. 117.

133 *Bernstein* v. *Bester NO*, at para. 150.

134 See s. 39 of the Constitution of South Africa (1996). See also Lourens Du Plessis, 'Interpretation', in Stuart Woolman, Michael Bishop and Jason Brickhill (eds.), *Constitutional Law of South Africa*, 2nd edn, Revision Series 4 (Cape Town: Juta, 2nd 2012) chapter 32.

135 For analysis of this overlap, see Woolman, 'Dignity', at 25; Botha, 'Human Dignity in Comparative Perspective', at 182.

136 See *National Coalition for Gay and Lesbian Equality* v. *Minister of Justice*; *National Coalition for Gay and Lesbian Equality* v. *Minister of Home Affairs*; *Government of the Republic of South Africa and Others* v. *Grootboom*; *Islamic Unity Convention* v.

At times, the right to human dignity conflicts with other constitutional rights. Thus, for example, the right to human dignity, including the right to reputation that constitutes part of the right to human dignity, might conflict with the right to freedom of expression.[137] At times a conflict might occur between two aspects of human dignity.[138] Narrowing the scope of one of the constitutional rights will not be the solution to all of these conflicts. The solution will be found in sub-constitutional law. Statutory and common law[139] that limits one of these rights, or both of them, or does not sufficiently protect them, will be constitutional only if it is proportional.

B. *The parties to the constitutional right to human dignity*

The right to human dignity is everyone's right.[140] Justice Nugent explained:

> Human dignity has no nationality. It is inherent in all people – citizens and non-citizens alike – simply because they are human. And while that person happens to be in this country – for whatever reason – it must be respected, and is protected, by s. 10 of the Bill of Rights.[141]

Every person is entitled to the constitutional right to human dignity, regardless of his attributes, his actions and crimes he has committed. Indeed, prisoners also have the right to human dignity.[142] The right is granted to a person: a human being. It is not granted to corporations.[143]

In most constitutions, human dignity, like the other constitutional rights, is only directed toward the state. That is not the case in South Africa. The Constitution of South Africa contains this special provision:

Independent Broadcasting Authority; *S* v. *Jordan*; *Khosa* v. *Minister of Social Development*; *NM* v. *Smith*.

137 See *Khumalo* v. *Holomisa*, at para. 27; *Le Roux* v. *Dey*, 2011 (3) SA 274 (CC) para. 72; Woolman, 'Dignity', at 56.

138 See *Christian Education South Africa* v. *Minister of Education*, at para. 15.

139 See *Bernstein* v. *Bester NO*, at para. 71; *Gardener* v. *Whitaker*, 1996 (4) SA 337 (CC) para. 9; *Carmichele* v. *Minister of Safety and Security*, 2001 (4) SA 938 (CC) para. 43; *Khumalo* v. *Holomisa*, at para. 27; *Rail Commuters Action Group v Transnet Ltd.*, 2005 (2) SA 359 (CC) para. 73; *NM* v. *Smith*, at para. 56.

140 See s. 10 of the Constitution of South Africa.

141 *Minister of Home Affairs* v. *Watchenuka*, at para. 25.

142 See *August* v. *Electoral Commission*, 1999 (3) SA 1 (CC), para. 18.

143 See Aharon Barak, 'The Corporation and Basic-Law: Human Dignity and Liberty' (2012) 8 *Mazney Mishpat* 49 (Heb.).

> A provision of the Bill of Rights binds a natural or a juristic person if, and to the extent that, it is applicable, taking into account the nature of the right and the nature of any duty imposed by the rights.[144]

According to this provision, every person has a constitutional right vis-à-vis any other person or corporation, so long as that such a right comports with the nature of the right and the nature of the duty it imposes on them. The fulfillment of this direct (or horizontal) relationship will be manifested in sub-constitutional norms (statute or common law). The reason is as follows: a person will raise the claim that he possesses a constitutional right vis-à-vis another. The obligee will then raise his own constitutional right vis-à-vis the possessor. Thus, for example, to counter a person's right to reputation (which is part of the right to human dignity) the obligee will raise his right to freedom of expression (which is recognized as an independent right). The solution to this clash of rights is not to be found at the constitutional level. The scope of the constitutional rights will remain unchanged. The solution will be found at the sub-constitutional level. Statute or common law will establish the appropriate balance between the clashing rights. This balance – being sub-constitutional – will be constitutional so long as it is proportional.

C. *The content of the constitutional right to human dignity*

(1) The external context and the internal context

In understanding the content of the right to human dignity two interpretational contexts must be considered. One is the "external" context, which pertains to understanding human dignity in light of the painful history of violations of human dignity during apartheid. The second context is "internal," which pertains to the structure of the constitutional Bill of Rights and the relationship between human dignity and the other constitutional rights.[145]

The first, external, interpretational context is apartheid. In order to understand human dignity in the Constitution of South Africa, one must understand the deep violation of human dignity under the

[144] S. 8(2) of the Constitution of South Africa. For an interpretation of this section see Ackermann, *Human Dignity*, at 255.

[145] See *Government of the Republic of South Africa and Others* v. *Grootboom*, at para. 22 ("Interpreting a right in its context requires the consideration of two types of context. On the one hand, rights must be understood in their textual setting. This will require a consideration of Chapter 2 and the Constitution as a whole. On the other hand, rights must also be understood in their social and historical context") (Yacoob J).

apartheid regime.[146] In *Makwanyane*, justice Mahomed[147] wrote that the Constitution of South Africa is characterized not by continuity in regards to the past, but rather by detachment from it:

> The South African Constitution … retains from the past only what is defensible and represents a decisive break from, and a ringing rejection of, that part of the past which is disgracefully racist, authoritarian, insular, and repressive and a vigorous identification of and commitment to a democratic, universalistic, caring and aspirationally egalitarian ethos, expressly articulated in the Constitution. The contrast between the past which it repudiates and the future to which it seeks to commit the nation is stark and dramatic. The past institutionalized and legitimized racism. The Constitution expresses in its preamble the need for a "new order … in which there is equality between … people of all races." Chapter 3 of the Constitution extends the contrast, in every relevant area of endeavour (subject only to the obvious limitations of section 33). The past was redolent with statutes which assaulted the human dignity of persons on the grounds of race and colour alone; section 10 constitutionally protects that dignity.[148]

In *Daniels*, Justice Ngcobo similarly wrote:

> The new constitutional order rejects the values upon which these decisions were based and affirms the equal worth and equality of all South Africans. The recognition and protection of human dignity is the touchstone of this new constitutional order. The new constitutional order is based on the recognition of our diversity and tolerance for other religious faiths. It is founded on human dignity, equality and freedom. These founding values have introduced new values in our society. The process of interpreting legislation must recognise the context in which we find ourselves and the constitutional goal of establishing a society based on democratic values, social justice and fundamental human rights.[149]

The second, internal, interpretational context is the structure of the Bill of Rights. This Bill of Rights recognizes a long and impressive list of political, civil, social and economic rights. Between the different rights there is overlap and conflict. Where there is overlap, the value of human dignity, which is the underlying value of the constitutional right to human dignity, serves as one value alongside others in the various rights. As a result,

[146] See section 1D above. [147] *S* v. *Makwanyane*, at para. 262.

[148] *Ibid.* See also *Bernstein* v. *Bester NO*, at para. 148 ("Our Constitution represents an emphatic rejection of a past in which human dignity was denied repeatedly by an authoritarian and racist government") (O'Regan J); *National Coalition for Gay and Lesbian Equality* v. *Minister of Justice*, at para. 125.

[149] *Daniels* v. *Campbell*, at para. 54.

most of the judgments do not dedicate the discussion solely to the constitutional right to human dignity. They discuss the constitutional right to human dignity alongside the discussion of the other constitutional rights, where the various constitutional rights overlap and reinforce each other.[150] At times, even when it was appropriate to examine whether the right to human dignity had been limited, no such examination was carried out, in light of the approach that the constitutional examination should be within the framework of the relevant particular right.[151] It is therefore difficult at times to know what the result of those judgments would have been if the other constitutional rights had not existed.

In light of these two interpretational contexts, I shall now examine the content of the right to human dignity. This examination will take place against the backdrop of the judgments that examined human dignity in the general context of the constitutional Bill of Rights. Note, in this context, that the right to human dignity is not only a negative right (i.e. – the right not to have human dignity limited). Human dignity as a constitutional right is also a positive right (i.e. – the right to have human dignity protected).[152] This is expressly determined in the constitutional right to human dignity ("the right to have their dignity respected and protected"), and it also derives from the general provision in the Bill of Rights of South Africa, which determines:

> The state must respect, protect, promote and fulfill the rights in the Bill of Rights.[153]

(2) The content of human dignity as a constitutional right in light of the Constitutional Court's jurisprudence

Human dignity as a constitutional right fulfills the constitutional value of human dignity. It thus fulfills the humanity of a human being. That humanity means that a person is not merely a means for satisfying the will of another. The humanity of a human being means his ability to exercise his autonomy and to develop his personality. That humanity recognizes the intrinsic self-worth of every person as a human being. Human dignity as a constitutional right thus expresses what it means to be a human being.

150 See *Khumalo* v. *Holomisa*, at para. 28.

151 See section 1F(2) above.

152 See *Carmichele* v. *Minister of Safety and Security*, at para. 44, 62; *Rail Commuters Action Group v Transnet Ltd.*, at para. 73.

153 S. 7(2) of the Constitution of South Africa.

Human dignity as a constitutional right protects the decision of the individual to marry or not to marry[154] and to choose in what way to marry.[155] The right protects family life and its fulfillment in South Africa.[156]

There is a close association and a great deal of overlap between human dignity and equality,[157] privacy,[158] freedom of expression,[159] freedom of faith,[160] individual freedom[161] and the social and economic rights.[162] Human dignity is limited if the right to participate in elections[163] or the freedom to work[164] or study[165] are denied. Human dignity covers a person's reputation.[166]

Human dignity rejects the death penalty,[167] whipping[168] and any other cruel punishment.[169] Imprisonment for a civil debt limits the human dignity of the debtor.[170] Human dignity protects a person from rape[171] and bodily threat.[172] Human dignity protects the intimate choices of a

154 See *Volks NO* v. *Robinson*, 2005 (5) BCLR 446 (CC) para. 154.

155 See *Hassam* v. *Jacobs NO*, 2009 5 (SA) 572 (CC) para. 46.

156 See *Dawood* v. *Minister of Home Affairs*, at para. 30; *Booysen* v. *Minister of Home Affairs and Another*, at para. 10.

157 See *President of the Republic of South Africa* v. *Hugo*, 1997 (4) SA 1 (CC) para. 41; *Prinsloo* v. *Van der Linde*, at para. 31; *Harksen* v. *Lane*, at para. 46; *National Coalition for Gay and Lesbian Equality* v. *Minister of Justice*, at para. 124; *National Coalition for Gay and Lesbian Equality* v. *Minister of Home Affairs*, at para. 31. See also Ackermann, *Human Dignity*, at 181; Cowen, 'Can "Dignity" Guide South Africa's Equality Jurisprudence?'; Rory O'Connell, 'The Role of Dignity in Equality Law: Lessons from Canada and South Africa' (2008) 6 *International Journal of Constitutional Law* 267.

158 See *Khumalo* v. *Holomisa*, at para. 27; *NM* v. *Smith*, at para. 133.

159 See *Islamic Unity Convention* v. *Independent Broadcasting Authority*, at para. 26.

160 See *Christian Education South Africa* v. *Minister of Education*, at para. 36.

161 See *Ferreira* v. *Levin NO*, at para. 47.

162 See *Government of the Republic of South Africa and Others* v. *Grootboom*, at para. 83; *Jaftha* v. *Schoeman*, at para. 21; *Khosa* v. *Minister of Social Development*, at para. 41, 104, 114.

163 See *August* v. *Electoral Commission*, at para. 17; *Minister of Home Affairs* v. *NICRO*, at paras. 28, 96; *Occupiers of 51 Olivia Road* v. *City of Johannesburg*, 2008 (3) SA 208 (CC), para. 16.

164 See *Minister of Home Affairs* v. *Watchenuka*, at para. 27.

165 See *ibid.*, at para. 36.

166 See *Khumalo* v. *Holomisa*, at paras. 27–28; *Gardener* v. *Whitaker*, at para. 9 ("He was balancing one fundamental right (dignity, including reputation) against another (freedom of speech) and developing (or altering) a common law rule in a manner which in his opinion struck the correct balance") (Kentridge AJ).

167 See *S* v. *Makwanyane*, at para. 214.

168 See *S* v. *Williams* 1995 (3) SA 632 (CC) para. 35.

169 See *S* v. *Dodo*, at para. 35.

170 See *Coetzee* v. *Government of the Republic of South Africa*, at para. 43.

171 See *Bothma* v. *Els*, 2010 (2) SA 622 (CC) para. 45.

172 See *National Coalition for Gay and Lesbian Equality* v. *Minister of Justice*, at para. 28.

person.[173] It thus protects homosexual relationships,[174] the right to same-sex marriage[175] and the right to adopt.[176] The human dignity of homosexual partners is limited if the rights to which they are entitled are denied them.[177]

(3) Human dignity and the autonomy of individual will

Human dignity includes the autonomy of individual will, and the individual's ability to develop his personality. Justice Ackermann discussed this in *Ferreira*:

> Human dignity cannot be fully valued or respected unless individuals are able to develop their humanity, their "humanness" to the full extent of its potential. Each human being is uniquely talented. Part of the dignity of every human being is the fact and awareness of this uniqueness. An individual's human dignity cannot be fully respected or valued unless the individual is permitted to develop his or her unique talents optimally. Human dignity has little value without freedom; for without freedom personal development and fulfillment are not possible. Without freedom, human dignity is little more than an abstraction. Freedom and dignity are inseparably linked. To deny people their freedom is to deny them their dignity.[178]

This was part of Justice Ackermann's dissent in *Ferreira*, and served as the basis of his view regarding the scope of the right to liberty. Does this reflect the approach of the Constitutional Court of South Africa regarding human dignity? It appears that this question has yet to be answered. Furthermore, even if it is determined that human dignity includes the ability to develop one's personality, the following question arises: what is the scope of that ability? Do the penal restrictions that the state puts on a person's ability to develop his personality in order to protect others, or the public interest in social life, limit this aspect of human dignity? In *Ferreira* Justice Sachs noted:

> The reality is that meaningful personal interventions and abstinences in modern society depend not only on the state refraining from interfering with individual choice, but on the state helping to create conditions

[173] See *Khumalo* v. *Holomisa*, at para. 27.

[174] See *National Coalition for Gay and Lesbian Equality* v. *Minister of Justice*, at para. 28.

[175] See *Minister of Home Affairs* v. *Fourie*, at paras. 48, 61.

[176] See *Khumalo* v. *Holomisa*, at paras. 28, 36.

[177] See *National Coalition for Gay and Lesbian Equality* v. *Minister of Home Affairs*, at para. 58.

[178] *Ferreira* v. *Levin NO*, at para. 49.

> within which individuals can effectively make such choices. Freedom and personal security are thus achieved both by protecting human autonomy on the one hand, and by acknowledging human interdependence on the other. The interdependence is not a limitation on freedom, but an element of it. It follows that the definition of freedom requires not the exclusion of inter-dependence, but its embodiment, bearing in mind that such incorporation should be accomplished in a manner which reinforces rather than undermines autonomy and upholds rather than reduces the value of maximising effective personal choice.[179]

In *Bernstein* that approach was quoted in agreement by Justice O'Regan, who added:

> It does not seem to me that this approach will render all regulatory laws or criminal prohibitions subject to constitutional challenge in terms of section 11(1). A purposive approach to section 11(1) recognises that it is aimed not at rendering constitutionally suspect all criminal prohibitions or governmental regulation. Our society, as all others in the late twentieth century, clearly requires government regulation in many areas of social life. It requires a criminal justice system based on the prohibition of criminal conduct. The need for effective government which can facilitate the achievement of autonomy and equality is implicit within the constitutional framework. Only when it can be shown that freedom has been limited in a manner hostile to the values of our Constitution will a breach of section 11(1) be established.[180]

This was written regarding the right to freedom, but it appears that it also applies regarding the parallel problem in the framework of human dignity. If the residual right to freedom is not recognized, will the residual human dignity right be recognized? Woolman raises this question,[181] noting that the recognition of autonomy ("self-realisation") as part of human dignity is directed toward the "negative" aspect of the right, and not the "positive" one. According to this approach, the autonomy of individual will and of the free will of the individual will not provide a basis for a positive right to protection of this autonomy and free will.[182] That approach is reinforced in light of the view of human dignity as the right of a person in the framework of society. In contrast, according to the South African Bill of Rights, every right has not only a "negative" aspect but also a "positive" aspect.[183] Furthermore, viewing a person as part of society does not conflict with recognition of a residual human dignity right, as it will always

[179] *Ibid.*, at para. 251. [180] *Bernstein* v. *Bester NO*, at para. 151.

[181] See Woolman, 'Dignity', at 11, footnote 4.

[182] See Haysom, 'Dignity', at 132.

[183] See s. 7(2) of the Constitution of South Africa.

be possible to ensure the recognition of the rights of others and the public interest through the limitations clause. That is also the case in Germany regarding the right to development of personality,[184] and there is no reason not to apply a similar approach regarding human dignity as a constitutional right in South Africa.

[184] See Art. 2(1) of the German Basic Law.

15

Human dignity in Israeli constitutional law

1. The normative traits of human dignity

A. *Articles 2 and 4 of the Basic Law*

Articles 2 and 4 of Basic Law: Human Dignity and Liberty recognize human dignity as a constitutional right. Section 2 of the Basic Law states:

> The life, body, or dignity of a person, as a human being, is not to be limited.

Article 4 of the Basic Law adds:

> Every person is entitled to protection of his life, his body and his dignity.

These articles have undergone comprehensive judicial interpretation. They have been employed by scores of judgments in various areas of law. These judgments share the approach that human dignity is not solely a constitutional value. It is also a constitutional right. The Israeli Supreme Court discussed this in one case:

> [T]he Basic Law does not merely declare "policy" or "ideals" (cf. art. 20(1) of the Basic Law of Germany). The Basic Law does not merely delineate a "plan of operation" or a "purpose" for the organs of government (cf. art. 27(2) of the constitution of South Africa; art. 39 of the constitution of India). It does not merely provide an "umbrella concept" with interpretive application ... Sections 2 and 4 of the Basic Law provide a right – a right that guarantees human dignity. This right corresponds with the duty of the organs of government to respect it (s. 11).[1]

[1] HCJ 366/03 *Commitment to Peace and Social Justice* v. *Minister of Finance*, IsrLR 335, 347 (Barak J) (2005). See also CA 294/91, *Jerusalem Chevra Kadisha* v. *Kestenbaum*, IsrSC 46(2) 464, 524 (1992) (Heb.) ("[H]uman dignity creates rights and duties, grants authority and powers and influences the interpretation of all legislation. Human dignity in Israel is not a metaphor") (Barak J); HCJ 6427/02 *The Movement for Quality Government in Israel* v. *Knesset*, IsrSC 61(1) 619, 681 (2006) (Heb.) ("However, human dignity in Israel is not just a basis and foundation for the various human rights. Human dignity in Israel is not just a

Basic Law: Human Dignity and Liberty recognizes a number of independent freestanding constitutional rights.[2] In addition to these is the constitutional right to engage in any occupation, profession or trade (freedom of occupation), which is enshrined in Basic Law: Freedom of Occupation. The rights determined in these two Basic Laws do not comprise the comprehensive list of the constitutional rights in Israel. The other Basic Laws also contain constitutional rights. Thus, for example, Basic Law: The Knesset contains provisions regarding the right to vote and run for office.[3] The provisions on this matter are not considered merely "institutional," but rather grant election rights pursuant to the conditions set out in the provisions, such as equality. Another example is the provision in Basic Law: The Judiciary, according to which "[a] court shall sit in public."[4] This is not only an institutional provision, but also an individual right for which there is a corresponding state duty. All these constitutional rights are at an equal constitutional level.

As it is in South Africa, in Israel human dignity in the Basic Law is characterized by the following four traits: first, human dignity is a relative right; second, human dignity is not an eternal right; third, human dignity is one of the supreme values; fourth, the constitutional right to human dignity at times overlaps complimentarily with other independent constitutional rights. At times the area it covers is exclusive to it and is not included within the scopes of any other independent constitutional rights. I shall discuss each of these traits separately.

B. *Human dignity as a relative right*

None of the rights set out in Basic Law: Human Dignity and Liberty and Basic Right: Freedom of Occupation are absolute. They are all relative rights; they can be limited. A general limitations clause provided in the Basic Laws applies to all of them. The limitations clause in Basic Law: Human Dignity and Liberty states:

> There shall be no limitation of rights under this Basic Law except by a law befitting the values of the State of Israel, enacted for a proper purpose, and to an extent no greater than is required.[5]

social value. Human dignity is an independent right which stands on its own two feet. It has its own existence, alongside the other human rights") (Barak P).

[2] See section 1E below.

[3] See Arts. 4, 5 and 6 of Basic Law: The Knesset.

[4] Art. 3 of Basic Law: The Judiciary.

[5] Art. 8. For its interpretation see Aharon Barak, *Proportionality: Constitutional Rights and their Limitations*, Doron Kalir trans. (Cambridge University Press, 2012) 143. This is

This provision, which establishes the rules of proportionality, applies to all "the rights under this Basic Law." All the rights determined in the Basic Law are therefore relative. This is also the case regarding the constitutional rights determined in Basic Law: Freedom of Occupation.[6]

The limitations clause in Basic Law: Human Dignity and Liberty applies only to "the rights under this Basic Law." What about the constitutional rights enshrined in the other Basic Laws? Certain Basic Laws contain specific provisions stating that some of these constitutional rights can be limited by statute.[7] Can any statute, whatever its content, limit such a constitutional right? Certain Basic Laws contain no provision regarding the limitation of the rights within them. Does that mean that those rights are absolute? These questions have been raised before the Supreme Court of Israel. The accepted approach is that all of the constitutional rights – even those that are not subject to express limitations clauses – are relative rights. In lieu of an express limitations clause, an implied (judicial) limitations clause should be recognized.[8]

A limitations clause by implication is an accepted phenomenon in comparative law. It seems that the levels of scrutiny in American law[9] may be based upon an implied limitation clause. The European Court of Human Rights took a similar approach, recognizing a limitations clause by implication,[10] as did the Constitutional Court of

my own, unofficial, translation. The Ministry of Justice's translation, which is inaccurate, reads: "There shall be no violation of rights under this basic law."

[6] Art. 3 of Basic Law: Freedom of Occupation.

[7] See Arts. 5 and 6 of Basic Law: The Knesset; Art. 3 of Basic Law: The Judiciary.

[8] See HCJ 3434/96 *Hoffnung* v. *The Chairman of the Knesset*, IsrSC 50(3) 57 (1996) (Heb.); EA 92/03 *Mofaz* v. *The Chairman of the Central Elections Committee*, IsrSC 57(3) 793 (2003) (Heb.); HCJ 1435/03 *Jane Doe* v. *the Disciplinary Tribunal of the Civil Service*, IsrSC 58(1) 529 (2003) (Heb.); HCJ 4593/05 *Bank HaMizrahi* v. *The Prime Minister*, (20.9.2006) (Heb.); HCJ 2605/05 *The Academic Center for Law and Business* v. *Minister of Finance*, paras. 15 and 16 of Justice Levy's Opinion (19.11.2009) (Heb.).

[9] See Note, 'Less Drastic Means and the First Amendment' (1969) 78 *Yale Law Journal* 464; Note, 'The First Amendment Overbreadth Doctrine' (1970) 83 *Harvard Law Review* 844; Jeffrey M. Shaman, 'Cracks in the Structure: The Coming Breakdown of the Levels of Scrutiny' (1984) 45 *Ohio State Law Journal* 161; Laurence H. Tribe, *American Constitutional Law*, 2nd edition (New York: Foundation Press, 1988) 832; Eugene Volokh, 'Freedom of Speech, Permissible Tailoring and Transcending Strict Scrutiny' (1996) 144 *University of Pennsylvania Law Review* 2417; Ian Ayres, 'Narrow Tailoring' (1996) 43 *UCLA Law Review* 1781; Adam Winkler, 'Fatal in Theory and Strict in Fact: An Empirical Analysis of Strict Scrutiny in the Federal Courts' (2006) 59 *Vanderbilt Law Review* 793; Richard H. Fallon, 'Strict Judicial Scrutiny' (2007) 54 *UCLA Law Review* 1267.

[10] *Golder* v. *United Kingdom*, App. No. 4451/70, 18 Eur. H. R. Rep. 524 (1975); Robin C. A. White and Clare Ovey, *Jacobs, White & Ovey: The European Convention on Human Rights*,

Germany.[11] Underlying the implied limitations clause is purposive interpretation. The structure of the Basic Laws and their inseparable constitutional values lead to the interpretational conclusion that these Basic Laws recognize a limitations clause by constitutional implication. Its elements are similar, if not identical, to those of the express limitations clause. This similarity is not the product of an analogy used to fill a lacuna, but rather of constitutional interpretation of the constitutional structure. Indeed, just as constitutional interpretation provides the basis for recognition of a constitutional implication, it also determines the content of that implication.[12] The same problems are involved in the limitation of all of the constitutional rights. Constitutional interpretation attempts to provide a solution for the internal tension in substantive democracy between majority rule and individual rights.

C. *Human dignity is not an eternal right*

(1) There is no express eternity clause

The Basic Laws of Israel do not include any express provision regarding eternality clauses. The result is that all the provisions in the Basic Laws

5th edition (Oxford University Press, 2010) 254, 527. See also Marc-Andre Eissen, 'The Principle of Proportionality in the Case-Law of the European Court of Human Rights', in Ronald Macdonald, Franz Metscher and Herbert Petzold (eds.), *The European System for the Protection of Human Rights* (Dordrecht: Martinus Nijhoff, 1993) 125; *Ashingdane* v. *United Kingdom*, App. No. 8225/78, 7 Eur. H. R. Rep. 528 (1985); *Mathieu-Mohin and Clerfayt* v. *Belgium*, App. No. 9267/ 81, 10 Eur. H. R. Rep. 1 (1987).

11 See Michael Sachs, *GG Verfassungsrecht II. Grundrechte* (Berlin: Springer, 2003), 71; BVerfGE 28, 243 (261) (1970). The translation is taken from Robert Alexy, *A Theory of Constitutional Rights*, Julian Rivers trans. (Oxford University Press, 2002) 188. See also I. M. Rautenbach, *General Provisions of the South African Bill of Rights* (Durban: Butterworths, 1995) 83, 106; Dieter Grimm, 'Human Rights and Judicial Review in Germany', in David M. Beatty (ed.), *Human Rights and Judicial Review: A Comparative Perspective* (Dordrecht: Martinus Nijhoff, 1994) 267, 275; Gerhard Van der Schyff, *Limitation of Rights: A Study of the European Convention and the South African Bill of Rights* (Nijmegen: Wolf Legal Publishers, 2005) 127; I. M. Rautenbach and E. F. J. Malherbe, *Constitutional Law*, 4th edn (Durban: LexisNexis Butterworths, 2004) 315.

12 Jeffrey Goldsworthy, 'Implications in Language, Law and the Constitution', in Geoffrey Lindell (ed.), *Future Directions in Australian Constitutional Law* (Sydney: Federation Press, 1994) 150; Jeremy Kirk, 'Constitutional Interpretation and a Theory of Evolutionary Originalism' (1999) 27 *Federal Law Review* 323; Matthew Palmer, 'Using Constitutional Realism to Identify the Complete Constitution: Lessons from an Unwritten Constitution' (2006) 54 *American Journal of Comparative Law* 587; Jeffrey Goldsworthy, 'Clarifying, Creating, and Changing Meaning in Constitutional Interpretation' (2013) 14 *German Law Journal* 1279.

are amendable; thus the provisions regarding human dignity are also subject to the possibility of Basic Law: Human Dignity and Liberty being amended by another Basic Law. The scope of the right to human dignity cannot be altered by a regular statute, regardless of the size of the majority that purports to do so.[13]

(2) Is there an eternity clause by implication?

There are no express restrictions to the Knesset's power to amend Basic Law: Human Dignity and Liberty. Are there restrictions by implication? As we have seen,[14] the Indian Supreme Court developed the unconstitutional constitutional amendment doctrine in cases where an amendment strikes at the basic structure of the constitution. According to this approach – which was also accepted by the South African Constitutional Court[15] – the authority to amend a constitution should not be turned into an opportunity to write a new constitution, or to include in the new constitution changes that conflict with the basic constitutional structure.

With this in mind, the question arises in the Israeli context: can an amendment to a Basic Law, such as Basic Law: Human Dignity and Liberty, be considered an unconstitutional amendment? It seems to me that, in terms of constituent power, the Knesset is not omnipotent in amending the existing constitution. It can be said that the Knesset, as a constituent power, must act within the framework of the fundamental principles and values of the Israeli constitutional structure. Thus it must act within the framework of the fundamental principles upon which the Israeli Declaration of Independence and constitutional enterprise are based. In accordance with this view, it was decided that a new Basic Law or amendment to a Basic Law containing provisions:

> which reject the character of Israel as a Jewish or democratic state is unconstitutional. The people – the sovereign – did not authorize our Knesset to do that. The authorization is to act within the fundamental principles of the regime, as they were expressed in the Declaration of Independence. It was not authorized to annul them.[16]

The Knesset was not authorized to amend fundamental principles and objectives "upon which our entire constitutional structure, including the Basic Laws themselves, are based, and the violation of which is substantial

[13] See CA 6821/93 *Bank Mizrahi* v. *Migdal Cooperative Village*, 1995-2 IsrLR 1, 207–209 (1995) (Barak P).

[14] See Chapter 14, section 1B. [15] *Ibid.*

[16] See *The Movement for Quality Government in Israel* v. *Knesset*, at 717 (Barak P).

and severe."[17] The Knesset was not authorized to strike at "the heart of democracy or the minimum requirement to retain the democratic character of the state."[18] Similarly, it was not authorized to strike at the heart of Israel as a Jewish state and the minimum requirements for that identity.

This approach is slightly different than the basic structure doctrine of the Indian Supreme Court. The Indian approach assumes a complete constitution and an amendment thereof. Israel is in the midst of a constitutional process based on basic laws, which has not yet been completed. Even if the basic approach that there are restrictions upon enacting or amending a constitution in Israel is accepted, it seems that until the enterprise of enacting basic laws is completed, these restrictions are narrower than those accepted in the Indian doctrine. Thus, for example, a constitutional amendment narrowing the scope of the right to human dignity might conflict with the Indian fundamental structure doctrine. However, it may not strike at the heart of democracy, and thus its annulment would not be possible in Israel.[19]

The difference between this position and that of the courts that found constitutional amendments to be unconstitutional is not a principled or qualitative difference. It is a difference in implementation, or a quantitative difference. The doctrine of unconstitutional constitutional amendment is recognized as a legitimate and suitable doctrine. However, in the current constitutional situation in Israel, and as long as the enterprise of enacting basic laws has not been completed, this doctrine acts within narrower confines. Be that as it may, in terms of the question at hand – the eternality of the right to human dignity – the answer is that, in principle, the right to human dignity is not eternal.

D. *Human dignity as a supreme value*

Human dignity is a constitutional value in Israel.[20] It has two sources: the first is the name of the Basic Law: "Basic Law: Human Dignity and Liberty." Human dignity in the name of the Basic Law, as well as the language of

[17] HCJ 4676/94 *Meatrael Ltd.* v. *The Knesset*, IsrSC 50(5) 15, 27 (1996) (Barak P) (Heb.).

[18] *Ibid.*

[19] See *The Movement for Quality Government in Israel* v. *Knesset*; but see also the dissenting opinion of Deputy President M. Cheshin.

[20] See HCJ 5688/92, *Wekselbaum* v. *Minister of Defense*, IsrSC 47(2) 812, 829 (1993) (Heb.); HCJ 6126/94 *Senesh* v. *Broadcasting Authority*, IsrSC 53(3) 817, 865 (1996) (Heb.); CA 3295/94 *Preminger* v. *Mor*, IsrSC 50(5) 111, 121 (1997) (Heb.); CrimFH 7048/97 *John Does* v. *Minister of Defense*, IsrLR 84, 99 (2000).

liberty in the name of the Basic Law, expresses the values upon which the Basic Law is based. It thus covers all the constitutional rights determined in the Basic Law and not only the right to human dignity. It expresses the value of human dignity, as well as the value of liberty, which is common to all the rights in the Basic Law. Second, Article 1 of Basic Law: Human Dignity and Liberty, the heading of which is "Fundamental Principles," states:

> The basic rights of a person in Israel are based upon the recognition of the value of a person, the sanctity of his life and his freedom as a person, and they shall be respected in the spirit of the principles in the declaration of the establishment of the State of Israel.

The value of a person is the dignity of a person (as a constitutional value); the sanctity of human life is life (as a constitutional value); and the freedom of a person is his liberty (as a constitutional value). The fundamental principles of Basic Law: Human Dignity and Liberty are thus human dignity, human life and liberty (as constitutional values).

E. *The area covered by human dignity as a constitutional right*

Basic Law: Human Dignity and Liberty includes a short list of independent freestanding rights: the rights to life,[21] dignity,[22] bodily integrity,[23] property,[24] personal liberty,[25] exit from and entrance into Israel[26] and privacy.[27] In addition to these are the freedom of occupation,[28] the right to vote and run for office[29] and the right to an open court.[30] Central civil, political, social and economic rights, such as equality, the right to health care, the right to housing, freedom of expression, freedom of demonstration and assembly, freedom of religion, the right to employment, and the rights of suspects and the accused in criminal proceedings are not recognized as independent freestanding rights. Some of them are recognized in "regular" legislation[31] and in common law.[32] But are they, or at least some

[21] Arts. 2 and 4. [22] *Ibid.* [23] *Ibid.*
[24] *Ibid.*, Art. 3. [25] *Ibid.*, Art. 5.
[26] *Ibid.*, Art. 6. [27] *Ibid.*, Art. 7.
[28] Art. 3 of Basic Law: Freedom of Occupation.
[29] Arts. 5 and 6 of Basic Law: The Knesset.
[30] Art. 3 of Basic Law: The Judiciary.
[31] See, for example, Equal Rights for Woman Law, 1951; Prohibition of Defamation Law, 1965; Protection of Privacy Law, 1981; The Law for Equal Opportunities in the Workplace, 1988.
[32] See Aharon Barak, *Interpretation in Law, Vol. 2: Statutory Interpretation* (Jerusalem: Nevo, 1993) 457 (Heb.).

of them, recognized as constitutional rights? Can they be derived from the constitutional right to human dignity?

The Supreme Court of Israel rejected a narrow approach to human dignity according to which only the core of human dignity is included in the scope of the right.[33] It thus rejected the approach that only physical and psychological harm, torture, humiliation and degradation constitute the full scope of human dignity. The broad approach, according to which all of the human rights recognized as independent rights in modern constitutions are included within the right to human dignity, was also rejected. The Court accepted an intermediate approach, according to which the right to human dignity expresses the constitutional value of human dignity.

What is the scope of the constitutional value of human dignity?[34] The Supreme Court's answer was that the value of human dignity reflects the humanity of a person as a human being. The humanity of a person means recognizing "the value of a person, the sanctity of his life and his freedom as a person."[35] Human dignity as a constitutional value is a person's free will and the autonomy of that will. It is his personality, his "I" that ensures his identity as a person. It is the freedom of the individual to write his life story and impact its content; it is the freedom from humiliation and degradation; it is the rejection of the idea that a person is a mere means for fulfilling the ends of others. This freedom acts within the framework of society. Human dignity sees the individual as a part of a family, a group and a society.

According to this approach, there is full overlap in the Basic Law between the scope of the constitutional value of human dignity and the scope of the constitutional right to human dignity. There is nothing in the language of the Basic Law or its architecture that leads to narrowing of the right to human dignity in comparison to the value of human dignity. Thus the Israeli approach is different than the approach of the German Constitution.

Human dignity as a constitutional right is a framework right or a mother-right. It is a bundle of daughter-rights which reflect the various aspects of the mother-right. The daughter-rights are the various categories that fulfill the mother-right. They protect the wide variety of the mother-right's attributes.

[33] *Ibid.*, at 682–3. [34] See Chapter 7, section 4B(1).

[35] Art. 1 of Basic Law: Human Dignity and Liberty.

The daughter-rights are not rights derived by implication; rather they are express rights, as each daughter-right comprises a part of the mother-right to human dignity.[36] It was further held that they are not unnamed rights, as their name is the name of the mother-right to human dignity.[37] Of course, the daughter-rights cover only the "dignitary" aspect that these rights would contain if they were recognized as independent freestanding rights.[38] Like their mother-right, the daughter-rights are both positive and negative rights; they cover both civil and political aspects; they cover both the core and the periphery of human dignity; they are relative rights – they can be limited, provided that the limitation is proportional; they are rights vis-à-vis the state alone. I shall now briefly discuss a number of daughter-rights of human dignity that have been recognized in the decisions of the Israeli Supreme Court.

2. The daughter-rights of human dignity

A. *The right to personality*

The Supreme Court of Israel has held, in a series of judgments, that certain aspects of human personality are derived from human dignity. It was held, for example, that a person's right to know the identity of his parents is part of his right to human dignity.[39] This is also true regarding a person's right to adopt an adult.[40] The court recognized a person's right to grow a beard as part of his right to human dignity.[41] On the basis of these "milestones," the door to recognition of the daughter-right to personality has been opened. This recognition has not yet arrived.

B. *The right to dignified human subsistence*

In a number of cases[42] the Supreme Court of Israel determined that a daughter-right to a minimum level of dignified human subsistence is derived from human dignity. It has been said that this right is "found at the heart and core of human dignity."[43] It has been emphasized that the right

[36] See Chapter 9, section 2A. [37] See Chapter 9, section 2C.

[38] See Chapter 9, section 2C.

[39] CA 5942/92 *John Doe* v. *John Doe*, IsrSC 35(1) 536 (1994) (Heb.).

[40] CA 7155/96 *A.* v. *the Attorney-General*, 13 IsrLR 115 (1997).

[41] HCJ 721/94 *Nof* v. *Ministry of Defense*, 13 IsrLR 1, 9–10 (1997).

[42] See, primarily, *Commitment to Peace and Social Justice* v. *Minister of Finance*; HCJ 10662/04 *Hasan* v. *the Social Security Institution*, (28.2.2012).

[43] *Hasan* v. *the Social Security Institution*, para. 35 of President Beinisch's opinion.

to dignified human subsistence is a condition for "exercise of the other human rights … Without minimal material conditions, a person does not have the ability to create, to aspire, to make his choices and to exercise his liberties."[44] "Without food, water, housing, health care and education, the individual would have difficulty filling his civil rights with true content and meaning."[45] "Without minimal living conditions a person cannot exercise his liberty … he cannot have an autonomous and full life, and cannot become an active member of his society and community."[46]

A key question is what minimum constitutes the content of the right to a minimum of dignified human existence. Certainly any material aspect without which a person cannot live is included in this minimum. Thus "access to sources of water for basic human use" is part of the minimum of dignified subsistence.[47] The same is true regarding food and provision of "emergency services to every person as a human being."[48] However, it was decided that minimum subsistence is not merely the minimum necessary to live and not die. It is not the minimum needed in order not to be hungry. The minimum in question is the minimum needed in order to live with dignity. It is the basic living conditions for dignified human existence.

A minimum dignified subsistence is therefore the minimal living conditions that enable a person in Israel to fulfill his personality. It is the minimum that is a prerequisite "for the exercise of the other human rights."[49] The minimum needed in order to live is an objective amount. It can be measured in medical terms. It is universal. However, the minimum needed to live with dignity – the minimum needed in order to fulfill the personality of a person as a human being, the minimum that fulfills a person's right "to live a proper life"[50] – cannot be determined by a medical measurement. It is the product of society's view regarding the minimum a person needs in order to express her personality in the framework of the society in which she lives. It is that minimum that will allow a person "to make his choices and to exercise his liberties."[51] It is the minimum that

[44] *Ibid.* [45] *Ibid.* para. 4 of Justice Arbel's opinion.

[46] *Ibid.*, para. 6 of Justice Jubran's opinion.

[47] CA 9535/06 *Abu Musa'ed* v. *The Water Commissioner*, para. 22 of Justice Procaccia's opinion (5.6.2011) (Heb.).

[48] See HCJ 5637/07 *Jane Doe* v. *The Minister of Health*, para. 10 of Justice Rubinstein's opinion (15.8.2010) (Heb.).

[49] *Hasan* v. *the Social Security Institution*, para. 35 of President Beinisch's opinion.

[50] HCJ 4542/02 *Kav LaOved* v. *Government of Israel*, 2006-1 IsrLR 260, 318 (2006) (Cheshin VP (ret.)).

[51] *Hasan* v. *the Social Security Institution*, at para. 35 of President Beinisch's opinion.

will grant a person "subsistence with economic dignity."[52] It is the same system that will ensure "'a protective net for persons in society with limited means, so that their physical position does not reduce them to a lack of subsistence."[53] It is the minimum that will allow a person "to fulfill his experience as a person."[54]

This level of welfare can be exemplified by a number of situations that arose in the judicial history. I shall begin with the question of food. The minimum amount of food for dignified human subsistence is not limited merely to the amount of food required to prevent a person from dying. Nor is it limited to the requirement to prevent "the shame of hunger."[55] Although it is true that "[a] person hungry for bread is a person whose dignity as a person has been limited,"[56] merely preventing hunger falls below the required minimum. "Every person must be satiated, so that he or she can enjoy human rights in actuality, and not just by law."[57] "A person struggling to attain minimal living conditions does not have real freedom to strive to attain any goals."[58] Therefore, the minimum level of food needed is the level that allows a person to fulfill himself in society. The right to food of course also includes the right to water. Indeed, the court has expressly recognized "the constitutional right to water as part of the right to a dignified minimal subsistence."[59] It has been held that "access to sources of water for basic human use falls within the right to dignified minimal subsistence."[60] "Every person has the basic right to be connected to the water and sewer systems of the state for the purposes of regular supply of potable water."[61]

A minimum of dignified human subsistence contains the right to housing. "Life ... without a roof over your head ... is not a dignified life."[62]

[52] HCJ 1181/03 *Bar-Ilan University* v. *the National Labor Court*, para. 37 of Justice Procaccia's opinion (28.4.2011) (Heb.).

[53] *Commitment to Peace and Social Justice* v. *Minister of Finance*, at 353 (Barak P). See also HCJ 11044/04 *Solomatin* v. *Minister of Health* (27.6.2011) (Heb.).

[54] *Abu Musa'ed* case, supra note *, at para. 22 of Justice Procaccia's opinion.

[55] *Hasan* v. *the Social Security Institution*, at para. 35 of President Beinisch's opinion.

[56] LCA 4905/98 *Gamzu* v. *Yeshayahu*, IsrSC 55(3) 360, 375 (2001) (Barak P.) (Heb.).

[57] HCJ 164/97 *Conterm Ltd.* v. *Finance Ministry*, 14 IsrLR 1, 62 (1998) (Zamir J.).

[58] Ruth Gavizon, 'On the Relationship Between Civic-Political Rights and Socio-Economic Rights', in Yotam Rabin and Yuval Shany (eds.,), *Economic, Social and Cultural Rights in Israel* (Tel Aviv: Ramot, 2004) 25, 45.

[59] HCJ 10541/09 *Yuvalim* v. *Government of Israel*, at para. 24 of Justice Jubran's opinion (5.1.2012) (Heb.).

[60] *Abu Musa'ed* v. *The Water Commissioner*, at para. 23 of Justice Procaccia's opinion.

[61] *Yuvalim* v. *Government of Israel*, at para. 24 of Justice Jubran's opinion (5.1.2012).

[62] *Hasan* v. *the Social Security Institution*, at para. 35 of President Beinisch's opinion.

However, the minimum needed for dignified human subsistence is not limited to a roof over one's head. A person's right to housing means "a place to live in which he can realize his privacy and his family life and be protected from the elements."[63]

The right to a minimum of dignified human subsistence includes the right to health care.[64] That right includes the right to health care in an emergency,[65] as well as "proper health care for a person in immediate bodily distress."[66] In addition, "[a] ward's right to receive proper treatment in an institution can be seen, without too much difficulty, as a derivative of human dignity."[67] However, a minimum of dignified human subsistence in regard to health care includes more than that. It covers not only "access to the facilities of modern medicine,"[68] but also access to "basic medical care."[69] These are "medical services which are necessary at the most basic level ... this is the most elementary level of medical services needed for preservation of life and health."[70] It is the right to be provided with health services "to the extent that they fall within the necessary minimum level for human subsistence in society."[71]

The right to a minimum of dignified human subsistence covers a person's right vis-à-vis the state to social security. This right has been recognized as "a social human right and as a necessary component of protecting human dignity."[72] "The right to social security as ensuring basic living

[63] *Commitment to Peace and Social Justice* v. *Minister of Finance*, at 353 (Barak P). This right of course includes the right to sleep in a bed – see HCJ 4634/04 *Physicians for Human Rights* v. *Minister for Internal Security*, IsrSC 62(1) 762, 772 (2007) ("A person's right to sleep on a bed is a basic condition for minimum subsistence"), 775; ("The right to a bed to sleep in is in the hard core of the basic right to minimal conditions of subsistence granted to a person as part of the protection of his dignity") (Procaccia J).

[64] On the right to health care in Israel see Carmel Shalev, *Health and Human Rights in Israeli Law* (Tel Aviv: Ramot, 2003) (Heb.); Guy I. Seidman and Erez Shaham, 'Symposium: Law and Medicine' (2007) 6 *Law and Business* 9; Ida Koch, *Human Rights as Indivisible Rights: The Protection of Socio-Economic Demands under the European Convention on Human Rights* (Leiden: Martinus Nijhoff, 2009) 59. See also John Tobin, *The Right to Health in International Law* (Oxford University Press, 2012).

[65] *Jane Doe* v. *the Minister of Health*, at para. 10 of Justice Rubinstein's opinion.

[66] *Solomatin* v. *Minister of Health*, at para. 13 of Justice Procaccia's opinion.

[67] HCJ 5631/01 *AKIM* v. *the Minister of Labor and Social Welfare*, IsrSC 58(1) 936, 948 (2003) (Cheshin J) (Heb.).

[68] *Commitment to Peace and Social Justice* v. *Minister of Finance*, at 481 (Barak P).

[69] *Abu Musa'ed* v. *The Water Commissioner*, at para. 22 of Justice Procaccia's opinion.

[70] *Solomatin* v. *Minister of Health*, at para. 16 of Justice Procaccia's opinion.

[71] HCJ 3071/05, *Louzon* v. *Government of Israel*, IsrLR 344 (2008), at 360–1 (Beinisch P).

[72] HCJ 890/99 *Halamish* v. *The National Insurance Institute*, IsrSC 54(4) 423, 429 (2000) (Dorner J) (Heb.).

conditions enjoys the constitutional protection of human dignity."[73] This right "includes the right to basic human subsistence, so that an employee will not need to rely on welfare benefits."[74] Social security as a constitutional right imposes upon the state "the duty to maintain a system that will ensure 'a protective net' for persons in society with limited means, so that their physical position does not reduce them to a lack of subsistence."[75]

C. *The right to reputation*

The Supreme Court has not seen any difficulty in recognizing the right to reputation as part of human dignity. It has granted this daughter-right significant constitutional consideration and importance. It is manifest in various contexts. Thus, for example, it has great importance in reinforcing other constitutional rights, whether these are other daughter-rights of human dignity or independent rights (such as property, personal liberty or privacy). In addition, it has significance where it conflicts with another constitutional right. Thus, for example, the importance of the right to reputation is expressed where it conflicts with the daughter-right to freedom of expression. These are both constitutional daughter-rights; they are both derived from human dignity; both have great significance in the Israeli constitutional system. The relative weight of each of them is reflected within the bounds of the limitations clause in general, and specifically in proportionality *stricto sensu* (balancing).[76]

The right to reputation is not recognized in Israel as an independent freestanding constitutional right. It is a daughter-right of human dignity. At the constitutional level it applies only to the (vertical) relations between individual and government. It does not apply to the (horizontal) relations between two individuals. Like all of the daughter-rights of human dignity, the daughter-right to reputation has both a positive and a negative aspect.

D. *The right to family life*

In a long series of judgments, the Supreme Court of Israel decided that the right to family life is a daughter-right of human dignity. It has been said of this daughter-right that it "is one of the fundamentals of human

[73] *Physicians for Human Rights* v. *Minister for Internal Security*, at 333 (Barak P).

[74] HCJ 3512/04 *Shezifi* v. *The National Labor Court*, IsrSC 59(4) 70 (2004) (Arbel P) (Heb).

[75] *Commitment to Peace and Social Justice* v. *Minister of Finance*, at 481 (Barak P). See also *Solomatin* v. *Minister of Health*, at para. 13 of Justice Procaccia's opinion.

[76] See Chapter 6, section 4.

existence. It is hard to describe human rights that are its equal in their importance and strength … Among human rights, the human right to family stands on the highest level. It takes precedence over the right to property, to freedom of occupation and even to privacy and intimacy."[77]

Within this framework it was decided that human dignity dictates that the state must create a system of laws that recognizes the right of every person to create a familial relationship as he desires. The right to family life thus includes "the right of the individual to choose his partner and to establish a family with him."[78] "The basic human right to choose a spouse and to establish a family unit with that spouse in our country is part of [a person's] dignity."[79]

> A person's right to create a relationship with a partner and to establish a family with him or her is connected by strong bonds to the value of human dignity, and is found at its core. It is among the fundamental components that determine a person's identity and his ability to fulfill himself. A person's right to choose the person with whom he will share his life is the ultimate expression of the autonomy of individual will.[80]

Thus a statute requiring a person to enter into a familial relationship against his will limits the constitutional right to human dignity.

Within the framework of the right to family life, the human right to parenthood vis-à-vis the state has been recognized. This right to parenthood is based upon "[a person's] existential instinct to establish the next generation bearing the genes of the parents."[81] In this light, the constitutional right requiring the state to apply the arrangements regarding surrogacy to a woman with no partner in order to enable her to become a parent was recognized.[82] Similarly, a prisoner's right to be allowed to artificially inseminate his partner has been recognized.[83] The right to parenthood is fulfilled if all methods of fertilization and birth are employed.[84] Indeed, "the right to parenthood … is derived from the protection of

[77] HCJ 7052/03, *Adalah* v. *Minister of Interior* 2006-1 IsrLR 443, 486–7, 690–1 (2006) (Procaccia J).

[78] AAP 4614/05 *State of Israel* v. *Oren*, IsrSC 61(1) 211, 231 (2006) (Beinisch J) (Heb.).

[79] *Adalah* v. *Minister of Interior*, at 660 (Beinisch J).

[80] HCJ 466/07 *MK Zahava Galon* v. *The Attorney General*, at para. 8 of Justice Arbel's opinion (11.1.2012).

[81] HCJ 2458/01 *New Family* v. *The Approvals Committee for Surrogate Pregnancies*, IsrSC 57(1) 419, 461 (2002) (Cheshin J) (Heb.).

[82] *Ibid.*

[83] HCJ 2245/06 *MK Neta Dobrin* v. *Israel Prison Service*, 2006-2 IsrLR 1 (2006). See also *MK Zahava Galon* v. *The Attorney General*, at para. 8 of Justice Naor's opinion.

[84] HCJ 4077/12 *Jane Doe* v. *The Ministry of Health*, para. 6 of Justice Barak-Erez's opinion (5.2.2013) (Heb.).

human dignity ... a person's decision regarding parenthood is an expression, *par excellence*, of his free will."[85]

The state "is not permitted to limit a person's right to parenthood without important relevant reasons."[86] Such reasons are found in the limitations clause. Of course, alongside the right of the individual vis-à-vis the state to be a parent, the individual also has a right vis-à-vis the state not to be a parent. Thus, for example, a statute prohibiting abortion limits the right not to be a parent. Limitation of that right is constitutional only if it fulfills the provisions of the limitations clause. The right to parenthood also includes, as a granddaughter-right of human dignity, the right to adopt. The state must ensure that there are adoption laws that allow an individual to adopt another individual. That right includes adoption by same-sex couples.[87]

In a number of judgments, the constitutional aspects of the right to a family within the framework of a family unit have been determined vis-à-vis the state. It has been held that the state must maintain a system of laws that preserves the family unit, allows realization of family life and ensures that the family "continu[es] to live together as one unit."[88] The fulfillment of the right to family "is a condition to fulfilling life and the essence of life; it is a condition to the self fulfillment of a person and his ability to tie his life to his partner's and his children's in a truly shared destiny. It reflects the essence of a person's life and the embodiment of his life's desires."[89] In this light it was held that an Israeli prisoner has a constitutional right to maintain contact with his family members who are outside of prison.[90] A prisoner also has a right to undergo fertility treatments.[91] Parents have a constitutional right vis-à-vis the state to raise and educate their children.

The family rights derived from human dignity are not restricted to the parents' rights vis-à-vis the state. They also include the children's rights vis-à-vis the state.[92] Indeed, the state has a constitutional duty vis-à-vis

[85] LFA 377/05 *John Doe and Jane Doe Designated Parent for Adoption of the Minor* v. *the Biological Parents*, IsrSC 60(1) 124, 186 (2005) (Procaccia J) (Heb.).

[86] *Jane Doe* v. *The Ministry of Health*, at para. 26 of Justice Rubinstein's opinion.

[87] See CA 10280/01 *Yaros-Hakak* v. *Attorney-General*, 2005-1 IsrLR 1 (2005).

[88] *Adalah* v. *Minister of Interior*, at 490 (Barak P).

[89] HCJ 7444/03 *Daka* v. *The Minister of Interior*, para. 15 of Justice Procaccia's opinion (22.2.2010) (Heb.).

[90] LHCJA 6956/09 *Yunes* v. *Israel Prison Service* (7.10.2010) (Heb.).

[91] See *MK Neta Dobrin* v. *Israel Prison Service*.

[92] See Judith Karp, 'Matching Human Dignity with the UN Convention on the Rights of the Child', in Ya'ir Ronen and Charles W. Greenbaum (eds.), *The Case of the Child: Towards a New Agenda* (Intersentia, 2008) 89.

the children to maintain a system of laws that ensures and preserves their relationship with their parents. The state has a duty to protect "the personal autonomy and the family of a child and his parent."[93] It has the duty of "preserving the natural family tie between parents and their child and the complicated tapestry of rights and duties that stem from that parental link. These rights and duties regard the natural right of the child to be in his parents' custody and to grow up and be educated by them."[94] Therefore, when the welfare agencies remove a child from the custody of his natural parents, they limit the child's constitutional right to remain with his parents. Indeed, the child has a right vis-à-vis the state "to grow up with his natural parents."[95] Thus a child also has the right to know who his parents are.[96]

E. *The right to equality*

The Supreme Court of Israel derived a daughter-right to equality from the right to human dignity. It held that "[t]he right to human dignity … includes those aspects of equality that guarantee protection of human dignity from violation, and that are closely related to it. Human dignity thus extends to those situations in which a limitation of equality is inextricably linked to human dignity and to a limitation thereof."[97] The court has found that "the right to equality dovetails with human dignity in those areas in which it regards human dignity."[98] That dovetailing is with respect to both the negative aspect (the prohibition of the limitation of equality) and the positive aspect (protection of equality).[99]

[93] LCA 3009/02 *Jane Doe* v. *John Doe*, IsrSC 56(4) 872, 893 (2002) (Procaccia J) (Heb.).

[94] *Ibid.*

[95] HCJ 4293/01 *New Family* v. *the Minister of Labor and Social Services*, para. 17 of Justice Procaccia's opinion (24.3.2009). See also *Adalah* v. *Minister of Interior*, at 690.

[96] See CA 5942/92 *John Doe* v. *John Doe*.

[97] HCJ 10203/03 *HaMifkad HaLeumi* v. *Attorney General*, IsrLR 402 (2008), at 555–6 (Procaccia J).

[98] HCJ 7426/08 *Tebka* v. *Minister of Education*, para. 12 of Justice Procaccia's opinion (6.2.2011) (Heb.).

[99] See *Hasan* v. *the Social Security Institution*, at para. 28 of President Beinisch's opinion. ("A person's right not to be discriminated against and not to be treated with bias requires … at times considerable allocation of resources. At times the right to equality has only a negative character, but many times it creates a positive duty to correct discriminatory

F. *The right to freedom of expression*

The Supreme Court recognized the right to freedom of expression as a daughter-right of human dignity.[100] This daughter-right covers all of the dignitary aspects of expressions whose protection fulfills the underlying principles of human dignity. Therefore, there is a broad area of protected acts and omissions that constitute the entirety of freedom of expression.

A question that has not yet been decided is whether or not human dignity also covers freedom of commercial expression. An opinion has been expressed, according to which this daughter-right should be derived from the constitutional right of freedom of occupation rather than from the constitutional right to human dignity.[101] That would not prevent the application of the right to human dignity to the "dignitary" aspects of commercial expression.

G. *The right to freedom of conscience and religion*

In a significant number of *obiter dicta* the court has held that the dignitary aspect of freedom of conscience can be derived from human dignity. This is also the case regarding the freedom of religion. The court determined that the freedom of religion – and the freedom of religious worship derived from it – is the freedom of every person to believe in God, to perform all of the acts his faith requires, and to refrain from all of the acts his faith prohibits in order to fulfill his faith in practice.[102] "Freedom of religion … encompasses the liberty of the individual to believe and his liberty to act according to his faith, while realizing its rules and customs ('freedom of worship')."[103] Parents have the right to determine the religion of their children.[104] Freedom of religion includes the right to convert to

distortions in society and to make facilities, services and public office equally accessible to the entire population").

100 See *HaMifkad HaLeumi* v. *Attorney General*, at 436; LCA 2687/92 *Geva* v. *Walt Disney*, IsrSC 48(1) 251, 265 (1993) (Heb.); CA 105/92 *Re'em Ltd.* v. *The Municipality of Nazareth-Illit*, IsrSC 47(5) 189 (1993) (Heb.); LCrimA 8295/02 *Biton* v. *Sultan*, IsrSC 59(6) 554 (2005) (Heb.).

101 HCJ 606/93 *Kidum* v. *Broadcasting Authority*, IsrSC 48(2) 1 (1994) (Heb.).

102 Amnon Rubinstein and Barak Medina, *The Constitutional Law in the State of Israel*, 6th edn (Jerusalem: Shocken, 2005) vol. I, 176 (Heb.).

103 See HCJ 1514/01 *Gur Aryeh* v. *Second Television and Radio Authority*, IsrLR 324, 333–4 (2001). See also HCJ 1890/03 *Bethlehem Municipality* v. *Ministry of Defense*, 2005-1 IsrLR 98, 116–17 (2005).

104 CA 5942/92 *John Doe* v. *John Doe*, at 233 (Shamgar P).

another religion and the right to preach religion and spread it, as well as the right not to belong to any religion.

The state limits freedom of religion when it forbids a person to do what his faith requires of him. Is freedom of religion limited when the state prohibits a person from doing what a religion does not command him to do, yet allows him to do? The approach of the courts is that such limitation is not a limitation of freedom of religion. Thus prohibition of polygamy is not a limitation of the freedom of religion of a Muslim man.[105] It was determined that television broadcasts on the Sabbath do not constitute a limitation of the freedom of religion of an individual who does not watch television on the Sabbath.[106] Similarly, importation of non-kosher meat and its consumption by Jews do not entail limitation of the freedom of religion of the observant Jews.[107] In the same spirit, allowing cars to be driven in a religious neighborhood does not limit the freedom of religion of the neighborhood's religious residents.[108] The court similarly held that the broadcast of a movie on the Sabbath does not limit the freedom of religion of the participants in the movie who asked that it not be broadcast on the Sabbath. The act of the broadcasters should not be seen as a limitation of the freedom of religion of the participants.[109]

The right of every person vis-à-vis the state not to have religious faith, not to belong to any religion and not to be subject to religious coercion is derived from the mother-right to human dignity.[110] The human dignity of the individual is also his freedom to be a heretic, agnostic or atheist. This is "the freedom from religion, which members of other religions or nonbelievers enjoy."[111] Indeed, just as protecting a person's conscience protects his freedom of religion, it also protects his freedom from religion. The autonomy of the individual, his free will and his ability to write his life story – that is the humanity of a person – are limited if his freedom of action is limited for religious reasons that are not part of his religious

[105] See CrimA 112/50 *Yosifof* v. *the Attorney-General*, 1 Selected Judgments Supreme Court Israel 174 (1951), at 188–9; HCJ 49/54 *Malhem* v. *Judge of the Sharia Tribunal, Acre*, IsrSC 8 910, 913 (1954) (Heb.).

[106] See HCJ 287/69 *Meron* v. *the Minister of Labor, the Broadcasting Authority and the Minister of the Post*, IsrSC 24(1) 337, 363 (1970).

[107] See HCJ 3872/93 *Meatrael* v. *the Prime Minister*, IsrSC 47(5) 485, 500 (1993).

[108] See HCJ 5016/96 *Horev* v. *The Minister of Transportation*, 13 IsrLR 149, 213–14 (1997).

[109] See *Gur Aryeh* v. *Second Television and Radio Authority*, at 335.

[110] HCJ 10907/04 *Soloduch* v. *City of Rehovot*, para. 73 of Justice Procaccia's opinion (1.8.2010) (Heb.).

[111] LPPA 4201/09 *Raik* v. *Israel Prison Service*, para. 2 of Deputy President Rivlin's opinion (24.3.2010) (Heb.).

beliefs.[112] For example, the conscience of a person who is not observant of religious commandments is limited if she is required, if marrying in Israel, to do so solely according to Jewish religious law.[113] This is the case regarding the conscience of a person who is not permitted to use the streets of his city on the Sabbath.[114] The same is true of the conscience of family members of a deceased person who are prohibited from inscribing the headstone with any language other than Hebrew for religious reasons.[115] Similarly, freedom from religion is limited if the individual is prevented, due to a religious prohibition, from purchasing non-kosher meat.[116] Just as it must be ensured that a religious person can live according to her faith, it must also be ensured that a non-religious person will not have a faith that is not her own forced upon her. The rule is: "each person shall live by his own beliefs."[117] "Religious commandments are not to be forced on a person who is not observant or a person who does not want to observe religious commandments; he is to be forced neither directly nor indirectly."[118]

H. The right to freedom of movement

Basic Law: Human Dignity and Liberty determines that every person has an independent right to exit the country, and that every Israeli citizen has the right to enter it.[119] There is no provision regarding the freedom of movement inside Israel. The Supreme Court held that this does not establish a negative implication that precludes the recognition of the right to freedom of movement within Israel, as derived from human dignity.[120]

112 *Horev* v. *The Minister of Transportation*, at 307 (Cheshin J).

113 See HCJ 80/63 *Gurfinkel and Haklai* v. *The Minister of the Interior*, IsrSC 17 2048, 2069 (1963) (Heb.); HCJ 51/69 *Rodnitzki* v. *The High Rabbinical Court of Appeals*, IsrSC 24(1) 704, 712 (1970); CA 450/70 *Rogozinski* v. *State of Israel*, IsrSC 26(1) 129, 134 (1971) (Heb.)

114 See HCJ 531/77 *Baruch* v. *The Supervisor of Transportation*, IsrSC 32(2) 160, 166 (1978) (Heb.); *Horev* v. *The Minister of Transportation*, at 254–5.

115 See CA 6024/97 *Shavit* v. *Rishon Lezion Jewish Burial Society*, 1998–9 IsrLR 259, 329 (1999) ("[T]he prohibition against foreign writing for religious reasons … constitutes religious coercion. It violates the free will of the deceased and her relatives. It violates their autonomy of personal choice on one of the most sensitive points – the relationship with a loved one who has passed away") (Barak P).

116 See HCJ 953/01 *Solodkin* v. *Beit Shemesh Municipality*, IsrLR 232, 246–7, 257–8 (2004).

117 *Meatrael* v. *The Prime Minister*, at 497 (Or J).

118 *Ibid.*, at 507 (Cheshin J).

119 Art. 6 of Basic Law: Human Dignity and Liberty.

120 See HCJ 6824/07 *Manaa* v. *Israel Tax Authority*, para. 40 of Justice Vogelman's opinion (20.12.2010) (Heb.).

Therefore, every person has a constitutional right, derived from human dignity, to move freely within Israel.[121] This daughter-right is not absolute. It can be limited, provided that the limitation is proportional.

I. The right to education

The Supreme Court held that a daughter-right to education can be derived from the mother-right to human dignity.[122] The court recognized the link "that cannot be broken ... between human dignity and a person's basic right to acquire knowledge, culture, values and skills which are all intertwined and all constitute conditions for a life with human dignity."[123]

J. The right to employment

The National Labor Court[124] and the Supreme Court[125] of Israel have recognized a daughter-right to labor relations, derived from the mother-right to human dignity. It includes the right to work, that is, that the state will ensure that every individual has the option of participating in the labor market. This daughter-right includes the right to a dignified wage, the right to fair working conditions (such as a suitable working environment, reasonable working hours and annual vacation) as well as the right not to have labor relations terminated for irrelevant reasons.

Another aspect of the constitutional daughter-right to labor relations regards the right to organize in labor unions or employer's associations. This right is not recognized as an independent freestanding right in Basic Law: Human Dignity and Liberty. The Supreme Court recognized the right of the employee and the employer to organize as a constitutional daughter-right of human dignity.[126] It was held that this right includes

[121] See *ibid*; HCJ 6358/05 *Vanunu* v. *Head of the Home Front Commander*, para. 10 of Justice Procaccia's opinion (12.1.2006) (Heb.).

[122] See *Tebka* v. *Minister of Education*; HCJ 5373/08 *Abu Levada* v. *The Minister of Education* (6.2.2011) (Heb.); HCJ 1067/08 *Noar KaHalacha* v. *the Minister of Education* (14.9.2010) (Heb.).

[123] *Tebka* v. *Minister of Education*, at para. 16 of Justice Procaccia's opinion.

[124] See LabCH 27–41/57 *Histadrut* v. *MCW*, IsrLabC 30, 449 (1997); LabApp 359/88 *Levin* v. *The Broadcasting Authority*, IsrLabC 36, 400, 408 (2001); CollDis 722-09-11 *State of Israel* v. *Medical Union* (4.9.2011); CollDisapp 25476-09-12 *Histadrut* v. *Pelephone* (2.1.2013).

[125] See HCJ 8111/96 *New Federation of Workers* v. *Israel Aerospace Industries Ltd.*, IsrSC 58(6) 481, 596 (2004); *Kav LaOved* v. *Government of Israel*; *Bar-Ilan University* v. *the National Labor Court*.

[126] See *Bar-Ilan University* v. *the National Labor Court*.

the right of the employees or the employers vis-à-vis the state to ensure a normative framework that enables them to organize in labor unions or employers' organizations,[127] the right to collective bargaining,[128] the employee's right to strike[129] and the employer's right to lockout.

K. *The right to due process*

It was held that the dignitary aspects of due process can be derived from human dignity.[130] This includes the right to judicial independence and the requirement of judicial objectivity, and applies to all proceedings: civil, criminal and administrative. Most of the jurisprudence deals with criminal due process. The court held that the right to due process covers all phases of a criminal proceeding. It held that the right of the defendant to sufficient time and means in order to prepare his defense, his right to be present at his hearing and the right to be represented by an attorney are derived from the mother-right of human dignity.

The right to remain silent[131] and the presumption of innocence[132] are derived from the right to criminal due process. The notion that a person is not to be convicted for a criminal offense unless his guilt has been proven beyond any reasonable doubt is also derived from this right. The

[127] See LabCH 4–10/98 *Delek* v. *Histadrut*, IsrLabC 33, 338 (1998).

[128] See *Bar-Ilan University* v. *the National Labor Court*, para. 40 of Justice Procaccia's opinion ("[T]he right to organize [is seen] as a framework right comprised of three complementary rights: the right to organize, the right to hold collective bargaining, and the right to strike").

[129] See *Histadrut* v. *MCW*, at 468.

[130] See CrimA 1741/99 *Yosef* v. *State of Israel*, IsrSC 53(4) 750, 767 (1999) (Heb.); RT 3032/99 *Baranes* v. *State of Israel*, IsrSC 56(3) 354, 375 (2002) (Heb.); HCJ 11339/05 *State of Israel* v. *Beer-Sheba District Court*, 2006-2 IsrLR 112, 152 (2006); CrimA 1903/99 *Hasin* v. *State of Israel*, para. 7 of Justice Levy's opinion (7.4.2008); CrimA 9956/05 *Shay* v. *State of Israel*, para. 9 of Justice Rubinstein's opinion (4.11.2009) (Heb.).

[131] See CrimA 6613/99 *Smirk* v. *State of Israel*, IsrSC 56(3) 529 (2002) (Heb.).

[132] See LCrimA 4212/04 *Milstein* v. *Chief Military Prosecutor*, 2006-2 IsrLR 534, 546 (2006) ("[T]he presumption of innocence and the right to remain silent are two of the foundations on which our criminal law is based … They are also an inextricable part of the defendant's right to due process … They are directly connected with the principles of fairness, justice and liberty … They reflect a recognition of the huge disparity of forces between the state, in its capacity as prosecutor, and the defendant standing trial. They impose on the state the burden of justifying the violation of human rights that is caused as a result of the conviction and sentencing of defendants. They reduce the risk of mistakenly convicting an innocent person. Therefore some authorities regard them as constitutional rights that are derived from the Basic Law: Human Dignity and Liberty") (Levy J).

right to criminal due process also leads to the conclusion that evidence that has been elicited through coercion is inadmissible.[133] Judicial stays of criminal proceedings are also derived from the right to judicial due process. None of these rights regarding due process in a criminal proceeding are absolute. They can be limited, provided that their limitation is proportional.

3. Parties to the right

A. *The bearer of the right to human dignity*

(1) A person

The right to human dignity is the right of every person as a human being. Young and old, man and woman, physically and psychologically healthy or ill, prisoner, detainee and upstanding member of society, citizen or resident of Israel or foreigner, each of them has the right to human dignity. Indeed, a person's very birth grants him the right to human dignity. There is no requirement that the right holder be able to exercise his own right. A person in a "vegetative state" has the right to human dignity. Regarding the right of a foreigner, it makes no difference if the foreigner is in Israel legally or illegally.[134] Of course, every person's right is in a constant state of conflict with the rights of other people or the public interest. That conflict is solved at the sub-constitutional level. Restrictions might be placed upon the human dignity of one person in order to ensure another person's right or the public interest. These restrictions, which are a product of the sub-constitutional law, are constitutional if they are proportional. Thus, both a person in prison and a free person enjoy a constitutional right to freedom of expression, as a daughter-right of human dignity. Nonetheless, the prisoner's ability to exercise this right is more restricted than that of a person outside of prison. The restrictions upon the right to human dignity of various types of people are the product of the sub-constitutional law. Their validity depends upon their proportionality.

A person's constitutional right to human dignity certainly begins no later than his birth. But should the date not be pushed back to the time of

[133] See CrimA 5121/98 *Yissacharov* v. *Chief Military Prosecutor*, 2006-1 IsrLR 320, 370 (2006).

[134] See HCJ 4542/02 *Kav LaOved* v. *The Ministry of the Interior*, 2006-1 IsrLR 260 (2006), para. 36.

conception? That question has not yet arisen in Israel. The issue is difficult and complex. Morality, law and religion are all mixed into it. The comparative jurisprudence is sparse. The Constitutional Court of Germany ruled that the moment of conception is decisive. It added that this does not recognize an independent legal personality of the fetus from that moment.[135] An opposing approach can be presented, according to which birth should be seen as the starting date for human dignity. That does not prevent recognition of the public interest in saving the life of the fetus. That interest will be examined to ascertain if it can justify limiting the woman's constitutional right to an abortion (as part of her right to human dignity or as part of her right to privacy). According to this approach, the fetus has no constitutional right (to life and dignity), but rather the public interest in saving the life of the fetus opposes the woman's constitutional right to have an abortion (as part of her right to human dignity or as part of her right to privacy). Therefore, abortion, whatever month pregnancy may have reached, does not limit the human dignity of the fetus. In in-vitro fertilization, the fertilized ovum does not have a right to human dignity. Human dignity begins only at birth.

When does the right to human dignity come to an end? Does a deceased person have the right to human dignity? The Supreme Court held that a deceased person has the right to human dignity.[136] An argument can be made that the right entitles a living person and not the dead. It is the right of a living person that the memory of the dead person be respected. There is also a public interest in preserving the memory of the dead.

Human dignity is interpreted in most constitutions as the right of a person. According to that interpretation, it is not the right of an animal. Statutes that do not sufficiently protect animals cannot be seen as infringing upon the human dignity of the animal. Should it not be said that this infringes upon human dignity of the person who is aware of the abuse done to the animal? Whatever form that infringement may take, it seems as though granting constitutional status to the protection of animals requires a constitutional amendment. It is possible to speak of the dignity of animals[137] – and I for one am of the opinion that they should receive

[135] See The First and Second Abortion Cases: BVerfGE 39, 1 (41) (1975); BVerfGE 88, 203 (252) (1993).

[136] See *Jerusalem Chevra Kadisha* v. *Kestenbaum*, at 520.

[137] See LCA 1684/96 *Let the Animals Live* v. *Hamat Gader*, IsrLR 445, 491 (1997) (Cheshin J) ("An animal, like a child, is a defenseless creature. Neither are able to defend themselves, nor can either stand up for their rights, honor and dignity").

constitutional protection[138] – but there should be no application of the constitutional provisions on human dignity to them.

(2) Groups

Is a group, as opposed to its members, entitled to human dignity? Do Romanian Jews or the students of the Interdisciplinary Center Herzliya have different human dignity than that of an individual who is a member of that group? The question whether a social group has group rights is an important question, the answer to which is relevant in various contexts.[139] In public discourse it is possible to speak of the human dignity of a group. That might have important implications.[140] Nonetheless, the constitutional right to human dignity is the right of the individual and not the right of a group.

A group does not have its own humanity. The humanity is that of the members of the group. The constitutional right to human dignity is that of each of its individuals.[141] The same is true regarding the daughter-rights of human dignity. For example, freedom of religion is the right of the individual and not the right of the members as a group.[142] There is an Arab minority living in Israel. It enjoys the rights that international law grants a minority within a nation state.[143] Regarding Basic Law: Human Dignity and Liberty, the rights enshrined in it – first and foremost human dignity – are not the rights of the minority, but rather the rights of every single person, including members of the minority.

(3) A corporation

Can a corporation enjoy the constitutional right to human dignity? Generally, the constitutional rights are also the rights of a corporation

[138] See Peter Singer, *Animal Liberation*, 2nd edn (New York: Harper Collins, 1990); David Bilchitz, 'Moving Beyond Arbitrariness: The Legal Personhood and Dignity of Non-human Animals' (2009) 25 *South African Journal on Human Rights* 38.

[139] See Koen De Feyter and George Pavlakos (eds.), *The Tension Between Group Rights and Human Rights: A Multidisciplinary Approach* (Oxford: Hart Publishing, 2008).

[140] See Jeremy Waldron, 'The Dignity of Groups' (2008) *Acta Juridica* 66. See also Dwight Newman, *Community and Collective Rights: A Theoretical Framework for Rights Held by Groups* (Oxford: Hart Publishing, 2011).

[141] Compare with Michael Ignatieff, *Human Rights as Politics and Idolatry* (Princeton University Press, 2001) 166.

[142] See Anat Scolnicov, *The Right to Religious Freedom in International Law: Between Group Rights and Individual Rights* (London: Routledge, 2011) 24.

[143] See Declaration on the Rights of Persons Belonging to National or Ethnic, Religious and Linguistic Minorities, A/Res/47/135 (1992). See also Natan Lerner, *Group Rights and Discrimination in International Law*, 2nd edn (The Hague: Martinus Nijhoff, 2003);

(a company, partnership, cooperative or society). For example, the constitutional right of property[144] is the right of a "person," and there is no reason to assume that a corporation does not have that right. Of course, the right must be, by its nature, the kind of right that a corporation can benefit from. Thus a corporation does not have the constitutional right to personal liberty.[145]

Does a corporation have a constitutional right to human dignity? The answer is no. The dignity of a person is the humanity of the person, and a corporation does not have "humanity." Indeed, the three rights in Articles 2–4 of the Basic Law – the right to life, the right to body and the right to human dignity – are rights of a "person as a human being." That condition is not fulfilled regarding a corporation.

The mother-right to human dignity includes, as daughter-rights, rights that in other constitutions are recognized as freestanding human rights, such as the right to equality and to freedom of expression. If these daughter-rights stood by themselves, they could, theoretically, apply to a corporation as well. That is not the case regarding Basic Law: Human Dignity and Liberty. In the framework of that Basic Law, the rights to equality and freedom of expression are the equality and expression of a human being – of a person characterized by humanity. They are not the equality and expression of a corporation. Indeed, it is a well-known phenomenon that daughter-rights have a narrower scope than they would have if they were freestanding rights. These constitutional "family ties" narrow their scopes to the outer limits of the scope of the mother-right. Thus equality and freedom of expression of a corporation will continue to apply at the sub-constitutional level.

B. *Obligee*

Toward whom is the right to human dignity directed? It is certainly directed toward every governmental authority, but is it directed only toward governmental authorities? Is it also directed toward other individuals? Is the right of a person to human dignity not only his right vis-à-vis governmental authorities but also toward any other person? This question was discussed extensively in comparative law,[146] where it is known as the

Steven Wheatley, *Democracy, Minorities and International Law* (Cambridge University Press, 2005).

144 Art. 3 of Basic Law: Human Dignity and Liberty.

145 *Bank HaMizrahi* v. *The Prime Minister*, at para. 10 of President Barak's opinion.

146 Many books and articles have been published on this subject since the late 1990s. The important books published during this period are Alfredo Mordechai Rabello and Petar

question of the third party effect (*Drittwirkung*) or the problem of vertical or horizontal application.

The vertical model (i.e. a right vis-à-vis the state alone) is the more appropriate one. The horizontal model[147] (i.e. a right vis-à-vis the state and other individuals) is not appropriate, because the right of the individual to human dignity vis-à-vis the state is different than the right of that same individual to human dignity vis-à-vis another individual. Whereas vis-à-vis the state the individual's right to human dignity has the full ideal scope it is intended to fulfill, the individual's right toward another individual is a right that has undergone balancing and narrowing in light of conflict with other constitutional rights or the public interest. This process takes place at the sub-constitutional level, and it thus reflects the vertical (indirect) model.

4. Temporal application

A. *Active application of the Basic Law*

The provisions of Basic Law: Human Dignity and Liberty apply to every sub-constitutional legal norm that existed in Israeli law on the eve of the enactment of the Basic Law (March 25, 1992) which limits a constitutional right. Such a provision will be constitutional only if it fulfills the requirements of the limitations clause. The fact that the sub-constitutional provision was enacted prior to the Basic Law (the fact that it is "old law") cannot inoculate it against the effect of the Basic Law.

Sercevic (eds.), *Freedom of Contracts and Constitutional Law* (Hebrew University of Jerusalem, 1998); Rosalind English and Philip Havers (eds.), *An Introduction to Human Rights and the Common Law* (Oxford: Hart Publishing, 2000); Daniel Friedmann and Daphne Barak-Erez (eds.), *Human Rights in Private Law* (Oxford: Hart Publishing, 2001); Andras Sajo and Renata Uitz (eds.), *The Constitution in Private Relations: Expanding Constitutionalism* (Utrecht: Eleven International Publishing, 2005); Tom Barkhuysen and Siewert D. Lindenbergh (eds.), *Constitutionalisation of Private Law* (Leiden: Martinus Nijhoff, 2006); Katja Ziegler (ed.), *Human Rights and Private Law: Privacy as Autonomy* (Oxford: Hart Publishing, 2006); Dawn Oliver and Jörg Fedtke (eds.), *Human Rights and The Private Sphere: A Comparative Study* (New York: Routledge, 2007); Chantal Mak, *Fundamental Rights in European Contract Law: A Comparison of the Impact of Fundamental Rights on Contractual Relationships in Germany, the Netherlands, Italy and England* (Alphen aan den Rijn: Kluwer Law International, 2008).

147 But see Mattias Kumm and Victor Ferreres Comella, 'What Is So Special About Constitutional Rights in Private Litigation? A Comparative Analysis of the Function of State Action Requirement and Indirect Horizontal Effect', in András Sajó and Renáta Uitz (eds.), *The Constitution in Private Relations: Expanding Constitutionalism* (Utrecht: Eleven International Publishing, 2005) 241.

However, Basic Law: Human Dignity and Liberty deviated from the interpretational assumption regarding active application. It contains a provision regarding validity of laws that states:

> Validity of Laws — This Basic Law shall not affect the validity of any law in force prior to the commencement of the Basic Law.[148]

The result is that the active application of the Basic Law cannot affect the validity of old law. The provision on validity of laws in Basic Law: Human Dignity and Liberty does not have an expiration date. The result is that all of the laws that were in effect on March 25, 1992 will continue to be valid, and their conflict with the provisions of Basic Law: Human Dignity and Liberty cannot lead to their invalidation. However, when a new law amends old law, the validity of the new law is contingent on it comporting with the provisions of the Basic Law. The new law is not protected by the Validity of Laws Clause.

B. A normative anomaly

The Validity of Laws Clause created a unique legal situation, in which two legal systems – old and new – exist alongside each other, without one of them changing or annulling the other. This normative array is the product of a political compromise. However, it creates a constitutional anomaly. It is not healthy for a legal system when one part of it (the old part) is not subject to constitutional scrutiny, whereas the other (new) part is subject to such scrutiny. A legal system aspires to harmony and unity. The Validity of Laws Clause disturbs that harmony and unity. Indeed, modern democratic constitutions do not include a provision on validity of old laws; quite the opposite. They are based on a break from the past, and the recognition of a better present and future.[149]

That does not reflect the constitutional development in Israel. The past is preserved. This causes tension between past, present and future. Therefore, all efforts must be made in order to ameliorate the internal tension created by this situation. As time passes, and new legislation

[148] Art. 10 of Basic Law: Human Dignity and Liberty.

[149] See Catherine Dupré, 'Dignity, Democracy, Civilisation' (2012) 33 *Liverpool Law Review* 263, 274–5 ("Codification of dignity in normative texts, particularly in codified constitutions, has therefore played a crucial role in this process in marking a clear break between two eras, i.e. the time before the constitution when there was no dignity and no democracy, and the time under the new constitution that guarantees dignity and democracy").

amasses, the tension will ebb. Nonetheless, and as long as the Validity of Laws Clause is in effect, the natural development of the legal system is prevented and the constitutional human rights do not receive their full and proper protection. This severe result was the product of the desire to achieve as broad a consensus as possible for Basic Law: Human Dignity and Liberty. Indeed, underlying the Validity of Laws Clause is a political compromise reflecting a lack of consensus regarding several issues, the central among them being the division of church and state. The "price of the compromise" was the preservation of the validity of laws.

The results of the Validity of Laws Clause are severe. Many areas of sub-constitutional Israeli law still continue, for the most part, to be how they were in the past. This is conspicuous, for example, in family law.

The Validity of Laws provision is intended to preserve the legal validity of old law that is not proportional. De facto it has protected old law from judicial review in light of Basic Law: Human Dignity and Liberty. It prevents the otherwise necessary examination of whether the old law limits a constitutional right disproportionally. The fact that the law is old is sufficient to block judicial review regarding its proportionality.

The Validity of Laws Clause does not raise the old law to constitutional status. That law remains at the sub-constitutional level. In effect, the Validity of Laws Clause creates an exception to the rule that a norm of higher status overcomes a norm of lower status.[150] Furthermore, the old law exists in a "new environment," shaped by the Basic Laws on human rights. Thus the old law is interpreted in the spirit of the provisions of the Basic Laws. The general purpose[151] of the old law is affected by the new normative array created by the Basic Laws. The balance between the fundamental values underlying the purposes of the old legislation will be performed under the influence of the constitutional status they received in the Basic Laws.[152] The new interpretation cannot, of course, change the language of an old law.

[150] CrimFH 2316/95 *Ganimat* v. *State of Israel*, IsrSC 49(4) 589, 653 (1995) (Heb.).

[151] See *Wekselbaum* v. *Minister of Defense* ("The law is that any legislation – including legislation to which the provision of the Validity of Laws Clause (Article 10) applies – will be interpreted in light of the fundamental principles enshrined in the basic law") (Barak J).

[152] *Ganimat* v. *State of Israel*, at 653 (Barak P).

BIBLIOGRAPHY

International documents

Additional Protocol to the American Convention on Human Rights in the Area of Economic, Social and Cultural Rights "Protocol of San Salvador," OAS Treaty Series No. 69 (November 17, 1988).

Additional Protocol to the Convention for the Protection of Human Rights and Dignity of the Human Being with regard to the Application of Biology and Medicine, on the Prohibition of Cloning Human Beings, CETS No. 168 (January 12, 1998).

Additional Protocol to the Convention on Human Rights and Biomedicine, Concerning Biomedical Research, CETS No. 195 (January 25, 2005).

Additional Protocol to the Convention on Human Rights and Biomedicine Concerning Transplantation of Organs and Tissues of Human Origin, CETS No. 186 (January 24, 2002).

Additional Protocol to the Convention on Human Rights and Biomedicine Concerning Genetic Testing for Health Purposes, CETS No. 203 (November 27, 2008).

African [Banjul] Charter on Human and Peoples' Rights, adopted June 27, 1981, OAU Doc. CAB/LEG/67/3 rev. 5, 21 ILM 58 (1982).

American Declaration of the Rights and Duties of Man, OAS Res. XXX, adopted by the Ninth International Conference of American States (1948).

American Jewish Committee Declaration of Human Rights (1944).

Cairo Declaration on Human Rights in Islam, August 5, 1990, UN GAOR, World Conference on Human Rights, 4th Session, Agenda Item 5, UN Doc. A/CONF.157/PC/62/Add.18 (1993).

Charter of Fundamental Rights of the European Union 01.

Charter of Fundamental Rights of the European Union, 7 December 2000, Official Journal of the European Communities, December 18, 2000 (2000/C 364/01).

Charter of the United Nations, 1 UNTS XVI (October 24, 1945).

Convention against Discrimination in Education (December 14, 1960).

Convention against Torture and Other Cruel, Inhuman or Degrading Treatment or Punishment, 1465 UNTS 85 (December 10, 1984).

Convention concerning Equal Opportunities and Equal Treatment for Men and Women Workers: Workers with Family Responsibilities, C156 (1981).

Convention for the Protection of Human Rights and Dignity of the Human Being with Regard to the Application of Biology and Medicine: Convention on Human Rights and Biomedicine (Oviedo Convention), CETS No. 164 (April 4, 1997).

Convention for the Protection of Human Rights and Fundamental Freedoms, CETS No. 005 (November 4, 1950).

Convention for the Protection of All Persons from Enforced Disappearance, UN Doc. A/61/488 (December 20, 2006).

Convention on the Protection of the Rights of All Migrant Workers and Members of their Families, 2200 UNTS 3 (December 18, 1990).

Convention on the Elimination of all Forms of Discrimination against Women, 1249 UNTS 13 (December 18, 1979).

Convention on the Elimination of all Forms of Racial Discrimination, 660 UNTS 195 (December 21, 1965).

Convention on the Rights of Persons with Disabilities, 2515 UNTS 3 (December 13, 2006).

Convention on the Rights of the Child, 1577 UNTS 3 (November 20, 1989).

Declaration Concerning the Aims and Purposes of the International Labour Organization (Declaration of Philadelphia), adopted at the 26th session of the ILO (May 10, 1944).

Declaration on the Rights of Persons Belonging to National or Ethnic, Religious and Linguistic Minorities, A/Res/47/135 (1992).

Dijon Declaration (1936).

Hague Regulations on the Laws and Customs of War on Land, October 18, 1907, 205 Consol. T.S. 277.

International Covenant on Civil and Political Rights, 999 UNTS 171 (December 16, 1966).

International Covenant on Economic, Social and Cultural Rights, 993 UNTS 3 (December 16, 1966).

League of Arab States, Arab Charter on Human Rights, September 15, 1994.

Organization of American States, American Convention on Human Rights, "Pact of San Jose," Costa Rica (November 22, 1969).

Organization of American States, Inter-American Convention on the Prevention, Punishment and Eradication of Violence against Women ("Convention of Belem do Para"), June 9, 1994.

Organization of American States, Inter-American Convention on the Elimination of All Forms of Discrimination against Persons with Disabilities, June 7, 1999, AG/RES. 1608 (XXIX–O/99).

Organization of American States, Inter-American Convention to Prevent and Punish Torture, December 9, 1985, OAS Treaty Series, No. 67.

Protocol Additional to the Geneva Conventions of 12 August 1949, and Relating to the Protection of Victims of International Armed Conflicts (Protocol I), June 8, 1977, 1125 UNTS 3.

Protocol Additional to the Geneva Conventions of 12 August 1949, and Relating to the Protection of Victims of Non-International Armed Conflicts (Protocol II), June 8, 1977, 1125 UNTS 609.

Protocol No. 13 to the Convention for the Protection of Human Rights and Fundamental Freedoms, Concerning the Abolition of the Death Penalty in All Circumstances, CETS No. 187 (May 3, 2002).

Protocol to the African Charter of Human and Peoples Rights on the Rights of Women in Africa (2000) (Maputo Protocol).

Rome Statute of the International Criminal Court, July 17, 1998.

Setting International Standards in the Field of Human Rights, GA Res. 41/120 (December 4, 1986).

Statute of the International Criminal Tribunal for the Prosecution of Persons Responsible for Genocide and Other Serious Violations of International Humanitarian Law Committed in the Territory of Rwanda and Rwandan Citizens Responsible for Genocide and Other Such Violations Committed in the Territory of Neighboring States, Between 1 January 1994 and 31 December 1994.

The Agreement for and Statute of the Special Court for Sierra Leone, January 16, 2002.

Treaty of Lisbon Amending the Treaty on European Union and the Treaty Establishing the European Community, December 13, 2007, 2007/C306/01.

Vienna Declaration and Programme of Action, A/CONF.157/23 (1993).

Universal Declaration of Human Rights, GA RES. 21A (III), UN DOC A/810 (1948).

Universal Declaration on the Human Genome and Human Rights, UNESCO Gen. Conf. Res. 29 C/Res.17, 29th Sess. (November 11 1997).

Constitutions and statutes

Basic Law: Freedom of Occupation (Israel).

Basic Law: Human Dignity and Liberty (Israel).

Basic Law: The Judiciary (Israel).

Basic Law: The Knesset (Israel).

Equal Rights for Woman Law, 1951 (Israel).

German Basic Law (*Grundgesetz*).

Prohibition of Defamation Law, 1965 (Israel).

Protection of Privacy Law, 1981 (Israel).

The American Constitution 1791.

The Canadian Bill of Rights, SC 1960 (RSC.1970).

The Canadian Constitution Act, 1982, being Schedule B to the Canada Act, 1982, c. 11 (UK).
The Canadian Criminal Code, RSC 1970.
The Citizenship and Entry into Israel Law (Temporary Provision), 5753-2003 SH 544.
The Constitution of Afghanistan.
The Constitution of Albania.
The Constitution of Angola.
The Constitution of Argentina.
The Constitution of Armenia.
The Constitution of Australia.
The Constitution of Azerbaijan.
The Constitution of Belarus.
The Constitution of Belgium.
The Constitution of Bhutan.
The Constitution of Bolivia.
The Constitution of Bosnia-Herzegovina.
The Constitution of Botswana.
The Constitution of Brazil.
The Constitution of Brunei.
The Constitution of Bulgaria
The Constitution of Burundi.
The Constitution of Cambodia.
The Constitution of Cameroon.
The Constitution of Cape Verde.
The Constitution of Chad.
The Constitution of Chile.
The Constitution of China.
The Constitution of Colombia.
The Constitution of Congo.
The Constitution of Costa Rica.
The Constitution of Croatia.
The Constitution of Cuba.
The Constitution of the Czech Republic.
The Constitution of the Democratic Republic of Congo.
The Constitution of Djibouti.
The Constitution of East Timor.
The Constitution of Ecuador.
The Constitution of Egypt.
The Constitution of El Salvador.
The Constitution of Eritrea.
The Constitution of Estonia.

The Constitution of Ethiopia.
The Constitution of Fiji.
The Constitution of Finland.
The Constitution of the French Fifth Republic.
The Constitution of Gambia.
The Constitution of Georgia.
The Constitution of Ghana.
The Constitution of Guatemala.
The Constitution of Guinea.
The Constitution of Greece.
The Constitution of Haiti.
The Constitution of Honduras.
The Constitution of Hungary.
The Constitution of India.
The Constitution of Indonesia.
The Constitution of Iraq.
The Constitution of Ireland.
The Constitution of Ivory Coast.
The Constitution of Japan.
The Constitution of Jordan.
The Constitution of Kazakhstan.
The Constitution of Kenya.
The Constitution of Kirgizstan.
The Constitution of Kosovo.
The Constitution of Laos.
The Constitution of Lebanon.
The Constitution of Liberia.
The Constitution of Lithuania.
The Constitution of Macedonia.
The Constitution of Madagascar.
The Constitution of Malawi.
The Constitution of Malaysia.
The Constitution of the Maldivian Islands.
The Constitution of the Marshall Islands.
The Constitution of Mauritania.
The Constitution of Mauritius.
The Constitution of Mexico.
The Constitution of Micronesia.
The Constitution of Moldova.
The Constitution of Mongolia.
The Constitution of Montana.
The Constitution of Morocco.

The Constitution of Mozambique.
The Constitution of Myanmar.
The Constitution of Namibia.
The Constitution of Nauru.
The Constitution of Nepal.
The Constitution of Nicaragua.
The Constitution of Nigeria.
The Constitution of Oman.
The Constitution of Pakistan.
The Constitution of Panama.
The Constitution of Papua New Guinea.
The Constitution of Paraguay.
The Constitution of Peru.
The Constitution of Poland.
The Constitution of Portugal.
The Constitution of Qatar.
The Constitution of Russia.
The Constitution of Rwanda.
The Constitution of Saudi Arabia.
The Constitution of Senegal.
The Constitution of Serbia.
The Constitution of Sierra Leone.
The Constitution of Singapore.
The Constitution of Slovakia.
The Constitution of Slovenia.
The Constitution of South Africa.
The Constitution of South Korea.
The Constitution of South Sudan.
The Constitution of Spain.
The Constitution of Sudan.
The Constitution of Swaziland.
The Constitution of Sweden.
The Constitution of Switzerland.
The Constitution of Syria.
The Constitution of Taiwan.
The Constitution of Tajikistan.
The Constitution of Tanzania.
The Constitution of Thailand.
The Constitution of Togo.
The Constitution of Tonga.
The Constitution of Turkey.
The Constitution of Turkmenistan.

The Constitution of Uganda.
The Constitution of Ukraine.
The Constitution of the United Arab Emirates.
The Constitution of Uruguay.
The Constitution of Uzbekistan.
The Constitution of Vanuatu.
The Constitution of Venezuela.
The Constitution of Vietnam.
The Constitution of Yemen.
The Constitution of Zaire.
The Constitution of Zimbabwe.
The Federal Constitution of Switzerland.
The Interim Constitution of South Africa (1993).
The Italian Civil Codex.
The Law for Equal Opportunities in the Workplace, 1988 (Israel).
The Province of Ontario Human Rights Code, RSO 1990.
The Quebec Charter of Human Rights and Freedoms, SQ 1975.

Books and Articles

'God's Honour', in *The Biblical Encyclopedia: A Treasury of Knowledge on the Bible and that Era* (Jerusalem: Bialik Institute, 1963) vol. IV, 3.

Abraham, Mathew, 'Judicial Role in Constitutional Amendments in India: The Basic Structure Doctrine', in Mads Andenas (ed.), *The Creation and Amendment of Constitutional Norms* (London: British Institute of International and Comparative Law, 2000) 195.

Ackerman, Bruce, *We The People: Foundations* (Boston, MA: Harvard University Press, 1991).

Ackermann, Laurie, 'Equality and Non-Discrimination: Some Analytical Thoughts' (2006) 22 *South African Journal on Human Rights* 597.

'Equality and the South African Constitution: The Role of Dignity' (2000) 63 *Heidelberg Journal of International Law* 537.

Human Dignity: Lodestar for Equality in South Africa (Cape Town: Juta, 2012).

'The Soul of Dignity: A Reply to Stu Woolman', in Stuart Woolman and Michael Bishop (eds.), *Constitutional Conversations* (Cape Town: Pretoria University Law Press, 2008) 217.

Ackermann, Lourens, 'The Legal Nature of the South African Constitutional Revolution' (2004) 4 *New Zealand Law Review* 633.

'The Significance of Human Dignity for Constitutional Jurisprudence', *Lecture Before Stellenbosch Law Faculty* (August 15, 2005).

Al-Ahsan, Abdullah, 'Law, Religion and Human Dignity in the Muslim World Today: An Examination of OIC's Cairo Declaration of Human Rights' (2009) 24 *Journal of Law and Religion* 569.

Albert, Richard, 'Constitutional Handcuffs' (2010) 42 *Arizona State Law Journal* 663.

'Nonconstitutional Amendments' (2009) 22 *Canadian Journal of Law and Jurisprudence* 5.

Alexander, Larry and Kress, Ken, 'Against Legal Principles', in Andrei Marmor (ed.), *Law and Interpretation: Essays in Legal Philosophy* (Oxford: Clarendon Press, 2007) 279.

Alexy, Robert, *A Theory of Constitutional Rights*, Julian Rivers trans. (Oxford University Press, 2002).

Allan, T. R. S., *Constitutional Justice* (Oxford University Press, 2001).

'Constitutional Justice and the Concept of Law', in Grant Huscroft (ed.), *Expounding the Constitution: Essays in Constitutional Theory* (Cambridge University Press, 2008) 219.

Al-Rahim, Muddathir Abd, *Human Rights and the World's Major Religions: The Islamic Tradition* (Westport: Praeger 2005).

Altmann, Alexander, 'Homo Imago Dei in Jewish and Christian Theology' (1968) 48 *Journal of Religion* 235.

Amar, Akhil Reed, 'Architexture' (2002) 77 *Indiana Law Journal* 671.

The Bill of Rights: Creation and Reconstruction (New Haven: Yale University Press, 1998).

'Foreword: The Document and the Doctrine' (2000) 114 *Harvard Law Review* 26.

'Intratextualism' (1999) 112 *Harvard Law Review* 747.

Anderson, Adrienne, 'On Dignity and whether the Universal Declaration of Human Rights Remains a Place of Refuge after 60 Years' (2009) 25 *American University International Law Review* 115.

Angle, Stephen, *Human Rights and Chinese Thought: A Cross Cultural Inquiry* (Cambridge University Press, 2002).

Anselm, Reiner, 'Human Dignity as a Regulatory Principle of Bioethics: A Theological Perspective', in Nikolaus Knoepffler, Dagmar Schipanski and Stefan L. Sorgner (eds.), *Human-Biotechnology as Social Challenge: An Interdisciplinary Introduction to Bioethics* (Aldershot: Ashgate Publishing, 2007) 109.

Arendt, Hannah, *The Origins of Totalitarianism* (New York: Harcourt, Brace & Co., 1951).

Arieli, Yehoshua, 'On the Necessary and Sufficient Conditions for the Emergence of the Dignity of Man and His Rights', in David Kretzmer and Eckart Klein (eds.), *The Concept of Human Dignity in Human Rights Discourse* (The Hague: Kluwer Law International, 2002) 1.

Aristotle, 'Ethica Nicomechea', in *The Works of Aristotle Translated into English*, ed. by William D. Ross and John A. Smith, (Oxford: Clarendon, 1912).

Ashford, Elizabeth, 'The Alleged Dichotomy between Positive and Negative Rights and Duties', in Charles R. Beitz and Robert E. Goodin (eds.), *Global Basic Rights* (Oxford University Press, 2009) 92.

Aubert, Jean François, *Traite de Droit Constitutionnel Suisse* (Neuchâtel: Ides et Calendes, 1967).

Avila, Humberto Bergmann (ed.), *Theory of Legal Principles* (Dordrecht: Springer, 2007).

Ayres, Ian, 'Narrow Tailoring' (1996) 43 *UCLA Law Review* 1781.

Baer, Susanne, 'Dignity, Liberty, Equality: A Fundamental Rights Triangle of Constitutionalism' (2009) 59 *University of Toronto Law Journal* 417.

Bagaric, Mirko and Allan, James, 'The Vacuous Concept of Dignity' (2006) 5 *Journal of Human Rights* 257.

Baker, Hershel, *The Dignity of Man: Studies in the Persistence of an Idea* (Cambridge, MA: Harvard University Press, 1947).

The Image of Man: A Study of the Idea of Human Dignity in Classical Antiquity, the Middle Ages, and the Renaissance (New York: Harper, 1961).

Balkin, Jack, *Living Originalism* (Cambridge, MA: Harvard University Press, 2011).

'The Rule of Law as a Source of Constitutional Change' (1989) 6 *Constitutional Commentary* 21.

Barak, Aharon, 'The Corporation and Basic-Law: Human Dignity and Liberty' (2012) 8 *Mazney Mishpat* 49.

Interpretation in Law, Vol. 2: Statutory Interpretation (Jerusalem: Nevo, 1993).

Interpretation in Law, Vol. 3: Constitutional Interpretation (Jerusalem: Nevo, 1994).

The Judge in a Democracy (Princeton University Press, 2006).

Judicial Discretion (New Haven: Yale University Press, 1989).

Proportionality: Constitutional Rights and their Limitations, Doron Kalir trans. (Cambridge University Press, 2012).

Purposive Interpretation in Law (Princeton University Press, 2005).

'The Right to Access to the Justice System', in Asher Grunis, Eliezer Rivlin and Michael Karayanni (eds.), Shlomo Levin Book (Jerusalem: Nevo, 2013) 31 (Heb.).

'Unconstitutional Constitutional Amendment' (2011) 44 *Israel Law Review* 321.

Barendt, Eric, *Freedom of Speech*, 2nd edn (Oxford University Press, 2005).

Barkhuysen, Tom and Lindenbergh, Siewert D. (eds.), *Constitutionalisation of Private Law* (Leiden: Martinus Nijhoff, 2006).

Barrett, Jonathan, 'Dignatio and the Human Body' (2005) 21 *South African Journal on Human Rights* 525.

Baxi, Upendra, 'The Constitutional Quicksands of Kesavananda Bharati and the Twenty Fifth Amendment' (1974) 1 *Supreme Court Cases Journal* 45.

Bayefsky, Rachel, 'Dignity, Honour, and Human Rights: Kant's Perspective' (2013) 41 *Political Theory* 809.

Beatty, David M., 'The Forms and Limits of Constitutional Interpretation' (2001) 49 *American Journal of Comparative Law* 79.

Becchi, Paolo, *Il Principio Dignità Umana* (Brescia: Morcelliana, 2009).

Bedau, Hugo A., 'The Eighth Amendment, Human Dignity, and the Death Penalty', in Michael J. Meyer and William A. Parent (eds.), *The Constitution of Rights: Human Dignity and American Values* (Ithaca, NY: Cornell University Press, 1992) 145.

Beltramo, Mario, Longo, Giovanni E. and Merryman, John Henry (trans.), *The Italian Civil Code* (Dobbs Ferry: Oceana Publications, 1969).

Benda, Ernst, 'The Protection of Human Dignity (Article 1 of the Basic Law)' (2000) 53 *SMU Law Review* 443.

Bendor, Ariel L. and Sachs, Michael, 'Human Dignity as a Constitutional Concept in Germany and in Israel' (2011) 44 *Israel Law Review* 26.

Bennett, Robert W., 'Objectivity in Constitutional Law' (1984) 132 *University of Pennsylvania Law Review* 445.

Bennion, Francis, *Statutory Interpretation*, 3rd edn (London: LexisNexis Butterworths, 1997).

Besson, Samantha, 'The Right to Have Rights: From Rights to Citizens and Back', in Marco Goldoni and Christopher McCorkindale (eds.), *Hannah Arendt and the Law* (Oxford and Portland, OR: Hart, 2012) 335.

Beyleveld, Deryck and Brownsword, Roger, 'Human Dignity, Human Rights, and Human Genetics' (1998) 61 *Modern Law Review* 661.

Human Dignity in Bioethics and Biolaw (Oxford University Press, 2001).

Bilchitz, David, 'Moving beyond Arbitrariness: The Legal Personhood and Dignity of Non-human Animals' (2009) 25 *South African Journal on Human Rights* 38.

Bishop, Michael and Woolman, Stuart, 'Freedom and Security of the Person', in Stuart Woolman, Michael Bishop and Jason Brickhill (eds.), *Constitutional Law of South Africa*, 2nd edn, Revision Series 4 (Cape Town: Juta, 2012) chapter 40.

Black, Charles L., *Structure and Relationship in Constitutional Law* (Baton Rouge: Louisiana State University Press, 1969).

Blackstone, William T., 'Human Rights and Human Dignity' (1971) 9 *Philosophy Forum* 3.

Blidstein Gerald I., '"Great is Human Dignity" – the Peregrination of a Law' (1982) 15 *Annual of the Institute for Research in Jewish Law* 127 (Heb.).

'The Honour of the Creations and the Dignity of Man', in Yosef David (ed.), *A Question of Dignity – Human Dignity as a Supreme Ethical Value in Modern Society* (Jerusalem: The Israel Democracy Institute, 2006) 97.

Bobbitt, Philip, *Constitutional Fate: Theory of the Constitution* (Oxford University Press, 1982).

Bognetti, Giovanni, 'The Concept of Human Dignity in European and US Constitutionalism', in George Nolte (ed.), *European and US Constitutionalism* (Cambridge University Press, 2005) 85.

Bollinger, Lee C., *The Tolerant Society* (Oxford: Clarendon Press, 1986).

Bomhoff, Jacco, 'Balancing, the Global and the Local: Judicial Balancing as a Problematic Topic in Comparative (Constitutional) Law' (2008) 31 *Hastings International and Comparative Law Review* 555.

Borghesi, Francesco, Papio, Michael and Riva, Massimo (eds.), *Giovanni Pico della Mirandola, Oration on the Dignity of Man: A New Translation and Commentary* (Cambridge University Press, 2012).

Bork, Robert, *The Tempting of America: The Political Seduction of the Law* (New York: The Free Press, 1990).

Borowski, Martin (ed.), *On the Nature of Legal Principles* (Stuttgart: Franz Steiner Verlag, 2010).

Botha, Henk, 'Equality, Dignity and the Politics of Interpretation' (2004) 19 *South African Public Law* 724.

'Human Dignity in Comparative Perspective' (2009) 2 *Stellenbosch Law Review* 171.

Bracey, Christopher A., 'Dignity in Race Jurisprudence' (2005) 7 *University of Pennsylvania Journal of Constitutional Law* 669.

Brandes, Tamar Hostovsky, 'Human Dignity as a Central Pillar in Constitutional Rights Jurisprudence in Israel: Definitions and Parameters', in Gideon Sapir, Daphne Barak-Erez and Aharon Barak (eds.), *Israeli Constitutional Law in the Making* (Oxford: Hart Publishing, 2013) 267.

Brennan, William J. Jr., 'The Bill of Rights and the States: The Revival of State Constitutions as Guardians of Individual Rights' (1986) 61 *New York University Law Review* 535.

'Color-Blind, Creed-Blind, Status-Blind, Sex-Blind' (1987) 14 *Human Rights* 30.

'The Constitution of the United States: Contemporary Ratification' (1986) 27 *South Texas Law Review* 433.

'Construing the Constitution' (1985) 19 *University of California Davis Law Review* 2.

'Rededication Address: The American Bar Association's Memorial to the Magna Carta' (1986) 19 *Loyola of Los Angeles Law Review* 55.

Brest, Paul, 'The Misconceived Quest for the Original Understanding' (1980) 60 *Boston University Law Review* 204.

Brewer-Carías, Allan R., *Constitutional Protection of Human Rights in Latin America: A Comparative Study of Amparo Proceedings* (Cambridge University Press, 2009).

Broberg, Margareta, 'A Brief Introduction', in Margareta Broberg and J. B. Ladegaard Knox (eds.), *Dignity, Ethics and Law* (Copenhagen: Centre for Ethics and Law, 1999) 7.

Brownsword, Roger, 'Bioethics Today, Bioethics Tomorrow: Stem Cell Research and the "Dignitarian Alliance"' (2003) 17 *Notre Dame Journal of Law, Ethics and Public Policy* 15.

'An Interest in Human Dignity as the Basis for Genomic Torts' (2003) 42 *Washburn Law Journal* 413.

Rights, Regulation and the Technological Revolution (Oxford University Press, 2008).

Brugger, Winfried, 'May Government Ever Use Torture – Two Responses from German Law' (2000) 48 *American Journal of Comparative Law* 661.

Buchanan, Allen, 'The Egalitarianism of Human Rights' (2010) 120 *Ethics* 679.

Buchhandler-Raphael, Michal, 'Drugs, Dignity and Danger: Human Dignity as a Constitutional Constraint to Limit Overcriminalization' (2013) 80 *Tennessee Law Review* 291.

Burgh, James, *The Dignity of Human Nature: Or, a Brief Account of the Certain and Established Means for Attaining the True End of Our Existence* (London: J. Johnson and J. Payne, 1767; New York: J. O. Ram 1812).

Byrd, B. Sharon and Hruschka, Joachim, *Kant's Doctrine of Rights: A Commentary* (Cambridge University Press, 2010).

Calabresi, Steven G. (ed.), *Originalism: A Quarter Century of Debate* (Washington DC: Regnery Publishing, 2007).

Caminker, Evan H., 'Judicial Solicitude for State Dignity' (2001) 574 *Annals of the American Academy of Political and Social Science* 81.

Canaris, Claus-Wilhelm, *Die Feststellung von Lücken im Gesetz: Eine Methodologische Studie über Voraussetzungen und Grenzen der Rechtsfortbildung Praeter Legem*, 2nd edn (Berlin: Duncker & Humblot, 1983).

Cancik, Hubert, '"Dignity of Man" and "Persona" in Stoic Anthropology: Some Remarks on Cicero, *De Officiis* I, 105–107', in David Kretzmer and Eckart Klein (eds.), *The Concept of Human Dignity in Human Rights Discourse* (The Hague: Kluwer Law International, 2002) 19.

Carbonari, Paulo C., 'Human Dignity as a Basic Concept of Ethics and Human Rights', in Berma K. Goldewijk, Adalid C. Baspineiro and Paulo C. Carbonari (eds.), *Dignity and Human Rights: The Implementation of Economic, Social and Cultural Rights* (Antwerp: Intersentia, 2002) 35.

Cardozo, Benjamin N., *The Nature of the Judicial Process* (New Haven: Yale University Press, 1921).

Carmi, Guy E., 'Dignity versus Liberty: The Two Western Cultures of Free Speech' (2008) 26 *Boston University International Law Journal* 277.

Carozza, Paolo G., 'Human Dignity and Judicial Interpretation of Human Rights: A Reply' (2008) 19 *European Journal of International Law* 931.

'Human Dignity in Constitutional Adjudication', in Tom Ginsburg and Rosalind Dixon (eds.), *Comparative Constitutional Law* (Cheltenham: Edward Elgar, 2011) 459.

Castiglione, John D., 'Hudson and Samson: The Roberts Court Confronts Privacy, Dignity, and the Fourth Amendment' (2007) 68 *Louisiana Law Review* 63.

'Human Dignity under the Fourth Amendment' (2008) 2008(4) *Wisconsin Law Review* 655.

Chalmers, Don and Ida, Ryuichi, 'On the International Legal Aspects of Human Dignity', in Jeff E. Malpas and Norelle Lickiss (eds.), *Perspectives on Human Dignity: A Conversation* (Dordrecht: Springer, 2007) 157.

Chapman, Audrey, 'A "Violations Approach" for Monitoring the International Covenant on Economic, Social and Cultural Rights' (1996) 18 *Human Rights Quarterly* 23.

Chaskalson, Arthur, 'Dignity and Justice for All' (2009) 24 *Maryland Journal of International Law* 24.

'Human Dignity as a Constitutional Value', in David Kretzmer and Eckart Klein (eds.), *The Concept of Human Dignity in Human Rights Discourse* (The Hague: Kluwer Law International, 2002) 133.

'Human Dignity as a Foundational Value of our Constitutional Order' (2000) 16 *South African Journal on Human Rights* 193.

Cheadle, Halton, 'Limitation of Rights', in Halton Cheadle, Dennis Davis and Nicholas Haysom (eds.), *South African Constitutional Law: The Bill of Rights* (Durban: Butterworths, 2002) 693.

Chibundu, Maxwell O., 'Structure and Structuralism in the Interpretation of Statutes' (1993–1994) 62 *University of Chicago Law Review* 1439.

Choudhry, Sujit, 'Globalization in Search of Justification: Toward a Theory of Comparative Constitutional Interpretation' (1999) 74 *Indiana Law Journal* 819.

Christiano, Thomas, 'Two Conceptions of the Dignity of Persons' (2008) 16 *Jahrbuch Fuer Recht Und Ethik* 101.

Cicero, Marcus T., *De Inventione: De Optimo Genere Oratorum: Topica* (London: W. Heinemann, 1949).

De Officiis (Cambridge, MA: Harvard University Press, 1975).

Clapham, Andrew, 'Human Rights Obligations of Non-State Actors', in Andrew Clapham, *Human Rights Obligations of Non-State Actors* (Oxford University Press, 2006) 535.

Clifford, Matthew O. and Huff, Thomas P., 'Some Thoughts on the Meaning and Scope of the Montana Constitution's Dignity Clause with Possible Applications' (2000) 61 *Montana Law Review* 301

Cohen-Eliya, Moshe and Porat, Iddo, 'The Hidden Foreign Law Debate in Heller: The Proportionality Approach in American Constitutional Law' (2009) 46 *San Diego Law Review* 367.

Collste, Göran, *Is Human Life Special? Religious and Philosophical Perspectives on the Principle of Human Dignity* (Berlin: Peter Lang, 2002).

Corder, Hugh, 'Comment', in George Nolte (ed.), *European and US Constitutionalism* (Cambridge University Press, 2005) 132.

Cornell, Drucilla, 'Bridging the Span toward Justice: Laurie Ackermann and the Ongoing Architectonic of Dignity Jurisprudence' (2008) *Acta Juridica* 18.

Cowen, Susie, 'Can "Dignity" Guide South Africa's Equality Jurisprudence?' (2001) 17 *South African Journal on Human Rights* 34.

Craven, Matthew, *The International Covenant on Economic, Social and Cultural Rights: A Perspective on its Development* (Oxford: Clarendon Press, 1998).

Cua, Antonio S., 'Dignity of Persons and Styles of Life' (1971) 45 *Proceedings of the American Catholic Philosophical Association* 120.

Currie, David P., *The Constitution of the Federal Republic of Germany* (University of Chicago Press, 1994).

Currie, Iain, de Waal, Johan and Hoexter, Cora, *The New Constitutional and Administrative Law* (Landsdowne: Juta, 2001).

Cuschieri, Andrew, 'Endorsement of Human Dignity in the Jurisprudence of the Sacred Roman Rota in the XVI–XVII Centuries' (1982) 42 *Jurist* 466.

Da Costa, Jose Manuel Cardoso, 'The Principle of Human Dignity in European Case-Law', in European Commission for Democracy through Law, *The Principle of Respect for Human Dignity* (Strasbourg: Council of Europe, 1999) 50.

Dales, Richard C., 'A Medieval View of Human Dignity' (1977) 38 *Journal of the History of Ideas* 557.

Dallner, James E. and Manning, D. Scott, 'Death with Dignity in Montana' (2004) 65 *Montana Law Review* 309.

Daly, Erin, 'Constitutional Dignity: Lessons from Home and Abroad', Widener Law School Legal Studies Research Paper 08-07 (2007).

'Dignity in the Service of Democracy', Widener Law School Legal Studies Research, Paper 11-07 (2010).

Dignity Rights: Courts, Constitutions and the Worth of the Human Person (Philadelphia: University of Pennsylvania Press, 2012).

'Human Dignity in the Roberts Court: A Story of Inchoate Institutions, Autonomous Individuals, and the Reluctant Recognition of a Right' (2011) 37 Ohio Northern University Law Review 381.

'The New Liberty' (2005) 11 Widener Law Review 221.

Dan-Cohen, Meir, 'A Concept of Dignity' (2011) 44 *Israel Law Review* 9.

Davis, D. M., 'Equality: The Majesty of Legoland Jurisprudence' (1999) 116 *South African Law Journal* 398.

Davis, William, *The True Dignity of Human Nature: Or, Man Viewed in Relation to Immortality* (London: General Books, 2009).

De Baets, Anton, 'A Successful Utopia: The Doctrine of Human Dignity' (2007) 7 *Historein* 71.

De Feyter, Koen and Pavlakos, George (eds.), *The Tension Between Group Rights and Human Rights: A Multidisciplinary Approach* (Oxford: Hart Publishing, 2008).

de los Reyes, Alberto Oehling, 'Algunas Reflexiones Sobre la Significación Constitucional de la Noción de Dignidad Humana' (2006) 12 *Pensamiento Constitucional* 327.

De Waal, Johan, 'A Comparative Analysis of the Provisions of German Origin in the Interim Bill of Rights' (1995) 11 *South African Journal of Human Rights* 1.

Delpérée, Francis, 'The Right to Human Dignity in Belgian Constitutional Law', in European Commission for Democracy through Law, *The Principle of Respect for Human Dignity* (Strasbourg: Council of Europe, 1999) 57.

Desai, Ashok, 'Constitutional Amendments and the "Basic Structure" Doctrine', in Venkat Lyer (ed.), *Democracy, Human Rights and the Rule of Law: Essays in Honour of Nani Palkhivala* (New Delhi: Butterworths India, 2000).

Devenish, G. E., *A Commentary on the South African Bill of Rights* (Durban: Butterworths 1999) chapter 5: 'Respect for Human Dignity', p. 79.

Dicke, Klaus, 'The Founding Function of Human Dignity in the Universal Declaration of Human Rights', in David Kretzmer and Eckart Klein (eds.), *The Concept of Human Dignity in Human Rights Discourse* (The Hague: Kluwer Law International, 2002) 111.

Dickerson, Reed, *The Interpretation and Application of Statutes* (Boston: Little Brown, 1975).

Donnelly, Jack, 'Human Rights and Human Dignity: An Analytic Critique of Non-Western Conceptions of Human Rights' (1982) 76 *American Political Science Review* 303.

Dorf, Michael C., 'Interpretive Holism and the Structural Method, or How Charles Black Might Have Thought about Campaign Finance Reform and Congressional Timidity' (2003) 92 *Georgetown Law Journal* 833.

Dreier, Horst, 'Does Cloning Violate the Basic Law's Guarantee of Human Dignity?', in Silja Vöneky and Rüdiger Wolfrum (eds.), *Human Dignity and Human Cloning* (Leiden: Martinus Nijhoff, 2004) 77.

GG Grundgesetz Kommentar (Tübingen: Mohr Siebeck, 2006).

Du Plessis, Lourens, 'Interpretation', in Stuart Woolman, Michael Bishop and Jason Brickhill (eds.), *Constitutional Law of South Africa*, 2nd edn, Revision Series 4 (Cape Town: Juta, 2012) chapter 32.

Dupré, Catherine, 'Dignity, Democracy, Civilisation' (2012) 33 *Liverpool Law Review* 263.

'Human Dignity and the Withdrawal of Medical Treatment: A Missed Opportunity?' (2006) 6 *European Human Rights Law Review* 678.

'Human Dignity in Europe: A Foundational Constitutional Principle' (2013) 19 *European Public Law* 319.

Importing Law in Post-Communist Transitions: The Hungarian Constitutional Court and the Right to Human Dignity (Oxford and Portland, OR: Hart Publishing, 2003).

'The Right to Human Dignity in Hungarian Constitutional Case-law', in European Commission for Democracy through Law, *The Principle of Respect for Human Dignity* (Strasbourg: Council of Europe, 1999) 68.

'Unlocking Human Dignity: Towards a Theory for the 21st Century' (2009) 2 *European Human Rights Law Review* 190.

Dürig, Günter, 'Der Grundrechtssatz von der Menschenwürde' (1956) *Archiv des öffentlichen Rechts* 81.

Düwell, Marcus, Braarvig, Jens, Brownsword, Roger and Mieth, Dietmar (eds.), *The Cambridge Handbook of Human Dignity: Interdisciplinary Perspectives* (Cambridge University Press, 2014).

Dworkin, Ronald, '*Freedom's Law: The Moral Reading of the American Constitution* (Oxford University Press, 1996).

Is Democracy Possible Here? Principles for a New Political Debate (Princeton University Press, 2006).

Justice for Hedgehogs (Cambridge, MA: Harvard University Press, 2011).

Law's Empire (Cambridge, MA: Harvard University Press, 1986) 229.

Life's Dominion: An Argument about Abortion, Euthanasia, and Individual Freedom (New York: Vintage Books, 1994).

Taking Rights Seriously (Cambridge, MA: Harvard University Press, 1978).

'Unenumerated Rights: Whether and How Roe Should Be Overruled' (1992) 59 *University of Chicago Law Review* 381.

Eberle, Edward J., *Dignity and Liberty: Constitutional Visions in Germany and the United States* (Santa Barbara: Praeger, 2002).

'Human Dignity, Privacy and Personality in German and American Constitutional Law' (1997) 4 *Utah Law Review* 963.

Eckart, Klein, 'Human Dignity in German Law', in David Kretzmer and Eckart Klein (eds.), *The Concept of Human Dignity in Human Rights Discourse* (The Hague: Kluwer Law International, 2002) 145.

Eckert, Joern, 'Legal Roots of Human Dignity in German Law', in David Kretzmer and Eckart Klein (eds.), *The Concept of Human Dignity in Human Rights Discourse* (The Hague: Kluwer Law International, 2002) 41.

Edel, Abraham, 'Humanist Ethics and the Meaning of Human Dignity', in Paul Kurtz (ed.), *Moral Problems in Contemporary Society: Essays in Humanistic Ethics* (Englewood Cliffs: Prentice-Hall, 1969) 232.

Eide, Asbjørn, 'Realization of Social and Economic Rights and the Minimum Threshold Approach' (1989) 10 *Human Rights Law Journal* 36.

Eissen, Marc-Andre, 'The Principle of Proportionality in the Case-Law of the European Court of Human Rights', in Ronald Macdonald, Franz Metscher and Herbert Petzold (eds.), *The European System for the Protection of Human Rights* (Dordrecht: Martinus Nijhoff, 1993).

Eklund, Amanda K., 'The Death Penalty in Montana: A Violation of the Constitutional Right to Individual Dignity' (2004) 65 *Montana Law Review* 135.

Elliot, Robin, 'References, Structural Argumentation and the Organizing Principles of Canada's Constitution' (2001) 80 *Canadian Bar Review* 67.

Elon, Menachem, Amit, Yaira, Shvid, Eliezer and Knohel, Israel, 'Human Dignity and Liberty in Hebraic Tradition', in *Human Dignity and Liberty in Hebraic Tradition* (Jerusalem: The President's House Press for Bible and Hebraic Liturgy, 1995) 15.

Emiliou, Nicholas, *The Principle of Proportionality in European Law* (Cambridge, MA: Kluwer Law International, 1996).

Enders, Christoph, *Die Menschenwürde in der Verfassungsordnung: zur Dogmatik des Art. 1 GG* (Tübingen: Mohr Siebck, 1997).

'A Right to Have Rights – The German Constitutional Concept of Human Dignity' (2010) 3 *NUJS Law Review* 253.

Englard, Izhak, 'Human Dignity: From Antiquity to Modern Israel's Constitutional Framework' (1999) 21 *Cardozo Law Review* 1903.

English, Rosalind, 'Ubuntu: The Quest for an Indigenous Jurisprudence' (1996) 12 *South African Journal on Human Rights* 641.

English, Rosalind and Havers, Philip (eds.), *An Introduction to Human Rights and the Common Law* (Oxford: Hart Publishing, 2000).

Essert, Christopher, 'Dignity and Membership, Equality and Egalitarianism: Economic Rights and Section 15' (2006) 19 *Canadian Journal of Law and Jurisprudence* 507.

Fallon, Richard, 'A Constructive Coherence Theory of Constitutional Interpretation' (1987) 100 *Harvard Law Review* 1189.

'Strict Judicial Scrutiny' (2007) 54 *UCLA Law Review* 1267.

Farber, Daniel A., 'The Originalism Debate: A Guide for the Perplexed' (1989) 49 *Ohio State Law Journal* 1085.

Feldman, David, 'The Developing Scope of Article 8 of the European Convention on Human Rights' (1997) 3 *European Human Rights Law Review* 265.

'Human Dignity as a Legal Value: Part 1' (Winter 1999) *Public Law* 682.

'Human Dignity as a Legal Value: Part 2' (Spring 2000) *Public Law* 61.

Finnis, John, *Aquinas: Moral, Political and Legal Theory* (Oxford University Press, 1998).

Fletcher, George P., 'Comparative Law as a Subversive Discipline' (1998) 46(4) *American Journal of Comparative Law* 683.

'In God's Image: The Religious Imperative of Equality under Law' (1999) 99 *Columbia Law Review* 1608.

Forkosch, Morris D., 'Privacy, Human Dignity, Euthanasia – Are These Independent Constitutional Rights?' (1974) 3 *University of San Fernando Valley Law Review* 1.

Foster, Charles, *Choosing Life, Choosing Death: The Tyranny of Autonomy in Medical Ethics and Law* (Oxford: Hart Publishing, 2009).

Human Dignity in Bioethics and Law (Oxford: Hart Publishing, 2011).

Frankenberg, Günter, 'Comparative Constitutional Law', in Mauro Bussani and Ugo Mattei (eds.), *The Cambridge Companion to Comparative Law* (Cambridge University Press, 2012) 171.

Frankfurter, Felix, *On The Supreme Court – Extrajudicial Essays on the Court and the Constitution*, ed. by Philip B. Kurland (Cambridge, MA: Harvard University Press, 1970).

'Some Reflections on the Reading of Statutes' (1947) 47 *Columbia Law Review* 527.

Fredman, Sandra, *Human Rights Transformed: Positive Rights and Positive Duties* (Oxford University Press, 2008).

Freund, Paul A., 'The Supreme Court of the United States' (1951) 29 *Canadian Bar Review* 1080.

Friauf, Karl Heinrich, 'Techniques for the Interpretation of Constitutions in German Law', in *Proceedings of the Fifth International Symposium on Comparative Law* (University of Ottawa Press, 1968).

Friedman, Gabrielle S. and Whitman, James Q., 'The European Transformation of Harassment Law: Discrimination versus Dignity' (2003) 9 *Columbia Journal of European Law* 241.

Friedmann, Daniel and Barak-Erez, Daphne (eds.), *Human Rights in Private Law* (Oxford: Hart Publishing, 2001).

Friedrich, Carl J., 'The Political Theory of the New Democratic Constitutions' (1950) 12 *Review of Politics* 215.

Fyfe, James, 'Dignity as Theory: Competing Conceptions of Human Dignity at the Supreme Court of Canada' (2007) 70 *Saskatchewan Law Review* 1.

Gardbaum, Stephen, 'The Myth and Reality of American Constitutional Exceptionalism' (2008) 107 *Michigan Law Review* 391.

Garg, Ramesh D., 'Phantom of Basic Structure of the Constitution: A Critical Appraisal of the Kesavananda Case' (1974) 16 *Journal of Indian Law Institute* 243.

Gauri, Varum and Brinks, Daniel E. (eds.), *Courting Social Rights: Judicial Enforcement of Social and Economic Rights in the Developing World* (Cambridge University Press, 2008).

Gearty, Conor A., *Principles of Human Rights Adjudication* (Oxford University Press, 2006).

Gertz, Elmer, *For the First Hours of Tomorrow: The New Illinois Bill of Rights* (Urbana: University of Illinois Press, 1972) 107.

Gewirth, Alan, 'Are There Any Absolute Rights?' (1981) 31 *Philosophical Quarterly* 1.

'Human Dignity as the Basis of Rights', in Michael J. Meyer and William A. Parent (eds.), *The Constitution of Rights: Human Dignity and American Values* (Ithaca, NY: Cornell University Press, 1992) 10.

Giakoumopoulos, Christos, 'Opening Speech', in European Commission for Democracy through Law, *The Principle of Respect for Human Dignity* (Strasbourg: Council of Europe, 1999) 25.

Glendon, Marry Ann, '*Propter Honoris Respectum*: Knowing the Universal Declaration of Human Rights' (1998) 73 *Notre Dame Law Review* 1153.

Goldford, Dennis, *The American Constitution and the Debate over Originalism* (Cambridge University Press, 2005).

Goldsworthy, Jeffrey, 'Clarifying, Creating, and Changing Meaning in Constitutional Interpretation' (2013) 14 *German Law Journal* 1279.

'Constitutional Cultures, Democracy and Unwritten Principles' (2012) *University of Illinois Law Review* 683.

'Constitutional Implications Revisited' (2011) 30 *University of Queensland Law Journal* 9.

'Implications in Language, Law and the Constitution', in Geoffrey Lindell (ed.), *Future Directions in Australian Constitutional Law* (Sydney: The Federation Press, 1994) 150.

Interpreting Constitutions: A Comparative Study (Oxford University Press, 2006).

'Originalism in Constitutional Interpretations' (1997) 25 *Federal Law Review* 1.

'Unwritten Constitutional Principles', in Grant Huscroft (ed.), *Expounding the Constitution: Essays in Constitutional Theory* (Cambridge University Press, 2008) 277.

Goodman, Maxine, 'Human Dignity in Supreme Court Constitutional Jurisprudence' (2006) 84 *Nebraska Law Review* 740.

Goolam, Nazeem M., 'Human Dignity – Our Supreme Constitutional Value' (2001) 4 *Potchefstroom Electronic Law Journal* 1.

Gottlieb, Stephen E. (ed.), *Public Values in Constitutional Law* (Ann Arbor: University of Michigan Press, 1993).

Grant, Evadne, 'Dignity and Equality' (2007) 7 *Human Rights Law Review* 299.

Grasso, Kenneth L., 'Saving Modernity from Itself: John Paul II on Human Dignity, the Whole Truth about Man, and the Modern Quest for Freedom', in Robert P. Kraynak and Glenn E. Tinder (eds.), *In Defense of Human Dignity: Essays for our Times* (University of Notre Dame Press, 2003) 207.

Greenawalt, Kent, 'Are Mental States Relevant for Statutory and Constitutional Interpretation?' (2000) 85 *Cornell Law Review* 1609.

Grey, Thomas C., 'The Constitution as Scripture' (1984) 37 *Stanford Law Review* 1.

Griffin, James, *On Human Rights* (Oxford University Press, 2008).

Grimm, Dieter, 'Human Rights and Judicial Review in Germany', in David M. Beatty (ed.), *Human Rights and Judicial Review: A Comparative Perspective* (Dordrecht: Martinus Nijhoff, 1994) 267.

Grodin, Joseph, 'Are Rules Really Better than Standards' (1993) 45 *Hastings Law Journal* 569.

Groppi, Tania and Ponthoreau, Marie-Claire (eds.), *The Use of Foreign Precedents by Constitutional Judges* (Oxford: Hart Publishing, 2013).

Häberle, Peter, *Europäische Verfassungslehre*, 6th edn (Baden-Baden: Nomos, 2009).

Häfelin, Ulrich, Haller, Walter and Keller, Helen, *Schweizerisches Bundesstaatsrecht*, 8th edn (Zurich: Schulthess, 2012).

Hamilton, Alexander, *The Federalist Papers* (New York: The Modern Library, 1937) No. 84, 6.

Hargrave, Lee, *The Louisiana State Constitution: A Reference Guide* (Westport: Greenwood Publishing Group, 1991) 23.

Harris, David J., O'Boyle, Michael, Bates, Edward P. and Buckley, Carla M., *Harris, O'Boyle & Warbrick: Law of the European Convention on Human Rights*, 2nd edn (Oxford University Press, 2009).

Hasson, Kevin J., 'Religious Liberty and Human Dignity: A Tale of Two Declarations' (2003) 27 *Harvard Journal of Law and Public Policy* 81.

Haysom, Nicholas, 'Dignity', in Halton Cheadle, Dennis Davis and Nicholas Haysom (eds.), *South African Constitutional Law: The Bill of Rights* (Durban: Butterworths, 2002) 131.

Helis, John, 'Hannah Arendt and Human Dignity: Theoretical Foundations and Constitutional Protection of Human Rights' (2008) 1 *Journal of Politics and Law* 73.

Henckaerts, Jean-Marie and Daswald-Beck, Louise, *Customary International Humanitarian Law* (New York: Cambridge University Press, 2005).

Hendriks, Aart, 'Personal Autonomy, Good Care, Informed Consent and Human Dignity – Some Reflections from a European Perspective' (2009) 28 *Medicine and Law* 469.

Henkin, Louis, 'Human Dignity and Constitutional Rights', in Michael J. Meyer and William A. Parent (eds.), *The Constitution of Rights: Human Dignity and American Values* (Ithaca, NY: Cornell University Press, 1992) 228.

Human Dignity and Human Rights (Jerusalem: The Israel Academy of Sciences and Humanities, 1995).

Hennette-Vauchez, Stéphanie, 'A Human Dignitas? Remnants of the Ancient Legal Concept in Contemporary Dignity Jurisprudence' (2011) 9 *International Journal of Constitutional Law* 32.

'When Ambivalent Principles Prevail: Leads for Explaining Western Legal Orders' Infatuation with the Human Dignity Principle' (2007) 10 *Legal Ethics* 193.

Henry, Leslie Meltzer, 'The Jurisprudence of Dignity' (2011) 160 *University of Pennsylvania Law Review* 169.

Herdegen, Mattias, 'Die Garantie der Menschenwürde: absolut und doch differenziert?', in Rolf Gröschner and Oliver W. Lembcke (eds.), *Das Dogma der Unantastbarkeit* (Tübingen: Mohr Siebeck, 2009) 93.

Herman, Barbara, 'Mutual Aid and Respect for Persons' (1984) 94 *Ethics* 577.

Herzog, Roman, Scholz, Rupert, Herdegen, Matthias and Klein, Hans H., *Maunz & Dürig Grundgesetz Kommentar* (Munich: C. H. Beck'sche Verlagsbuchhandlung, 2007) 12.

Hesse, Konrad, *Grundzüge des Verfassungsrechts der Bundesrepublik Deutschland* (Heidelberg: C. F. Muller, 1999).

Heun, Werner, *The Constitution of Germany: A Contextual Analysis* (Oxford University Press, 2011) 204.

Hill, Thomas E., 'Humanity as an End in Itself' (1980) 91 *Ethics* 84.

Hogg, Peter W., 'Canadian Law in the Constitutional Court of South Africa' (1998) 13 *South African Public Law* 1.

Constitutional Law of Canada, 5th edn (Toronto: Thomson Carswell, 2007).

'Interpreting the Charter of Rights: Generosity and Justification' (1990) 28 *Osgoode Hall Law Journal* 817.

Hogg, Peter W. and Bushell, Alison A., 'The Charter Dialogue between Courts and Legislatures' (1997) 35 *Osgoode Hall Law Journal* 75.

Holland, Sharon, 'Equality, Dignity and Rights of the Laity' (1987) 47 *Jurist* 103.

Hörnle, Tatjana and Kremnitzer, Mordechai, 'Human Dignity as a Protected Interest in Criminal Law' (2011) 44 *Israel Law Review* 143.

Howard, Rhoda E., 'Dignity, Community, and Human Rights', in Abdullahi Ahmed An-Na'im (ed.), *Human Rights in Cross-Cultural Perspectives – A Quest for Consensus* (Philadelphia: University of Pennsylvania Press, 1992) 81.

Howard, Rhoda E. and Donnelly, Jack, 'Human Dignity, Human Rights, and Political Regimes' (1986) 80(3) *American Political Science Review* 801.

Hruschka, Joachim, 'Kant and Human Dignity', in B. Sharon Byrd and Joachim Hruschka (eds.), *Kant and Law* (Aldershot: Ashgate, 2006) 69.

Hughes, Glenn, 'The Concept of Dignity in the Universal Declaration of Human Rights' (2011) 39 *Journal of Religious Ethics* 1.

Huscroft, Grant and Miller, Bradley, *The Challenge of Originalism: Theories of Constitutional Interpretation* (Cambridge University Press, 2011).

Huxley, Andrew, 'The Pali Buddhist Approach to Human Cloning', in Silja Vöneky and Rüdiger Wolfrum (eds.), *Human Dignity and Human Cloning* (Leiden: Martinus Nijhoff, 2004) 13.

Iacobucci, Frank, 'The Charter: Twenty Years Later' (2002) 21 *Windsor Yearbook of Access to Justice* 3.

Iglesias, Teresa, 'Bedrock Truths and the Dignity of the Individual' (2001) 4 *Logos* 114.

'The Dignity of the Individual in the Irish Constitution: The Importance of the Preamble' (2000) 89 *Studies: An Irish Quarterly Review* 19.

Ignatieff, Michael, *Human Rights as Politics and Idolatry* (Princeton University Press, 2001).

Jackman, Martha, 'Poor Rights: Using the Charter to Support Social Welfare Claims' (1993–1994) 19 *Queen's Law Journal* 65.

Jackson, Vicki C., 'Ambivalent Resistance and Comparative Constitutionalism: Opening Up the Conversation on "Proportionality", Rights and Federalism' (1999) 1 *University of Pennsylvania Journal of Constitutional Law* 583.

'Constitutional Comparisons: Convergence, Resistance, Engagement' (2005) 119 *Harvard Law Review* 109.

'Constitutional Dialogue and Human Dignity: States and Transnational Constitutional Discourse' (2004) 65 *Montana Law Review* 15.

Constitutional Engagement in a Transnational Era (Oxford University Press, 2010).

Jackson, Vicki C. and Mark V. Tushnet, *Comparative Constitutional Law* (New York: Foundation Press, 1999).

Jacobs, Francis and White, Robin, *Jacobs & White: The European Convention on Human Rights*, 3rd edn (Oxford University Press, 2002).

Jacobsohn, Gary J., 'An Unconstitutional Constitution? A Comparative Perspective' (2006) 4 *International Journal of Constitutional Law* 460.

Jochen, Frowein Abr., 'Human Dignity in International Law', in David Kretzmer and Eckart Klein (eds.), *The Concept of Human Dignity in Human Rights Discourse* (The Hague: Kluwer Law International, 2002) 121.

Jones, Harry W., 'Statutory Doubts and Legislative Intention' (1940) 40 *Columbia Law Review* 957.

Jones, Jackie, '"Common Constitutional Traditions": Can the Meaning of Human Dignity under German Law Guide the European Court of Justice?' (Spring 2004) *Public Law* 167.

Jooss, Alexander, 'Life after Death? Post Mortem Protection of Name, Image and Likeness under German Law with Specific Reference to "Marlene Dietrich"' (2001) 12 *Entertainment Law Review* 141.

Joseph, Sarah, Schultz, Jenny and Castan, Melissa, *International Covenant on Civil and Political Rights*, 2nd edn (Oxford University Press, 2005).

Kalb, Johanna, 'Litigating Dignity: A Human Rights Framework' (2011) 74 *Albany Law Review* 1725.

Kamali, Mohammad Hashim, *The Dignity of Man: An Islamic Perspective* (Kuala Lumpur: Ilmiah Publishers, 1999).

Kamir, Orit, *Israeli Honor and Dignity: Social Norms, Gender Politics and the Law*, 2nd edn (Jerusalem: Carmel, 2004).

Kaplan, Yehiel, 'Basic Law: Human Dignity and Liberty – Balance between Conflicting Jewish Values and Conflicting Human Rights' (2009) 8 *Kiryat HaMishpat* 145.

Kaplow, Louis, 'Rules Versus Standards: An Economic Analysis' (1992) 42 *Duke Law Journal* 557.

Karp, Judith, 'Matching Human Dignity with the UN Convention on the Rights of the Child', in Ya'ir Ronen and Charles W. Greenbaum (eds.), *The Case of the Child: Towards a New Agenda* (Antwerp: Intersentia, 2008).

Kass, Leon R., 'Defending Human Dignity', in President's Council on Bioethics, *Human Dignity and Bioethics* (Washington DC: President's Council on Bioethics, 2008) 297.

Life, Liberty and the Defense of Dignity: The Challenge for Bioethics (New York: Encounter Books, 2002).

Kelman, Herbert C., 'The Conditions, Criteria, and Dialectics of Human Dignity: A Transnational Perspective' (1977) 21 *International Studies Quarterly* 529.

Kelsen, Hans, *Pure Theory of Law*, 2nd edn, Max Knight trans. (Berkeley: University of California Press, 1967).

Kende, Mark S., 'Stereotypes in South African and American Constitutional Law: Achieving Gender Equality and Transformation' (2000) 10 *Southern California Review of Law and Women's Studies* 3.

Kesby, Alison, *The Right to Have Rights: Citizenship, Humanity, and International Law* (Oxford University Press, 2012).

Kirby, Michael, 'Australian Law – After 11 September 2001' (2001) 21 *Australian Bar Review* 253.

'Constitutional Interpretation and Original Intent: A Form of Ancestor Worship?' (2000) 24 *Melbourne University Law Review* 1.

Kirk, Jeremy, 'Constitutional Implications (I): Nature, Legitimacy, Classification, Examples' (2000) 24 *Melbourne University Law Review* 645.

'Constitutional Interpretation and a Theory of Evolutionary Originalism' (1999) 27 *Federal Law Review* 323.

Kleinig, John, 'Humiliation, Degradation and Moral Capacity' (2011) 44 *Israel Law Review* 169.

Klopfer, Michael, 'Leben und Würde des Menschen', in Peter Badura and Horst Dreier (eds.), *Festschrift 50 Jahre Bundesverfassungsgericht* (Tübingen: Mohr Siebeck, 2001) 82.

Klug, Heinz, 'The Dignity Clause of the Montana Constitution: May Foreign Jurisprudence Lead the Way to an Expanded Interpretation?' (2003) 64 *Montana Law Review* 133.

Koch, Ida Elisabeth, *Human Rights as Indivisible Rights: The Protection of Socio-Economic Demands under the European Convention on Human Rights* (Leiden: Martinus Nijhoff, 2009).

Kokott, Juliane, 'From Reception and Transplantation to Convergence of Constitutional Models in the Age of Globalization – With Particular Reference to the German Basic Law', in Christian Starck (ed.), *Constitutionalism, Universalism and Democracy: A Comparative Analysis* (Baden-Baden: Nomos Publication, 1999), 71.

Kolnai, Aurel, 'Dignity' (1976) 51 *Philosophy* 251.

Kommers, Donald P., *The Constitutional Jurisprudence of the Federal Republic of Germany*, 2nd edn (Durham, NC: Duke University Press, 1997).

'The Value of Comparative Constitutional Law' (1976) 9 *John Marshall Journal of Practice and Procedure* 685.

Kommers, Donald P. and Miller, Russell A., *The Constitutional Jurisprudence of the Federal Republic of Germany*, 3rd edn (Durham, NC: Duke University Press, 2012).

Kraynak, Robert P., 'Made in the Image of God: The Christian View of Human Dignity and Political Order', in Robert P. Kraynak and Glenn E. Tinder (eds.), *In Defense of Human Dignity: Essays for our Times* (University of Notre Dame Press, 2003) 81.

Kremnitzer, Mordechai and Kramer, Michal, *Human Dignity as a Supreme and Absolute Constitutional Value in German Law – In Israel Too?* (Jerusalem: The Israel Democracy Institute, 2011).

Kretzmer, David, 'Human Dignity in Israeli Jurisprudence', in David Kretzmer and Eckart Klein (eds.), *The Concept of Human Dignity in Human Rights Discourse* (The Hague: Kluwer Law International, 2002) 161.

Krishnaswamy, Sudhir, *Democracy and Constitutionalism in India: A Study of the Basic Structure Doctrine* (Oxford University Press, 2009).

Kristeller, Paul Oskar, *Renaissance Concepts of Man and Other Essays* (New York: Harper & Row, 1972).

Kroeze, Irma J., 'Doing Things with Values: the Role of Constitutional Values in Constitutional Interpretation' (2001) 12 *Stellenbosch Law Review* 265.

'Doing Things with Values (Part 2): The Case of Ubuntu' (2002) 13 *Stellenbosch Law Review* 252.

'Human Dignity in Constitutional Law in South Africa', in *The Principle of Respect for Human Dignity* (European Commission for Democracy Through Law, Council of Europe Publishing, 1999).

Krotoszynski, Ronald J., 'A Comparative Perspective on the First Amendment: Free Speech, Militant Democracy, and the Primacy of Dignity as a Preferred Constitutional Value in Germany' (2004) 78 *Tulane Law Review* 1549.

Kumm, Mattias and Comella, Victor Ferreres, 'What is so Special about Constitutional Rights in Private Litigation? A Comparative Analysis of the Function of State Action Requirement and Indirect Horizontal Effect', in András Sajó and Renáta Uitz (eds.), *The Constitution in Private Relations: Expanding Constitutionalism* (Utrecht: Eleven International Publishing, 2005) 241.

Langford, Malcolm, 'Domestic Adjudication and Economic, Social and Cultural Rights: A Socio-Legal Review' (2009) 6 *Sur International Journal of Human Rights* 91.

Lasswell, Harold D. and McDougal, Myres S., *Jurisprudence for a Free Society: Studies in Law, Science and Policy* (Dordrecht: Martinus Nijhoff, 1992).

Law, David S. and Versteeg, Mila, 'The Evolution and Ideology of Global Constitutionalism' (2011) 99 *California Law Review* 1163.

Lebech, Mette, 'What Is Human Dignity?', in Mette Lebech (ed.), *Maynooth Philosophical Papers* (National University of Ireland Maynooth, 2004) 59.

Leckey, Robert, 'Embodied Dignity' (2005) 5 *Oxford University Commonwealth Law Journal* 63.

Lee, Man Yee Karen, 'Universal Human Dignity: Some Reflections in the Asian Context' (2008) 3 *Asian Journal of Comparative Law* 1932.

Lee, Tanya, 'Section 7 of the Charter: An Overview' (1985) 43 *University of Toronto Faculty Law Review* 1.

Legrand, Pierre, 'European Legal Systems are not Converging' (1996) 45 *International Comparative Law Quarterly* 52.

Leibowitz, David and Spitz, Derek, 'Human Dignity', in Stuart Woolman, Michael Bishop and Jason Brickhill (eds.), *Constitutional Law of South Africa*, 2nd edn, Revision Series 4 (Cape Town: Juta, 2012) chapter 12.

Lepsius, Oliver, 'Human Dignity and the Downing of Aircraft: The German Federal Constitutional Court Strikes Down a Prominent Anti-terrorism Provision in the New Air-transport Security Act' (2006) 7 *German Law Journal* 761

Lerner, Natan, *Group Rights and Discrimination in International Law*, 2nd edn (The Hague: Martinus Nijhoff, 2003).

Levitsky, Serge, 'Protection of Individual Honour and Dignity in Pre-Petrine Russian Law' (1972) 40 *Legal History Review* 341.

Lewaszkiewicz-Petrykowska, Biruta, 'The Principle of Respect to Human Dignity', in European Commission for Democracy through Law, *The Principle of Respect for Human Dignity* (Strasbourg: Council of Europe, 1999) 15.

Lewis, Milton, 'A Brief History of Human Dignity: Idea and Application', in Jeff E. Malpas and Norelle Lickiss (eds.), *Perspectives on Human Dignity: A Conversation* (Dordrecht: Springer, 2007).

Liebenberg, Sandra, *Socio-Economic Rights: Adjudication under a Transformative Constitution* (Claremont: Juta, 2010).

'The Value of Human Dignity in Interpreting Socio-Economic Rights' (2005) 21 *South African Journal on Human Rights* 1.

Lloyns, David, 'Original Intent and Legal Interpretation' (1999) 24 *Australian Journal of Legal Philosophy* 1.

Locke, John, *An Essay Concerning Human Understanding* (London: The Baffet, 1690).

Two Treatises of Government (London: Awnsham Churchill, 1690).

Lorerboim, Yair, *Image of God: Halakhah and Aggadah* (Tel Aviv: Shoken, 2004).

McAllister, Marc C., 'Human Dignity and Individual Liberty in Germany and the United States as Examined through Each Country's Leading Abortion Cases' (2004) 11 *Tulsa Journal of Comparative & International Law* 491.

McCrudden, Christopher, 'A Common Law of Human Rights? Transnational Judicial Conversations on Constitutional Rights' (2000) 20 *Oxford Journal of Legal Studies* 499.

'Human Dignity and Judicial Interpretation of Human Rights' (2008) 19 *European Journal of International Law* 655.

'A Part of the Main? The Physician-Assisted Suicide Cases and Comparative Law Methodology in the United States Supreme Court', in Carl E. Schneider (ed.), *Law at the End of Life* (Ann Arbor: University of Michigan Press, 2000) 125.

McGinnis, John O., 'The Limits of International Law in Protecting Dignity' (2003) 27 *Harvard Journal of Law and Public Policy* 137.

McGirr, Daniel, 'Liberty in an American and German Constitutional Context through the Lens of Isaiah Berlin and Lord Acton' (Forthcoming, available at http://papers.ssrn.com/sol3/papers.cfm?abstract_id=1872626).

McLachlin, Beverley M., 'The Charter: A New Role for the Judiciary' (1990) 29 *Alberta Law Review* 540.

Macklin, Ruth, 'Dignity Is a Useless Concept' (2003) 327 *British Medical Journal* 1419.

Magiera, Siegfried, 'The Interpretation of the Basic Law', in Christian Starck (ed.), *Main Principles of the German Basic Law* (Baden-Baden: Nomos, 1983) 89.

Mahlmann, Matthias, 'The Basic Law at 60 – Human Dignity and the Culture of Republicanism' (2010) 11 *German Law Journal* 9.

Elemente einer ethischen Grundrechtstheorie (Berlin: Nomos, 2008).

'Human Dignity and Autonomy in Modern Constitutional Orders', in Michael Rosenfeld and Andras Sajo (eds.), *The Oxford Handbook of Comparative Constitutional Law* (Oxford University Press, 2012) 372.

Mak, Chantal, *Fundamental Rights in European Contract Law: A Comparison of the Impact of Fundamental Rights on Contractual Relationships in Germany, the Netherlands, Italy and England* (Alphen aan den Rijn: Kluwer Law International, 2008).

Malpas, Jeff and Lickiss, Norelle, 'Human Dignity and Human Being', in Jeff Malpas and Norelle Lickiss (eds.), *Perspectives on Human Dignity: A Conversation* (Dordrecht: Springer, 2007) 19.

Manglapus, Raul S., 'Human Rights Are Not a Western Discovery' (1978) 21(10) *Worldview* 4.

Margalit, Avishai, *The Decent Society* (Cambridge, MA: Harvard University Press, 1996).

Maritain, Jacques, *The Rights of Man and Natural Law* (University of Chicago Press, 1951).

Mason, Anthony, 'The Interpretation of the Constitution in a Modern Liberal Democracy', in Charles Sampford and Kim Preston (eds.), *Interpreting Constitutions: Theories, Principles and Institutions* (Sydney: The Federation Press, 1996) 13.

'The Role of a Constitutional Court in a Federation: A Comparison of the Australian and the United States Experience' (1986) 16 *Federal Law Review* 1.

'Trends in Constitutional Interpretation' (1995) 18 *University of New South Wales Law Journal* 237.

Mehlmann, Mattias, 'Human Dignity and Autonomy in Modern Constitutional Orders', in Michael Rosenfeld and Andras Sajo (eds.), *The Oxford Handbook on Comparative Constitutional Law* (Oxford University Press, 2012) 370.

Melchior, Michel, 'Rights Not Covered by the Convention', in R. Macdonald, F. Matscher and H. Petzold (eds.), *The European System for the Protection of Human Rights* (Dordrecht: Martinus Nijhoff, 1993) 593.

Melden, Abraham I., 'Dignity, Worth, and Rights', in Michael J. Meyer and William A. Parent (eds.), *The Constitution of Rights: Human Dignity and American Values* (Ithaca, NY: Cornell University Press 1992) 29.

Mendes, Errol P., 'Taking Equality into the 21st Century: Establishing the Concept of Equal Human Dignity' (2000) 12 *National Journal of Constitutional Law* 3.

Meron, Theodor, 'The Martens Clause: Principles of Humanity and Dictates of Public Conscience' (2000) 94 *American Journal of International Law* 78

Merryman, John Henry, 'The Italian Legal Style III: Interpretation' (1966) 18 *Stanford Law Review* 583.

Meyer, Michael J., 'The Constitution of Rights: Human Dignity and American Values – Introduction', in Michael J. Meyer and William A. Parent (eds.), *The Constitution of Rights: Human Dignity and American Values* (Ithaca, NY: Cornell University Press, 1992) 6.

'Dignity as a (Modern) Virtue', in David Kretzmer and Eckart Klein (eds.), *The Concept of Human Dignity in Human Rights Discourse* (The Hague: Kluwer Law International, 2002) 195.

Michalowski, Sabine and Lorna, Woods, *German Constitutional Law: The Protection of Civil Liberties* (Sudbury, MA: Dartmouth Publishing, 1999).

Miguel, Carlos R., 'Human Dignity: History of an Idea' (2002) 50 *Jahrbuch des öffentlichen Rechts der Gegenwart* 281.

Miller, Jeremy M., 'Dignity as a New Framework, Replacing the Right to Privacy' (2007) 30 *Thomas Jefferson Law Review* 1.

Millon, David, 'Objectivity and Democracy' (1992) 67 *New York University Law Review* 1.

Milo, Dario, Glenn Penfold and Anthony Stein, 'Freedom of Expression', in Stuart Woolman, Michael Bishop and Jason Brickhill (eds.), *Constitutional Law of South Africa*, 2nd edn, Revision Series 4 (Cape Town: Juta, 2012) chapter 42.

Minai, Maryam, Conrad, Helen and Lynch, Philip, 'The Right to a Fair Hearing and Access to Justice: Australia's Obligations', Human Right's Law Resource Centre Ltd. (Submission to the Senate Legal and Constitutional Affairs

Committee: Inquiry into Australia's Judicial System, the Role of Judges and Access to Justice, 2009).

Mirandola, Giovanni Pico della, *Oration on the Dignity of Man* (Washington DC: Regnery Publising, 1996; The University of Adelaide, 2005).

Mokgoro, Yvonne, 'Ubuntu and the Law in South Africa' (1998) 4 *Buffalo Human Rights Law Review* 15.

Möller, Kai, *The Global Model of Constitutional Rights* (Oxford University Press, 2012).

'On Treating Persons as Ends: The German Aviation Security Act, Human Dignity, and the German Federal Constitutional Court' (Autumn 2006) *Public Law* 457.

Möllers, Christoph, 'Democracy and Human Dignity: Limits of a Moralized Conception of Rights in German Constitutional Law' (2009) 42 *Israel Law Review* 416.

Moltmann, Jurgen, *On Human Dignity: Political Theology and Ethics* (Minneapolis: Alban Books Limited, 2007).

Mongham, Henry Paul, 'Stare Decisis and Constitutional Adjudication' (1996) 88 *Columbia Law Review* 877.

Monsalve, Viviana Bohrquez and Romcan, Javier Aguirre, 'Tensions of Human Dignity: Conceptualization and Application to International Human Rights Law' (2009) *International Journal on Human Rights* 39.

Moon, Gay and Allen, Robin, 'Dignity Discourse in Discrimination Law: A Better Route to Equality?' (2006) 11 *European Human Rights Law Review* 610.

Moreso, Jose J., *Legal Indeterminacy and Constitutional Interpretation* (Dordrecht and Boston: Kluwer Academic Publishers, 1998).

Morgan, David G., 'The Indian "Essential Features" Case' (1981) 30 *International and Comparative Law Quarterly* 307.

Morris, Bertram, 'The Dignity of Man' (1946) 57 *Ethics* 57.

Morsink, Johannes, *Inherent Human Rights: Philosophical Roots of the Universal Declaration* (Philadelphia: University of Pennsylvania Press, 2009).

'The Philosophy of the Universal Declaration' (1984) 6 *Human Rights Quarterly* 309.

The Universal Declaration of Human Rights: Origins, Drafting and Intent (Philadelphia: University of Pennsylvania Press, 1999).

Müller, Jörg Paul and Müller, Stefan, *Grundrechte: Besonderer Teil* (Bern: Stämpfli & Cie, 1985).

Munster, Ralf F., 'A Critique of Blackstone's Human Rights and Human Dignity' (1971) 9 *Philosophy Forum* 65.

Murkens, Jo Eric Khushal, 'Comparative Constitutional Law in the Courts: Reflections on the Originalists' Objections', Law, Society and Economics Working Papers No. 15–2008 (Department of Law, LSE, London, 2008).

Murphy, Walter, 'The Art of Constitutional Interpretation: A Preliminary Showing', in Mont J. Harmon (ed.), *Essays on the Constitution of the United States* (Port Washington, NY: Kennikat Press, 1978), 130.

Constitutional Democracy: Creating and Maintaining a Just Political Order (Baltimore: The Johns Hopkins University Press, 2007).

'An Ordering of Constitutional Values' (1979–80) 53 Southern California Law Review 703.

Naske, Nina and Nolte, Georg, 'Legislative Authorization to Shoot Down Aircraft Abducted by Terrorists if Innocent Passengers Are on Board – Incompatibility with Human Dignity as Guaranteed by Article 1(1) of the German Constitution' (2007) 101 *American Journal of International Law* 466.

Neuhäuser, Christian, 'Humiliation: The Collective Dimension', in Paulus Kaufmann, Hannes Kuch, Christian Neuhäuser and Elaine Webster (eds.), *Humiliation, Degradation, Dehumanization: Human Dignity Violated* (Dordrecht: Springer, 2011).

Neuman, Gerald, 'Human Dignity in United States Constitutional Law', in Dieter Simon and Manfred Weiss (eds.), *Zur Autonomie des Individuums: Liber Amicorum Spiros Simitis* (Baden-Baden: Nomos, 2000), 249.

The New Shorter Oxford English Dictionary, ed. by Lesley Brown (Oxford: Clarendon Press, 1993).

Newman, Dwight, *Community and Collective Rights: A Theoretical Framework for Rights Held by Groups* (Oxford: Hart Publishing, 2011).

Nishihara, Hiroshi, 'The Significance of Constitutional Values', in Faculty of Law, Potchefstroom University for Christian Higher Education, *Constitution and Law IV: Developments in the Contemporary Constitutional State* (Johannesburg: Konrad-Adenauer-Stiftung, 2001) 11.

Note, 'Less Drastic Means and the First Amendment' (1969) 78 *Yale Law Journal* 464.

'The First Amendment Overbreadth Doctrine' (1970) 83 *Harvard Law Review* 844.

UN Covenant on Civil and Political Rights: CCPR Commentary (Arlington: N. P. Engel Verlag, 1993).

Nussbaum, Martha C, *Hiding from Humanity: Disgust, Shame, and the Law* (Princeton University Press, 2004).

Nwabueze, Remigius N., *Legal and Ethical Regulation of Biomedical Research in Developing Countries* (Farnham: Ashgate, 2013).

O'Connell, Rory, 'Guardians of the Constitution: Unconstitutional Constitutional Norms' (1999) 4 *Journal of Civil Liberties* 48.

'The Role of Dignity in Equality Law: Lessons from Canada and South Africa' (2008) 6 *International Journal of Constitutional Law* 267.

O'Mahony, Conor, 'There is No Such Thing as a Right to Dignity' (2012) 10 *International Journal of Constitutional Law* 551.

'There is No Such Thing as a Right to Dignity: A Rejoinder to Emily Kidd White' (2012) 10 *International Journal of Constitutional Law* 585.

Oliver, Dawn and Fedtke, Jörg (eds.), *Human Rights and the Private Sphere: A Comparative Study* (New York: Routledge, 2007).

Oxford, Roderick, 'Eighth Amendment ETS Claims: A Matter of Human Dignity' (1993) 18 *Oklahoma City University Law Review* 505.

Pagán, Luis Aníbal Avilés, 'Human Dignity, Privacy and Personality Rights in the Constitutional Jurisprudence of Germany, the United States and the Commonwealth of Puerto Rico' (1998) 67 *Revista Juridica Universidad de Puerto Rico* 343.

Palkhivala, Nani A., 'Fundamental Rights Case: Comment' (1973) 4 *Supreme Court Cases Journal* 57.

Palmer, Matthew, 'Using Constitutional Realism to Identify the Complete Constitution: Lessons from an Unwritten Constitution' (2006) 54 *American Journal of Comparative Law* 587

Parent, William A., 'Constitutional Commands of Human Dignity: A Bicentennial Essay in Honor of Mr. Justice William J. Brennan, Jr.' (1992) 5 *Canadian Journal of Law and Jurisprudence* 237.

'Constitutional Values and Human Dignity', in Michael J. Meyer and William A. Parent (eds.), *The Constitution of Rights: Human Dignity and American Values* (Ithaca, NY: Cornell University Press, 1992) 47.

Patapan, Haig, 'The Dead Hand of the Founders? Original Intent and the Constitutional Protection of Rights and Freedoms in Australia' (1997) 25 *Federal Law Review* 211.

'Politics of Interpretation' (2000) 22 *Sydney Law Review* 247.

Patrick, Glenn H., 'Persuasive Authority' (1987) 32 *McGill Law Journal* 261.

Paust, Jordan J., 'Human Dignity as a Constitutional Right: A Jurisprudentially Based Inquiry into Criteria and Content' (1984) 27 *Howard Law Journal* 145.

'Human Dignity, Remedies, and Limitations in the Convention' (1989) 7 *New York Law School Journal of Human Rights* 116.

Perales, Kathryn A., 'It Works Fine in Europe, So Why Not Here? Comparative Law and Constitutional Federalism' (1999) 23 *Vermont Law Review* 885.

Perelman, Chaim, *Le Problème des Lacunes en Droit* (Brussels: Établissements Émile Bruylant, 1968).

Perez, Jesus Gonzalez, *La Dignidad de la Persona* (Madrid: Civitas Ediciones S.L., 1986).

Perry, Michael J., 'The Legitimacy of Particular Conceptions of Constitutional Interpretation' (1991) 77 *Virginia Law Review* 669.

Toward a Theory of Human Rights: Religion, Law, Courts (Cambridge University Press, 2007).

Petersen, Niels, 'Human Dignity, International Protection', in Rüdiger Wolfrum (ed.), *Max Planck Encyclopedia of Public International Law* (Oxford University Press, 2007).

Pieroth, Bodo and Schlink, Bernhard, *Grundrechte Staatsrecht II* (Heidelberg: C. F. Müller Verlag, 2006).

Platt, Thomas W., 'Human Dignity and the Conflict of Rights' (1972) 2 *Idealistic Studies* 174.

Pollak, Louis H., '"Original Intention" and the Crucible of Litigation' (1989) 57 *University of Cincinnati Law Review* 867.

Porat, Iddo, 'The Use of Foreign Law in Israeli Constitutional Adjudication', in Gideon Sapir, Daphne Barak-Erez and Aharon Barak (eds.), *Israeli Constitutional Law in the Making* (Oxford: Hart Publishing, 2013) 151.

Posner, Richard, 'Legal Reasoning from the Top Down and from the Bottom Up: The Question of Unenumerated Constitutional Rights', in Geoffrey R. Stone, Richard A. Epstein and Cass R. Sunstein (eds.), *The Bill of Rights in the Modern State* (University of Chicago Press, 1992) 433.

Post, Robert C., *Constitutional Domains: Democracy, Community, Management* (Boston, MA: Harvard University Press, 1995).

Powell, H. Jefferson, 'Rules for Originalists' (1987) 73 *Virginia Law Review* 659.

President's Council on Bioethics, *Human Dignity and Bioethics: Essays Commissioned by the President's Council on Bioethics* (Washington DC: President's Council on Bioethics, 2008).

Pufendorf, Samuel, *De Jure Naturae et Gentium Libri Octo* (Amsterdam: David Mortier, 1684).

Rabello, Alfredo Mordechai and Sercevic, Petar (eds.), *Freedom of Contracts and Constitutional Law* (Hebrew University of Jerusalem, 1998).

Rabkin, Jeremy, 'What We Can Learn about Human Dignity from International Law' (2003) 27 *Harvard Journal of Law and Public Policy* 145.

Rakove, Jack N., *Original Meanings: Politics and Ideas in the Making of the Constitution* (New York and Toronto: Random House, 1996).

Rakover, Nahum, *Human Dignity in Jewish Law* (Jerusalem: Library of Jewish Law, 1998).

Rao, Neomi, 'On the Use and Abuse of Dignity in Constitutional Law' (2008) 14 *Columbia Journal of European Law* 201.

'Three Concepts of Dignity in Constitutional Law' (2011) 86 *Notre Dame Law Review* 183.

Rao, Pavani P., 'Basic Features of the Constitution' (2002) 2 *Supreme Court Cases Journal* 463.

Ratnapala, Suri, *Australian Constitutional Law: Foundations and Theory*, 2nd edn (South Melbourne: Oxford University Press, 2007).

Rautenbach, I. M., *General Provisions of the South African Bill of Rights* (Durban: Butterworths, 1995).

Rautenbach, I. M. and Malherbe, E. F. J., *Constitutional Law*, 4th edn (Durban: LexisNexis Butterworths, 2004).

Rawls, John, *Political Liberalism* (New York: Columbia University Press, 2005).

Raz, Joseph, *The Morality of Freedom* (Oxford University Press, 1986).

Rehnquist, William H., 'The Notion of a Living Constitution' (1976) 54 *Texas Law Review* 693.

Reimann, Mathias, 'Prurient Interest and Human Dignity: Pornography Regulation in West Germany and the United States' (1987) 21 *University of Michigan Journal of Law Reform* 201.

Reinbold, Jenna, 'Political Myth and the Sacred Center of Human Rights: The Universal Declaration and the Narrative of "Inherent Human Dignity"' (2011) 12 *Human Rights Review* 247.

Reinhardt, Stephan, 'The Conflict Between Text and Precedent in Constitutional Adjudication' (1988) 73 *Cornell Law Review* 434.

Resnik, Judith and Suk, Julie Chi-Hye, 'Adding Insult to Injury: Questioning the Role of Dignity in Conceptions of Sovereignty' (2003) 55 *Stanford Law Review* 1921.

Rhonheimer, Martin, 'Fundamental Rights, Moral Law, and the Legal Defense of Life in a Constitutional Democracy' (1998) 43 *American Journal of Jurisprudence* 135.

Ripstein, Arthur, *Force and Freedom: Kant's Legal and Political Philosophy* (Cambridge, MA: Harvard University Press, 2009).

Robbin, Tia R., 'Untouched Protection from Discrimination: Private Action in Montana's Individual Dignity Clause' (1990) 51 *Montana Law Review* 553.

Robert, Jacques, 'The Principle of Human Dignity', in European Commission for Democracy through Law, *The Principle of Respect for Human Dignity* (Strasbourg: Council of Europe, 1999) 43.

Roederer, Christopher, 'Founding Provisions', in Stuart Woolman, Michael Bishop and Jason Brickhill (eds.), *Constitutional Law of South Africa*, 2nd edn, Revision Series 4 (Cape Town: Juta, 2012) chapter 15.

Rose, Dennis, 'Judicial Reasonings and Responsibilities in Constitutional Cases (1994) 20 *Monash University Law Review* 195.

Rosen, Michael, *Dignity: Its History and Meaning* (Cambridge, MA: Harvard University Press, 2012).

Rosenberg, David and Levy, Ken, 'Capital Punishment: Coming to Grips with the Dignity of Man' (1978) 14 *California Western Law Review* 275.

Rotenstreich, Nathan, *Man and His Dignity* (Jerusalem: Magnes Press, Hebrew University, 1983).

Roznai, Yaniv, 'Unconstitutional Constitutional Amendment – The Migration and Success of a Constitutional Idea' (2013) 61 *American Journal of Comparative Law* 657.

Rubenfeld, Jed, 'Reading the Constitution as Spoken' (1995) 104 *Yale Law Journal* 1119.

Rubinstein, Amnon, 'The Story of the Basic Laws' (2012) 13 *Law and Business* 79 (Heb.).

Rubinstein, Amnon and Medina, Barak, *The Constitutional Law in the State of Israel, 6th edn* (Jerusalem: Shocken, 2005).

Runzo, Joseph, Martin, Nancy and Sharma, Arvind (eds.), *Human Rights and Responsibilities in the World Religions* (Oxford: Oneworld, 2003).

Sachs, Albie, 'Equality Jurisprudence: The Origin of the Doctrine in the South African Constitutional Court' (1999) 5 *Review of Constitutional Studies* 76.

Sachs, Michael, *GG Verfassungsrecht II. Grundrechte* (Berlin: Springer, 2003).

Grundgesetz Kommentar (Berlin: Springer, 2003).

Sadurski, Wojciech, *Rights Before Courts: A Study of Constitutional Courts in Postcommunist States of Central and Eastern Europe* (Dordrecht: Springer, 2005).

Sajo, Andras and Uitz, Renata (eds.), *The Constitution in Private Relations: Expanding Constitutionalism* (Utrecht: Eleven International Publishing, 2005).

Sajo, Andras and Uitz, Renata (eds.), *Constitutional Topography: Values and Constitutions* (Utrecht: Eleven International Publishing, 2010).

Salehi, Hamidreza and Abbasi, Mahmoud, 'Human Dignity: The Final Word on the Religious Ideas and Moral Thinking' (2012) 1 *Iranian Journal of Medical Ethics* 14.

Sandalow, Terrance, 'Constitutional Interpretation' (1981) 79 *Michigan Law Review* 1033.

Sathe, P. A., 'Amendability of Fundamental Rights: Golaknath and the Proposed Constitutional Amendment' (1969) 33 *Supreme Court Cases Journal* 42.

Scalia, Antonin, 'Originalism: The Lesser Evil' (1989) 57 *University of Cincinnati Law Review* 849.

Scalia, Antonin and Garner, Bryan A., *Reading Law: The Interpretation of Legal Texts* (St. Paul: West Publishing, 2012).

Schachter, Oscar, 'Human Dignity as a Normative Concept' (1983) 77 *American Journal of International Law* 848.

Schauer, Frederick, 'The Convergence of Rules and Standards' (2003) 3 *New Zealand Law Review* 303.

Free Speech: A Philosophical Inquiry (Cambridge University Press, 1982).

Thinking Like a Lawyer: A New Introduction to Legal Reasoning (Cambridge, MA: Harvard University Press, 2009).

Schlag, Pierre J., 'Rules and Standards' (1985) 33 *UCLA Law Review* 379.

Schlieter, Jens, 'Some Aspects of the Buddhist Assessment of Human Cloning', in Silja Vöneky and Rüdiger Wolfrum (eds.), *Human Dignity and Human Cloning* (Leiden: Martinus Nijhoff, 2004) 23.

Schopenhauer, Arthur, *On the Basis of Morality* (Indianapolis: Bobbs-Merrill, 1965) 100.

Schroeder, Doris, 'Human Rights and Human Dignity: An Appeal to Separate the Conjoined Twins' (2012) 15 *Ethical Theory Moral Practice* 323.

Schwelb, Egon, 'Civil and Political Rights: The International Measures of Implementation' (1968) 62 *American Journal of International Law* 827.

Scolnicov, Anat, *The Right to Religious Freedom in International Law: Between Group Rights and Individual Rights* (London: Routledge, 2011).

Scott, Dodson, 'Dignity: The New Frontier of State Sovereignty' (2003) 56 *Oklahoma Law Review* 777.

Seidman, Guy I. and Shaham, Erez, 'Symposium: Law and Medicine' (2007) 6 *Law and Business* 9.

Sensen, Oliver, 'Human Dignity in Historical Perspective: The Contemporary and Traditional Paradigms' (2011) 10 *European Journal of Political Theory* 71.

Shalev, Carmel, *Health and Human Rights in Israeli Law* (Tel Aviv: Ramot, 2003).

Shaman, Jeffrey M., 'Cracks in the Structure: The Coming Breakdown of the Levels of Scrutiny' (1984) 45 *Ohio State Law Journal* 161.

Sheikholeslami, Reza, 'The Creation and the Dignity of Man in Islam', in Silja Vöneky and Rüdiger Wolfrum (eds.), *Human Dignity and Human Cloning* (Leiden: Martinus Nijhoff, 2004) 3.

Shepherd, Lois, 'Dignity and Autonomy after Washington v. Gluckberg: An Essay about Abortion, Death and Crime' (1998) 7 *Cornell Journal of Law and Public Policy* 431.

Sher, Jeremy M., 'A Question of Dignity: The Renewed Significance of James Wilson's Writings on Popular Sovereignty in the Wake of Alden v. Maine' (2005) 61 *New York University Annual Survey of American Law* 591.

Shultziner, Doron, 'Human Dignity – Justification, not a Human Right' (2007) 11 *Hamishpat* 527.

'A Jewish Conception of Human Dignity: Philosophy and its Ethical Implications for Israeli Supreme Court Decisions' (2006) 34 *Journal of Religious Ethics* 663.

Siegel, Reva B., 'Dignity and Sexuality: Claims on Dignity in Transnational Debates over Abortion and Same-Sex Marriage' (2012) 10 *International Journal of Constitutional Law* 355.

'Dignity and the Politics of Protection: Abortion Restrictions Under Casey/Carhart' (2008) 117 *Yale Law Journal* 1694.

Simmonds, Andrew R., 'Measure for Measure: Two Misunderstood Principles of Damages, Exodus 21:22–25, "Life for Life, Eye for Eye," and Matthew 5:38–39, "Turn the Other Cheek"' (2004) 17 *Saint Thomas Law Review* 123.

Singer, Peter, *Animal Liberation*, 2nd edn (New York: Harper Collins, 1990).

Slaughter, Anne-Marie, 'A Typology of Transjudicial Communication' (1994) 29 *University of Richmond Law Review* 99.

Small, Joan and Grant, Evadne, 'Dignity Discrimination and Context: New Directions in South African and Canadian Human Rights Law' (2005) 6 *Human Rights Review* 25.

Sommer, Hillel, 'Background Paper on: Human Dignity as a Constitutional Right', submitted to the Knesset's Constitution, Law and Justice Committee (The Interdisciplinary Center, Herzliya, 2005).

Sontheimer, Kurt, 'Principles of Human Dignity in the Federal Republic', in Paul Kirchhof, Donald P. Kommers and American Institute for Contemporary German Studies (eds.), *Germany and its Basic Law: Past, Present, and Future: A German–American Symposium*, Dräger-Stiftung Publication (Baden-Baden: Nomos, 1993) 213.

Sossin, Lorne, 'The "Supremacy of God", Human Dignity and the Charter of Rights and Freedoms' (2003) 52 *University of New Brunswick Law Journal* 227.

Soulen, R. Kendall and Woodhead, Linda (eds.), *God and Human Dignity* (Michigan: Wm. B. Eerdmans Publishing, 2006).

Spiegelberg, Herbert, 'Human Dignity: A Challenge to Contemporary Philosophy', in Rubin Gotesky and Ervin Laszlo (eds.), *Human Dignity: This Century and the Next* (New York: Gordon and Breach, 1970) 39.

Starck, Christian, 'The Religious and Philosophical Background of Human Dignity and its Place in Modern Constitutions', in David Kretzmer and Eckart Klein (eds.), *The Concept of Human Dignity in Human Rights Discourse* (The Hague: Kluwer Law International, 2002) 179.

Statman, Daniel, 'Humiliation, Dignity, and Self Respect', in David Kretzmer and Eckart Klein (eds.), *The Concept of Human Dignity in Human Rights Discourse* (The Hague: Kluwer Law International, 2002) 209.

'Two Concepts of Dignity' (2001) 24 *Tel Aviv University Law Review* 541 (Heb.).

Strange, Steven K. and Zupko, Jack (eds.), *Stoicism: Traditions and Transformation* (Cambridge University Press, 2004).

Strauss, David A., 'Common Law Constitutional Interpretation' (1996) 63 *University of Chicago Law Review* 877

The Living Constitution (Oxford University Press, 2010).

Sullivan, Kathleen M., 'The Supreme Court 1991 Term – Forward: The Justices of Rules and Standards' (1992) 106 *Harvard Law Review* 22.

Taylor, George H., 'Structural Textualism' (1995) 75 *Boston University Law Review* 321.

Teifke, Nils, 'Human Dignity as an "Absolute Principle"?', in Martin Borowski (ed.), *On the Nature of Legal Principles* (Stuttgart: Franz Steiner Verlag, 2010) 93.

Tobin, John, *The Right to Health in International Law* (Oxford University Press, 2012).

Tribe, Laurence H., *American Constitutional Law*, 2nd edn (New York: Foundation Press, 1988).

American Constitutional Law, 3rd edn (New York: Foundation Press, 2000).

The Invisible Constitution (New York: Oxford University Press, 2008).

'Taking Text and Structure Seriously: Reflections on Free-Form Method in Constitutional Interpretation' (1995) 108(6) *Harvard Law Review* 1221

Tribe, Laurence H. and Dorf, Michael, 'Levels of Generality in the Definition of Rights' (1990) 57 *University of Chicago Law Review* 1057.

On Reading the Constitution (Boston, MA: Harvard University Press, 1991).

Tripathi, P. K., 'Kesavanda Bharati v. State of Kerata: Who Wins?' (1974) 1 *Supreme Court Cases Journal* 3.

Tucker, David, 'Textualism: An Australian Evolution of the Debate between Professor Ronald Dworkin and Justice Antonin Scalia' (1999) 21 *Sydney Law Review* 567.

Tushnet, Mark V., 'Can You Watch Unenumerated Rights Drift' (2006) 9 *University of Pennsylvania Journal of Constitutional Law* 209.

'Critical Legal Studies and Constitutional Law: An Essay in Deconstruction' (1984) 36 *Stanford Law Review* 623.

'Following the Rules Laid Down: A Critique of Interpretativism and Natural Principles' (1983) 96 *Harvard Law Review* 781.

'Justification in Constitutional Adjudication: A Comment on Constitutional Interpretation' (1994) 72 *Texas Law Review* 1707.

'The Possibilities of Comparative Constitutional Law' (1999) 108 *Yale Law Journal* 1225.

'Some Reflections on Method in Comparative Constitutional Law', in Sujit Choudhry (ed.), *The Migration of Constitutional Ideas* (Cambridge University Press, 2006) 67.

Ullrich, Dierk, 'Concurring Visions: Human Dignity in the Canadian Charter of Rights and Freedoms and the Basic Law of the Federal Republic of Germany' (2003) 3 *Global Jurist Frontiers* 1.

Van der Schyff, Gerhard, *Limitation of Rights: A Study of the European Convention and the South African Bill of Rights* (Nijmegen: Wolf Legal Publishers, 2005).

Venter, Francois, 'Human Dignity as a Constitutional Value: A South African Perspective', in Jörn Ipsen, Dietrich Rauschning and Edzard Schmidt-Jortzig (eds.), *Recht, Staat, Gemeinwohl: Festschrift für Dietrich Rauschning* (Munich: Heymann, 2001) 341.

'Utilising Constitutional Values in Constitutional Comparison', in Potchefstroom University for Christian Higher Education, Faculty of Law, *Constitution and Law IV: Developments in the Contemporary Constitutional State* (Johannesburg: Konrad-Adenauer-Stiftung, 2001) 33.

Vermeule, Adrian and Young, Ernest A., 'Hercules, Herbert, and Amar: The Trouble with Intratextualism' (2000) 113 *Harvard Law Review* 730.

Vila, Marisa Iglesias, *Facing Judicial Discretion: Legal Knowledge and Right Answers Revisited* (Dordrecht: Kluwer, 2001)

Volokh, Eugene, 'Freedom of Speech, Permissible Tailoring and Transcending Strict Scrutiny' (1996) 144 *University of Pennsylvania Law Review* 2417.

von der Pfordten, Dietmar, 'On the Dignity of Man in Kant' (2009) 84 *Philosophy* 371.

Von Overbeck, Alfred E., 'Some Observations on the Role of the Judge under the Swiss Civil Code' (1977) 37 *Louisiana Law Review* 681.

Vöneky, Silja and Wolfrum, Rüdiger (eds.), *Human Dignity and Human Cloning* (Leiden: Brill, 2004).

Wagner, William J., 'Universal Human Rights, the United Nations and the Telos of Human Dignity' (2005) 3 *Ave Maria Law Review* 197.

Waldron, Jeremy, 'Dignity and Defamation: The Visibility of Hate' (2010) 123 *Harvard Law Review* 1596.

'Dignity and Rank' (2007) 48 *European Journal of Sociology* 201.

'The Dignity of Groups' (2008) *Acta Juridica* 66.

The Dignity of Legislation (Cambridge University Press, 1999).

Dignity, Rank, and Rights, ed. by Meir Dan-Cohen (Oxford University Press, 2012).

'Dignity, Rights, and Responsibilities' (2011) 43 *Arizona State Law Journal* 1107.

'Does "Equal Moral Status" Add Anything to Right Reason', New York University School of Law Working Paper No. 11-52 (2011).

'Foreign Law and the Modern Ius Gentium' (2005) 119 *Harvard Law Review* 129.

The Harm in Hate Speech (Cambridge, MA: Harvard University Press, 2012).

'How Law Protects Dignity' (2012) 71 *Cambridge Law Journal* 200.

'The Image of God: Rights, Reason, and Order', New York University Public Law and Legal Theory Working Papers, Paper 246 (2010).

'Is Human Dignity the Foundation of Human Rights?', New York University School of Law Research Paper No. 12–73 (2013).

'Partly Laws Common to All Mankind: Foreign Law in American Courts' (New Haven: Yale University Press, 2012).

Walter, Christian, 'Human Dignity in German Constitutional Law', in European Commission for Democracy through Law, Venice Commission, CDL-STD 26, *The Principle of Respect for Human Dignity* (Strasbourg: Council of Europe, 1999) 25.

Walters, Mark D., 'Written Constitutions and Unwritten Constitutionalism', in Grant Huscroft (ed.), *Expounding the Constitution: Essays in Constitutional Theory* (Cambridge University Press, 2008) 245.

Walton, Luanne A., 'Making Sense of Canadian Constitutional Interpretation' (2001) 12 *National Journal of Constitutional Law* 315.

Wechsler, Herbert, 'Toward Neutral Principles of Constitutional Law' (1959) 73 *Harvard Law Review* 1.

Weinrib, Lorraine E., 'Constitutional Conceptions and Constitutional Comparativism', in Vicki C. Jackson and Mark V. Tushnet (eds.), *Defining the Field of Comparative Constitutional Law* (Westport: Praeger, 2002) 23.

'Human Dignity as a Rights-Protecting Principle' (2004) 17 *National Journal of Constitutional Law* 325.

Weisstub, David, 'Honor, Dignity and the Framing of Multiculturalists Values', in David Kretzmer and Eckart Klein (eds.), *The Concept of Human Dignity in Human Rights Discourse* (The Hague: Kluwer Law International, 2002) 263.

Wellington, Harry H., *Interpreting the Constitution: The Supreme Court and the Process of Adjudication* (New Haven: Yale University Press, 1992).

Wermiel, Stephen J., 'Law and Human Dignity: The Judicial Soul of Justice Brennan' (1998) 7 *William & Mary Bill of Rights Journal* 223.

Westover, Casey L., 'Structural Interpretation and the New Federalism: Finding the Proper Balance between State Sovereignty and Federal Supremacy' (2005) 88 *Marquette Law Review* 693.

Wheatley, Steven, *Democracy, Minorities and International Law* (Cambridge University Press, 2005).

'Human Rights and Human Dignity in the Resolution of Certain Ethical Questions in Biomedicine' (2001) 3 *European Human Rights Law Review* 312.

White, Robin C. A. and Ovey, Clare, *Jacobs, White & Ovey: The European Convention on Human Rights*, 5th edn (Oxford University Press, 2010).

Whitman, James Q., 'Enforcing Civility and Respect: Three Societies' (2000) 109 *Yale Law Journal* 1279.

'"Human Dignity" in Europe and the United States: the Social Foundations', in George Nolte (ed.), *European and US Constitutionalism* (Cambridge University Press, 2005) 108.

'On Nazi "Honour" and the New European "Dignity"', in Christian Joerges and Navraj S. Ghaleigh (eds.), *Darker Legacies of Law in Europe: The Shadow of National Socialism* (Oxford: Hart Publishing, 2003) 243.

'The Two Western Cultures of Privacy: Dignity Versus Liberty' (2004) 113 *Yale Law Journal* 1151.

Wildhaber, Luzius, 'Limitations on Human Rights in Times of Peace, War and Emergency: A Report on Swiss Law', in Armand L. C. De Mestral *et al.* (eds.), *The Limitation of Human Rights in Comparative Constitutional Law* (Cowansville: Yvon Blais, 1986) 41.

Wilson, Bertha, 'Decision-Making in the Supreme Court' (1986) 36 *University of Toronto Law Journal* 227.

Winkler, Adam, 'Fatal in Theory and Strict in Fact: An Empirical Analysis of Strict Scrutiny in the Federal Courts' (2006) 59 *Vanderbilt Law Review* 793.

Winnacker, Ernst L., 'Human Cloning from a Scientific Perspective', in Silja Vöneky and Rüdiger Wolfrum (eds.), *Human Dignity and Human Cloning* (Leiden: Martinus Nijhoff, 2004) 55.

Witte, John, 'Between Sanctity and Depravity: Human Dignity in Protestant Perspective', in Robert P. Kraynak and Glenn E. Tinder (eds.), *In Defense of Human Dignity: Essays for our Times* (University of Notre Dame Press, 2003) 119.

Jr. and Alexander, Frank (eds.), *Christianity and Human Rights: An Introduction* (Cambridge University Press, 2010).

Wittreck, Fabian, 'Menschenwürde und Folterverbot' (2003) 56 *Die Öffentliche Verwaltung* 873.

Wolterstorff, Nicholas P., 'Modern Protestant Developments in Human Rights', in John Witte, Jr. and Frank Alexander (eds.), *Christianity and Human Rights: An Introduction* (Cambridge University Press, 2010) 155.

Wood, Allen, 'Humanity as an End in Itself', in Paul Guyer (ed.), *Kant's Groundwork of the Metaphysics of Morals: Critical Essays* (Lanham: Rowman and Littlefield, 1998), 165.

Woolman, Stuart, 'Dignity', in Stuart Woolman, Michael Bishop and Jason Brickhill (eds.), *Constitutional Law of South Africa*, 2nd edn, Revision Series 4 (Cape Town: Juta, 2012) chapter 36.

Woolman, Stuart and Botha, Henk, 'Limitations', in Stuart Woolman, Michael Bishop and Jason Brickhill (eds.), *Constitutional Law of South Africa*, 2nd edn, Revision Series 4 (Cape Town: Juta, 2012) chapter 34.

Wright, R. George, 'Dignity and Conflicts of Constitutional Values: The Case of Free Speech and Equal Protection' (2006) 43 *San Diego Law Review* 527.

Young, Ernest A., 'Alden v. Maine and the Jurisprudence of Structure' (1999–2000) 41 *William and Mary Law Review* 1601.

Young, Margot, 'Section 7 and the Politics of Social Justice' (2005) 38 *University of British Columbia Law Review* 539.

Youngs, Raymond, 'Germany: Shooting Aircraft and Analyzing Computer Data' (2008) 6 *International Journal of Constitutional Law* 331.

Ziegler, Katja (ed.), *Human Rights and Private Law: Privacy as Autonomy* (Oxford: Hart Publishing, 2006).

Zucca, Lorenzo, *Constitutional Dilemmas: Conflicts of Fundamental Legal Rights in Europe and the USA* (Oxford University Press, 2007).

A Secular Europe: Law and Religion in the European Constitutional Landscape (Oxford University Press, 2012).

Zúñiga, Gloria L., 'An Ontology of Dignity' (2004) 5 *Metaphysica* 115.

INDEX